# Speedway to Sunshine

### The Story of the Florida East Coast Railway

# Speedway to Sunshine

### THE STORY
### OF THE FLORIDA
### EAST COAST
### RAILWAY

SETH H. BRAMSON

The BOSTON
MILLS PRESS

A BOSTON MILLS PRESS BOOK

Published by Boston Mills Press, 1984
Copyright © Seth Bramson, 1984, 2003

Reprinted with revisions. Third printing, January 2003.

**Cataloging in Publication Data**

Bramson, Seth, 1944-
  Speedway to sunshine / Seth Bramson. — Rev. ed.

Includes bibliographical references.
ISBN 1-55046-358-6

1. Florida East Coast Railway—History.
2. Railroads—Florida—Florida Keys—History. I. Title.

HE2791.F53B73 2003     385'.09759'41     2003-901601-0

**Publisher Cataloging-in-Publication Data (U.S.) is available.**


Published by
BOSTON MILLS PRESS
132 Main Street
Erin, Ontario, N0B 1T0
Tel. (519) 833-2407
Fax (519) 833-2195
books@bostonmillspress.com
www.bostonmillspress.com

IN CANADA:
Distributed by Firefly Books Ltd.
3680 Victoria Park Avenue
Toronto, Ontario M2H 3K1

IN THE UNITED STATES:
Distributed by Firefly Books (U.S.) Inc.
P.O. Box 1338, Ellicott Station
Buffalo, New York 14205



Jacket design by Gillian Stead
Printed and bound in Canada by Friesens, Altona, Manitoba

To the memory of my parents—Jess Allen Bramson (who took me to see "Toodles" the steam engines at Miami's Buena Vista Yards from 1947 until 1949) and Selma (Sally) Bramson Middleton (who allowed the collection to outgrow our beloved former family home on Cecil St.)—this book is lovingly dedicated.

Daddy with Seth at Buena Vista, 1948.

Mom with Bennett at FEC Miami Station, June 1962.

# TABLE OF CONTENTS

"Along the Indian River." For some miles between Jensen Beach and Melbourne the famous double track main line paralleled the Indian River. 451 is shown southbound. The park like appearance of the right of way as shown in this photo leaves little doubt that the FEC was a first class railroad in all respects.

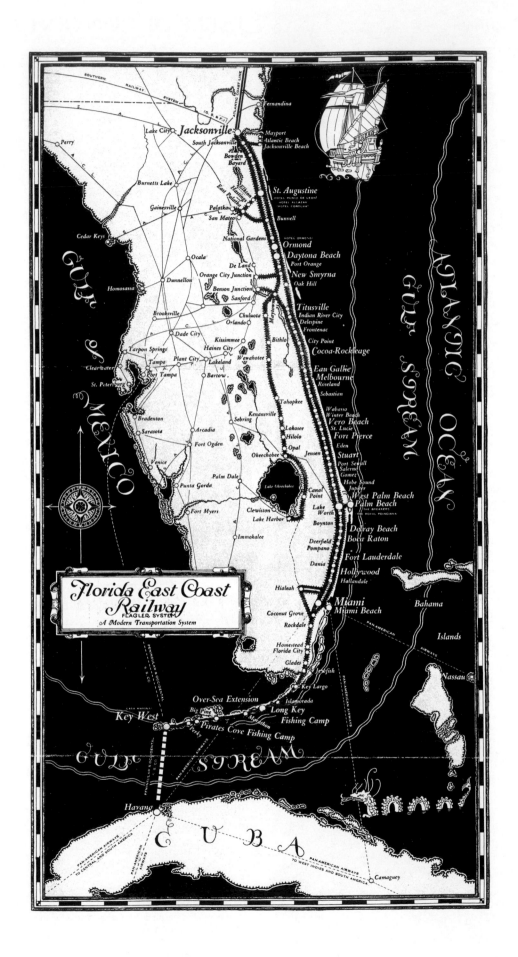

# PREFACE

The Florida East Coast Railway is America's greatest railroad, totally different and completely unique from any other railroad in the United States or Canada. From Henry M. Flagler to W. R. Kenan to Edward Ball to W. L. Thornton, Raymond W. Wyckoff, Carl F. Zellers, Jr., and Robert W. Anestis and John D. McPherson, this railroad has been the maverick, doing what it had to do when it had to do it, going it alone when necessary, but always operating with one thought uppermost in the corporate mind: service to the people of the east coast of Florida.

After the first edition of *Speedway to Sunshine* was published, no small number of people intimated that I had written the book from a personal perspective. How could I not? From my father's taking me to Buena Vista Yard every Sunday beginning in 1947 to my involvement as Company Historian in the joint FEC Railway–Miami Centennial celebration in 1996, my association with the Florida East Coast has been up close, personal, and, yes, even familial, for over 54 years. There is now, and will ever and only be, one Florida East Coast Railway.

Although the passage of time, in and of itself, was reason enough for a revised, expanded edition, one event after another kept adding to the FEC legacy, whether it was the retirement of a president, a short-lived foray outside Florida, the company's centennial, or the appointment of a new Chairman and CEO, each event, in turn, pushed back the publication date for the new edition — an eager and supportive wife, innumerable FEC fans and railroad notwithstanding. Finally, the time has come.

The charge has been leveled that I am both chauvinistic about and prejudiced toward the subject; those allegations are totally true. Knowing the people, riding the trains, photographing the subject, and watching the FEC develop into the best-kept, best-managed, best-run railroad in America has been a rare privilege. The late, beloved editor of *Trains* Magazine, David P. Morgan, wrote that the FEC's evolution took it from "a slumbering potential super-railroad to the most admired and respected railroad in the country."

Since the first publication of *Speedway to Sunshine* in 1984, much has occurred, and the railroad has continued to evolve. At one point, there were rumors that the railroad might be sold; it wasn't. Instead, the company's leadership continues to insist on dedication and productivity, and that ethic is in no place stronger than in the executive suites of the company's St. Augustine General Offices.

FEC trains, formerly short, fast and frequent, are now long, fast and frequent. The precision of the operation is, simply put, a model most other American railroads attempt to emulate.

Since the original edition was published, new and enlightening material has been brought forward, from names of individual employees to incidents that have affected the company's history. Photos, correspondence, maps, drawings, blueprints, timetables, brochures and meetings with past and present employees have helped to provide both new information and additional documentation about the FEC's history.

This edition contains four new chapters to cover the years from 1984 through 2001, giving the reader information on the "Georgia-Florida Xpress," the appointment of new corporate officers, the great Centennial event, and the changes as the new millennium begins. New information has also been added to the appendices, and a variety of new photos further enhance this edition.

As in the previous edition, while every effort was made to be as accurate as possible, readers are asked to share with the author any inaccuracies that they may find in the text.

And now, welcome aboard—and happy reading!

The East Coast that is no more. When Harry Wolfe focused his enormous Graphlex Press Camera on the Florida East Coast Railway near his home in St. Augustine, the results were striking. He long considered this picture to be an unqualified failure, due to the fact that he had tripped the curtain shutter too soon. Few photographs, however, better illustrate the changes experienced by the East Coast of Florida since the depression of the 30's. The phenomenal perspective, in which wide open Florida flatlands were bisected by the famous doubletrack main has been obliterated by thousands of hastily constructed cubicles on postage stamp sized lots. The charming rurality is gone and crabgrass and oil slicks are the only harvest the mutilated woods now yield. Although hemmed in, devoid of the river views and robbed of the beautiful steam locomotives which once traversed it, the FEC is one of the few major physical ties to Florida's halcyon yesterdays that still remain.

# INTRODUCTION

The story of the FEC, unlike that of many other railroads, is, almost in its entirety, a "modern" story, taking place primarily within the 20th Century. As these words are written in 1984, there are individuals who remember, with clarity, Flagler's arrival in Key West; who recall in detail riding trains on the Oversea Railroad; who can visualize almost to exactness six sections of the "Florida Special" departing Miami on four separate occasions in 1936; and who watched the last pre-strike passenger train leave Jacksonville on January 22, 1963.

There is little about the history of the FEC that is not exciting: completion of the road to Miami; extension to Key West; double tracking to cope with the 1920's Boom; the depression and subsequent receivership; the Hurricane of 1935 which destroyed the Key West Extension; World War II and record passenger and freight movements; the loss of service to Cuba via the car ferries due to Castro; and the ending of the receivership under the new ownership of the Florida Dupont interests.

Through all of this, the FEC has continued to operate with a single-minded toughness that few other American businesses could sustain. There is a fascination of, to, for and about the FEC. Concrete crossties; cabooseless trains; non-union operations since 1963; a first class passenger train service during the strike, from 1965 until 1968; and a resilient and innovative executive department and sales force continue to keep the railroad in the forefront of national railroad news.

In the main—and on the mainland—the FEC is not, topographically speaking, a remarkable railroad. It crosses no great bodies of water, and the scenery is undiversified: flat land, minimal curves, modest rivers. There are no mountains or majestic scenic vistas.

Geographically, with one exception, the East Coast of Florida is totally unremarkable. But that exception—the chain of islands that form the Florida Keys and the building of the Key West Extension over miles of open water—imprinted indelibly upon the minds and consciousness of the American people the gutsiness, stamina, and beyond belief stick-to-it-iveness that have, ever since, been the hallmark of the FEC.

But even without the Key West Extension, the FEC would be remembered for elegant passenger trains; for the Palm Beach resorts; for laying out and developing Miami; for the private cars that came from across America to be where summer spends the winter; for its Mountain type steam engines; for what was arguably America's most beautiful diesel color scheme...

How many railroads spawned land companies, a hotel company, a steamship line, a horsecar line, a concrete crosstie manufacturer, and, almost phoenix like, a multi-hundred million dollar commercial colossus scheduled to rise on and adjacent to the long fallow site of the Miami passenger station and yards?

All this has combined to make the FEC what *Railway Age* publisher Robert Lewis calls "that tough little railroad with the concrete crossties that has shown the whole country how to do it." Interestingly enough, earlier fears that the FEC would become part of another major railroad have vanished, and W.L. Thornton, chairman of the FEC, is far from shy about paraphrasing Vince Lombardi when talking about the road he has commanded since 1960: "On this road," he says, "the future is now."

Dramatic, melodramatic, violent, exciting, and filled with a sense of history-in-the-making, the FEC has become an operating legend in its own time. The railroad has gone it alone, and this book is that saga.

"Speedway to Sunshine" begins at the beginning, exploring the early histories of the FEC's predecessors, and continues through to the present day. In so doing, it becomes the first book written which covers the entire history of the railroad, and incorporates material found in the Company's 1916 Corporate history. There may be, in the course of the book, errors in dates, names or places. In such cases, where same can be verified by the reader, corrections are, of course, welcome and appreciated. In a few instances, where details are sketchy, approximations have been given, and are so noted. In any case, "Speedway to Sunshine" presents a new vista of information, not just to the railroad buff, but to any student of Florida's long and glorious history.

On the Miami River, Fla.
Compliments of the Land Department of the Florida East Coast Railway, St. Augustine, Fla.

From its inception the FEC and its predecessors had a deep commitment to the land and it's people. Besides having their own Land and Industrial Development Departments, FEC officers served as the management of other Flagler System endeavors, including the Perrine Grant Land Co., Model Land Co. and the Chuluota Land Co. Besides issuing a now much sought after publication entitled "The Florida East Coast Homeseeker" and numerous booklets, brochures and pamphlets extolling the virtues of the rich agricultural opportunities that were available, the Land Dept. of the railroad issued a set of post cards showing the beauty of the East Coast. Emblazoned with the words "Compliments of the Land Department of the Florida East Coast Railway. St. Augustine, Florida", the photographer is unknown; unlike the Extension series cards, this group is NOT numbered and, as with so much else relating to the history of the East Coast Line the number of different cards that were printed remains a mystery. All of the cards in this series are printed in sepia tone, and 24 different scenes are known to exist.

# CHAPTER 1

# BEFORE THE COMING OF THE RAILROAD

The scene was almost idyllic. Over 500 miles of untrodden beaches; stunning sunset vistas; a land undesecrated by what we now call civilization. Such was the appearance of the East Coast of Florida.

While most school children are aware that the first permanent settlement in the United States was at St. Augustine, our purview, of necessity, must focus on the years immediately preceding the coming of the railroad to the East Coast.

As the effects of the Civil War gradually wore away, an increasing number of winter visitors began venturing south to Jacksonville and nearby St. Augustine. Picturesque river steamers plied up and down the St. Johns River, along the banks of which there grew a number of small towns and resorts. But travel to Florida was difficult. To reach Jacksonville by train from the North and Mid-West, involved many changes and delays due to the different gauges of the railroads. Three to four days were required to make the trip by railroad from New York, and many preferred to take the coastal steamers to Charleston or Savannah, and then change to railroad or a smaller steamer to complete the trip to Jacksonville.

One G. W. Nichols wrote in Harpers Magazine for October, 1870, "There are two ways of getting to Jacksonville from Savannah, and whichever you choose, you will be sorry you had not taken the other. There is the night train by railroad, which brings you to Jacksonville in about sixteen hours and there is the steamboat line, which goes inland nearly all the way, and which may land you in a day, or you may run aground and remain on board a week."

(Author's Note: Until a direct line between Savannah and Jacksonville was completed, trains between the two cities operated on a circuitous routing that took them south and west from Savannah to Dupont, Georgia, and Live Oak, Florida, via the Atlantic & Gulf RR, thence east to Jacksonville via the Jacksonville, Pensacola & Mobile RR. Later, a shorter, but still indirect route was opened when the Savannah, Florida & Western RR built a 75 mile line connecting Waycross and Jacksonville. However, it was not until Jan. 1, 1894 that a direct line via Everett, Georgia, and Yulee, Florida, was finally completed. The Plant System (SF&W) line via Jesup and Folkston was not finished until late 1901–early 1902.)

Until 1870 there were also two ways of travelling from Jacksonville to St. Augustine. A little steamer operated up the coast once a week and might give the traveler a very rough trip, or he might take a river steamer down the St. Johns to a place called Picolata, and then be transported by horse-drawn stage over a miserable eighteen mile road to the Ancient City. Most travelers of the day used the latter route, which they also unanimously condemned for its crudeness and discomforts.[1]

South of St. Augustine, travel was almost nil. The only settlement of consequence was Key West, and the only means of travel to the Island City were the steamboats that plied the coast, putting in at Titusville or Daytona, or one of the Upper Keys before reaching Key West. Key West, for a time the largest city in Florida, had no difficulty "exporting" its "produce"—tobacco in different forms; liquors and liqueurs; crafts and jewelry, and other handcrafted items—via Tampa and Florida's West Coast.

Before the railroad extended its twin ribbons of steel along the East Coast, there was no industry, no agriculture, no amusements, and a miniscule number of settlers. The Indians, sole inhabitants of the area for hundreds of years, were, especially when compared to their brothers in the Northeast and on the Western Plains, small in both numbers and impact.

The Seminoles and Miccousoukees, rich in culture and heritage, did maintain burial grounds, hunting areas, rudimentary settlements and "trading posts." They were widely scattered, and, well before the coming of the railroad, either ensconced to the West of what would become the populated areas or willing to live in harmony with the changes that befell them. As in other areas of the United States, many of the names of cities and landmarks are derivatives of Indian names, readily recognizable today. Osceola County was named for the fabled Chief; the great lake, Okeechobee, bears an Indian name; May-a-mi meant sweet water, and was the name of a pristine river, with clear and beautiful shallows, free running rapids, and tributaries that led to Indian hunting grounds.

There was little, if any, reason to come to Florida before the coming of the railroad. The land was hostile, the mosquitoes voracious, the crocodiles and alligators numerous, the commerce nearly nonexistent, the settlements few and far between, and the weather, especially during what we now know as "hurricane season," wickedly unpredictable.

Following the panic of 1873, most of the country was engaged in "railroad fever." Lines were being built anywhere and everywhere, with Florida being the notable exception. It was quite simple: there was no need to build an extensive system of railroads in and through Florida. Commerce, such as it was, was expedited by freighters of the oxen and buckboard variety, or by the various inland steamers that followed the banks of the St. Johns or Ocklawaha Rivers, depositing and receiving freight, mail and passengers.

In St. Augustine, several merchants, annoyed at the inconveniences of travel to their city, contracted for the construction of what became known as the St. Johns Railway. The road, originally chartered in 1858, was graded to within 1¼ miles of St. Augustine, having originated at Tocoi Landing on the St. Johns River. Due to the outbreak of the Civil War, the right of way lay fallow and weed grown until 1866. When the road finally reopened, the improvement in either speed or freighting ability over the former line from Picolata was minimal at best.

In 1881, most of the claims of the few early railroads of Florida, bankrupt since the Civil War, were settled. One of the prime areas of litigation centered around State owned lands that had been deeded to some of the original railroads to aid them in speeding up the construction of their lines in the sparsely settled territory. With final settlement of these claims, the State again began to grant lands to encourage railroad and population expansions, and the railroad era of most of Florida began to emerge.

Very little of this affected the East Coast. Though railroad building and planning proceeded apace during the late 1870s and into the 80s, it was not until June of 1883 that the initially narrow gauge Jacksonville, St. Augustine & Halifax River Railroad extended its rails southward as far as St. Augustine.

While the negatives concerning Florida's East Coast in those days were many, there was one constant positive: the warmth. Even though the weather was quite unpredictable, it was, winter or summer, almost always warm. Snow was so infrequent to the region south of Jacksonville that it was almost unknown, and, because of this (and this alone) people began to take their holidays as far south as decent transportation would take them.

Getting to St. Augustine became a great deal easier. River and ocean voyages were unnecessary, but many people were not overwhelmed by the new all-rail route. The ties were laid directly on the sandy soil, with no roadbed, and the schedules were infrequent and unreliable. Motive power was not in the best of condition due to the distance involved in getting replacement parts. There was hardly the skill required to operate the new railroad.

Transportation south of St. Augustine was such an "iffy" proposition that few would attempt to travel.

In the early 1880s, the coast south of St. Augustine was still very sparsely settled. At Daytona there was a village, tiny and unstable, of about 100 people. South of that point, nothing in the way of settlement worthy of mention existed. Here and there, along the bays and rivers, a few hardy pioneers had either homesteaded or purchased a tract of land and built some form of domicile.[2]

Transportation in this section was almost exclusively by means of sailboat on the bays and inland rivers, subject to the hazards and uncertainties of wind and weather. The natural thoroughfares were the lakes and rivers, and Lake Worth, Bay Biscayne, Indian River and Halifax River were the main routes of travel. Roads did not exist, except for the old King's Road, built during Florida's English period between St. Augustine and New Smyrna, and this 'supposed road' was barely a sandy trail.

The few pioneers who inhabited this section enjoyed very few conveniences and fewer luxuries. They had no ice for preservation of meat or perishables, necessitating the simplest of fare, and while the woods west of the coast contained game in abundance, and the rivers and inlets were full of fish, these foods were more of a delicacy than part of a regimen. Even the game birds had to be cooked and eaten almost immediately to prevent them from rotting away.

While there was a dearth of population and scarcely a settlement large enough to support a general store, several enterprising merchants loaded their goods aboard sloops and sailed up and down the rivers, through the inlets and around the bays in order to call on the widely scattered residents. These hardy souls were glad to lay in a stock of necessities, as it might be months before the floating general merchandise emporium returned to their locale.[3]

Daytona Beach, Fla. Seabreeze Ave.

Along the scenic ocean shore the Florida East Coast was, unequivocably the developer of what has become a 365 mile super-megalopolis. A person standing on a main street of an East Coast city today would be hard put to recognize the way we were. It all began with Flagler and since 1892 the FEC and its predecessors have been, in many cases, the sole reason that people came to the East Coast of Florida.

South of Daytona, as previously mentioned, there was little in the way of settlement or civilization. Along the shores of Lake Worth, over 150 miles south of Daytona, a small group of people had settled near the present Palm Beach. Still further south, a few families had cleared land at the point at which the present day Miami River opens into Biscayne Bay. Five miles below them, directly on the bay, another small group established a clearing at the "coconut grove," a name which stuck with the area when it became an incorporated village, and, later, as a section of Miami proper.

The original County of Dade was eventually partitioned into a total of three counties: Palm Beach to the North, Broward in the middle, and Dade in the South. In being aware of that fact, one may then appreciate the census statistics of 1880 showing Dade County with 527 counted heads, and, in 1890, still unpartitioned, with only 861. Dade today, with 27 incorporated municipalities, and its metropolitan government is the second largest county (in terms of area) in the state, with over 2,000 square miles, and the largest in population with more than two million people.

It is not difficult, then, to comprehend the stark isolation of living south of Daytona during the last two and one-half decades of the nineteenth century, not to mention the dangers associated with that isolation. Besides disease, the vagaries of weather, fugitives from the law seeking refuge in the Everglades, poisonous snakes, and animals of prey, there were the mosquitoes. Ever present, ever omnivorous, ever noisome, the foul pests seemed to be of a clear and unconscionable single-mindedness regarding homo sapiens: bite them, buzz them, and in every way possible, make their lives miserable. In a Jerry Reed song, one line is, "If the skeeters don't getcha, then the gators will." In South and East Florida, if everything else didn't get them, then the skeeters would.

The railroad builders, men of money, vision, and glib promises, were undeterred. The land, barren and untilled though it might be, was good for something, and that something, of course, was development. But development, in those days, was accomplished in only one way: by building a railroad.

FOOTNOTES:

1. "The Story of a Pioneer," FEC Ry., St. Augustine, FL, September, 1946 edition, p. 5
2. Ibid, P.6.
3. Ibid, P.6.

The woodcut, showing the horse drawn passenger and freight cars was, if anything, kind to the surrounding territory, for from one terminus to the other, in either direction, the term "nothingness" is actually mild when used to describe the surroundings that the right of way passed through.
*—Florida State Archives: Author's Collection*

EN ROUTE FOR ST. AUGUSTINE, FLORIDA.

G 15656 Lemon Street, Palatka, Fla.

# CHAPTER 2

# THE PREDECESSOR RAILROADS

As is the case with most railroads, the FEC did not spring into existence with the corporate name, "Florida East Coast Railway." While there were numerous mergers, buy-outs, leases and trackage rights agreements, the FEC had, in name, only two predecessors: the Florida Coast & Gulf Ry., and its successor, the Jacksonville, St. Augustine & Indian River Ry. (After the first use of a railroads name in full, initials will be used thereafter.)

The first CONSTRUCTED segment of what was to become the FEC, however, was also the first abandoned, and, for that reason alone, may be considered one of the most interesting of the FEC's descendants.

The St. Johns Ry. was originally conceived as a "light," or mule-operated tram-type railroad from Tocoi Landing, 14½ miles due west of St. Augustine on the St. Johns River, to the outskirts of town. As first constructed, the line, with Dr. John Westcott as its president, was intended for freighting, but began carrying passengers shortly after its opening in 1859.

Westcott, a man of vision and money, was a member of the legislature and one of the projectors of the Internal Improvement System of Florida. According to early patrons of the road, the mules that were the motive power had a habit of lying down frequently to rest, so that the 15 mile trip often took four to five hours to negotiate. The fare was two dollars, and to those who complained that the tariff was exorbitant, Dr. Westcott retorted that there was no other road in the United States on which a man could ride that long for so little money.[4]

In 1860, Westcott, along with two other major stockholders, graded and rebuilt the roadbed, and replaced the original wooden rail with iron track. A steam locomotive, passenger coach and some freight cars were received in late 1860.

All went well for the road until early March, 1862, when Federal gunboats came down the St. Johns River and burned the Tocoi depot, destroyed the locomotive and rolling stock, and tore up much of the iron track. In 1866, using a makeshift steam engine constructed from scrap, the line was again put into operation.

In 1870 Westcott sold the line to William Astor, the New York millionaire, and upon the elder Astor's death in 1875, it was ably financed and improved by his son, William, Jr., with Dr. Westcott remaining on as one of the directors of the road. The line was again upgraded and rebuilt, receiving new passenger and freight cars in the process.

In 1888, Flagler purchased the St. Johns Railway and converted the track to standard gauge of 4 feet 8½ inches. The St. Johns, along with the St. Augustine and Palatka, which shared trackage with the St. Johns from St. Augustine to Tocoi Junction, a distance of about six miles, gave Flagler a double-pronged access to the St. Johns River.

It soon became apparent that Palatka, about 12 miles south of Tocoi, was to be a far more important point. Plans were in progress for a Union Station there, and crossing the St. Johns River at East Palatka would be far less expensive than at Tocoi.

In 1883, the Jacksonville, St. Augustine & Halifax River Railroad was completed, operating between the south side of the St. Johns River in Jacksonville, and St. Augustine. The St. Johns struggled gamely along, but could not compete with the JStA&HR's route. In 1892, the Jacksonville, St. Augustine & Indian River Ry. became the major Flagler railroad operating company, and in 1895 discontinued service on the former St. Johns Railway. In early April of 1896, the line was formally abandoned, and the earliest segment of the FEC, originally incorporated December 31, 1858, ceased to exist.

With the exception of a few tickets, several passes, and some timetables, the only tangible reminder of the St. Johns existence is a St. Augustine Historical Society marker standing on Florida State Road 214, near the site of Tocoi Junction, commemorating the little road's existence.[5]

**NO 15**
THE HALIFAX AND INDIAN RIVER
RAILWAY COMPANY
*Letters Patent issued*
*Sept 3, 1891*
*Right of Way Through Titusville*
*Deeded to Florida Coast and Gulf Railway Company*
*August 16, 1892*

1

**NO 16**
FLORIDA COAST & GULF RAILWAY COMPANY
*Letters Patent Issued*
*May 28, 1892*
*Line Constructed*
*Daytona to Smyrna 15.07 Miles*
*Name Changed to*
*Jacksonville, St. Augustine &*
*Indian River Railway Co.*
*by*
*Letters Patent Issued*
*Oct 31, 1892*

2

**NO 17**
JACKSONVILLE, ST. AUGUSTINE
& INDIAN RIVER RAILWAY CO.
*Name Changed from Florida Coast and*
*Gulf Railway Company*
*by letters patent issued Oct 31, 1892*
*Line Construction*
*New Smyrna to West Palm Beach*
*174.69 miles*
*Name changed to*
*Florida East Coast Railway Co.*
*by letters patent issued Sept 13, 1895*

3

**NO. 19**
FLORIDA EAST COAST RAILWAY COMPANY
FLAGLER SYSTEM
*Name Changed from*
*Jacksonville, St. Augustine and Indian River*
*Railway Company*
*by letters patent issued September 13, 1895*
*Capital Stock 10,000,000.00*
*Funded Debt 37,300,000.00*
*Mainline Jacksonville to Key West   522.17 miles*
*Branches                                          217.01 miles*
*Total      739.18 miles*
*Compiled as of June 30, 1916*

4

**NO 13**
JACKSONVILLE BRIDGE COMPANY
*Incorporated Nov 9, 1888*
*Bridge across St Johns River*
*Between*
*Jacksonville and South Jacksonville*
*0.54 miles*
*Deeded to*
*Florida East Coast Railway Company*
*May 5, 1896*

5

**NO 3**
JACKSONVILLE, ST AUGUSTINE AND
HALIFAX RIVER RAILWAY CO.
*Letters Patent Issued Jan 24, 1881*
*Line Conveyed*
*South Bank of St. Johns River*
*to St. Augustine 36.24 miles*
*Deeded to*
*Florida East Coast Railway Company*
*April 4, 1896*

6

**NO 18**
JACKSONVILLE AND ATLANTIC RAILWAY CO.
*Letters Patent issued January 15, 1893*
*Line Conveyed*
*South Jacksonville to Pablo 16.54 miles*
*Deeded to Florida East Coast Railway Company*
*September 25, 1900*

7

**NO 11**
PALATKA BRIDGE COMPANY
*Incorporated Aug 15, 1888*
*Bridge*
*from East Bank St Johns River*
*to West Bank at Palatka*
*1.81 miles*
*Deeded to*
*Florida East Coast Railway Company*
*May 5, 1896*

10

**NO 14**
ST. AUGUSTINE AND HALIFAX RIVER
RAILWAY COMPANY
*Letters Patent issued April 15, 1889*
*for Maintenance and Operation of the*
*St. Augustine and Palatka*
*Railway Company*
*from Junction with St. Johns Railway*
*Company to East Palatka 20.38 miles*
*Deeded to Florida East Coast*
*Railway Company April 4, 1896*

11

**NO 7**
JACKSONVILLE AND ATLANTIC
RAILROAD CO.
*Letters Patent issued Aug 6, 1883*
*Line Constructed*
*South Jacksonville to Pablo 16.54 miles*
*Sold by Special Matter to M.W. Drew, under*
*Forclosure Dec 5, 1892*
*Deeded by M.W. Drew to the Jacksonville*
*and Atlantic Railway Company Jan 18, 1893*

12

**NO 21**
ATLANTIC COAST LINE RAILWAY COMPANY
*Trackage Rights*
*79 miles*
*for Joint Operations*
*of Freight Yard Terminals*
*at Palatka*
*Agreement dated Sept 27, 1888*

15

**NO 8**
THE ST. AUGUSTINE AND
PALATKA RAILWAY COMPANY
*Letters Patent issued February 5, 1886*
*Line Constructed*
*Tocoi Junction to East Palatka*
*21.75 miles*
*Deeded to St. Augustine and Halifax*
*River Railway Company*
*March 1, 1889*

16

**NO 5**
ARLINGTON AND ATLANTIC
RAILWAY COMPANY
*Letters Patent issued Aug 29, 1882*
*Proposed Line*
*Arlington to Atlantic Coast*
*Name changed to Jacksonville and Atlantic*
*Railroad Company Sept 23, 1882*

17

**NO. 22**
JACKSONVILLE TERMINAL COMPANY
*Trackage Rights.*
*1.57 miles*
*For Operation of Passenger Terminals*
*and Freight Interchange*
*at Jacksonville*
*Agreement Dated*
*July 1, 1911*

20

**NO 23**
ATLANTIC AND EAST COAST
TERMINAL COMPANY
*Trackage Rights 1.48 miles*
*For operation of*
*Freight Terminals at Jacksonville*
*50% Stock Ownership*

21

**NO 1**
ST. JOHNS RAILWAY
*Incorporated Dec 31, 1858*
*Line Constructed*
*Tocoi to St. Augustine 15.25 miles*
*Deeded to Florida East Coast Railway Company*
*April 6, 1896*

22

18

# Florida East Coast Ry.

## NOTES

The Chart Numbers shown in the Index appear at the top of the rectangles, circles and octagons in the order of date of incorporation or issuance of Letters Patent.

The Place Numbers in the small circles at the bottom of each rectangle, circle and octagon refers to its position on the chart.

Rectangles indicate Ownership
Circles indicate Trackage Rights.
Octagons indicate Lease

---

**NO 12**
**ST JOHNS AND HALIFAX RIVER RAILWAY COMPANY**
*Letters Patent Issued Oct 11, 1888*
*Constructed Line Changed*
*East Palatka to Daytona 50.59 miles*
*Deeded April 4, 1896 to Florida East Coast Railway Company. Corrected deed June 18, 1901*

8

---

**NO 4**
**THE ST. JOHNS AND HALIFAX RAILWAY COMPANY**
*Letters Patent Issued Dec 12, 1881*
*Line Constructed*
*Rollestowe to Daytona 51.89 miles*
*Deeded to*
*St. Johns and Halifax River Railway Co. Oct 1, 1888*

13

---

**NO 10**
**ATLANTIC AND WESTERN RAILROAD COMPANY**
*Letters Patent Issued Mar 7, 1888*
*Line Conveyed Blue Spring to New Smyrna 28.48 miles*
*Deeded to Florida East Coast Railway Co. April 4, 1896*

18

---

**NO 2**
**BLUE SPRING, ORANGE CITY AND ATLANTIC RAIL ROAD COMPANY**
*Letters Patent Issued Aug 28, 1878*
*Line Constructed*
*Blue Spring to New Smyrna 28.48 miles*
*Deeded to*
*Atlantic and Western Railroad Company Nov 29, 1887*

23

---

**NO 20**
**SOUTHEASTERN RAILWAY COMPANY**
*Letters patent issued May 10, 1899*
*Enterprise to Titusville 35.71 miles*
*Deeded to Florida East Coast Railway Company July 18, 1902*

9

---

**NO 6**
**THE ATLANTIC COAST, ST. JOHNS AND INDIAN RIVER RAILWAY COMPANY**
*Letters Patent Issued Jan 25, 1883*
*Enterprise to Titusville 35.7 miles*
*Foreclosed and deeded by*
*Special Master April 21, 1889*
*to T. S. Beatty*
*Deeded to A. V. S. Smith April 22, 1889*
*Deeded by A. V. S. Smith to Southeastern Railway Co. June 1, 1899*

14

---

**NO 9**
**ORMOND BRIDGE COMPANY**
*Incorporated June 16, 1887*
*Bridge Across Halifax River*
*Ormond to Ormond Beach 1.76 miles*
*Deeded to Florida East Coast Railway Co. Feb 16, 1893*

19

---

**NO 24**
**ATLANTIC COAST LINE RAILWAY COMPANY**
*Enterprise to Enterprise Junction—Leased Line*
*4.83 miles*
*Lease dated Dec 7, 1910*

24

---

In order to reconstruct the history of the FEC, consideration was given to the use of either chronology or geography as the superior method. In order to show the progression of lines into other lines that eventually became the Florida East Coast Railway, it was decided to attempt the reconstruction geographically, in order that a continuum of companies could be established. There were actually a total of 20 companies involved. However, the FECs 1916 Corporate History, published by the Railroad under ICC mandate, makes no reference at all to one them (St. Johns & Indian River RR). It is, therefore, a possibility that one or more "earlier predecessors" could exist.

## ARLINGTON & ATLANTIC RAILWAY CO.

This Company was incorporated under the general laws of the State of Florida and received letters patent August 29, 1882, for the purpose of constructing, maintaining, and operating a line of narrow gauge railway from a point on the St. Johns River near Arlington (Duval County) to a point on the Atlantic Coast (in Duval County). Articles of Incorporation were filed in the office of the Secretary of State, Tallahassee, Florida, and recorded in Book "B," pp 336 and 337. Date of organization is unknown. The original incorporators were John Q. Burbridge, George B. Griffin and J. C. Greeley.

There are no records available from which to determine the original costs or dates of construction, or the date when the road was first opened for commercial service. The exact mileage constructed by the Company is also not a matter of available record.

By a resolution of its stockholders, the name of the Corporation was changed September 25, 1882, to the Jacksonville & Atlantic Railroad Co., and the change in name was filed in the office of the Secretary of State on September 23, 1882.[6]

## JACKSONVILLE & ATLANTIC RAILROAD CO.

This Company was the successor, by change of name, of the Arlington and Atlantic Ry. Co. The Arlington & Atlantic had filed a resolution of its stockholders with the Secretary of State to change its name to the Jacksonville & Atlantic RR Co. on September 23, 1882, but letters patent do not appear to have been issued to the latter Company until August 6, 1883. Articles of Incorporation were filed in the office of the Secretary of State in Book "B," pages 450 and 451. The date of organization is unknown. The original incorporators were James M. Schumacher, John Q. Burbridge, and W. M. Ledwith.

There are no records available from which to determine the original cost, date of construction or the date when the road was first opened for commercial service. The owned mileage at the date of sale was 16.54 miles.

The mortgage or trust deed on the road, lands and other properties, was foreclosed in 1890 and the property was sold at Master's Sale to W. M. Drew on December 5, 1892 (Deed recorded in Book #83, page 690, Duval County records). W. M. Drew deeded the property to the Jacksonville & Atlantic Railway Co. under date of January 18, 1893 (Deed recorded in book #84, page 341, Duval County).[7]

## JACKSONVILLE & ATLANTIC RAILWAY CO.

This company was incorporated and received letters patent on January 10, 1893, for the purpose of acquiring and operating the properties of the J. & A. Railroad Co., extending from the south bank of the St. Johns River to Pablo, a distance of 16.54 miles. Articles of incorporation were filed and recorded in Book "C," pp. 67, 68, 69 and 70. The original incorporators were W. M. Drew, W. A. Macduff, B. P. Hazelton and J. W. Archibald.

Under date of January 23, 1893, the J&A Railway Co. obtained the right to use the tracks of the JStA&IR Ry. Co. from the point of intersection of its tracks with the JStA&IR Ry. Co., South Jacksonville Yard, to the ferry dock at South Jacksonville.

The bonds of the J&A Railroad Co. were assumed by the J&A Railway Co. These bonds and the capital stock of the J&A Railway Co. were purchased by Flagler in 1899. The property, rights and franchises of the J&A Railway Co. were deeded to the FEC Rwy. Co., September 25, 1900.

Improvements on the tracks acquired from the J&A Railway were begun immediately by the FEC. A station building and track scales were erected at South Jacksonville, the road was re-graded and standard gauged. New rails and ties were laid, turnouts, shelter stations at all flag stops, buildings and section houses erected and the line extended to Mayport, a distance of about 8 miles, where extensive docks and wharves were constructed.[8]

## JACKSONVILLE BRIDGE CO.

This Company was incorporated November 9, 1888 for the construction, maintenance and operation of a bridge at Jacksonville, across the St. Johns River, a distance of .54 miles. Articles of incorporation were filed in Tallahassee. The original incorporators were R. H. Mason, J. P. Kelly and J. R. Parrott. The date of organization is unknown.

The construction of the bridge was commenced in January, 1889, and was completed and opened for service January 20, 1890.

THE HARBOR AND "EAST COAST LINE" BRIDGE.—JACKSONVILLE.

The substructure was contracted for by Anderson & Barr on November 12, 1888; the superstructure was built by the Keystone Bridge Co. under contract covered by File 890,[9] December, 1888. The turning gear and draw were built by the Excelsior Iron works covered by contract of December 13, 1889.

The bridge was operated by the JStA&HR Ry. Co. from its completion until October 31, 1892. On November 1, 1892 the JStA&IR Ry. Co. assumed control, through purchase of the stock of the Bridge Company.

The property, rights and franchise of the Jacksonville Bridge Co. were transferred by deed dated May 5, 1896 to the FEC Rwy. Co.[10]

## JACKSONVILLE, ST. AUGUSTINE & HALIFAX RIVER RAILWAY CO.

This Company was incorporated and received letters patent January 24, 1881 for the construction, operation and maintenance of a narrow gauge line of railway from the south bank of the St. Johns River opposite the City of Jacksonville to some point at or near St. Augustine, thence southwardly to within about 15 miles of the Atlantic Ocean, at a point near the headwaters of the Halifax River, a distance of about 80 miles.[11] Articles of Incorporation were filed in Secretary of State's Book "B," pp. 228 and 229. The Company was organized on February 1, 1881, and the principal office was located at St. Augustine.

The road was constructed from the south bank of the St. Johns to St. Augustine, a distance of 36.24 miles. The cost and the dates of the original construction, as well as the date the road first opened for commercial service are indeterminate, though it appears that the road opened for business in June, 1883. The road was standard gauged on January 20, 1890. The bonds and stocks of the Company were purchased by Flagler on December 31, 1885.

From April, 1885 until 1888, a large amount of additional construction was performed. On April 1, 1888, a contract was entered into with the Savannah, Florida & Western Rwy. for terminal facilities at Jacksonville. Upon the completion of the bridge over the St. Johns River on January 20, 1890, the contract with the SF&W was terminated, and through freight and passenger service over the JStA&HR Rwy. Co. was inaugurated to Jacksonville.

On October 31, 1892, the JStA&HR Rwy. Co. secured control of the Jacksonville Bridge. On November 1, 1892, the property of the JStA&HR Rwy. Co. was leased to the JStA&IR Rwy. Co. On April 4, 1896, the property, rights and franchise of the JStA&HR Rwy. Co. were deeded to the FEC.[12]

SAINT JOHNS RAILWAY COMPANY
OF FLORIDA

Pass E. Vonder Pass Ticket Agt.

**1883**

Until December 31st, 1883, unless otherwise ordered.
NOT TRANSFERABLE.

R. McLaughlin

No.                                    President.

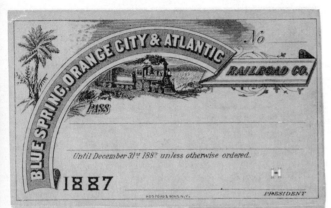

BLUE SPRING ORANGE CITY & ATLANTIC RAILROAD CO.

No

PASS

Until December 31st 1887 unless otherwise ordered.

**1887**

ROSFORD & SONS, N.Y.                    PRESIDENT

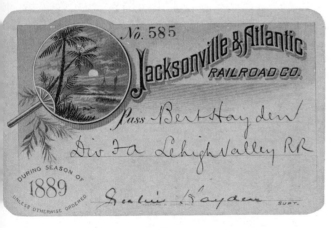

No. 585

Jacksonville & Atlantic RAILROAD CO.

Pass Bert Hayden

Div J.a Lehigh Valley RR

DURING SEASON OF
1889
UNLESS OTHERWISE ORDERED

Julia Hayden

SUPT.

Pass Mr. W. E. Pearson

President

B & SS Co.

Good During the Year
1893
Unless otherwise ordered.

INDIAN RIVER STEAMBOAT CO.

No A 57

R B Cable,

General Manager

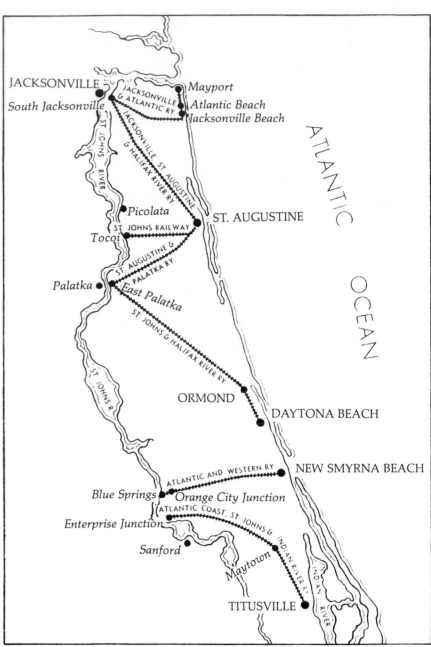

FLORIDA EAST COAST RAILWAY

PASS H. Murphy

FROM Jax TO

ACCOUNT Pass

ISSUED Oct 27th EXPIRES Oct 1905

STOP-OVER PERMITTED AT
INTERMEDIATE STATIONS.

No. 10578

COUNTERSIGNED BY

J. R. Parrott

Vice-President & General Manager

8235   A FLORIDA EAST COAST RAILWAY STATION.

COPYRIGHT, 1904, BY DETROIT PHOTOGRAPHIC CO.

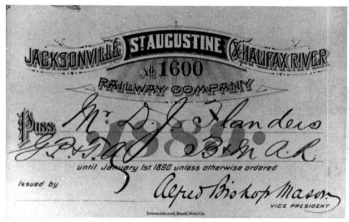

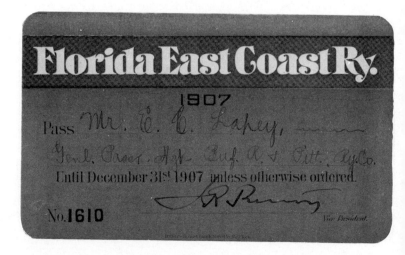

## ST. AUGUSTINE & PALATKA RAILWAY CO.

This company was incorporated under the laws of the State of Florida and received letters patent February 5, 1885, for the purpose of constructing a line of railway from Tocoi Jct. to East Palatka,[13] a distance of about 25.3 miles. Articles of Incorporation are filed with the Secretary of State in Book "B," pp. 590 and 591. Date of organization of the company is unknown.

There are no records available from which to determine the original cost and dates of construction.[14]

The bonds secured by a mortgage on the railway properties and lands were purchased by Flagler on July 23, 1893.

The rights, property and franchise of the Company, which included 21.75 miles of railway, were deeded to the St. Augustine & Halifax River Railway Co., March 1, 1889.[15]

## ST. AUGUSTINE & HALIFAX RIVER RAILWAY

This Company was incorporated and received letters patent April 15, 1889 for the purpose of operating and maintaining an existing line of railway known as the St. Augustine & Palatka Rwy. Co. The original incorporators were Mason Young, Charles C. Deming and Alfred B. Mason. Articles of incorporation are recorded in Book "B," P. 733. The organization of the company was perfected July 16, 1889.

On November 1, 1892, the road was leased to the JStA&IR Rwy. Co. The bonds of the St. Augustine & Palatka Rwy. Co. were purchased by the St. Augustine & Halifax River Rwy. Co. on July 16, 1889. They came into ownership of H. M. Flagler on July 23, 1895.

The property, rights and franchise of this Company, including 20.38 miles of track, were deeded to the FEC on April 4, 1896.[16]

## PALATKA BRIDGE COMPANY

This Company was incorporated April 15, 1888 for a period of 99 years, for the purpose of constructing and operating a bridge from the east to the west bank of the St. Johns River at Palatka, with the right to construct tracks from E. Palatka to the west end of Palatka Bridge, a distance of 1.81 miles. With its principal office in Jacksonville, the Company was organized August 15, 1888.

On October 1, 1888, J. P. Kelly, as president of the Company, made a contract with T. E. Brown and Co. for the construction of the bridge, same to be built by December 10, 1888.

Funds for the construction work were secured from the sale of St. Johns & Halifax River Rwy. Co's. Palatka Bridge bonds, which were secured by a mortgage with the Mercantile Trust Co. of New York, dated December 10, 1888. The bonds were acquired by Flagler on May 2, 1895. In that same year, the drawbridge was rebuilt to conform to more modern requirements.

The property, rights and franchise of the Palatka Bridge Co. were deeded to the FEC on May 5, 1896.[17] [18]

## THE ST. JOHNS & HALIFAX RAILWAY CO.

This Company was incorporated and letters patent issued December 12, 1881, for the purpose of constructing a narrow gauge line of railway from Rollestown[19] to Daytona, a distance of about 45 miles. Articles of Incorporation are in Book "B," P. 307. The date of organization is unknown.[20]

The original cost and dates of construction, as well as the date when the road first opened for operation cannot be determined.[20]

Its property, rights and franchises, which included 51.99 miles of railway, were deeded to the St. Johns and Halifax River Rwy. Co. on October 1, 1888.[21]

## ST. JOHNS & HALIFAX RIVER RAILWAY

This Company was incorporated and received letters patent October 11, 1888, for the purpose of operating and maintaining a 3 foot gauge railway, known as the St. Johns & Halifax Railway Co., and to complete the construction of that road from Rollestown to Palatka. Articles of Incorporation are recorded in Book "B," page 719. The original incorporators were Mason Young, Charles C. Deming, and Alfred B. Mason. The Company was organized September 12, 1888.

The Company constructed the bridge at Palatka, connecting East Palatka with Palatka, and re-constructed the line to standard gauge, the re-gauging apparently being done between October 1, and December 10, 1888 in order to coincide with the opening of the bridge and enabling through service to begin.

On November 1, 1892 the property of the St. Johns & Halifax River Rwy. Co. was leased to the JStA&IR Rwy. Co. for operation and maintenance.

The rights, property and franchise of the St. Johns & Halifax River Rwy. Co., which included the 50.59 miles of railway, were transferred to the FEC Rwy. Co. by deed dated April 4, 1896. Supplement deed dated June 18, 1901 corrected certain omissions in the original deed.[22]

## ORMOND BRIDGE CO.

The Ormond Bridge Company was incorporated and received its charter on June 18, 1887 for a period of 50 years for the purpose of constructing a bridge across the Halifax River at Ormond, and the connection of tracks from Ormond Station to Ormond Beach, a distance of 1.76 miles. The original incorporators were Charles McNary, president; J. A. Bostrom, vice president; and James Carnell, secretary. The date of organization is unknown.

On September 2, 1887, the St. Johns & Halifax Rwy. Co. entered into an agreement with the Ormond Bridge Co. for the construction of a bridge across the Halifax River at Ormond to provide passage of steam engines with trains, also wagons, carriages and other vehicles and stock and for persons on foot. The St. Johns & Halifax Rwy. Co. was to operate, maintain and keep the bridge in repair for a ten year period.

On December 1, 1890, the Ormond Bridge Co. entered into a contract with Anderson & Price[23] for the leasing and operation of said bridge for a period terminating October 1, 1897.[24]

No records are available showing original cost or dates of construction or when the bridge was first opened for service.[25]

Flagler secured 60 shares of the stock of the Bridge Co. and assumed control in January, 1898, electing J. R. Parrott, president; Charles McNary, treasurer; and J. A. Bostrom, secretary.

On February 16, 1898, a deed conveyed to the FEC all property and appurtenances of the Bridge Co., and the railroad assumed all outstanding obligations of the Company.[26]

## THE HALIFAX & INDIAN RIVER RAILWAY

This company was incorporated under the laws of the State and letters patent issued on September 3, 1891, to construct, maintain and operate a standard gauge line of railway from Daytona on the Halifax River to some point on the Indian River near Titusville, a distance of about 50 miles. Articles of Incorporation are in Book of Incorporation (no letter issued), P. 716. The date of organization is unknown.

No mileage was constructed by this company and none of its records are available. (Or are known to exist in 1984). On June 14, 1892, the Company secured a franchise from the Town Council of Titusville to run its tracks through DeSoto Street, in the Town of Titusville.

Its property, rights and franchise were transferred to the Florida Coast & Gulf Rwy. Co. by deed dated August 16, 1892, and the president and secretary of the Halifax & Indian River Rwy. tendered their resignations as directors and as president and secretary respectively, on August 20, 1892.[27]

## BLUE SPRING, ORANGE CITY & ATLANTIC RAILROAD CO.

This company was incorporated and received letters patent dated August 26, 1878,[28] for the purpose of constructing a standard gauge line of railroad from a point on the St. Johns River near Blue Spring to New Smyrna, a distance of about 30 miles. Articles of Incorporation are recorded in books of records (no letter listed) pages 108 to 111. The date of organization is unknown.

In 1883 construction began and 3 miles of track were laid. The entire road, comprising 26.48 miles of track was completed in 1886. The exact date that operation began is not known.

The books of accounts or records covering original construction are not in our possession, and the original cost of this property cannot be ascertained.[29]

The property, rights and franchise of the B S, O C & A RR CO. were deeded to the Atlantic & Western RR Co. on November 29, 1887.[30]

## ATLANTIC & WESTERN RAILROAD CO.

This Company was incorporated and letters patent issued to it on March 7, 1888, for the purpose of acquiring the property of the B S O C & A RR Co. Articles of Incorporation are recorded in Book "B," pp 676 and 677, April 18, 1888. The original incorporators were W. R. Chapman; Dexter Hunter; John G. Moore; Calvin S. Brice; Samuel Thomas, and others. The date of organization is unknown.

The Company assumed payment of the outstanding mortgage and bond issues of the B S, O C & A RR Co. in a deed of transfer dated November 29, 1887. A mortgage was executed by the A & W RR Co. to secure its issue of bonds dated December 20, 1887 to the Central Trust Co. of New York. This issue was acquired by Flagler on June 12, 1893.[31]

Its property, rights and franchise were deeded to the FEC Rwy. Co. April 4, 1896. Its outstanding bonds were cancelled and mortgage satisfied.[32] [33]

## ST. JOHNS & INDIAN RIVER RAILROAD[34]

The St. Johns & Indian River RR was incorporated in 1876 as the St. Johns River RR, Tram or Iron RR Co.[35] The road extended from Titusville to Salt Lake, a distance of 8.25 miles, being built to 5 foot gauge and laid with 40 pound rail. The original section of the road was opened late in 1876, but almost immediately the line was extended 13 miles to Lake Henry (sic).[36]

There remains little record of the operational activities of the Company, but it is known that, in 1883, the trackage from Titusville to Lake Henry (sic)[36] was taken over by the newly organized ACStJ&IR Rwy. Under the latter organization the line was extended to Enterprise Jct. and today forms a part of the FEC Rwy. branch to that town.[37] [38]

## THE ATLANTIC COAST, ST. JOHNS AND INDIAN RIVER RWY. CO.

This Company was incorporated and received letters patent January 25, 1883, for the purpose of constructing, maintaining and operating a line of wide gauge railway from Enterprise, Volusia County, to Titusville, Brevard County, a distance of about 36 miles.[39] Articles of Incorporation were filed in Book "B," pp 308 and 309. Date of organization is unknown. The road was changed from wide (or broad) to standard gauge in August, 1886.

There are no records available from which to determine the original cost, dates of construction, or the date when the road first opened for service. The Company constructed 35.71 miles of railway, extending from Enterprise to Titusville.[40]

The property of the ACStJ&IR Rwy. was sold April 3, 1899, under foreclosure proceedings by Charles S. Adams and Dennis Egan, special masters appointed by the U.S.Court, and deeded to T. S. Beatty on April 21, 1899. On April 22, 1899, the property was deeded to A. V. S. Smith. On June 1, 1899 it was deeded to the Southeastern Rwy. Co.[41]

Pettengill, writing in Bulletin 86 of the Railway & Locomotive Historical Society managed to contradict himself in discussing this road and its predecessor, the St. Johns & Indian River. Whereas, on page 41 he had given a history of the StJ&IR and states that it was taken over by the ACStJ&IR in 1883, he stated the following on page 107: "This road, having been built as the ACStJ&IR Ry. had for a time been operated as the Indian River Division of the JT&KW but had been relinquished by that road, when that Company became involved in financial difficulties."[42]

## SOUTHEASTERN RAILWAY COMPANY

This Company was incorporated and received letters patent on May 10, 1899 for the purpose of acquiring and operating the property of the ACStJ&IR Rwy. Co. The original incorporators were J. R. Parrott; A. G. Hamlin; J. P. Beckwith[43]; A. V. S. Smith and H. S. Jenison. Articles of Incorporation are in Book "F," pp 309 to 313. The date of organization is unknown.

From June 1, 1899 until July 18, 1902, the road was reconstructed and connected with the FEC at Titusville.[44]

Its property, rights and franchise were deeded to the FEC Rwy. Company on July 16, 1902.[45]

Unlike most other major railroads, which continued merging other roads into their own systems through the late 20s and into the 30s, the merging of the Southeastern Rwy. Co. into the FEC in 1902 was the last amalgamation that the FEC was to experience. While connections included lumber and rock companies, the FECs only intrastate connection (not including Jacksonville Terminal Co. or the "port" railroads), the Trans Florida Central (originally built as the Fellsmere Farms RR) was abandoned by its owners in October, 1952, after receiving ICC permission to do so on September 29.

## FLORIDA COAST & GULF RAILWAY

As noted in the beginning of the Chapter, the FEC had only two predecessors in name, hence the history of the two roads is a fitting end to the chapter. Though the road was built from Daytona to New Smyrna (and perhaps could have been grouped geographically) it was the sole predecessor, in name, to the JStA&IR Rwy., which became, in 1895, the FEC. It is for this reason that the FC&G is being listed next to last in this chapter.

The Company was incorporated and received letters patent May 28, 1892, for the purpose of constructing, maintaining and operating a line of standard gauge railway, from Jacksonvile to a point on the Gulf of Mexico, at or near Tampa, a distance of about 325 miles. The Company was organized June 26, 1892.

The road was authorized to pass through Duval, St. Johns, Putnam, Volusia, Brevard, Orange, Osceola, Dade, Polk and Hillsborough Counties.

The original incorporators were John Bushnell; George Cheesboro; L. B. Dryer; George W. Colton and W. A. Harris, with Bushnell serving as trustee. Articles of Incorporation are in Book "C," pp 538 to 540, dated May 25, 1892.

The Company started immediate survey, and the construction of a line from Daytona to New Smyrna, a distance of 16.07 miles.

At a meeting of the stockholders of the FC&G Rwy. Co., held October 6, 1892, a resolution was adopted to change the name of the Railway to the Jacksonville, St. Augustine & Indian River Rwy. Co., and this amendment to its charter was authorized by letters patent dated October 31, 1892, and were filed in the Office of the Secretary of State, in Book "H," page 8.[46]

The stage was set for the final predecessor.

## JACKSONVILLE, ST. AUGUSTINE & INDIAN RIVER RWY. CO.

On October 6, 1892, at a general meeting of the stockholders of the Florida Coast & Gulf Rwy. Co., a resolution was passed to change the name of the Corporation to JStA&IR Rwy. Co. and letters patent authorizing this change were issued October 31, 1892.

At the meeting of the Board of Directors on November 21, 1892, John Bushnell and G. W. Colton resigned as directors and as president and secretary-treasurer, respectively, and the vacancies were filled by the election of Henry M. Flagler as president, J. C. Salter as secretary and S. W. Crichlow as treasurer.

On November 1, 1892, the Railway Company entered into a contract for the leasing, operation and maintenance of certain properties of the following companies: Jacksonville, St. Augustine & Halifax River Rwy.; St. Johns & Halifax River Rwy. Co.; St. Augustine & Halifax River Rwy. Co.; St. Johns Rwy. Co.; Palatka Bridge Co., and Jacksonville Bridge Co.

This contract provided a continuous operation from Jacksonville to Daytona, a distance of about 110 miles.

Survey for an extension from Daytona to West Palm Beach was begun on May 10, 1892, by the FC&G Rwy., and track laid to New Smyrna, a distance of 15.07 miles. The track of the Atlantic & Western RR at New Smyrna was crossed on September 22, 1892. On November 2, 1892, through train service to New Smyrna was inaugurated by the JStA&IR Rwy.

On January 13, 1893, track laying to the wharf at Cocoa was completed and on February 1, 1893 through freight and passenger traffic was extended to Rockledge, a distance of 64.78 miles from Daytona.

Eau Gallie, 80 miles from Daytona was reached May 16, 1893, and Ft. Pierce, 131.62 miles from Daytona was reached in January, 1894. On January 29, 1894, regular train service was operated over the newly constructed line from New Smyrna to Ft. Pierce for the first time.

The next objective, West Palm Beach, a distance of 58.14 miles from Ft. Pierce, was reached on March 22, 1894, and regular service established on April 2, 1894. The bridge across Lake Worth, connecting Palm Beach to West Palm Beach, was begun during June of 1895, with regular train service commencing on November 12, 1895, two months and three days after the railroad had become the FEC.

On September 9, 1895, at a meeting of the stockholders of the JStA&IR Rwy. Co., a resolution was adopted to change the name of the Corporation to the Florida East Coast Railway and letters patent authorizing this change were issued September 13, 1895.[47]

Ironically, though the final predecessor of the FEC did not have its name for a full three years, it issued a copious amount of descriptive and promotional material, and, because of that, historians of the East

Coast of Florida are able to avail themselves of a wide range of material describing the various towns and villages "along the Gulf Stream." The FEC, as a Florida Industry and Institution, had a strong, well-rounded base from which to make its entry and impact on Florida, the United States, and, ultimately, the World.

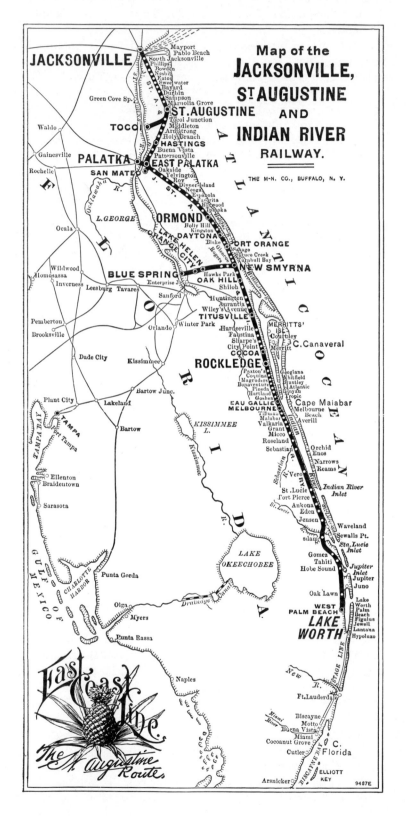

This incredibly rare view, from the authors' collection, shows the original Rockledge depot built by the J.St.A.&I.R. Railway and completed on February 1, 1893. It is likely that this scene, taken from a postcard was copied from an earlier photo and used by the printer around 1905.

*FOOTNOTES*

4. Pettengill, G. W., Jr. "The Story of the Florida Railroads," published as Bulletin 86 of the Railway and Locomotive Historical Society, Boston, Mass., July, 1952, P. 26.
5. For more information on the St. Johns Railway, the reader is referred to Bathe, Greville, "A Brief Account of the Saint Johns Railway of Florida," published May, 1961, by the Saint Augustine Historial Society.
6. FEC Railway Corporate History, St. Augustine, FL, June 30, 1916, P. 23.
7. Ibid, P. 24.
8. Ibid, P. 25
9. A file number is used in several places in the Corporate History, and it is believed that this file number refers to Corporate files formerly stored in Miller Shop Storehouse, and now dispersed to unknown locale or destroyed.
10. Op Cit. FEC Corporate History, P. 21.
11. Interestingly enough, the Halifax River is actually a part of the Inland Waterway and parallels the East Coast of Florida in the area of Daytona Beach. While the name of the Railway ended with "Halifax River," it is possible that the historian compiling the Corporate History meant the Tomoka River; it is, of course, also possible that the charter meant the Tomoka, but it is further within the realm of possibility that the mileage given (15) is wrong.
12. Op Cit, FEC Corporate History, P. 14.
13. Tocoi Jct. was the point at which the St. Augustine & Palatka Rwy. connected with the St. Johns Railway.
14. It is to the credit of early FEC historians such as Arthur Marsh and others that anything at all of the early days of the FEC was saved. If, in 1916, when the Corporate History was written, the official record is replete with phrases such as "There are no records available . . . ." can the modern day historian take umbrage at latter day managements?
15. Op Cit, FEC Corporate History, P. 12.
16. Ibid, P. 13.
17. Ibid, P. 16
18. As a historical footnote, the FEC was granted permission by the ICC to abandon service from E. Palatka to Palatka on November 9, 1949. From 1944 until abandonment, service was operated by a bus-truck vehicle over the highway bridge in place of train service.
19. Rollestown does not appear on modern highway maps, but early Florida railroad maps place it on the St. Johns River, about equidistant between Palatka and San Mateo.
20. Again, the "unknown" phraseology. Fortunately, George Pettengill, in Bulletin 86 of the Railway & Locomotive Historical Society, states that the St. Johns & Halifax Rwy. was organized in 1882, and that it reached Daytona in 1886. Page 11 of the 1946 edition of the FEC's "The Story of a Pioneer" also mentions the 1886 date for the road having reached Daytona.
21. Op Cit, FEC Corporate History, P. 18

22. Ibid, P. 19
23. Anderson & Price were associated with Flagler as partners and later managers of the Ormond Hotel.
24. There is no footnote in the Corporate History explaining this obvious conflict in dates. The St.J.&H. became the St.J.&H R. in 1888, but the St.J.&H.R. did not become part of the JStA&IR until 1892. We must surmise, at this point in time, and with the retrospective of history on paper, that Flagler was already involved with the railroads named, and that the transfer was a "paper" transaction, most likely done to facilitate accounting procedures. Company records from this period are so sparse as to be nonexistent.
25. It appears that the bridge was opened in 1888. FEC service over the bridge ceased in 1926, and in 1932 the bridge was sold by the FEC for $10,000.00 and service abandoned.
26. Op cit, FEC Corporate History, P. 20.
27. Ibid, P. 22.
28. The BS,OC&A was the third railroad built that would eventually became part of the FEC.
29. If the records and other material were not in the FECs possession in 1916, there is little chance that the Company's material has survived to the present day, with the exception of the pass shown in this chapter.
30. Op cit, FEC Corporate History, P. 26.
31. Though no mention is made in the Corporate History, the A&W was apparently operated by the JStA&IR Rwy. following the purchase of the bonds by Flagler. JStA&IR passenger brochures bear out this fact. It appears that the A&W maintained its own identity until the April 4, 1896 amalgamation with the FEC.
32. Sometime in late 1894 or early 1895, an epidemic of some sort struck Blue Spring, killing many of the residents and causing the town to be abandoned. The A&W was then cut back to Orange City Jct., a distance of about four miles. On September 22, 1933, the Federal Court approved the abandonment of the A&W branch in its entirety, subject to ICC approval. Same was granted on April 6, 1934 and service on the branch ended on May 7, with dismantling completed by the end of that year.
33. Op cit, FEC Corporate History, P. 27.
34. The St.J&IR RR is probably the most enigmatic and least known of the predecessors. It does not appear in the Corporate History, and, in fact, this material is taken from another source (see footnote 38). It may be that, due to the fact that the StJ&IR had been completely "ingested" by the ACStJ&IR Rwy., the FEC was (possibly) unaware of the StJ&IR's existence at the time of the writing of the Corporate History.
35. The name of the railroad is shown as printed in Bulletin 86 of the Railway and Locomotive Historical Society. See footnote 38.
36. The rails did not go to Salt Lake, but passed relatively close. The nearest to Lake Henry that can be found close to the route of the StJ&IR was (is) Lake Harney, however, the name "Lake Henry" has been left intact in the text.
37. Between December 2, 1924 and December 2, 1925, the name "Enterprise Jct." was changed to "Benson Jct." and the reason today is unknown.
38. Pettengill, George W. Jr., "The Story of the Florida Railroads," Published as Bulletin 86 of the Railway and Locomotive Historical Society, Boston, July, 1952, P. 41.
39. As will be noted, the FEC Corporate History of 1916 appears to either ignore or be unaware of the St. Johns & Indian River Rwy. as a predecessor to the ACStJ&IR Rwy. It also ignores the Jacksonville, Tampa and Key West Railway Company whose 1893 map indicates ownership of the Enterprise Junction to Titusville line which connects to the Indian River Steamboat Company at Titusville.
40. It seems that this statement (as noted in Footnote 39) is incorrect, due to the existence of a predecessor road that had constructed at least some of the railroad.
41. Op cit, FEC Corporate History, P. 28.
42. Another mention of the road is on Page 83 of Bulletin 86.
43. Beckwith and Parrott were FEC vice presidents.
44. The February 11, 1901 FEC timetable shows service from Titusville to Sanford (for several years the FEC had trackage rights on the Atlantic Coast Line from Enterprise Jct. to Sanford and operated their trains from Titusville through to Sanford) as part of its branch line service. It appears that the Southeastern maintained a corporate identity but was operated by the FEC from the time of the 1899 takeover until the 1902 merger.
45. Op cit, FEC Corporate History, P. 29.
46. Ibid, P. 9.
47. Ibid, pp. 10 and 11.

The original segment of what was to become known as the Florida East Coast Railway was the St. Johns Railway. This view of 2-4-0 "J.H. Flagler" is indicative of the minimal motive power requirements of that railroad. J.H. Flagler was not related to Henry M., who, in fact, did not arrive in St. Augustine until 1883. The photo is circa 1870.

There is no question as to the ancestry of this noble looking 4-4-0. FEC 9 originally came to the J.St.A.&H.R. as the former St. Johns Ry. 5. There is, among historians, some discrepancy as to the year, with some saying 1887 and others swearing the correct date to be 1889. Needless to say, the rarity of the engine itself on film overwhelms the academic points, and, perforce, renders them quite moot. (Though the photograph is dated 1910, Company records indicate that 9, nee Number 5, was sold in 1903.).

—(J. Nelson Collection)

So little...so very little...remains of what once was on the Florida East Coast. The records—written, photographic, concrete—have almost all been lost or destroyed in the century passed since that fateful December 31, 1885 when Flagler purchased the bonds of the narrow gauge Jacksonville, St. Augustine and Halifax River Railroad. What remains must be cherished, for it is all we have.

Though obviously made from a copy negative, StJ&H #3 warrants the East Coast historian's close attention as it sits patiently at Daytona, after having brought the first train into that sleepy little village in 1886. Number 3, built by Baldwin early in 1886, was named "Bulow," and, later became St. Johns & Halifax River #3. Since there was no "Bulow" listed among the incorporators of either the St. Johns & Halifax River Rwy., or its predecessor, the St. Johns & Halifax Railway, we can only blindly conjecture on who "Bulow" was. But, most importantly, we do know that, sadly, the little 4-4-0 never made it to the FEC, but was sold by the J.St.A.&H.R. to a Mexican short line for use on the Yucatan peninsula.

—(J. Nelson Collection)

A Jacksonville, St. Augustine and Halifax River passenger train near Daytona Beach.

The St. John's Railway was the earliest constructed segment of what would become, in 1895, the Florida East Coast Railway. As such, it was more than just a pioneer. The St. John's was, in effect, the Christopher Columbus of the railroads of the East Coast of Florida. Tracks were laid in and through a wilderness, with the promise of fiscal success being minimal. Though the St. John's, first built of the FEC predecessors, was also the first to be abandoned, it was a solution to a problem of the times, and provided St. Augustine with its first rails. Ultimately, the connection to the steamboats at Tocoi would be its undoing, as Palatka was a far superior dockage, with revenue producing towns and sidings enroute to the St. Johns River, of which the railroad of the same name had none. The view of the cars themselves is a revelation, for this photograph is the only known picture of a piece of St. Johns Railway passenger equipment. This picture, taken prior to 1890 shows the cars and a "coupling" device, which may well have been the horse harness hookup. As it was, in the end, with so many of the FEC predecessors, most all of the records were discarded prior to 1916, and it was only because of the researchings of the late Greville Bathe that we are able, today, to piece together anything at all in the way of a history on this important link to today's FEC.

—*Florida State Archives: Author's Collection*

Since the very last of the FEC predecessors has been completely amalgamated into the Flagler System road by 1902, it is easy to understand the dearth of historic records or photographs of the predecessor lines. Therefore, it becomes a matter of celebration, when, in the course of study and research, a clear and fine view of so obscure a road as the Jacksonville and Atlantic is unearthed. It becomes even more momentous when, unlike many other shots of so many of the predecessors, the photography is an engine, clear and unblurred, with human beings visible to lend proportion. Happily, on November 19, 1898, a man, his camera, two railroad emloyees, an onlooker, and a J&A train were simultaneously at Pablo Beach, on what became the Jacksonville Beaches branch of the Florida East Coast.

*—(J. Nelson Collection)*

The Jacksonville, St. Augustine and Halifax River Railway ferry boat "Armsmear."

—*Florida State Archives: Author's Collection*

The FEC's connections south of Jacksonville were limited to a few lumber roads and one common carrier the Fellsmere Farms Company's Fellsmere Railroad (later Trans Florida Central). Traffic and equipment on the road was small, and contributions to revenue (much less net) bordered on positively insignificant. Fellsmere Farms 101 is shown here at the Fellsmere Muck Plant, and its origin is unknown.

A rare view of the Jacksonville, St. Augustine and Halifax River Station at Ormond Beach.

In this view from an early postcard, South Jacksonville Station, known then as Union Depot because it served the trains going to the beaches, as well as the main line, awaits the arrival of a northbound FEC train. This station survived in more or less its original configuration until it was demolished in the late 1970s.

Jackson and Sharp built many of the FECs, and its predecessors, passenger cars. This extremely rare photo is Jacksonville and Atlantic combination car 1, "Pablo Beach." The J. and A. was originally a narrow gauge road, as attested to by the trucks sitting on the flat car at the left of the passenger car body. One can only imagine the elegance of the interior of this car, including the baggage areas. The sheen of the fresh paint, the striping, and the outlining of the door panels are an indication of the craftsmanship and care which went into the manufacture of the early railroad passenger cars. The year was 1885.

Trans Florida Central 103, shown here abandoned at Fellesmere in 1936 is rich in Florida history. Built at Schenectady by American Locomotive in November, 1888, the engine was sold to the J.St.A.&H.R., where it became their #4. It became FEC 4 (one of 5 FEC engines with that number!) and was sold in 1918 to a succession of Florida lumber, construction and equipment dealers, going to Missouri in 1921 and, finally, returning to Florida as TFC 103 on April 4, 1924.

Due to the wholesale destruction of historic records through the intervening years, little exists in the way of complete rosters of the FEC predecesors. Fortunately many of the Jackson and Sharp negatives have been preserved. In this view Jacksonville, St. Augustine and Halifax River car 4 is resplendent in its brand new livery. Particular attention should be paid to the ornate panels at the exterior corners of the car body and the entrance doorways. Imagine what the interior must have been like!

JACKSONVILLE & ATLANTIC RAILROAD.

BAGGAGE.    PABLO BEACH.    1

338

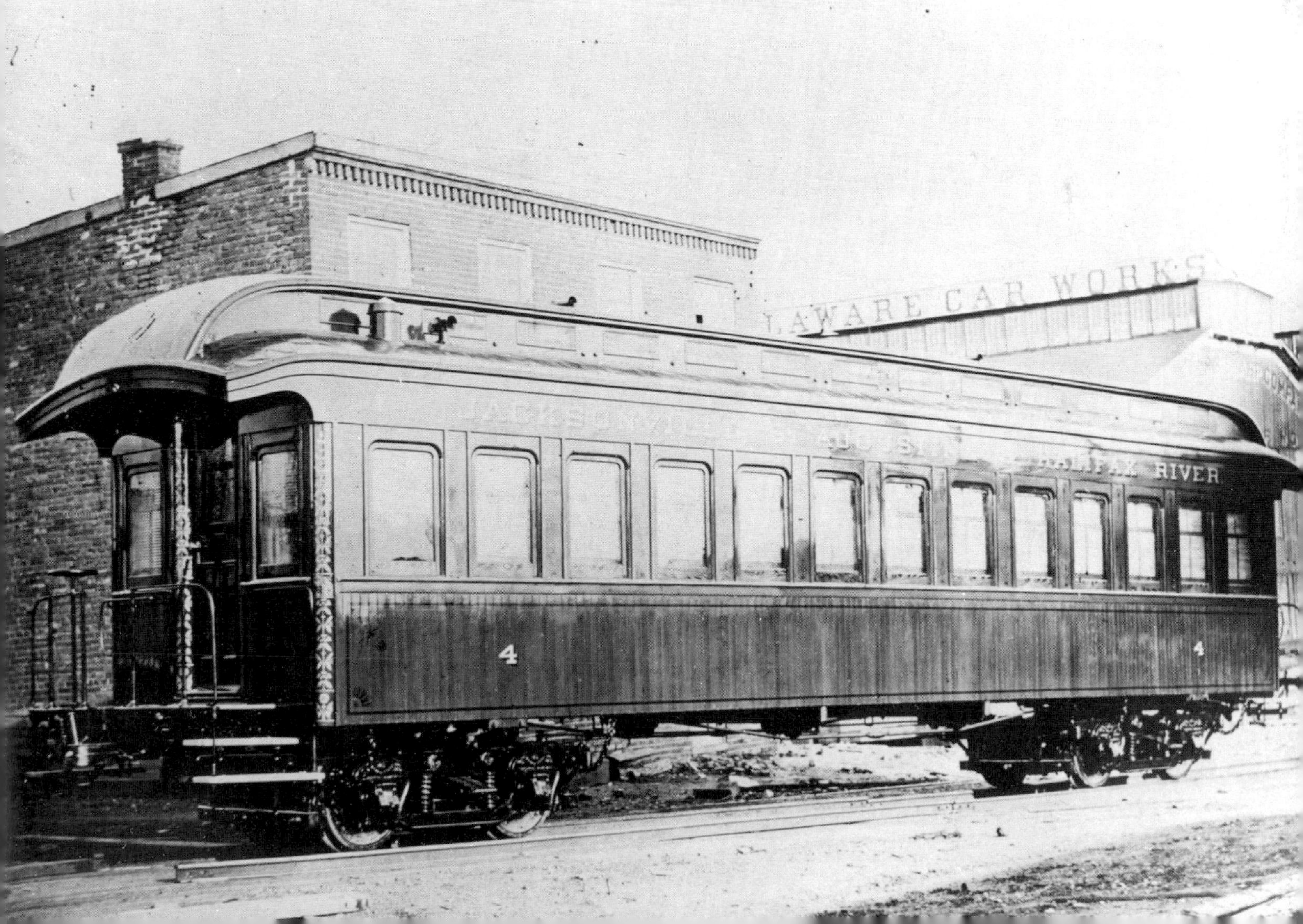

LAWARE CAR WORKS

JACKSONVILLE & AUGUSTINE    HALIFAX RIVER

4    4

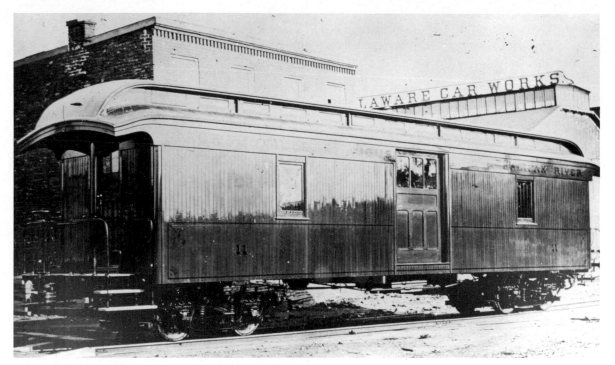

Car 11 is just a lowly baggage car yet the gloss of the varnish is evident in this builder's photograph taken just before shipment to the new owner in 1883.

In contrast to the preceding photo, the Jacksonville, St. Augustine and Halifax River Railroad has changed their passenger color scheme and in this 1888 picture of a two door baggage car, the Jackson and Sharp photograph clearly indicates the workmanship of the times.

The successor to the Jacksonville, St. Augustine and Halifax River was the Jacksonville, St. Augustine and Indian River. The Halifax River is located near Daytona Beach in Volusia County while the Indian River is much further south paralleling among others, the county of the same name. In these views, newly constructed (1892) Jackson and Sharp products, made for the J., St.A. and I.R. reflect the extension of the railroad well south of the Halifax River.

On the branch lines that were formed from the main lines of the FEC predecessors, the railroad inherited the then existing facilities. The line from New Smyrna to Orange City was once the Blue Spring, Orange City and Atlantic Railroad. It later became the Atlantic and Western Railroad and then the A & W branch of the FEC. The station at Orange City (once the predecessor road's headquarters) was a delightful mixture of Victorian gingerbread and American Railroad practicality.

The FEC purchased the line of the Jacksonville, Tampa and Key West Railway from Titusville to Enterprise (later Benson) Junction. J.T. & K.W. 4-4-0 #5 was typical of the motive power on that sparsely settled line. A product of the Baldwin Locomotive Works of Philadelphia. The locomotive builder's plate indicates that it was builder's 7487 and came from Baldwin in 1884.

West Palm Beach, Fla.
City and Ferry Docks, Lake Worth and F. E. C. Railway Bridge.

At two locations — Palm Beach and Ormond Beach, Flagler built hotels that were separated from the mainland by wide bodies of water. To reach the Hotel Ormond on Ormond Beach across the Halifax River the railroad constructed the trestle shown here. And to reach the Royal Poinciana and the Breakers on Palm Beach, the railroad made its way across Lake Worth. In 1926 the FEC ceased service on the Ormond bridge and in 1932 received permission to sell the 1.7 mile branch for $10,000. The company purchasing the branch simply abandoned the rail portion and operated the bridge as a toll bridge. On June 12, 1935 the receiver filed an application with the I.C.C. to abandon the branch to Palm Beach. On August 7, 1935 permission was granted and the 1.47 miles dismantled by December 31, 1935.

Florida East Coast Railroad Bridge at Ormond, Fla.

44

Dock At Fort Pierce, Fla.

Motor Railway, Melbourne Beach, Fla.

For some reason, at several cities along the right of way, there was trackage leading to the city's docks; at Fort Pierce, Melbourne and Titusville, there was something called a "motor railway" and while all of them seem to have been gone by 1929 or 1930, tangible evidence of their existence remains today as noted in these photos. Whether or not they actually connected with the FEC and who operated them is unknown to us at this time.

The Dock, Titusville, Fla.

"Our Founder"

# CHAPTER 3

# CONFLUENCE AND CATALYST

Confluence, according to Webster, is an act or instance of congregating.[48] A catalyst is " . . . . an agent introducing catalysis," which is any reaction brought about by a separate agent.[49]

There are, throughout history, those things that occur when, for whatever unknown reason, forces gather as if in a chemical experiment and are then ignited by a person acting as a catalyst. The history of the FEC and its predecessors from 1883 on is the result of just such an occurrence: the time, the events, and the location converging; coming together as if pre-ordained in order that one man—a man of influence, wealth, power, intelligence, foresight and (perhaps most of all) the desire to create—could turn a barren, unpopulated, and pestilential subtropical wilderness into what became known as 'The American Riviera.'

It was then, in the winter of 1883-84,[50] that one Henry M. Flagler, multi-millionaire industrialist, late of Standard Oil, partner of John D. Rockefeller and seeker of a clime of warmth, journeyed to St. Augustine.

Arriving in the 'Ancient City', Flagler found a sleepy, almost dilapidated town of about 2,500 inhabitants. While he was charmed with the climate and beauty of the old place, he found the hotel facilities quite inferior to the accommodations he and his circle of friends were accustomed to in northern cities.

Many wealthy Americans were then going to the Mediterranean each winter to sun themselves on the shores of Southern France and Italy, a section known as "the Riviera." Flagler became convinced that these wealthy Americans could be induced to come to Florida, which offered an even better winter climate, if proper facilities were provided for their accommodation. He was determined to create an 'American Riviera'.[51]

Flagler, who had remarried in June of 1883, had already retired from Standard Oil as a man of immense wealth, and could have been content to spend his remaining years travelling or "resorting." That, of course, was not to occur.

The winter of 1883-84 was particularly bitter in the north and the Flaglers remained in St. Augustine until the end of February. At first, Flagler was certain that he would retire to a life of ease in St. Augustine, but one thing worried him. Why did St. Augustine, with such lovely weather, have such poor lodging? Why wasn't a hotel built or planned to entice weather-weary Northerners?

To say that Flagler had any intention of playing the role of a developer this early would be a mistake. His thoughts, however, were soon to turn in that direction. He began to have visions of what St. Augustine might be if only a little money were lavished on her. Destiny had intervened to shape a new career for the oil magnate.[52]

Flagler was not born a railroad builder, and there is little evidence that he was interested in hotels until he saw the need for better accommodations in St. Augustine. Transportation facilities were in poor shape as were the hotels.

Flagler was well aware of Florida's poor railroads, but it was brought to his attention very distinctly when he began construction of the Ponce de Leon Hotel. The Jacksonville, St. Augustine and Halifax River Railroad, which had reached St. Augustine in June, 1883, was a rickety, little narrow gauge road, built with 30 pound rail, and, consequently, proved of minimal value to Flagler in the ongoing hotel construction.

There was, in 1884, little thought in Flagler's mind of operating a railroad. Unfortunately, however, the ownership of the JStA&HR showed little inclination to upgrade their railroad or its facilities. Flagler, with a small fortune being invested in his St. Augustine building enterprise knew that better transportation facilities were an absolute must, both for the immense quantities of building materials the hotels (he had begun a second hotel, the Alcazar, and purchased a third, the Casa Monica, before the Ponce de Leon was completed) would require, and later for the elegant class of people he hoped to attract to St. Augustine when the hotels were completed.

A rare confluence of forces was now at work. On very few occasions in the history of American Industrial Enterprise have person, place and time coincided so perfectly, and so remarkably, as the events that led Flagler back to St. Augustine determined to build a magnificent hotel. It was that determination that forced Flagler's decision to improve the transportation to and from his Hotel, and that decision, in turn, set the stage for the single most important event in the industrial history of the East Coast of Florida: on December 31, 1885, Henry M. Flagler purchased the stocks, bonds, and all assets of the Jacksonville, St. Augustine & Halifax River Railway.

The die was cast; the stage was set. Henry Flagler had figuratively thrown the dice, and with that roll unknowingly prepared himself to become a legend—a larger than life character—in his own lifetime. The fortunes of the East Coast—the State—of Florida had, prior to the roll, hung in the balance.

Now, in that moment, at that time, Flagler had taken upon himself the fate of the East Coast of Florida. Without accepting, admitting or acknowledging, he had become Florida's Empire Builder.[53]

## FOOTNOTES

48. Webster's Seventh New Collegiate Dictionary, G. & C. Merriam Co., Springfield, MA. P. 175
49. Ibid, P. 131
50. Akin, Edward Nelson, "Southern Reflections of the Gilded Age: Henry M. Flagler's System, 1885-1913," PhD Thesis, University of Florida, Gainesville, 1975, P. 19
51. Op cit, "Story of a Pioneer," P. 9
52. Martin, Sidney Walter, "Florida's Flagler," University of Georgia Press, Athens, GA, 1949, P. 95.
53. For details regarding Flagler's early years, and his Standard Oil ventures "Florida's Flagler" (see Footnote 52) is recommended reading. "Speedway to Sunshine" is a history of the FEC and it's predecessors, and Flagler is very much a part of that history; however, his importance to this book is his interaction with the FEC and not his earlier years.

*The Casa Marina (Castle by the Sea), Key West*

# CHAPTER 4

# THE EMPIRE BUILDER

Flagler did not consider himself a railroad man, nor did he come to Florida to build railroads or hotels. But because of the circumstances with which he was confronted, magnified by his need to create, Henry M. Flagler, the Standard Oil magnate, became Flagler the railroad builder, and Flagler the hotel builder, and Flagler, the land magnate. Most importantly, through design or otherwise, the man became Flagler the Empire Builder, with most of the East Coast of Florida south of St. Augustine owing its existence to him.

In addition to having a County named after him, and a monument built in his memory on an island between Miami and Miami Beach, almost every town and city on the East Coast has a street, school, park, playground, church or library named after him. It is from this man, this legend, that the story of the FEC and its predecessors springs.

## THE HOTELS

As the predecessor railroads were purchased, and further extended down the East Coast, Flagler built or bought what he and his associates felt would be or was the finest hostelry in the area. The Ponce de Leon opened in January of 1888. In April of that year he purchased the new Casa Monica and renamed it the Cordova. The following year the Alcazar was opened. In 1890, Flagler bought the Hotel Ormond, originally built in 1876. The first three were in St. Augustine, and the Ormond was, of course, at Ormond Beach.

In May of 1893, ground was broken for the Royal Poinciana at Palm Beach, and the hotel opened in February of 1894. The Palm Beach Inn was begun in the summer of 1895 and opened in January of 1896. At the time of the opening the railroad was being extended to Miami, and, as part of Flagler's agreement with the Brickell and Tuttle families, who were Miami's leading commercial people, he agreed to build one of his fine hotels in the settlement around Biscayne Bay. Work began on the Royal Palm Hotel on February 15, 1896 and the big frame structure opened its doors for the first time on January 16, 1897.[54] In the meantime, through negotiation with the British government in Nassau, Flagler purchased the Royal Victoria and the Carthagena hotels, the latter being renamed the Royal Victoria Annex. These purchases were made in 1898, and the Royal Victoria did not open after the 1901 season although it was advertised for several years afterward in Flagler promotional material.[55] The construction of the Colonial, also in Nassau, was begun in the spring of 1898 and completed in 1899.

In addition to the Royal Palm, the Flagler hotel company operated the Hotel Biscayne in Miami. This hotel, built in 1896, was owned by a Flagler lieutenant, Joseph A. McDonald. This association ended when McDonald sold the hotel prior to the 1899 winter season.[56] In the fall of 1900, Flagler commissioned his builder, J. A. McGuire, to begin plans for a hotel at Atlantic Beach. The Continental was to be an ignoble failure, and was the least successful of Flagler's hotels. It opened in time for the summer season of 1901[57] and after losing over $50,000.00 in its first five years the name was changed to the Atlantic Beach Hotel in 1907. In 1909, Flagler sought to rid himself of its operating expenses by renting it to another party. Finally, in 1919, the structure burned.[58]

In 1901, the name of the Palm Beach Inn was changed to "The Breakers." The hotel burned on June 9, 1903 and on June 24, Flagler announced that the hotel would be completely rebuilt. In 1906, the hotel reopened and in 1925–26 was rebuilt following another conflagration. The rebuilt hotel opened on December 29, 1926. The Royal Palm, meanwhile, outmoded and expensive to operate, had been severely damaged in the 1926 hurricane. The hotel closed after a much less than successful 1928 season, never to reopen and was torn down in 1928.

Following Flagler's death in 1913, the Long Key Fishing Camp[59] was completely rebuilt as a rustic and off the beaten path sportsmen's lodge and the Casa Marina in Key West was opened in 1922.

It was following the onset of the depression, and the railroad's fall into receivership in 1931 that the FEC Hotel Company began to crumble. In 1932, the Cordova (nee Casa Monica) was permanently shuttered and Royal Poinciana, by this time termite ridden and a fire hazard, closed for the last time. By 1934

HOTEL PONCE DE LEON, ST. AUGUSTINE

THE CORDOVA AND THE ALCAZAR, ST. AUGUSTINE

THE ORMOND

THE ROYAL POINCIANA, PALM BEACH

THE BREAKERS, PALM BEACH

THE ROYAL PALM, MIAMI

LONG KEY FISHING CAMP

THE COLONIAL, NASSAU

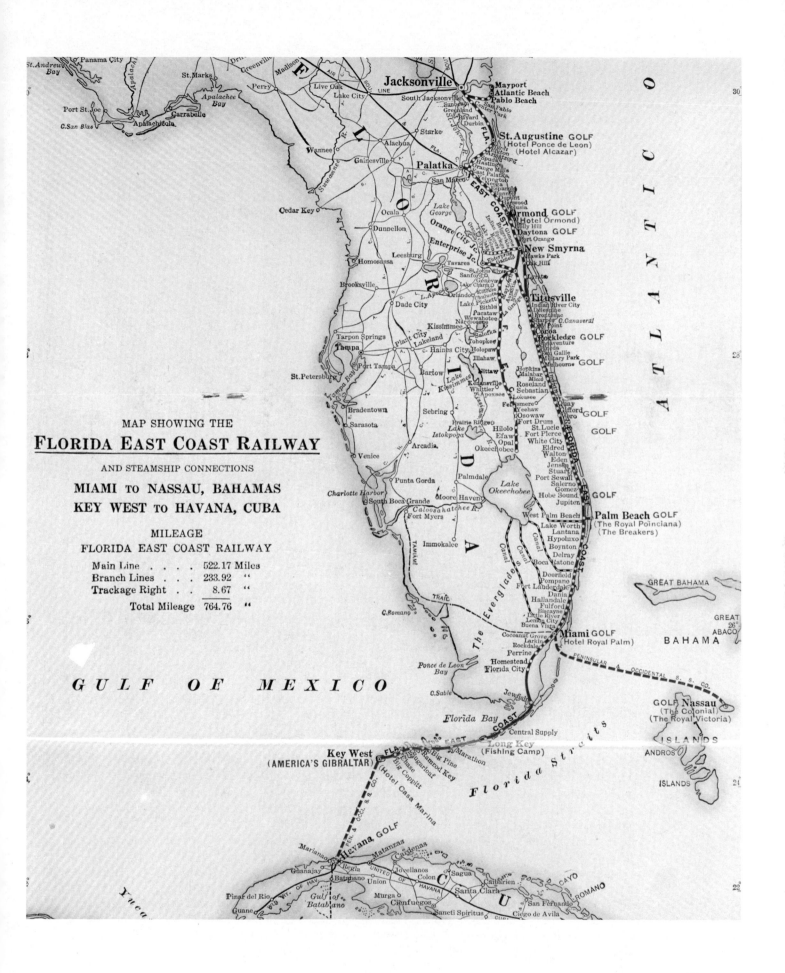

MAP SHOWING THE

# FLORIDA EAST COAST RAILWAY

AND STEAMSHIP CONNECTIONS

## MIAMI TO NASSAU, BAHAMAS
## KEY WEST TO HAVANA, CUBA

MILEAGE
FLORIDA EAST COAST RAILWAY

| | | |
|---|---|---|
| Main Line | . . . . | 522.17 Miles |
| Branch Lines | . . . | 233.92 " |
| Trackage Right | . . | 8.67 " |
| Total Mileage | 764.76 | " |

only the Ponce de Leon, Ormond, Breakers, Casa Marina, and Long Key Fishing Camp were still open. In 1935 the Long Key Fishing Camp was destroyed by the terrible Labor Day Hurricane and would, along with the railway properties in the keys, be disposed of in short order. In 1936, the Royal Poinciana was razed. The Cordova was converted into the St. John's County courthouse while the Alcazar had its hotel section converted to the St. Augustine City Hall and the casino section into the Lightner Museum of Hobbies. The Ponce de Leon closed its doors as a hotel in 1965, but continues to function in a new role as Flagler College, with the statue of Flagler, formerly on display in Station Park just north of the FEC General Offices, now prominently placed in front of the College's main entrance. During the late 1960s the revitalized Flagler System built or acquired thriving new properties: a new Ponce de Leon Motor Hotel on US 1 North in St. Augustine, and Flagler Inn Resort Motels in Gainesville and Nassau.

In the 1970s, the Company[60] sold all of its properties[61] except the Breakers, and this magnificent four star hotel, still considered by many to be the 'grande dame' of American resort hostelries, is the sole survivor of the once far-flung Florida Fast Coast Hotel Co.

## THE LAND COMPANIES

One of Flagler's most profitable pursuits was the acquisition and subsequent sale of large tracts of land along the east coast. The State, under an act passed by the legislature, gave to railroad builders a certain number of acres of land for each mile of track laid. Thousands of acres had been granted to the various railroads between Jacksonville and Daytona which Flagler had purchased prior to 1890. After Flagler began his railroad building in 1892, he claimed from the state, under a law passed in 1893, 8,000 acres per mile of railroad. His total claims amounted to over 2,040,000 acres. This was in addition to the alternate sections of land previously granted.[62]

In November 1892, Flagler hired James E. Ingraham as general manager of the JStA&IR Rwy. and placed him in charge of its land department.[63] Ingraham had been associated with other Florida railroads and had been president of H. S. Sanford's South Florida Railway from 1879 until November 1892. As each of the Flagler land companies was organized, Ingraham was appointed to its presidency.[64]

On either February 6, 1896 or June 1 of that year, the Model Land Company (MLC) was organized as the first of the Flagler System Land Companies.[65] An initial paper stock issue was made of 30 shares, 28 of which went to Flagler. Ingraham, and Flagler's confidante and vice president, J. R. Parrott, each received one share. Later, other issues were made to Flagler.

Other subsidiary land companies were the Okeechobee Company (charter date unknown); The Ft. Dallas Land Company, chartered March 17, 1896; Perrine Grant Land Company, chartered May 6, 1899; and Chuluota Land Company, chartered in 1912.

The Model Land Company and its associated organizations controlled land from Jacksonville to Key West, and contributed in a large measure to the agricultural and industrial growth of the East Coast of Florida. The company and its experts gave liberally of time, money, and experience in assisting the development of the soil areas. Expert agriculturalists, horticulturists, and stockmen were employed to give years of attention to the practical development of the east coast country.[66]

The only less than successful land venture was the Chuluota Company. MLC set aside 11,000 acres for an agricultural colony at Chuluota but the land company was not able to sell it.[67] Even today, there are vast stretches of unoccupied land in the area of the Chuluota Company. US 441, which parallels the former FEC Kissimmee Valley Division from Okeechobee (at the top of the Lake) to Holopaw (the junction of US 192 west of Melbourne) passes through villages once served by the FEC but which no longer exist today.

Ingraham had complete charge of the FEC land department and later the MLC. More than anyone else, Ingraham was credited with advertising Flagler and his developments all over the nation through his official position. Ingraham published booklets, pamphlets, brochures and a magazine called the "Homeseeker," in which he told of the advantages of the east coast and described the lands which were for sale. These lands sold for relatively low prices, ranging from $1.50 to $5.00 per acre. The terms were three to four yearly payments at eight per cent interest. Special prices were given on large tracts of land, and for land paid for in cash, or for groups of people wanting to colonize.[68]

During the winter season of 1898, Flagler invited President William McKinley to visit him in Florida. Aware of his own power and position, Flagler boasted, "My domain begins at Jacksonville."[69]

It was almost as if a Biblical scene was being recounted. What he (Flagler) saw was good. Flagler said, "Let there be hotels," and, lo, there were hotels. Then Flagler said, "Let there be railroads—and land companies—and cities—and paved roads—and water works—and visitors—and lo, there were all of these things.

But, most importantly, there was Flagler. And today's promotions, by cities, by airlines, by hotels, and by development companies, as well as by Amtrak, the bus lines and the cruise companies, is derived, in both concept and appeal, from the groundwork laid by Flagler's promotions of the East coast of Florida as the 'American Riviera', a superb place to farm, to fish, to plant, to vacation, and to live.

The campaigns to encourage the Northern populace to seek sunshine and good health in a Florida that was inhabited by a minority of men when compared to the mosquitoes was engendered by the Flagler people. There was not, nor has there been, anything to compare with the artistry and eloquence of the early FEC publicists.

In the words of the FEC, "The East Coast of Florida is Paradise Regained." This was the supreme apex of the publicist's prose, for nothing else, before or since, has been able to compare with the image of the sun shining out of the clouds on the East Coast of Florida.

Volume after volume heaped praise on the East Coast in general and the Southeast corner in particular. Palm Beach became "The Beautiful," and Miami, "The Magic City." Promotions continued unabated, because Flagler, in his wisdom, had established a hotel company, several land companies, a steamship company and an agricultural company, and all with a singular purpose: bring the people to Florida. Cajole them, plead with them, promote them, but, above all, bring them![70]

## STEAMSHIP LINES AND OTHER INTERESTS

To connect the mainland and Island portions of his empire Flagler created the FEC Steamship Company. In 1897 a contract was signed for the construction of its first new ship, "S. S. Miami." It began its schedule to Nassau after a banquet and ball in Miami on January 17, 1898.[71] On July 1, 1900, the FEC Steamship Co. combined assets with the Plant Steamship Company in order to form the Peninsula & Occidental Steamship Company.

While it is not the purpose here to detail the history of the P&O, it is important to note that the company continued operating as an integral part of the Flagler System until the mid 1960s. Finally, with the moving of Miami's port and the inroads of newer and faster ships, the P&O's "S.S. Florida" was retired and the Company ceased to exist.[72]

In 1913, following Flagler's death, the System's only other steamship operation was incorporated. The Florida East Coast Car Ferry Co. plied the waters from Key West to Havana until the Labor Day, 1935 hurricane destroyed much of the extension. Late in 1936, according to Flagler's brother-in-law William R. Kenan, the car ferry operation was moved to Port Everglades (Broward County, between Hollywood and Ft. Lauderdale) with service operating from that point to Havana until World War II, when the Navy appropriated the ferries for use as minesweepers.

Following the war, service was re-instituted from the Port of Palm Beach (actually at Riviera Beach, just above West Palm Beach) to Havana and continued until 1960, when shipments to Cuba were embargoed. The postwar service was operated by the West India Fruit and Steamship Company, and, though not a part of the FEC Railway or the Flagler System, the Railway maintained the WIF&SS Co's. freight car fleet and promoted the through service to Havana.

Other corporations in the Flagler System were the Miami Electric Light Co., the West Palm Beach Water Co., a one-half interest in the FEC Drainage and Sugar Company, and an intertwining with and in the affairs of the Florida Coast Line Canal and Transportation Co. Additionally, Flagler purchased controlling interest in various Florida Newspapers during his lifetime, including "The Miami Herald," the "St. Augustine Record," and the (Jacksonville) "Florida Times-Union."

Although of a personal nature, Flagler's magnificent Palm Beach mansion, "Whitehall," was one of his "other interests," and for that reason warrants mention. On August 24, 1901, Flagler married for the third time. His wife, the cultured and elegant Mary Lily Kenan, was an ideal mate for him. She was Flagler's equal, socially and intellectually, and she was a good wife to him. In return, Flagler spared no expense to give her anything that money could buy.

She had always wanted a marble palace for a home, so her aging husband built a mansion costing $2,500,00 in Palm Beach. In December 1900, the plans were completed, and in 1902, the mansion itself was ready to receive the Flagler household. After being sold by Flagler's Estate and being partially converted to a hotel in 1926, the building was repurchased by the Estate in 1959, the hotel wing torn down, and the mansion restored to its original magnificence. Today, Whitehall is the home of the Henry Morrison Flagler Museum as well as the Palm Beach County Historical Society.

This fascinating 1931 map shows the FEC wye at West Palm Beach, and the bridge and trackage on Palm Beach itself. The two largest buildings shown on this map are the Royal Poinciana Hotel and the Breakers Hotel. While the Royal Poinciana has been torn down and is now a shopping center, the Breakers, still under Flagler System ownership is considered one of America's premiere resort hotels. The dark line shown on Oleander Ave. is the FEC mule-car line that connected the two hotels. Whitehall was Flagler's mansion and this palatial residence was later used as the lobby and offices for the Whitehall Hotel which was constructed directly behind and connected to the mansion. The Whitehall Hotel opened for the season of 1926: it had been sold as a house by Louis C. Wise in 1924 and operated as a private club. Since it was not a financial success as a private club it was changed to a hotel and remained in operation until 1959 when Jean Flagler Matthews, Flagler's granddaughter, contributed the bulk of the funds necessary to enable the Flagler Foundation to repurchase the buildings and property. This purchase culminated in the re-opening of Whitehall as the Henry Morrison Flagler Museum with a restoration ball being held on February 6th, 1960. The hotel section was finally torn down in the summer of 1963.

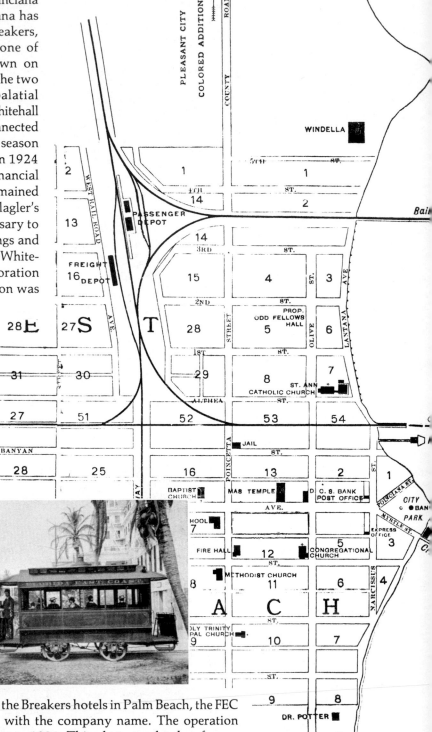

Following the construction of the Royal Poinciana and the Breakers hotels in Palm Beach, the FEC constructed a mule car line and painted the one car with the company name. The operation started in 1895 and was known to have operated as late as 1926. This photograph taken from a postcard shows the 'Palm Beach Trolley' in all its glory. When the railroad built the north bridge to Palm Beach and rerouted the trains coming to the two hotels, it also built a station and a baggage depot at the end of the bridge as the railroad came onto the island. To expedite passenger baggage destined for the Royal Poinciana Hotel, the railroad built a three foot narrow gauge railway between the baggage depot and the hotel. No known photographs are available but the FEC Engineering Drawings of existing trackage at Palm Beach in 1916 clearly indicate this "short line". Drawings in 1931 show that this line was removed.

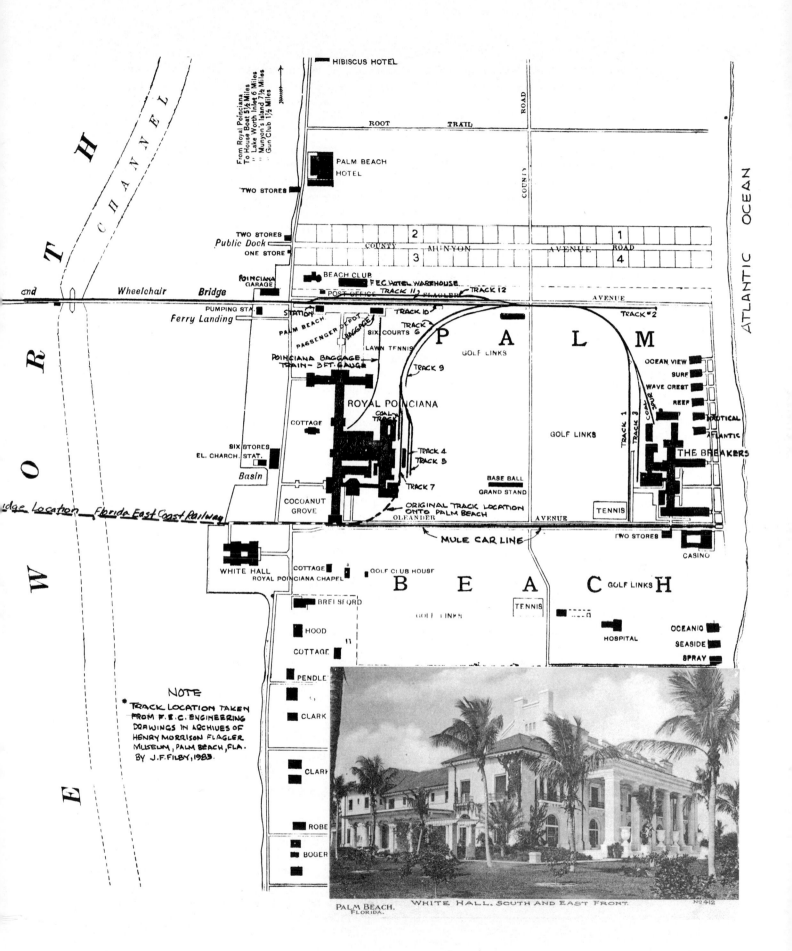

NORTH CHANNEL

NORTH LAKE WORTH

From Royal Poinciana
To House Boat 5½ Miles
" Lake Worth Inlet 6 Miles
" Munyon's Island 7½ Miles
" Gun Club 1½ Miles

HIBISCUS HOTEL

ROOT TRAIL

COUNTY ROAD

PALM BEACH HOTEL

TWO STORES

TWO STORES

Public Dock

ONE STORE

2

3

COUNTY MUNYON AVENUE ROAD

1

4

ATLANTIC OCEAN

BEACH CLUB

POINCIANA GARAGE

FEC HOTEL WAREHOUSE

POST OFFICE

TRACK 11½

SEMINOLE

TRACK 12

and

Wheelchair Bridge

AVENUE

PUMPING STA.

Ferry Landing

STATION

PALM BEACH

PASSENGER DEPOT BAGGAGE

TRACK 10

SIX COURTS

TRACK 6

LAWN TENNIS

TRACK #2

POINCIANA BAGGAGE
TRAIN - 3 FT. GAUGE

P A L M

GOLF LINKS

OCEAN VIEW

SURF

WAVE CREST

REEF

TRACK 9

ROYAL POINCIANA

COAL TRACK

COTTAGE

GOLF LINKS

NAUTICAL

ATLANTIC

THE BREAKERS

SIX STORES

EL. CHURCH. STAT.

Basin

TRACK 4

TRACK 5

TRACK 7

BASE BALL

GRAND STAND

TRACK 1

TRACK 3

COAL SPUR

COCOANUT GROVE

ORIGINAL TRACK LOCATION
ONTO PALM BEACH

OLEANDER

AVENUE

TENNIS

TWO STORES

MULE CAR LINE

CASINO

WHITE HALL

ROYAL POINCIANA CHAPEL

COTTAGE

COTTAGE

GOLF CLUB HOUSE

B E A C H

GOLF LINKS

TENNIS

GOLF LINKS

BRELSFORD

GOLF LINKS

OCEANIC

HOOD

COTTAGE

HOSPITAL

SEASIDE

SPRAY

PENDLETON

LAKE WORTH

Bridge Location Florida East Coast Railway

CLARK

CLARK

NOTE

* TRACK LOCATION TAKEN
FROM F.E.C. ENGINEERING
DRAWINGS IN ARCHIVES OF
HENRY MORRISON FLAGLER
MUSEUM, PALM BEACH, FLA.
BY J.F.FILBY, 1983.

ROBE

BOGER

PALM BEACH.
FLORIDA.

WHITE HALL, SOUTH AND EAST FRONT.

No 412

# THE FLORIDA EAST COAST RAILWAY

On September 9, 1895, the name of the Jacksonville, St. Augustine and Indian River Railway was changed to "Florida East Coast Railway." Having reached West Palm Beach on March 22, 1894, Flagler, it appeared at first, was now content to "set and rest," and did not seem, on the surface, to have any interest in extending the railroad any further south—not to Ft. Lauderdale, not to Miami, and certainly not to Key West.

While it has been the contention of historians for many years that Flagler came to Miami only because of the actions of Miami pioneer Julia Tuttle, it is very possible that Flagler planned all along to continue the railroad at least to Miami and possibly further south. As an astute businessman, however, and with the keen insightfulness into human nature that made Flagler the master of all he surveyed, it now seems extremely likely that Flagler was simply awaiting the best opportunity to extend the railroad to Biscayne Bay, an opportunity that would afford him the chance to receive great amounts of land without cost to himself or his companies, and to minimize his outlay in extending the railroad.

In the early 1890s, Mrs. Tuttle made an offer of land for a town site to Flagler—not once, but frequently. The Brickell family, another pioneering Miami family, joined her, and offered some of their land for a town.[73] The offer was taken under consideration by Flagler, but not acted upon. The opportunity (to act) came soon enough. The "Big Freezes" of December 24 and 28, 1894, and February 6, 1895, had, by their combined disastrous effects upon the citrus and vegetable industry, brought ruin and suffering at every turn.[74]

Not since January 3, 1766, when the ice was an inch thick in Florida as far south as nine degrees North Latitude, had such a catastrophe occurred. All the delicate plants from Palm Beach to the Georgia border were either killed outright or so badly blighted that it would require an indefinite length of time for them to get back to normal again. Rich men became paupers and poor men almost lost their self respect. Most of the state was in a turmoil: there were no jobs, there was no business and there was nothing for the destitute to eat.[75]

Mrs. Tuttle took advantage of this situation, sending word to Flagler that these freezing temperatures had not touched the Miami River area.[76]

Following "the freeze," Flagler's vice president, James E. Ingraham, was in the Biscayne Bay settlement reconnoitering. Mrs. Tuttle sent a box of fresh citrus flowers[77] to Flagler to show him that the temperate climate of the region surrounding Biscayne Bay would be ideal for agriculture, necessitating a railroad to haul out all that high tariff tonnage. No fanciful dreamer, she![78]

Mr. Flagler's response to the compliment of this box of flowers was a trip to Miami. This called for a voyage down the canal from Palm Beach to Ft. Lauderdale and then by carriage to Biscayne Bay. Flagler was accompanied by J. R. Parrott, Joseph A. McDonald, and James A. McGuire, his contractor. After several months of negotiations and discussions, terms were arranged.[79]

Mr. Flagler and Mrs. Tuttle met on June 1, 1895. In consideration of her gift of 100 acres for a railway station, yards and warehouses, and each alternate lot in a tract of 45 acres as well as a similar donation by the Brickells of all alternate lots in a hundred acre tract south of the (Miami) river, a contract was signed by which the railroad would be brought to Miami. Mr. Flagler also agreed to build one of his fine hotels not far from Mrs. Tuttle's residence, to provide waterworks for the hoped-for city, to have a survey made for new streets, and to clear existing ones.

The Tuttles and the Brickells were excited. They were commercial people and the undertaking of a great commercial enterprise was at hand. Well before the first train arrived, a city was being laid out by the Flagler forces and the Royal Palm Hotel was under construction. Miami, like West Palm Beach, quickly became a town of shacks and tents until more substantial buildings could be constructed.

On December 27, 1895, Flagler wrote to the president of the Lehigh Valley Railroad. "I sincerely hope," he said, "that you will make us a visit during the winter." But it is the offhanded manner in which he puts the next three sentences that makes one truly cognizant of the magnitude of the man. "I am extending the railroad to Biscayne Bay. It is under contract to be completed Feb. 1st, but like many such enterprises may be delayed ten to fifteen days. Florida is very beautiful at this season of the year."[80]

The railroad had reached as far south as the site of Ft. Lauderdale when on March 3, 1896, Flagler sent John Sewell[81] with a crew of twelve Negroes to "start the City," as Sewell describes his assignment in his book, "Memoirs and History of Miami, Florida."[82]

The surveys for the extension south of West Palm Beach began in June, 1895. The actual laying of track began in September. The distance of nearly seventy miles was covered in record time.[83]

The revered "Mother of Miami," Julia Tuttle. It was due to her frequent urgings that Flagler finally consented to extend the railroad to Biscayne Bay.

—*(Historical Association of Southern Florida.)*

Although, in "Florida's Flagler" author Sidney Martin states, "The coming of the railroad to Miami was the biggest single event in the City's history," the fact is that there is truth to that view only in perspective. What history? First, other than Indian raids, there was no "white man's" or "industrial" history. The "City" was not incorporated until July 28, 1896, over three months after the railroad arrived, and, prior to that, was not an incorporated area of any kind. 502 people simply voted it into existence.

There was another, more technical point that caused the enthusiasm to be less than it could have been for the arrival of the first train. The forces of the railroad were building in two directions: south from West Palm Beach and north from Miami, having barged material and equipment into the community around the Miami River in order to begin work on the Royal Palm Hotel. The railroad was completed to Miami on April 15, 1896 and the first regularly scheduled passenger train operated into Miami on April 22. So, the astute reader may ask, "what is the connection?"

The connection, basically, is this: the FEC didn't build into Miami—it closed a gap connecting Miami with the rest of the railroad. And, with that connection being made on April 15, the steam cars were arriving daily with special trains. The first *scheduled* train arrived a week later and by that time the steam cars were old hat.[84]

Following the railroad's arrival, the Ft. Dallas Land Company (FDLC)[85] was the agency used for Flagler's development. Flagler paid $8,000.00 for 80 percent of the stock in the company. The other 20 per cent was divided between Parrott and Ingraham. Miami lots sold by the FDLC ranged from $50.00 to $1,000.00 and buyers were permitted to pay one-quarter in cash, with the balance in three annual payments at eight per cent interest. The company also built cottages from three basic designs with an average cost of $1,500.00 each.[86]

The years following completion of the railroad to Miami were relatively quiescent, though Flagler's fertile mind was rarely at rest when it came to his ever growing business interests.

Determined to extend the sway of the FEC and to enable the rich but unsettled lowlands south of Miami to begin to develop as viable farming acreage, Flagler tapped this fine growing country with a twelve mile line in 1903. This 'short line' was used primarily for the shipping of fruits and vegetables north, and proved successful enough that the road was extended to what would become known as Homestead, on June 11, 1904. As in the case of many of the other small towns which Flagler had built, Homestead derived its existence primarily from the railroad.

For the moment—for only a moment—construction was complete.

54. Op cit, "Florida's Flagler," P. 162
55. Op cit, "Southern Reflections of the Gilded Age . . . ." P. 105
56. FEC Hotel System files, St. Augustine Historical Society Library
57. Unlike the remainder of the Flagler System (FEC Hotel Co.) Hotels, the Continental was a summer only resort, and (perhaps) for that reason, could not attract either the level of clientele or the volume to enable it to become a success.
58. Op cit, "Southern Reflections of the Gilded Age . . . ." pp 114-115.
59. The exact date of the opening of the Long Key Fishing Camp is January 11, 1909. A Long Key Fishing Camp brochure in the author's collection states "The Long Key Fishing Club was reorganized in 1917 . . . ." But the 1909 date is correct.
60. The railroad's entry into receivership in 1931 did not affect the other Flagler System units solvency, although the depression itself certainly forced all of them to retrench. The Hotel Company carried on as a separate company after 1931. When they (the Hotel company) moved their offices from St. Augustine to Palm Beach they thoughtfully donated most of their historical files to the Flagler Museum in Palm Beach and the St. Augustine Historical Society.
61. The Ormond was sold by the Company in 1950.
62. Op cit, "Florida's Flagler," pp 239-240.
63. Op cit, "Southern Reflections of the Gilded Age . . . ." p. 142
64. Ibid, p. 142
65. An interesting discrepancy appears between Akin and Martin. Martin, in "Florida's Flagler" lists the February date in 1896 while Akin, in "Southern Reflections of the Gilded Age . . . ." shows the June date. Each quotes a different source, and either may be correct.
66. Op cit, "Florida's Flagler," P. 240.
67. "The Miami Herald," September 2, 1948
68. Op cit, "Florida's Flagler," p. 241
69. Quoted from a letter to John Porter, McKinley's private secretary, February 15, 1898. The original is in the McKinley papers in the Library of Congress, with a microfilm copy at the University of Florida Library in Gainesville.
70. Bramson, Seth H., "It all Began with Flagler," article in "Update," published by Historical Association of Southern Florida," Vol. III, Number 4, April, 1976.
71. Op cit, "Southern Reflections of the Gilded Age," p. 108
72. The P&O Steamship Company is featured in an article by Edward Mueller, former Director of the Jacksonville Port Authority, in "Steamboat Bill," the publication of the Steamship Historical Society of America. (Summer 1984)
73. Carson, Ruby Leach, "Miami: 1896 to 1900," in "Tequesta," Published annually by Historical Association of Southern Florida, Vol. XVI, p. 5, 1956.
74. Ibid, p. 5
75. Nash, Charles Edgar, "The Magic of Miami Beach," David McKay Co., Philadelphia, 1938, pp 80-81
76. Op cit, "Tequesta," Vol. XVI, p. 5
77. The type of blossoms sent to Flagler are a source of controversy among South Florida historians. In the book "Magic of Miami Beach," (see Footnote 75.) it is stated that orange, lime and lemon blossoms were sent. In a booklet published in 1911, entitled "Coconut Grove," the statement is made that lime blossoms were sent. It is likely that some of each were sent, and that in later years, FEC publicists, mindful of the public's perception of oranges as a sweet fruit and limes or lemons as tart, changed the story and made it appear that orange blossoms were sent.
78. Bramson, Seth H., "The Coming of the Railroad to Miami and Key West," in National Railway Historical Society Bulletin, Volume 48, Number 5, 1983, p. 38.
79. The written contract has been preserved and is in the files of the Historical Association of Southern Florida, Miami.
80. Ibid, NRHS, Volume 48, Number 5, p. 38.
81. John Sewell moved to Miami and served as one of the inner circle to Flagler, being in charge of street construction. He later served as Mayor of the City of Miami. (See also Footnote 82)
82. Op cit, "Tequesta," Vol. XVI, p. 6. Sewell's book was published by the Franklin Press, Miami, in 1933. Though there is some question as to the exactness of some of Sewell's recollections in the book, it is considered one of the most important of the early histories of the City and is long out of print.
83. Op cit, "Florida's Flagler," p. 157
84. Op cit, NRHS, Vol. 48, Number 5, p. 40
85. The land company was named after the US Army fort built for the protection of settlers around Biscayne Bay during the Seminole uprisings.
86. Op cit, "Southern Reflections of the Gilded Age . . . . : p. 96

# FLORIDA EAST COAST RAILWAY

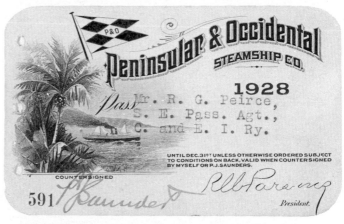

Shortest Sea Route to Cuba
THE PENINSULAR and OCCIDENTAL STEAMSHIP CO.

Menu

---

Summer Schedule No. 44. Season 1910.

HAVANA, NASSAU, PORT TAMPA, MIAMI, KNIGHTS KEY, KEY WEST

## Peninsular & Occidental S. S. Company.

United States Fast Mail Routes for

### KEY WEST, CUBA AND THE WEST INDIES

Via Miami, Knights Key and Port Tampa, Fla.

Proposed sailings in effect on dates shown. Subject to change and individual postponement without notice.

**PORT TAMPA—KEY WEST—HAVANA LINE**

(Touching at Key West)

Effective from Port Tampa, Florida, March 31st, 1910,

| Lv. | Port Tampa, | Sundays, | Thursdays, | 11:00 p. m. |
|---|---|---|---|---|
| Ar. | Key West, | Mondays, | Fridays, | 5:00 p. m. |
| Lv. | Key West, | Mondays, | Fridays, | 8:00 p. m. |
| Ar. | Havana, | Tuesdays, | Saturdays, | 6:30 a. m. |
| Lv. | Havana, | Tuesdays, | Saturdays, | 12:00 Noon |
| Ar. | Key West, | Tuesdays, | Saturday, | 8:00 p. m. |
| Lv. | Key West, | Tuesdays, | Saturdays, | 10:00 p. m. |
| Ar. | Port Tampa, | Wednesdays, | Sundays, | 5:30 p. m. |

**KNIGHTS KEY—KEY WEST—HAVANA LINE**

(Touching at Key West)

Effective from Knights Key, Florida, April 3rd, 1910,

| Lv. | Knights Key, | Sundays, | Tuesdays, | Thursdays, | 2:00 p. m. |
|---|---|---|---|---|---|
| Ar. | Key West, | Sundays, | Tuesdays, | Thursdays, | 6:00 p. m. |
| Lv. | Key West, | Sundays, | Tuesdays, | Thursdays, | 9:00 p. m. |
| Ar. | Havana, | Mondays, | Wednesdays, | Fridays, | 6:30 a. m. |
| Lv. | Havana, | Mondays, | Wednesday, | Fridays, | 3:00 p. m. |
| Ar. | Key West, | Tuesdays, | Thursdays, | Saturdays, | 5:30 a. m. |
| Lv. | Key West, | Tuesdays, | Thursdays, | Saturdays, | 7:30 a. m. |
| Ar. | Knights Key, | Tuesdays, | Thursdays, | Saturdays, | 11:30 a. m. |

Above hours are based on 90th Meridian Standard time.

Information regarding freight and pass... rates to all points in the United States, Cuba or the West Indies, cheerfully furnished upon application.

CHAS. L. MYERS,                                    P. J. SAUNDERS,
MANAGER.          JACKSONVILLE, FLA.          G. F. & P. A.
This abrogates previous notice.                March 18th, 1910.

FEC 4-6-2 91 is on the docks at Key West in this pre-1920 photograph.

A view of the docks at Key West with the P. & O. Steamship "Governor Cobb" and an FEC train on the docks.

It's December 22, 1926 and business was so heavy that the FEC was using both the "Governor Cobb" (left) and the "Miami" (right) for transporting their passengers to Havana. This photo was taken at Key West.

Until the end of service on the Key West Extension FEC car ferries plied the waters between Key West and Havana. Following the hurricane of Sept. 2, 1935, the car ferries sat unused and forlorn by the docks at Key West. Car ferry "Henry M. Flagler" is shown in Key West on April 26th, 1936.

Among the many steamships owned and/or operated by the P&O Steamship Company were the "Cuba," "Governor Cobb," (shown here at Key West), "Mascotte," "Olivette," and "Florida." Most of the P&O ships spent summers in New England, in various services there, and then returned to warmer waters for the winter tourist season in South Florida.

—*All Photographs: Collection of Edward A. Mueller*

This aerial view of the Port of Palm Beach finds two of the Florida-Havana Railroad Car Ferries awaiting their next load. At the bottom right of the photo are two of the steam locomotives that serviced the port. The photo was taken on January 16, 1953 for the West India Fruit and Steamship Co.

It was a spiffy little 4-4-0 that pulled up to the Lake Helen Station in 1910 with the train (one of two each day) to Orange City. The 4-4-0's that worked the branch were most likely from the predecessor Atlantic & Western (nee Blue Spring, Orange City and Atlantic), but may have been from any of the lines that operated 4-4-0's and were amalgamated into the Flagler System. This photograph is particularly tantalizing for several reasons. We can see the builder's plate (just under the classification lamp, below the bell) and we can see the words "Schenectady Locomotive Works" on it, so we know the engine was made by American Locomotive, but the builder's number is just too indistinct to read, which means that, since the engine number is also indistinguishable, we don't know the origins of the engine. And the other enigma? For as many years as those who made note of such things can remember, FEC trainmen's hat badges carried only the occupation, but not the railroad name. FEC buttons adorned the sides of the caps, but, unlike the ACL or Seaboard or hundreds of other railroads, the FEC didn't adorn their hat badges with their company name. Or did they. Are the trainmen in this picture wearing caps with company name? They might be, but, as with the vagaries of so many FEC "mysteries" the individuals pictured are just a few steps too far from the camera for us to be able to determine the answer. Some day, maybe, but not today...

*—Florida State Archives: Author's Collection*

"Sea Level II," owned by the WIF&SS Co., was based at the FEC's West Palm Beach yards. The "FEC Ry." markings at either end of the letterboard indicate this car is serviced by its home road, the FEC.

*—(Charles & Richard Beall collection)*

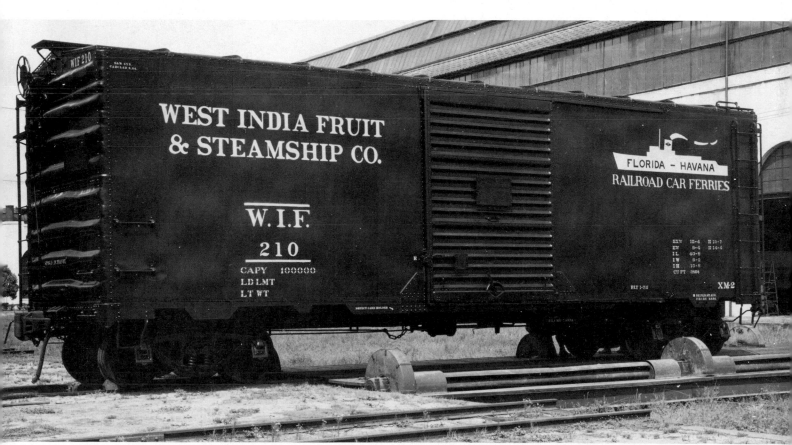

This West India Fruit and Steamship Company 40 foot steel box car is typical of the modern freight cars of this once active associate of the FEC. This car had been repainted before it returned to 'active duty.'

To stand...to remember.

# CHAPTER 5

# "GENTLEMEN: THE RAILROAD WILL GO TO SEA"

They stood, or so the apochryphal story goes, at the very edge of land, on the very bottom of the Florida peninsula, gazing southwestward. There were four of them, and one of the four was, even in his day, accorded a Godlike reverence. His name was Henry M. Flagler and it is told that he turned to the other three and said, "Gentlemen: the Railroad will go to Sea!"

It is, in fact, unknown exactly what Flagler's words were; or if there were four of them present. But one thing is certain: the Railroad went to Sea.

In one fell swoop, Flagler became a legend. This incredibly wealthy man, who was already credited with developing the East Coast of Florida, made the decision to press onward to America's Gibraltar, Key West, oblivious to problems, inured to criticism and indifferent to the encroaching infirmities of age, but totally capable of funding the Key West Extension by himself, as he had the entire railroad.

Various articles, booklets and books have had slightly differing versions of Flagler's exact conversation, as well as different listings of those present when the order was given to extend the railroad south of Homestead, but what seems to be generally agreed upon is that after all of the surveys were made, and the various routes considered, the line via the Keys to Key West appeared to be the most feasible. Flagler, in late 1904, called in his chief engineer for the project, J. C. Meredith, and asked him when he could start. Meredith answered, "immediately!" Flagler was not totally convinced and wished to confer further with his vice president, Joseph R. Parrott.

On January 30, 1905, Flagler and a group of his associates left Miami by steamer for a tour of the proposed route of the Extension.[87] On their return from the Keys, Flagler consulted with Parrott. The old man looked up from the clutter of blueprints and survey maps to say, "Joe, are you sure the railroad can be built?" Parrott looked up and caught Flagler's eye with his own. The two men looked at each other and Parrott replied, "Yes sir. I am sure."[88]

It is at this point that some anomalies creep in. The "Miami Metropolis," according to Martin in "Florida's Flagler," carried a special Key West edition on July 31, 1905 to announce the plans and untold the entire scheme.[89] However, all other sources, including the Company's "Official Announcement Key West Extension" state that construction commenced in April of 1905. What appears to have caused the difference in dates between Martin and the others is that, while the April, 1905 date is correct, the "Metropolis" *did* publish a special edition on the last day of July, 1905, which, apparently, was what we today would call a "media announcement." Additionally, 35 years after Martin's book was published, numerous new sources and manuscripts have become available that Martin did not have access to or that did not exist at that time.

The idea of a railroad to the Island City was far from new when the Flagler people announced their plans. It had, in fact, been brought up by Key West's newspapers as early as the 1830s. The first survey of a railroad route to Key West was made by Civil Engineer J. C. Bailey for the International Ocean Telegraph Co. in 1866.[90] In 1883, former Confederate General John B. Gordon of Georgia was granted a charter for a Key West railroad. He built 50 miles of railroad on the mainland, but the project was halted before the road reached the coast.[91]

In 1894, Jefferson B. Browne, Collector of Customs for the Port of Key West laid out an almost complete route for the railroad to follow in an article in "National Geographic." In his final paragraph, Browne wrote:

A railroad to Key West will assuredly be built. While the fact that it has no exact counterpart among the great achievements of modern engineering may make it, like all other great enterprises, a subject for a time of incredulity and distrust, it presents, as has been shown, no difficulties that are insurmountable. It is, however, a magnificent exercise of qualities of the very highest order. Who will be its Cyrus W. Field? The hopes of the people of Key West are centred in Henry M. Flagler, whose financial genius and public spirit have opened up to the tourist and health seeker 300 miles[92] of the beautiful east coast of the state. The building of a railroad to Key West would be a fitting consummation of Mr. Flagler's remarkable career, and his name would be handed down to posterity linked to one of the greatest achievements of modern times.[93]

In 1895, an item in "Railway World" stated that Flagler had bought the lower half of Key Largo, as well as parts of some of the other islands. The property purchased followed Browne's route plans closely.[94]

Flagler cogitated on all of these things, but committed to nothing. Finally, the United States Government announced that it would take on the task of completing the Panama Canal. It was this decision that enabled Flagler to declare that the Extension would be built.

There is one more fact, from the 1984 perspective, that does need to be considered and is, for the most part, glossed over in most of the booklets and pamphlets describing the building of the Extension.

In 1904, when construction had reached Homestead, the short extension south of Miami was but the forecast of what was in Flagler's mind: a deep water port somewhere (Miami's harbor at that time was not nearly deep enough) but not necessarily at Key West. Certainly, as far south on the Florida peninsula as was possible, but, again, not necessarily at Key West. It was never the intention after 1902 to end the road at Homestead. A surveying party was based there and the scouts and linksmen explored in a southwest direction through the trackless wastes of swamp and jungle in the Everglades—that blending of water and land which one hesitates to call either one or the other.

The surveyors studied channels and water courses, wind, wave and storm and quietly mapped, during two years of effort, a trail which led to Cape Sable, and along which financiers and engineers were certain no enterprise could ever venture to build a railroad. That the extension would not be built on this route was determined with finality in 1904, when the survey was collated and the engineers advised Parrott and Flagler that it simply could not be done.

All through the pathless wastes that hedged in the abandoned route to Cape Sable, and the accepted route to Key West, the surveyors were led by a young man little known to his profession at that time. He was William J. Krome, and he would, in time, have final responsibility for the completion of the extension to Key West. When the extension began the long jaunt south-southwest in 1905, J. C. Meredith, an engineer of splendid reputation and ability was put in charge and Krome became his first assistant and confidante.[95]

**ENGINEERING CORPS, KEY WEST EXTENSION.**
Left to right—P L. Wilson, Division Engineer; C. S. Coe, Division Engineer; W. J. Krome, Constructing Engineer; Ernest Cotton, Division Engineer; Edward Sheeran, General Foreman; R. W. Carter, Bridge Engineer.

Meredith was, above all, an engineer with sufficient courage to undertake the mission and with enough skill to meet and overcome the innumerable difficulties he was about to face. When Flagler found him, Meredith was building immense docks in Tampico Harbor, Mexico. The Overseas Extension proposition was outlined to him and he accepted and was made chief construction engineer, beginning his assignment on July 2, 1904.

In April, 1905, construction had begun on the mainland. On Thursday, November 2, 1905, ground was broken at Key West, in the largest ceremony that had ever been held on the island city up until that time. Though Flagler was at his northern home in Mamaroneck, NY, he sent the following telegram, dated November 1, to George Allen, president of the Chamber of Commerce: "Please express to the citizens of Key West as also to the officers of the army and navy, my appreciation of their interest in the extension of the Florida East Coast Railway to your city."[96]

An understaking of this magnitude required an army of labor. Men from almost every nation on earth were summoned to the service and welded into a single, vital, human machine which responded to the orders of the high command. There were hardy northerners of Swedish and Norwegian blood who served mostly as foremen and overseers. Spaniards from the Northern provinces went to work in great numbers, enlisting by way of Cuba. American and Caribbean Negroes came, as did divers from Greece and a horde of nondescripts, many of whom had known and loved the Bowery all of their lives.[97]

Almost all of these men were immigrants. They were rough stuff and worked none too contentedly for several dollars a day, plus room and board. Many were the fist fights, many the bloody noses. This was an experience that was to be repeated all the way along the line in the early days of the construction. It was a rough country, and the men were rougher, products of the day and generation. There were few niceties of life and fewer kindnesses. More than once the right of way was marked with human blood.

There were camps on the Keys, principally at Long Key and at Marathon. The food and the sleeping quarters in every camp were provided under contract, and were strictly supervised, and absolutely no lowering of fixed standards was countenanced. Menus were substantial and wholesome. No better proof could be needed of the care the workers received and of the healthfulness of the climate than in the fact that in more than seven years of construction, involving thousands of men, some of them none too well when they arrived, there was never an epidemic and, indeed, no prevailing sickness. In fact, the percentages of illness were a good bit lower than in the regular Army of the United States.

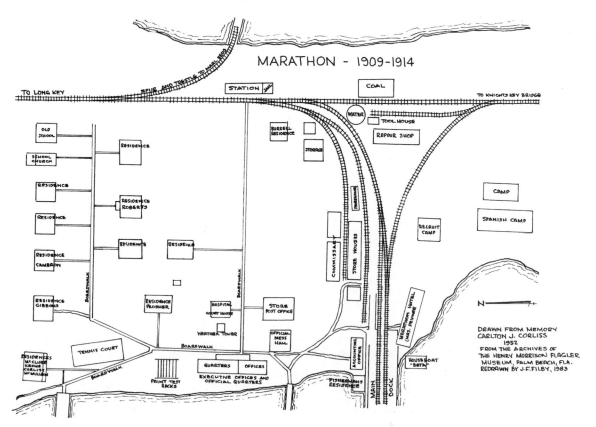

MARATHON - 1909-1914

DRAWN FROM MEMORY
CARLTON J. CORLISS
1952
FROM THE ARCHIVES OF
THE HENRY MORRISON FLAGLER
MUSEUM, PALM BEACH, FLA.
REDRAWN BY J.F.FILBY, 1983

Foremost among the medical problems was that of water for drinking and domestic purposes. Borings as deep as 2,000 feet failed to locate fresh water on the Keys, necessitating the building by the railroad of two trains of tank cars. These were flat cars with wooden or metal tanks, and were loaded with fresh water daily at a platform station called "Everglade," south of Homestead, where a wooden tank with a capacity of 100,000 gallons was erected and supplied with clear, fresh water from the Everglades, pumped in by powerful engines. This pumping station was the sole source of fresh water for the work along the Keys.

The Flagler people attempted to anticipate, and solve, as many problems in advance as were possible. Unfortunately hurricanes were unpredictable.

With construction proceeding apace, and in order to keep on schedule, engineers decided to work through the hurricane season, which is always at its height during September and October. The advance camp on Long Key had scant weather information from Miami and Key West. Foremen depended on crude barometers made from water-filled glass tubes with weeds in the bottom. They looked at these almost as often as they looked at their watches. If the pressure of the surrounding air decreased, the weed would rise. On the evening of October 17, 1906, the weed rose steadily.[98]

By the time the hurricane had spent itself, the Extension, particularly in the area around Long Key, had been pummeled and more than 140 men died in the storm. Long Key viaduct, already in the process of construction, was badly damaged.

It was a staggering setback. Yet when young Meredith surveyed the ruin, he straightened his shoulders and said, "No man has any business connected with this work who can't stand grief."[99] Flagler, when advised of the damage, ordered construction continued without delay.

Although hurricanes were still unpredictable, one lesson was learned. The labor force would no longer be housed in quarter boats adjacent to the construction camps. From 1906 on, wooden barracks were constructed on land for all workers to live in. Hurricanes thrice lashed the extension, and following each storm, in 1906, 1909, and 1910, the engineers gained valuable experience. Unhappily, this experience was always at a cost almost beyond estimate. And, following each storm, Flagler would give the same order: "On to Key West!"

Every part of the construction of the Extension was complex and demanding. Almost as soon as the Extension began south of Homestead, the engineers were faced with an immediate problem: the water level for the first twenty or so miles, from Homestead to Jewfish Creek, passing mostly through marsh and mangrove swamp, was insufficient to float dredges. Conversely there was not enough solid ground for wheelbarrows. The engineer's solution was to build channels to accommodate dredges, in order that a roadbed could be built up. Two excavations were made, each wide enough to contain a dredge, and each two and one-half feet deep. The dredges then made their way down either side of the embankment and dug their own channels. The material excavated was then used to form new embankment, and the dredges continued in this fashion south to Jewfish Creek.[100]

Throughout 1907, work continued. Going was uncertain, because work was a webfooted proposition, and the engineers expected marsh and swamp on each key. The first and largest of the keys is immediately below the mainland. Key Largo is twenty seven miles long at its longest point, and construction here was not as difficult as it was to be at other places along the route. Construction continued towards Key West. Long Island (not to be confused with Long Key) and Windly's Island were crossed and then Upper Matecumbe. The builders worked across Indian Key and then Lower Matecumbe and then onto Long Key, where the first of the three great viaducts began.

The Long Key Viaduct, with 186 eighty foot reinforced concrete arches is 2.68 miles long, 2.15 miles of which are over water. This bridge, one of the most expensive, had been interrupted in its construction by the 1906 hurricane. Construction was intricate, with concrete being mixed on barges and placed by derricks in some places, while, at other locations, molds were formed by driving piling which held watertight framework in place. The spans, giving the appearance of a Roman aqueduct, rest on piers set into solid rock. Long Key Viaduct required 286,000 barrels of cement, 177,000 cubic yards of crushed rock, 106,000 cubic yards of sand, 612,000 feet of piling, 5,700 tons of reinforcing rods and 2,600,000 feet of dressed timber.[101]

The arches gave the bridge such a beautiful and picturesque look that the railroad's emblem soon became a stylized drawing of a passenger train on the Long Key Bridge with an attached "sign" bearing the legend, "The Over-Sea R.R."

Long Key, with its sandy beaches and thick plantings of coconut palms was an ideal spot for a rustic

Long Key, Fla. Long Key Fishing Camp, Post Office and Cottages, view from Railway Station.

Rural and rustic, and reached only by FEC trains, Long Key Fishing Camp was a tropical paradise.

Knights Key Bridge piers in place. The railroad commissioned and gave to a select handful of privileged clientele, models of these piers to be used as paperweights. At this writing the only one known to exist is in the author's collection.

475A. Piers for the Knights Key Bridge. Florida East Coast Railway.
Published by Willis M. Huber.

resort or fishing camp. The Long Key Fishing Camp became nationally famous when such notables as Zane Grey came via rail to spend their vacations there. Some of the wealthy patrons came by boat and docked on the Gulf side of Long Key. A little narrow gauge railroad, one-half mile long, picked the guests up at dockside and transported them, via a tunnel under the main line, to the Atlantic side, where cottages, dining hall, post office, and recreation facilities awaited them.[102]

From Long Key, the railroad ran to Grassy Key, about 15 miles long, and then onto Knight's Key, which is less than a mile long. On January 22, 1908, the first train reached Knight's Key, and passenger service was extended to that point on Februry 5, 1908. At this spot, 18 miles below Long Key, 83 miles south of Homestead, 112 miles south of Miami and 477 miles south of Jacksonville, the work halted.

The reason for the complete stoppage of work was the temporary setback suffered by the Flagler forces at Key West. Work on the Key West terminal had been proceeding until word was received from the naval department that the railroad people could not dredge the Key West harbor for material to build up the dock area. This dredge work was planned to provide additional land for the terminal facilities as well as to deepen the harbor for ocean going commerce. Without these improvements, Flagler had no need to expend the funds to complete the road to Key West. Knight's Key Dock gave the railroad an excellent connection point for steamships enroute to Key West, Nassau or Havana, as it could accommodate ships with a nineteen foot draw. Knight's Key allowed the Company to operate daily service to Havana, rather than thrice weekly out of Miami, as the water route was now 112 miles shorter.[103]

The vagaries of history have left us without an exact date for the resumption of construction, but it appears to have been sometime in the fall of 1908, as the first pier for the Knight's Key Viaduct was completed at three in the morning on February 27, 1909. There were hopes for 1909, and it appeared that major progress would be made. Progress was made, but at terrible cost. [104]

On April 20, 1909, Joseph C. Meredith, the man upon whose shoulders the total engineering responsibility had been placed, died suddenly. Although Extension employees knew that Meredith had not been well, his death came as a shock to all on the railroad.

William J. Krome, at 32, was thrust into the position of chief engineer. Krome took up the torch, assumed the burden with his predecessors's courage and with his own great ability and determination, and saw the vast project through to its completion. In 1932, at the age of 55, Krome died in Homestead, where the steel trail to Key West had begun.[105]

On June 28, 1909, with Krome in command, the final concrete pier for Knight's Key viaduct was put in place at 5:00 PM.[106] In mid August, Flagler confidently announced that trains would be running to Key West by February of 1910, and his confidence appeared well placed when the first span for the bridge was positioned on August 21.

The second of the tribulations came to a close in 1909. For some time, the FEC had been accused of brutality and peonage (slavery). Such was far from fact, but with so many men involved, working in the blazing sun, fighting mosquitoes day and night, without female companionship, and working through hurricane season, seeds of discontent were bound to be sown, and trouble arose from the "United Nations" of people employed in the construction. There were hearings and trials and charges and countercharges. Finally, on November 10, 1908, the case was brought to trial in United States Court, southern district of New York. The government called about forty witnesses, most of whom were brought from Florida at great expense to the government. At the close of the government's presentation, the FEC attorneys moved that the court direct the jury to find a verdict of "Not guilty" on the ground that the government did not prove by its own evidence that a crime had been committed by the defendants. The court granted this motion, and instructed the jury to find a verdict of "Not guilty."

Of the forty witnesses called by the government in the attempt to substantiate its charges, only one was even cross-examined by defense attorneys.[107] The defense had cost Flagler approximately $80,000 and both he and the railroad were disappointed that they did not have an opportunity to present their case, as they planned to charge the government with an attack on Standard Oil and its owners.

National magazines and periodicals carried the story and by mid 1909 it was laid to rest with finality.

The final blow of 1909 was the hurricane of October 10. Remembering the great loss of life in 1906, FEC officials took extra precautions, after that devastating blow. Telegraph wires were strung from Miami to give fast weather information and men were quartered in strong, wooden barracks. No women were allowed to remain in camp homes later than August, and transportation was held ready to evacuate all but those who volunteered to stay.[108]

In 1909, the FEC thought they were ready. And they almost were. But almost doesn't count, and while the concrete viaducts, which had been built with enough strength to withstand a wind pressure 400 per cent greater than had ever been recorded in the Keys were proving their muscle (as they would do time and again) the filled embankments proved to be vulnerable. More than 40 miles of embankment and track washed out in the Upper Keys. The only positive point in this hurricane was the minimum loss of life. Although about 3,000 workers were exposed to the hurricane, the only loss of life was the crew of thirteen on the tug "Sybil."[109]

Original plans had contemplated only six miles of bridges. But Krome learned quickly that the words of "the conchs"[110] were to be heeded. Tropical storms force the water ahead of them, but along the Keys so great an influx as rides the tidal wave cannot get back to sea the way it came. It has to find an outlet between and across the islands rather than through the narrow, bridged passages. The return drag of the wave is greater than its flow. With these hardlearned lessons in mind, the engineers built 18 miles of bridges instead of six.[111]

It would cost extra millions in dollars and two additional years to repair the damage. Flagler answered the storm and the queries of the press and the public in the only way he knew how: "Go ahead."

On November 8, service was resumed to Knight's Key, with passenger, rock and supply trains arriving daily.[112]

In front row center is the first Station Agent at Knight's Key, which was the terminus for the FEC from 1909 until 1912 while the railroad was enroute to Key West. Unfortunately, the names and occupations of the other individuals have been lost in the mists of history.

The railroad continued to advance. It inched past Little Duck, Ohio and Missouri Keys until it came to the mighty Bahia Honda channel. Here, another great bridge, 5,055 feet in length, including approaches, would have to be built over water which ranged between 23 and 35 feet in depth. The Spaniards had correctly named this "Deep Bay."[113] The Bahia Honda bridge was built of steel lattice trusses defined by bridge engineers as "through trusses," erected in pairs on either side of the roadway.

In the Bahia Honda bridge, there are thirteen spans of 128 feet, six inches long, 13 spans of 186 feet long, and nine cement arches each eighty feet long, with the roadbed carried thirty feet above the ordinary level of low tide.[114]

As with the other bridges, both cofferdam and caisson types of construction were used for foundation piers. Cofferdams were floated into place by a catamaran and made to rest on the bottom. After all soft mud was pumped out, 24 piles for each pier were driven into bedrock as far as they could be forced. German cement that hardened underwater was piped in, forming a union with the bedrock and making the cofferdam essentially watertight.

The piling was sawed off at low-tide level. Then the form for the pier base was put in place. This, too, was filled with German cement, taking seven days to dry. Upon this foundation, each pier was built.[115]

Work continued through the end of 1909, and into 1910. Krome continued to work through the summer. Then, in September, another large storm struck. This time, it was the lower Keys that received the punishment. Unfortunately, it was in that area that construction was concentrated. Roadbeds between the Summerland Keys reverted to sea-filled channels and on Bahia Honda Key, tracks were washed 600 feet west of the roadbed. The worst blow to the engineers was the discovery that the combined strength of wind and water had displaced a foundation of the center span of Bahia Honda Bridge. It was this particular span which had taken a full shipload of material to anchor.[116]

As with the other hurricanes, the men of the Florida East Coast picked themselves up, assessed the damage, rolled up their collective sleeves and went back to work.

There was much to work with. Besides Central Supply, at Marathon, the railroad maintained a complete marine railway at Boot Key for the overhaul of its floating equipment. In addition, complete boiler and machine shops, sawmill and welding plant operated as needed, much of the time on a 24 hour schedule. The plant was so complete that it was able to both repair its own equipment and to build almost anything it lacked. All of the floating equipment had been equipped with dynamos for generating light, because so much of the work could not be interrupted by nightfall and had to go on to completion nonstop.[117]

As the work drew towards its conclusion, Niles Channel was bridged, and Pine, Kemp, Bow and Boca Chica viaducts were being built, when Krome learned that the "Old Man" was beginning to fade. At the end of February, 1911, Parrott contacted Krome.

Krome recorded the discussion in his diary. "It was near the end of February, 1911," he wrote, "when we were asked, 'Can you finish the road in time to put the chief there in his private car by his next birthday, January 2nd? I did some close figuring," he continued, "and finally replied that we could complete the road by January 22 of the coming year should no storm overtake us, or no unforeseen delay set us back."[118] Since the target for completion of the extension had been 1913, this meant shortening the schedule by a full year.

To accomplish such a speed-up, work was pressed on both ends of the line. Electric lights blazed all night as dredging and filling went on nonstop. At the Key West end, aching muscles, directed by tired foremen, extended fill to Stock Island and laid track. J. R. Parrott took personal responsibility for building the Key West terminal and docks. One anecdote tells that Parrott reported to Flagler that there wasn't enough dry land left in Key West for the terminal, and Flagler calmly replied, "Then make some." And Parrott did—134 acres of it! 1911 turned out to be the best year for construction since the inception of the project!

Trumbo Island (named for the terminal project's chief engineer, Howard Trumbo) was completed in time for the arrival of Flagler's special train. The gala day, though, was to be 20 days following Flagler's birthday,

As a sidelight to the coming of the first train to Key West, it appears that engines 10 and 12, both 4-4-0 American standard types had actually been in either Key West or Stock Island since early September of 1911. According to the "Key West Citizen" for Saturday, September 17, 1911, "Yesterday afternoon at 5:00 PM the first railroad train to run into Key West pulled up to the commissary building on Trumbo

Mr. H. M. Flagler's arrival with First Train to enter
Key West, Fla. Jan. 22nd, 1912.

Copyrighted 1912 by Harris.

Island and thereby marked another epoch in the history of this City. The engine was #12 of the FEC Railway and was manned by Engineer Joseph Knowles, Fireman Ernest Miller and Conductor G. W. Payne. A few minutes after the arrival of #12, engine #10, which was unloaded on Stock Island on September 3, ran up to the Commissary. #10 was pulling three cars and was manned by Engineer C. S. Mitchell, Fireman W. A. Parker and Conductor A. McRoe."[119]

Finally, all was ready. Trumbo Island was complete, with station and facilities, including a permanent pier, 1,700 feet long by 134 feet wide, where trains could pull up next to waiting steamships, which were ready to receive freight and passengers.

On the afternoon of January 21, 1912, the bridge foreman closed the crossover span at Knights Key trestle, the last link in the line of rails connecting the overseas road with the main line, and soon thereafter the pilot train from Knight's Key left for Key West. It gave the road a thorough testing and found it in prime condition for the opening. Engineers J. F. Norton and Ed Goehring, Pilot William Nichols and Fireman Jack Basskopp had the distinction of having carried the first train into the Island City."[120]

The "Over The Sea Railroad Celebration" began on January 20. A bright, warm sun shone steadily on the East Coast of Florida, and 15 years and nine months to the day after the first scheduled passenger train had arrived in the tiny village by Bay Biscayne, Henry M. Flagler, his eyes dim, his hearing diminished, his back bent, and his body withered from his 82 years, was helped off his private car, "Rambler," after the first official train arrived in Key West at 10:43 AM on January 22, 1912. Flagler whispered to his aides, "Now I can die fulfilled."

Bands played; the mayor spoke; ships in harbor blew their whistles; the Chamber of Commerce president presented Flagler with two plaques, and a chorus of school children threw roses in Flagler's path while they sang welcoming songs. Flagler replied with a short speech and ten thousand people cheered and shouted themselves hoarse, clapping and waving and babbling in Spanish, French and English. Many, having been born in the Caribbean or living in the Keys since birth, were seeing a train for the first time. The aging Flagler was overcome with emotion by the demonstration given him. "Flagler's Folly" had become a reality!

There was still work to do. Fine-tuning, cleanup and spit and polish had to be added. But the FEC had triumphed, and regular service south of Miami began immediately.[121]

Flagler returned to his beloved and beautiful Whitehall. On January 15, 1913, while descending the long marble staircase to the first floor, his leg gave way on the third stair from the bottom and he fell the remaining distance. He was badly bruised and shaken, and his right hip was broken. Flagler was in great pain and, though he rallied slightly after several days, he was too enfeebled to improve further. At 10:00 AM, on May 20, 1913, at the age of 83, the Empire Builder died peacefully, as though he were sinking into slumber.

A special train brought his remains to St. Augustine in the early hours of May 23, and he was laid to rest in the mausoleum of the beautiful church he had erected to the memory of his daughter. During the funeral services, shortly after 3:00 PM on the 23rd, every wheel on the Florida East Coast Railway stopped and every human being paused in silence for a period of ten minutes, in tribute to his memory.

## FOONOTES

87. "Miami Metropolis," February 2, 1905 (Microfilm files of the paper are kept by its successor, "The Miami News")
88. Parks, Pat, "The Railroad that Died at Sea," The Stephen Greene Press, Brattleboro, VT, 1968, p. 8
89. Op cit, "Florida's Flagler," p. 207
90. Browne, Jefferson B. "Across the Gulf by Rail to Key West," Article in National Geographic Magazine, Vol. VII, p.204, 1894
91. Op cit, "Southern Reflections of the Gilded Age . . . ." pp 194-195
92. The actual mileage was somewhat more if the branch lines were included. The railroad had been built only as far as West Palm Beach by this time (1894).
93. Loc cit, "Across the Gulf by Rail to Key West," pp. 203-207.
94. "Railway World," April 6, 1895, p. 270
95. Abercrombie, John, "Reporter in Paradise, Chapter 11" (Unpublished manuscript in the author's collection) Pages not numbered
96. "Key West Interocean" (Newpaper) Volume 28, Number 10, Friday, November 3, 1905
97. Op cit, "Reporter in Paradise," page not numbered
98. Op Cit, "The Railway that Died at Sea," pp 9-10.
99. Ibid, p. 10
100. Compass direction south of Key Largo is generally southwest. There are, in fact, several locations where the railroad (now the Highway) is going east and west. However, railroad direction does not take this into account. Direction from Homestead (or north to Jacksonville) to Key West is south, and, of course, anything above Key West is north.
101. Op cit, "The Railroad that Died at Sea," p. 14
102. The station at Long Key was close to the South end of the island, and, as such, was on an embankment leading to the Long Key Viaduct. The narrow gauge railroad went under the embankment somewhat south of the station, and it is unclear today if the narrow gauge tram line was originally built to aid in the construction of the railroad and Fishing Camp, or if it was added "for the convenience of guests arriving by yacht." At the entrance to Long Key State Park, which is roughly on the site of the Fishing Camp, a wheel set from the narrow gauge is on display.
103. Another benefit of having extended the tracks to Knight's Key was that the Post Office Department increased the pay to the FEC by $15,000 yearly due to the extension of Railway Post Office service to Knight's Key. "Miami & Key West RPO" operated to Knight's Key via rail and thence via steamer to Key West. While the steamers were not car ferries, the clerks and the mail was transferred from the train to the boat and vice versa, depending on direction of travel.
104. Flagler Diary (in Flagler Museum, Whitehall), February 27, 1909. The Diary is part of the Flagler papers at the Henry Morrison Flagler Museum, Palm Beach.
105. Lovering, Frank, "Hurricane Between . . . ." Published by the Author, St. Augustine, FL, 1946, p. 12
106. Loc cit, Flagler Diary, June 29, 1909
107. Houston, Hamilton, article in "Leslie's Weekly," January, 1909, p. 630.
108. Op cit, "The Railroad that Died at Sea," p. 19.
109. Op cit, "Southern Reflections of the Gilded Age . . . ." p. 209
110. Generally, "conchs" refers to people of and from the Florida Keys, though in the early days the reference was primarily to those of Bahamian origin.
111. Op cit, "Hurricane Between . . . ." p. 13.
112. Loc cit, Flagler's diary, November 8, 1909
113. Op cit, "The Railroad that Died at Sea," p. 21
114. Op cit, Abercrombie manuscript
115. Op cit, "The Railroad that Died at Sea," p. 23
116. Ibid, p. 24
117. For a complete list of the floating equipment used in the building of the Extension, see Appendix 3b.
118. This entry from Krome's diary quoted in numerous sources
119. There is an obvious implication here that the FEC had off-loaded locomotives and cars at Stock Island for at least five full months prior to the arrival, on January 21, 1912, of the pilot train. Unfortunately, no record seems to exist of the exact location of the "last spike" or the closing of the final gap.
120. Op cit, "Florida's Flagler," p. 222
121. FEC passenger timetable No. 91, in the author's collection, indicates two trains daily to Key West effective January 22, 1912. It is most likely, however, that only Train 37, the "Key West Express," due to arrive Key West at 6:30 PM, operated that day.

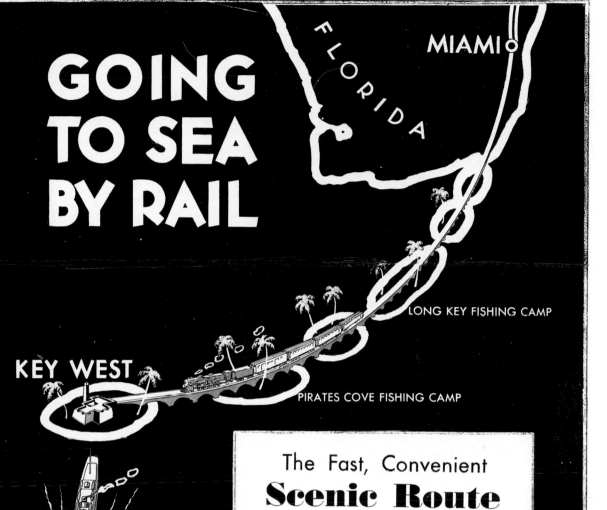

GOING TO SEA BY RAIL

MIAMI

FLORIDA

LONG KEY FISHING CAMP

KEY WEST

PIRATES COVE FISHING CAMP

The Fast, Convenient
## Scenic Route
TO
# Havana
Via Rail to Key West, Florida, thence
directly connecting steamship service
to and from Havana

HAVANA

CUBA

## FLORIDA EAST COAST RAILWAY
In connection with
Peninsular & Occidental S. S. Company

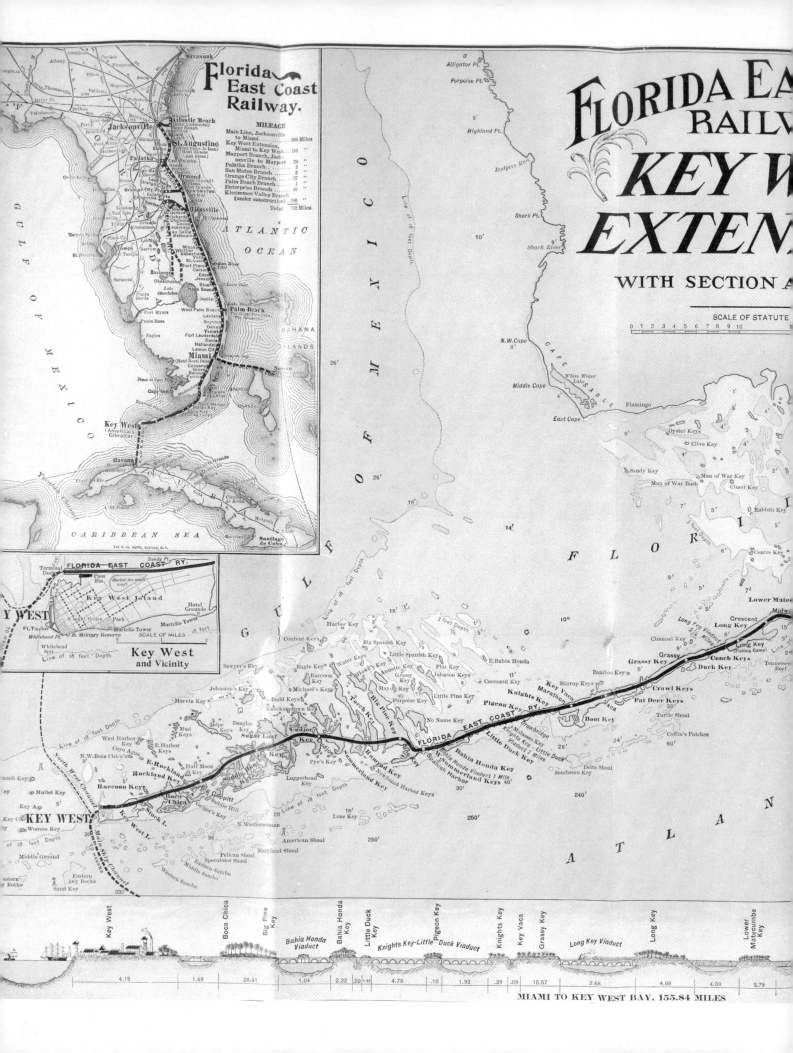

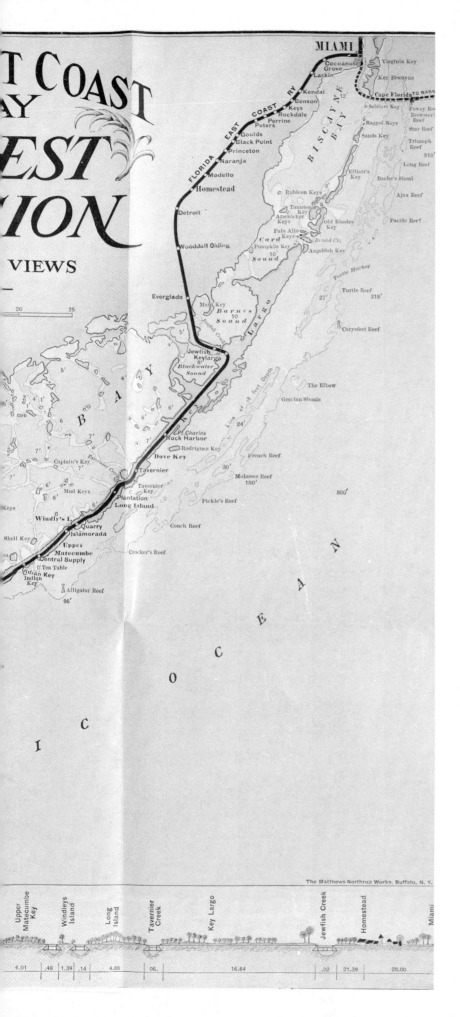

# ST COAST
## AY
## EST
## ION
#### VIEWS

44  EXCAVATOR THROWING UP FILL THRO EVERGLADES, FLA.  F. E. C. RY. EXTENSION SERIES

29  FRESH WATER SUPPLY BARGE TAKING WATER, MANETTE CREEK, FLA.  F. E. C. RY. EXTENSION SERIES

36  COFFERDAMS FOR CONCRETE PIERS, LONG KEY, FLA.  F. E. C. RY. EXTENSION SERIES

41  THREE STAGES OF CONCRETE CONSTRUCTION, LONG KEY, FLA.  F. E. C. RY. EXTENSION SERIES

42  LONG KEY VIADUCT COMPLETED, LONG KEY, FLA.  F. E. C. RY. EXTENSION SERIES

Quarter Boat No. 1, floating hotels or construction camps, Boot Key Harbor, Fla.

Quarter boat 1, one of the floating dormitories is shown here at Boot Key Harbor.

The FEC depot at Long Key. Completely obliterated by the Labor Day, 1935, hurricane, not a trace of either the station or the much-loved Long Key Fishing Camp survived the storm.

The station at Marathon was a small structure having an agent capable of handling express shipments. Look at the surrounding territory!!! Today, this area encompasses the bustling town of Marathon and nothing remains to attest to the hardy agents and their remote stations.

A section of the arched Long Key Viaduct under construction.

An infinity of arches on the Long Key Viaduct.

FEC 3, a 4-4-0 was used during the construction of the Overseas Extension as a work and switch engine. Behind and to the right of the tender of 3 is the permanent trestle that was to be used upon completion.

At Knight's Key dock, transfer was made to the P&O Steamship Company's boats to continue the journey to Key West. A group of what appears to be FEC employees is taking a break at the 'snack shack.' Apparently that familiar term derived from buildings such as this. Note the sign of a longtime American favorite above the first open window on the left. Behind the two story building in the background is a section of the Knight's Key bridge. All of the facilities at Knight's Key were removed shortly after the completion of the Railroad to Key West.

The temporary trestle at Knights Key. What was to become the FEC main line to Key West is shown at the right while the temporary trestle which was used to loop the trains at Knights Key is shown left. It was used from 1909 to 1912.

One of the FECs major stocking points for building and construction material was at Knight's Key. Material was stored as far as the eye can see and was moved as needed via the temporary trackage on the left. In the far left background, construction continues apace.

435 on Seven Mile Bridge is posed for this official photograph.

The Moser Channel Drawbridge looked like this when opened.

The breathtaking magnificence of a ride on the Railroad that went to sea is nowhere more graphically depicted than from the bridge tenders' house on the drawspan of the Seven Mile Bridge. The Railroad direction is north (compass direction N.W.) as a track gang works busily in the foreground. The tiny island visible in the picture is Pigeon Key, which was a supply depot during the construction period and a stop for passenger trains thereafter.

Bahia Honda Bridge was the only structure on the overseas railway in which trains passed through girder sections.

Florida East Coast Railway, Key West Extension, Bird's Eye View of Bahia Honda Bridge, Florida.

Builders Plate from 7 Mile Bridge.

It's June 21st, 1938 and trains to Key West have been a memory for almost three years. After the FEC sold the right of way from Florida City to Key West to the State of Florida, the State immediately began construction on what was to become known as the Overseas Highway. In what was probably the most unusual, if not difficult piece of construction, the State Road Department engineers elected to build the new road *on top of the girder span of the Bahia Honda Bridge.* Where the trains operated through the girder work, the autos rode above it.

This 1947 view shows the abandoned embankment of the railroad crossing Garrison Bight from left to right as it enters the island city of Key West.

For those passengers going on to Havana, the Havana Special pulled up alongside the steamers at Key West and Pullman passengers disembarked from the train to find the gangplank waiting to continue them on their journey to romantic Cuba.

A train of cypress tanks full of fresh water, Long Key Viaduct, 1912

The FEC maintained city ticket offices in New York, Chicago (closed by 1930) Jacksonville, West Palm Beach, Fort Lauderdale, Miami and Miami Beach. In this view of the Miami passenger office, located in the downtown Ingraham building until 1960, the railway prior to the abandonment of the Key West Extension was far from shy in announcing its presence.

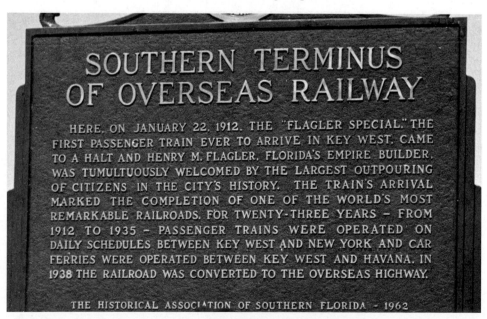

In 1962 to commemorate the coming of the railroad to Key West, the Historical Association of Southern Florida erected this plaque at the point at which the train had actually arrived on the island city. This location was not, however, the station site as that area was farther south.

In one of the most poignant photos Wolfe ever took, Mountain 431 is on the docks at Key West with a train of water tank cars. Before the completion of the water pipeline all fresh water for the island city was hauled by the FEC.

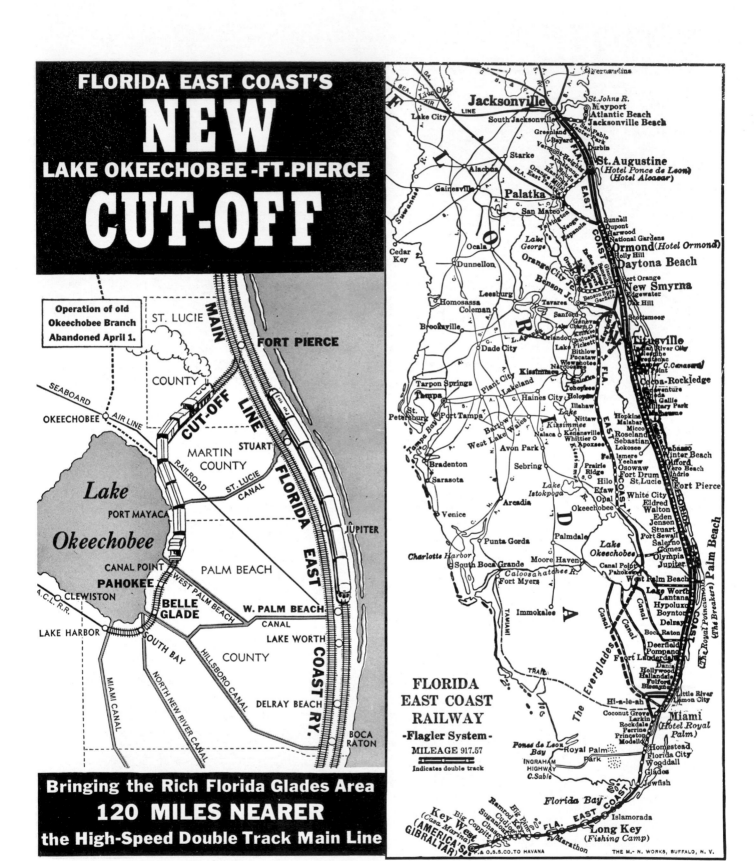

# FLORIDA EAST COAST'S
# NEW
## LAKE OKEECHOBEE -FT. PIERCE
# CUT-OFF

Operation of old Okeechobee Branch Abandoned April 1.

**Bringing the Rich Florida Glades Area**
# 120 MILES NEARER
**the High-Speed Double Track Main Line**

FLORIDA EAST COAST RAILWAY
-Flagler System-
MILEAGE 917.57
Indicates double track

# CHAPTER 6

# RESPITE

The teens themselves were to be, basically, a period for the railroad to recoup and regroup from the frantic machinations of the building of the Key West Extension.

In 1909, Parrott was named president of the FEC Railway; he was already president of the hotel company. On October 28, 1913, the trustees of the Estate[122] added the words "Flagler System" to the title of the railroad, and all passenger equipment and stationery carried those words until the end of the receivership.

Sadly, Joseph R. Parrott passed away in October of 1913. The year was a tragic one for the Flagler System: its two strongest and most important leaders were taken from active roles in its development.

Following Parrott's death, W. H. Beardsley, longtime Flagler employee, and vice president and treasurer of the System, was named president.

The FEC had, for some time, desired to tap the fertile growing areas around the Everglades and Lake Okeechobee. The former goal was achieved in 1904, and the latter in 1915. To reach Lake Okeechobee, the construction of a branch line from Maytown, near New Smyrna Beach, was started following the signing of a contract dated November 7, 1910. Work on what became known as the Kissimmee Valley branch (later Kissimmee Valley line, and then Okeechobee branch) began shortly after the contract was signed. The builder of the line was the Kissimmee Valley Construction Co., though a good deal of work was performed by the railroad's own forces.

Actual movement of earth began at Maytown on February 25, 1911. Various segments, aggregating 122.33 miles, opened between March 11, 1912 and January 5, 1915.[123] For many years, FEC maps showed the projection of the branch to continue to Miami, but the final extension of the line turned out to be to Lake Harbor, and a connection with the Atlantic Coast Line, at the south end of the Lake, in 1929. A further proposed extension, and one that showed on FEC maps for only a few years in the mid teens, was a line from Kenansville to Bassinger. No files or information have ever been uncovered to determine the reason for extending the line to Bassinger.

Since the Okeechobee branch passed through such hamlets as Bithlo, Holopaw, Yeehaw, Nittaw, Ilahaw and Solofka, it is not hard to understand the eventual demise of the line (in 1947) between Maytown and a point below Okeechobee where a connection was built to the truncated line from Ft. Pierce.[124]

Kenansville, about midway on the line, was to be a bustling city, named after Flagler's wife, Mary Lily Kenan. But Kenansville never quite got off the drawing board and today is barely a wide spot in the road, with a state department of transportation name sign on either side of the area.

The Chuluota Land Company was the only one of the Flagler System Land Companies that did not show a profit. Today, Chuluota, about 15 miles east of Orlando, is on the verge of a boom, but the Flagler System no longer owns any of the land.

## MOTIVE POWER CHANGES

Though the changes made in the teens were not earth shattering, three things occurred that were (or would be) of importance. Between 1913 and 1919, 20 locomotives were sold to scrap dealers or other railroads, including some of the Company's earliest engines. During this same period 38 new engines were purchased.[125]

The second thing that was of import, in regard to motive power in the teens, was the purchase by the railroad of a gasoline-electric car in 1915 from General Electric. On August 1, 1916, the Mayport Branch passenger timetable of the FEC carried, above the actual schedules, the notation "Steam and Electric Passenger Train Service," in bold letters. This note was not carried again on any timetable, and the use of the car from that point, until its sale to the Minneapolis, Northfield & Southern in 1920 is unknown,

# Florida
## STRING BEANS

*String Beans*
*And how they are grown on the*
*East Coast of Florida*

*Compiled by*
MODEL LAND COMPANY
FLAGLER SYSTEM
ST. AUGUSTINE, FLORIDA

PINERY, EAST COAST, FLA.

Compliments of the Land Department of the Florida East Coast Railway, St. Augustine, Fla.

This small brochure is an example of a series of Agricultural promotions done on an ongoing basis by the FEC and its numerous associated land and hotel companies.

FEC DEPOT 1940
NITTAW, FLA.

Stations on the FEC branch lines were a fascinating conglomeration of styles and designs. The branch from Maytown to the Lake Okeechobee area was replete with sheds, various station styles and two-story buildings. The stations at Nittaw and Holopaw are excellent examples.

*(Monypenny photos)*

FEC DEPOT 1940
HOLOPAW, FLA.

39                                                                          40

though the likelihood is that it continued in branch line service. Its early demise indicates that the FEC motive power people were less than pleased with the car's performance.

Finally, the item of greatest importance in the teens, and one that boded well for passenger train users on the FEC was the inauguration of oil-burning steam engines. The "St. Augustine Record," of July 7, 1915, reported that the first oil-burning engines had been put into use, and the railroad planned to convert "about two locomotives per week from coal to oil." The ramifications were quite clear.

From that point on, FEC passengers would never again be smudged or dusted by coal cinders, and the FEC could truly advertise "clean, oil-burning locomotives." Coal, as a source of power of the FEC, was no longer.

When the FEC extended its line around Lake Okeechobee to Lake Harbor, the country was so forbidding that it was necessary for the railway to provide living quarters for its station agents and their families. The depot at South Bay is a typical example of the two story construction.

## UNITED STATES RAILROAD ADMINISTRATION

While war had been raging in Europe since 1914, the United States did not enter the conflict until 1917. On December 28, 1917, by order of the President of the United States, William Gibbs McAdoo, Director General of Railroads for the Government, took control of America's railroads, effective January 1, 1918.

Unlike most other railroads, the FEC did not suffer the ravages of government misuse and neglect. All the FECs operating officials remained in their respective capacities while the road was in Federal hands, and, because of this, the road was cared for during the stewardship and returned to the Corporate entity in good condition on March 1, 1920. As of December 31, 1920, the balance due to the Florida East Coast from the Government was over $918,000.[126]

After several years of carrying asset and liability accounts, an agreement was entered into with the Director General of Railroads on April 6, 1923, providing for a final settlement of all matters arising out of the operation of the FEC by the USRA from January 1, 1918 to February 29, 1920. Under the terms of the agreement, the FEC received cash in the amount of $750,000.00, with a balance of over $253,700.00 remaining. This balance was, in accordance with an Order of the ICC dated January 26, 1922, credited to Profit and Loss.

During the period of Federal Control, the FEC received from the USRA $3,825,000 in cash for the use of the road (partial payment) and paid to the Government $1,400,000.00 in partial reimbursement of expenditures for Additions and Betterments made by the USRA.[127]

As the teens ended, the railroad was in better shape physically than it had been before the Government operation. But even with this improvement, the road was hardly in a position of readiness to handle the onslaught of business that was just around the corner! The term "Roaring 20's" was to prove to be an understatement on Florida's East Coast!

### FOOTNOTES

122. Besides Parrott, the other two trustees were Beardsley and Flagler's brother-in-law, William R. Kenan.
123. It is a measure of the strength of the Flagler System (obviously, Flagler, himself) that the Kissimmee Valley Line could be contracted for, and construction started a full year prior to the completion of the Key West Extension.
124. See Chapter 9
125. See Appendix 2 for complete FEC locomotive roster.
126. FEC Annual report for the year ending December 31, 1920.
127. FEC Annual Report for the year ending December 31, 1923, p. 9

One of the rarest birds on the FEC was the gas electric car 200, built for the railroad by Westinghouse and used on the branch lines. For several years the FEC used this car for service to the Jacksonville Beaches. In an extremely rare photograph, 200 is shown in front of the trainshed at the old Union Station in Jacksonville.

# CHAPTER 7

# BOOM, BUST AND BANKRUPTCY

The prelude to the "Roaring 20's" was three-pronged, as far as the American people living in that era were concerned. On November 11, 1918, the Armistice was signed and the First World War was ended. On July 1, 1919, the Volstead Act became effective, and the sale of alcoholic beverages became illegal. Finally, on March 1, 1920, the railroads of the United States were returned to their owners, basically intact, but, in most cases, much the worse for wear. Happily, this was not the case on the FEC.

As soon as the war ended, the tempo of America changed. The placid "it'll get done" attitude quickened, and the theme soon became "do it now!" The East Coast of Florida, and the southeast corner in particular, became the epitome of "flaming youth," as Miami bobbed her hair, shortened her skirts, raised the height of her once frowsy heels, lowered her neckline and hollered for joy. Neither Miami, nor the Florida East Coast, nor the nation, would ever again be the same!

The railroader and hotelier became almost indistinguishable from one another, for the FEC had been designed with passengers uppermost in the builder's mind, while the carriage of freight seemed to be secondary.

Because of the incredible plethora of publicity generated by the railroad, the state, and the communities along the way, particularly Miami and environs, along with the simple fact that the FEC had been built "that way," everything about the FEC bespoke the style and quality which were available to a company spawned by a Standard Oil partner with a mind to go first class and take a large number of people with him.

The FEC contrived to convey the impression that patrons were already registered and in residence at the Ponce de Leon, Royal Poinciana, Breakers, Royal Palm or some other Flagler Hotel of their choice when they boarded the Pullmans at Dearborn or Pennsylvania or South Station. The transition from their drawing rooms aboard the "Havana Special" to suites on the ocean side of the Ormond Hotel, or the Casa Marina was made to seem no more than the passage from one room to another in a well-appointed private house.

Evidence of the grand manner in which the affairs of the FEC were conducted in the specious days of rail travel survive to this day in company literature, brochures, and timetables—all printed on heavily coated book stock and illustrated with fine screen halftones and handsomely drawn art maps. To people the road's publicity photographs, professional models were posed with the cars rather than the often seedy groups of employees recruited (mostly against their wishes) from the general offices of the railroad, which was the practice elsewhere. As a result, the FEC publicity releases depicted passengers who looked the part of the dowagers, clubmen, and debutantes who did in fact ride the trains but were not available to advertising matter. In no instance on record were the roles of hotel operator and railroader more explicitly fused,[128] and at no time was this intermingling of professions more evident, obvious, or important, than in the operations of the Florida East Coast Railway and Hotels in the 1920's.

The decade began modestly. The FEC, in company with their major connections, the Atlantic Coast Line and Seaboard Air Line Railroads, published, in 1920-21, a 162 page "Directory and Guide of Florida Railways . . . . Commercial/Industrial & Agricultural Opportunities." It was an impressive volume, listing citrus growers, shippers, fruit packers, saw mills, and the like, as well as a modest compendium of the cities served by the three railroads, and filled with the still somewhat stilted and formal language that seemed to be "proper" in late 1919 and early 1920, when the book was being compiled. But this book was barely a harbinger of things to come, because the FEC *on its own*, published, for the 1926-27 season, a hard cover, 452 page "encyclopedia" telling you *everything* you could or would ever want to know about the East Coast of Florida. This superb volume, filled with listings, descriptions and advertisements, was dedicated strictly to the cities and towns served by the FEC.

In 1920, the railroad began the replacement of the seventy pound main line rail with 90 pound rail, and built new stations at Atlantic Beach and Long Key. Ten Pacific type (4-6-2) engines and two 0-6-0 switchers were purchased new along with two secondhand diners (re-named "Ormond" and "Alcazar"), all of which entered revenue service that year.

The East Coast was pulsating, and the FEC responded, quickening its pace of purchases as revenues increased. By 1922, gross revenues were 13½ million dollars for the year, compared to 10.8 million in 1920.

The railroad completed the first unit of the General Office Building in St. Augustine and authorized a second unit. 10 more locomotives, 10 baggage cars and 11 steel tank cars came on line in '22.

Early in 1923, the FEC suffered another loss. J. P. Beckwith, a loyal and trusted Flagler employee, died on January 4. He joined the FEC in 1896 as Traffic Manager, serving in that capacity until 1909; thereafter as Vice President in charge of Operation and Traffic. As Beardsley put it, "He leaves behind a record of many accomplishments, well and faithfully done."[129]

1923 passenger schedules provided five daily trains each way between Jacksonville and Miami. Two of these trains, the "Havana Special" and the "Key West Express" provided service through to the Island City. Numbers 37 and 38 were certainly given the name "Express" with tongue in cheek, making 43 stops, including scheduled and "flag" between Miami and Key West. Scheduled running time was 5 hours 50 minutes, while the "Havana Special" with only six northbound stops scheduled (only two of them being "flags") took five hours.

On January 10, 1923, the ICC authorized the construction of a new line from Okeechobee, at the top of the lake, around the east side of the lake, and partially around the south end to Lemon City (now NE 61st-62nd Street area in Miami, approximating the east end of what has become the Miami Belt Line of the railroad) and a branch from Hialeah to Larkin, which was the earlier name for the City of South Miami.[130] At a point near Hialeah, where the line from the north was supposed to come into the Greater Miami area, a line was built to what is now the Kendall-Dadeland area of Miami, and the Miami Belt was constructed.

1923 also saw the completion of the second unit of the General Office Building in St. Augustine and the receiving on-line of 15 Mountain type locomotives, 4-8-2's 301-315, along with 200 flat cars and the tug "R. M. DeGarmo", at a cost of $17,000.00, for use on the Key West Extension.

The 300 series are particularly noteworthy, as they were the first engines on the FEC larger than the Pacific types.

It was in 1924 that the "Boom" began to explode. People were pouring into Florida at such a rate that the January, 1924 passenger timetable showed eight trains daily between Jacksonville and Miami in each direction. Such famed names as the "Miamian" and the "Floridan" became regulars on FEC winter season timetables for years to come. Service was lush, and four of the eight trains were Pullman Cars only. Amenities were constantly increasing, and the FEC had this to say about its then renowned dining car service: "All Florida East Coast Railway[131] trains, except the strictly locals, are now served by dining cars and an unusual feature is that they are operated by the different railroads; for example, the diner of the Floridan is under the supervision of the Illinois Central; diners on the Florida Special and Havana Special by the Atlantic Coast Line, and the diner on the Seaboard Limited by the Seaboard Air Line.[132]

"This arrangement gives the traveler on the East Coast the almost certain knowledge that he might expect on each diner the best to be had in both food and service, varying in the little refinements, of course, as may be indicated by the several supervising agencies.

"The local trains carry Broiler Buffet Pullman cars, Parlor cars on the day trains and Sleepers on the night trains.

"Dining cars are in service between Jacksonville and Miami on trains Nos. 33-34, 35-36, 39-40, 85-86, 9-10, 87-88, also between Jacksonville and Key West on trains Nos. 85-86.

"Broiler Buffet cars are operated on trains Nos. 29-30, 37-38, 41-42. Trains Nos. 37, 38 and 41 also stop for meals at the famous Long Key Fishing Camp.

"Dining cars are of the latest design with attractive finish and are manned by experienced stewards, chefs and waiters. Kitchens are equipped with up-to-date appliances for the preparation and serving of meals, including steam tables, and, of course, model broilers and ovens. Dining car menus show a wide variety from which to make a selection, and delicious foods, including the famous citrus fruits of Florida, are served promptly by competent waiters. Special combinations on all menu cards provide meats, fowl or fish, vegetables, dessert and tea, coffee or milk for the moderate price of $1.00." [133]

It was in 1924 that total revenues jumped to over $20 million. And the railroad made news in other

## HAVANA SPECIAL LOUNGE CAR

**YOU ARE INVITED TO ENJOY THE LOUNGE CAR IN THE CENTER OF THIS TRAIN**

THERE YOU WILL FIND A DRAWING ROOM LOUNGE; A LADIES' LOUNGE AND BATH; GENTLEMEN'S LOUNGE AND BATH. THERE IS A WELL-EQUIPPED SODA FOUNTAIN WITH A TRAINED FILIPINO ATTENDANT

## ATLANTIC COAST LINE
"THE STANDARD RAILROAD OF THE SOUTH"

The printed invitation to visit the Havana Special's Lounge Car must have been a most tempting inducement to pamper oneself hedonisticly. In all likelihood, this card was from the 30's But the single most unique sybaritic lure to the potential passenger operated on the "Florida Special" during the 1932-33 season. As with many other tidbits of railroad lore and legend, the verification of the swimming pool operated on Trains 87 and 88 was long and difficult. However, the following appears on page 32 in the 1933 edition, "The Gimlet", published in Miami, John Ashe Scott, Publisher.

"A special recreation car is attached to the "Florida Special" each week as a feature of the Florida Year Round Clubs of Henry L. Doherty at Miami. (Author's note: Did they mean to say "of Miami?") Here the south-bound vacationist finds a gymnasium, dance floor, orchestra, bridge room with hostess-instructor in charge, a barber shop *and even a portable swimming pool.*" (Italics are the authors.) And in "Popular Mechanics," March, 1933, in a filler titled "Bathing Pool in Railroad Car Entertains Passengers," the following: "One railroad operating between New York and Florida has installed a recreation car on its southern run so passengers will not need to wait until they reach Miami to begin their sports. The club car is equipped with a small bathing pool, mechanical horses, a punching bag and other equipment for the entertainment of passengers who want exercise."

Though no mention is made of the pool in timetables of any of the roads involved in the operation of the Florida Special, Harold K. North, retired Assistant General Passenger Agent of the railroad remembers the car with the tiny pool in it. "It was," he recalls, "a real nuisance, as the constant motion of the train caused the pool to constantly need refilling. I was a ticket agent at the (Miami) depot that winter and remember the curiosity the pool generated. I don't think it ran after that one year." And, indeed, the pool never made a known trip after 1933, but, as with so much else in the annals and lore of the Florida East Coast Railway it remains a legend that turned out to have been a fact.

ways! In a story in the Miami "News", November 3, 1924, relating to the capture of the infamous Ashley gang, it was stated that "Joe Tracy, another member of the gang, was taken prisoner a few weeks ago at Kissimmee, having given himself up on a Florida East Coast branch line train. Tracy had deserted Ashley in the Everglades west of Salerno."

A little over a week before the exciting capture, another of the FEC's "pioneers" passed from the scene. The death of James E. Ingraham, vice president of lands and industries, and a director of the System who had been with Flagler and the Company since 1893 died on October 25, 1924. The announcement, made with great sadness by William R. Kenan, Jr., who had been named President of the road in 1923, following Beardsley's elevation to Board Chairman, shocked all who had known and loved the ebullient and gracious Ingraham.

All of this was but a harbinger of what was to come. The single track main line, overworked and overburdened, could no longer handle the load. By order of the Board of Directors, the FEC was to be double-tracked from Miami to Jacksonville. The work had actually begun in 1924, when 26 2/3 miles were completed. 230 miles were completed in 1925 with the remaining 114 miles due to be completed in 1926.

For several years, a cutoff had been planned between a point just south of St. Augustine (to be known as Moultrie Junction) and Bunnell (to be known as Bunnell Junction) in order to substantially reduce the running time of through trains which, since the original building of the St. Augustine & Palatka and the St. Johns & Halifax Railways had operated between St. Augustine and Bunnell via East Palatka. In 1925, this cutoff (known as the Moultrie Cutoff) was built on a direct line from Moultrie Junction to Bunnell Junction, a distance of slightly over 29 miles, eliminating 20 miles from the old route. By the winter season of 1925-26, 9 of 11 first class passenger trains between Jacksonville and either Miami or Key West had been re-routed via the new cutoff. East Palatka was left with two trains per day (29 & 30 and 37 & 38) as well as service to San Mateo and Palatka via shuttle trains, making four round trips to Palatka and two to San Mateo.

The list of improvements for 1925 had, however, just begun. In addition to double-tracking including the Moultrie Cutoff, the railroad completed the Belt Line between Lemon City and Hialeah by adding a second track to the single track that had been laid in 1924. A number of passing tracks were added, and the original Hialeah yard was completed with a 1300 car capacity in anticipation of the extension of the Okeechobee branch to Hialeah. Bowden Yard, south of Jacksonville was opened with a 2,120 car capacity, and work begun on Miller Shops, just north of St. Augustine, which was to be noted in FEC publicity as the most modern car and locomotive repair facilities in the South. [134]

One of the major improvements to the system, others notwithstanding, was the completion of the double-track bridge over the St. Johns River at Jacksonville, enabling a major increase in both freight and passenger capacity at that point.

Finally, in the way of equipment, the Company took delivery of 49 steam engines, including 4-8-2s, 2-8-2s and 0-8-0 switchers, 50 passenger cars, 15 baggage cars, 20 cabooses and a 150 ton wrecking crane.

By 1925, the Boom had become an epidemic! Miami's own four year boom had spread across Florida. But then, in August, the unthinkable occurred. The FEC, in the midst of double-tracking, found that every yard, every dray track and every siding on the system was filled with freight or passenger cars. There was barely room to turn the daily passenger trains at Miami. The trains couldn't be lengthened, and, if they could, there was no place to put the cars. The superintendent of transportation, with the approval of H. N. Rodenbaugh, Vice President of Operations, Traffic and Construction (who had received his approval from Kenan and the Board) announced a temporary freight embargo. The edict cut off the arrival of building materials, which forced draymen and contractors to reduce or idle their crews, and all manner of ships, steam, sail or oar, was used to get lumber and building materials into the ports along the length of the East Coast. Lumber bootleggers became welcome and honored members of society, along with their brethren, the rumrunners.

Freight was moved only by permit following the embargo, and only urgent or emergency cargo was allowed to move. Even the City of Miami Beach, awaiting ten cars of sewer pipe, was refused a permit for the movement of the cargo.[135]

It was, in today's vernacular, "a helluva year!" Once again the unkind hand of death struck at the Company near the end of the year, as President Kenan announced the passing of another of Flagler's faithful. W. H. Beardsley, former treasurer and president of the railroad, and, at the time of his death, Chairman of the Board and a member of the Executive Committee, died on December 13, 1925.

In 1926 at the height of the Florida boom the FEC committed to a myriad of capital improve-ments. Among these improvements was the General Office Building on Malaga Street in St. Augustine. The three four-story buildings were constructed next to what became known as the passenger annex, shown at far right in this photo. The annex housed passenger, dining and advertising departments and contained the passenger station. Just north of the annex is Flagler Park, where a statue of Flagler stood for many years. Following the takeover of the railroad by Edward Ball and the Florida Dupont interests the statue was given to Flagler College, which, itself is housed in the former Hotel Ponce de Leon, the first of Flagler's hostelries. The three office buildings, are connected by graceful, arched walkways and between each of the buildings, centered on the archway facing the street, is a full-color, overseas extension logo made entirely of concrete and Mediterranean tiles. On the north building facing both north and southwest are neon signs bearing the words "Florida East Coast Railway." These signs were removed from the North Miami and Fort Lauderdale stations following the complete cessation of passenger train service in 1968. The two signs were shipped to St. Augustine and add a tasteful and finished look to the buildings.

—(H. Wolfe)

At the close of the year, the road had 207 steam engines and 217 pieces of passenger equipment on hand, including 10 dining cars. [136]

Like 1925, 1926's revenues were over $29 million. The final 114 miles of double-track was completed, and the automatic block system was installed in both directions. Between Bowden, New Smyrna, Ft. Pierce and Hialeah Yards, car capacity was increased by a total of 8,445 units. The Ol' Hoss warehouse in Miami was completed for use as a freight station and a new passenger station was built at Little River (NE 79th Street) in Miami. Miller Shops were completed, and served, until 1963, as the FEC's main car and locomotive repair facilities. The third and final building of the General Offices was completed and occupied, as was the new passenger and freight office on Datura Street in West Palm Beach.

The passenger timetable of February 2, 1926, carried 12 main line trains, 11 between Jacksonville and Miami, with two of those continuing on to Key West, and a new train, "Tropical Limited," operating an all daylight schedule three times weekly between Miami and Key West in either direction. Numbers 98 and 99 carried coaches and a parlor car, as well as a diner and made a 30 minute stop at Long Key Fishing Camp "for those who wish to take lunch at this novel camp." Not considering "extras," "specials," or additional sections of scheduled trains, this was the largest number of first class main line trains that the FEC would ever operate.

In April, the FEC took the unusual step of terminating Mayport branch trains to and from the Jacksonville Beaches at the South Jacksonville ferry terminal rather that at Jacksonville Union Terminal. The FEC ballyhooed it as "Improved Mayport Branch Service," stating that "Trains on the Mayport Branch now depart and arrive at the new South Jacksonville Ferry Station, connecting directly with the ferry service from Main Street, Jacksonville, and thereby providing more rapid and convenient service to the popular Beach resorts, including Jacksonville Beach, Neptune, Atlantic Beach, Manhattan Beach and Mayport. One train daily has been continued in service to and from the Jacksonville Union Station and on Sundays one additional train departs and arrives at this point."[137] [138] Again, the lack of correspondence or records to indicate the reason for the change frustrates the modern day historian, but it likely had to do with terminal and usage charges at Jacksonville Union Terminal.

Jacksonville Terminal Co., of which FEC was a partial owner, operated as a separate company, and, as such, charged each railroad that operated into the Terminal a set fee for each arrival and departure. As history has shown, over and over, passengers do whatever is necessary to avoid changing from one conveyance to another, and, in retrospect (again) it appears that the FECs desire to save terminal charges for certain of the more lightly patronized trains may have signalled the beginning of the end for the Mayport branch.

It is doubtful that the embargo on freight had anything to do with the cutback of Mayport branch trains, but, as of mid February, the embargo was still very much in force. From letters now in the author's files, it appears that a mechanism was initiated by the railroad for shippers to enter statements of requirements with the railroad, listing items to be shipped and reasons therefor, and then apply for permits, which, in effect, were requests for permission to ship. If the permit was approved, the shipment could then be made.[139]

The FEC was doing all possible to build up business on the Key West Extension and by 1926 had reached almost 3,500 carloads of Cuban pineapples annually. All freight from Cuba was not as sweet smelling as the pineapples and on June 1, 1926, customs inspectors, after overseeing the removal from one of the carferries of several carloads of the fruit, began opening the cars, as was legally required. Much to their horror, three aliens, (two Hungarians and a Bulgarian) were sealed in with the pineapples. Needless to say, they were much less fragrant![140]

And then—again—it happened. Out of the blue expanse of the vast Caribbean, a whirling, howling wind-fury swooped mercilessly down upon the gayest, brightest playground in all the world—that sixty mile strip of Florida's East Coast with Palm Beach at one end and Miami at the other—and, on Friday and Saturday, September 17th and 18th, lashed the golden coast into a battleground of the elements, strewn with death and debris.

Because it had been so long since Miami had been hit by a major storm, and because the booming population was so uneducated about the ways and wiles of these horrific dervishes, terrified thousands, thinking the storm had spent its fury, and preparing to begin the work of counting the toll and cleaning up the death and debris, ventured outside, not knowing that they were in the eye of the storm. Without warning or alert, the other side of the 'cane struck again with redoubled intensity, completing the devastation of its first blow and leaving even vaster ruin in its wake.

The Hurricane of September 17th and 18th, 1926 was a horror previously unmatched by any other Florida storm. Roaring out of the Caribbean, the Hurricane devastated South Florida, leaving the FEC far from untouched. It took the FEC almost a full week to throw off the effects of the storm, with the center of damage being in the area from Dania, north of Hollywood, to South Miami. The Hollywood station, a beautiful, mission style building was ripped asunder by the monster 'cane, losing its roof, all electrical connections and the fence between the tracks. A concerted effort by the FEC totally rehabilitated the station, and from then until its demolition in 1967 it remained one of the most picturesque edificia on the railroad.

In the sixty mile swath it cut on Florida's seacoast, before roaring inland, the hurricane's toll was 220 dead and 6,328 injured. So complete was the ruin wrought in Miami and it's sister communities that nearly 24 hours elapsed before the first word of the disaster reached the outside world. When the remainder of the nation learned of the frightful destruction, a national outpouring of food, clothing, money and supplies streamed into Miami. Each of the municipal administrators moved quickly to assure the nation that the lower East Coast would be back in business in time for "the season." By and large, they were, but the shock waves and the apprehension brought about by this storm crashed the "house of cards" that the Florida boom had been built on.

During the year, the hurricane notwithstanding, the FEC was making every effort to "get caught up" and to eliminate the embargo. To this end, the double-tracking of the entire Jacksonville-Miami line was completed, and 10 more 400 series passenger engines, 23 800 series freight engines and 12 more 0-8-0 switchers were added to the roster. Additionally, Business Cars 93, 94 and 95, and dining cars "Daytona" and "Key West" were put into service, along with 40 cabooses, 15 coaches, 2 RPO's, 8 baggage cars and 18 tank cars.

Due to the Florida boom, and the FEC's inability to handle the vast amounts of traffic overpowering it, the Seaboard Air Line initiated, in 1925, extensions from the center of the state to Naples on the West Coast and Miami on the East Coast. The Miami line would not actually reach the East Coast until West Palm Beach, using a circuitous inland routing that took it through West Lake Wales and Sebring to Okeechobee, at the top of the Lake and on a beeline to West Palm Beach, where, from that point, it would parallel the FEC to Miami and continue to Homestead. Discussion was carried on regarding trackage rights to Key West from a connection at either Homestead or Florida City, but nothing came of that.

The FEC was in no position to contest the Seaboard's move, and on January 8, 1927, the famed "Orange Blossom Special" arrived in Miami's Seaboard depot. Seaboard trains now moved via their own rails, and the "Seaboard Florida Limited," via the FEC from Jacksonville to Miami, was no more. Ironically, the Florida extensions were one of the major causes of the Seaboard's bankruptcy during the depression.

Because of the all time high in revenues, the over purchase of equipment and double-tracking to cope with the boom, the hurricane in September and subsequent land bust, 1926 turned out to be a year like no other had ever been. 1926 was the year the FECs fortunes began to change. Unaware though they were at the time, a prince-to-pauper metamorphosis was about to begin.

1927 was a year to hold the line, a difficult task with revenues of $17.8 million compared to $29.4 million in '26. '27 was clearly a holding action with 1 less locomotive on the roster, 24 fewer freight cars and 8 fewer passenger cars by the end of the year. No new motive power or rolling stock was bought. Kenan put it tersely: "The construction and real estate activity of the recent Florida boom period was reflected in the Company's earnings for 1925 and 1926. The marked deflation and lack of buying power following, was also reflected in our earnings for 1927."[141]

Although a mild recovery was made after the 1926 hurricane, it did not begin to approach the land boom and spectacular increases in real estate prior to that disaster. The FEC was not to be deterred.

A strong effort was made to solicit and increase freight business, but with huge stocks on hand, shipments were less than robust. The railroad continued to seek new business and with full-page ads ballyhooed 24 hour reductions in freight movement from shipper to market. Passenger service, while far from being neglected, was reduced markedly, with the five trains that had operated through the summer of 1927 being reduced to three on September 26. Winter season service, which had been up to 12 main line trains in the winter of 1926, was down to nine trains daily each way between Jacksonville and Miami for the winter of 1927-28.

Revenues in 1928 dropped another $4 million to $13.8 million. The bottom line net deficit, even with the drop in revenues, had improved slightly and was $77,000.00 better than in 1927. Again, no equipment or rolling stock was purchased and equipment on hand remained relatively stable. In fact, no steam engines were sold or retired that year.

Miami was struggling to get back on its feet, and the BPOE—Elks—favored the City with their 1928 convention, the Elks first national convention to be held in the Magic City. The FEC went all out! Besides publishing a richly illustrated and elegantly worded (as was their bent) booklet, the railroad advertised heavily to encourage Elks from all over the country to come to Miami via the FEC. While the convention was a smashing success, and the FEC tracks were overladen with special cars and special trains, the four day "shot in the arm" was not enough to stem the tide. And, even with the FEC advertising that "You arrive in the heart of the Magic City," the new Seaboard route attracted a goodly share of the sun-bound travellers, before, during and after the conclave.

In 1929, though revenues dropped another $430,000.00, this was much less precipitous than the drop of the preceding two years. But it was obvious that the debt service and interest on the funded debt were brutalizing the railroad. For 1929, the FEC showed a loss of over $1.3 million.

The picture was not yet totally bleak. The final 10 miles of the Okeechobee branch, from Belleglade-Chosen to Lake Harbor were completed. For the 1929-1930 winter season, eight main line trains were scheduled, none of which operated via East Palatka. The FEC initiated the "Hastings—Bunnell Local," numbers 45 and 46 to operate through from Jacksonville to Bunnell via East Palatka, thereby serving those communities on the former main line with direct service from Jacksonville, while at the same time speeding up all other schedules.

Further, the FEC, in connection with Pan American Airways, announced New York—Miami—Havana service with transfer from train to plane at Miami. Flying time, Miami—Havana, in the tri-motored Fokkers, with accommodations for 12 and a crew of four, was two hours, fifteen minutes. The trip to Havana via the Oversea Railroad to Key West, thence by P&O steamer, was no less interesting or exciting, but it required twelve hours and fifteen minutes.

Again, comparing '29 to '28, changes in equipment were minimal. By December 31, 1929, the FEC had 248 engines, compared to 249 the previous year, 198 passenger cars compared to 208, 2,655 freight cars compared to 2,902, and 587 pieces of work equipment, including 6 office cars, compared to 616 the previous year.

There was, or so they thought, hope for the coming year.

As hopefully as 1930 dawned (notwithstanding the effects of the 1929 Wall Street stock market "crash") the Company knew, by the end of the year, that only the darkness lay ahead. 1930s net loss was only $2,000.00 short of $2 million, and, in 1930 dollars, no company could sustain that type of fiscal pounding for long.

In order to save many expenses through reduction of taxes and insurance, a program of retiring

# FLYING THE ROMANTIC CARIBBEAN

**Pan American Airways Passenger Terminal, Miami, Fla.**

## THROUGH
### RAIL - AIR - SERVICE
## TO
### HAVANA, WEST INDIES
### CENTRAL AND SOUTH AMERICA

### Only **36** hours
### from New York to Havana

Fast, direct train service to Miami, thence swift, safe, tri - motored cabin planes

### West Indies Air Limited

| Mon.-Wed.-Fri. | | | Sun.-Wed.-Fri. |
|---|---|---|---|
| 7.00 am | Lv. Miami.....................Ar. | | 5.30 pm |
| 10.50 am | Lv. Camaguey..................Lv. | | 2.30 pm |
| 3.30 pm | Lv. Port au Prince............Lv. | | 10.20 am |
| 5.10 pm | Ar. Santo Domingo.............Lv. | | 8.40 am |
| 6.00 am | Lv. Santo Domingo.............Ar. | | ........ |
| 8.25 am | Ar. San Juan..................Lv. | | 6.00 am |
| **Tuesday** | | | **Saturday** |
| 8.30 am | Lv. San Juan..................Ar. | | 5.00 pm |
| 9.30 am | Lv. St. Thomas, V. I..........Lv. | | 4.20 pm |
| 1.00 pm | Lv. St. Johns, Antigua........Lv. | | 2.00 pm |
| 4.00 pm | Lv. Port Castries, St. Lucia..Lv. | | 10.25 am |
| 6.00 pm | Ar. Port of Spain, Trin.......Lv. | | 7.00 am |
| **Wednesday** | | | **Friday** |
| 7.00 am | Lv. Port of Spain, Trin.......Lv. | | 6.00 pm |
| 12.15 pm | Lv. Georgetown, B. G..........Lv. | | 3.00 pm |
| 2.00 pm | Lv. Nickerie, D. G............Lv. | | 1.15 pm |
| 3.15 pm | Ar. Paramaribo, D. G..........Lv. | | 12.00 noon |
| **Thursday** | | | **Thursday** |
| 6.00 am | Lv. Paramaribo, D. G..........Ar. | | 11.30 am |
| 9.15 am | Lv. Cayenne, F. G.............Ar. | | ........ |
| 3.00 pm | Lv. Belem, Para...............Lv. | | 5.00 am |

### Miami - Jamaica - Canal Zone

| Tues.-Fri. | | | Mon.-Thurs. |
|---|---|---|---|
| 3.00 pm | Lv. Miami.....................Ar. | | 10.45 am |
| 5.15 pm | Ar. Cienfuegos................Lv. | | 8.15 am |
| **Wed.-Sat.** | | | **Sun.-Wed.** |
| 6.00 am | Lv. Cienfuegos................Ar. | | 5.15 pm |
| 10.30 am | Lv. Kingston..................Lv. | | 1.45 pm |
| 5.30 pm | Ar. Panama....................Lv. | | 6.00 am |

Also passenger and mail routes down the east and west coasts of South America, including service to Buenos Aires and Rio de Janeiro.

### Via the Havana Special

| 10:15 pm | Lv. New York (Penn.)................Ar. | 6:30 am |
|---|---|---|
| b3:10 am | Lv. Washington.................Ar. a1:10 am |
| 9:15 pm | Lv. Jacksonville (F.E.C.)...........Ar. | 7:15 am |
| a6:30 am | Ar. Miami (F.E.C.)..............Lv. 10:00 pm |
| 8:00 am | Lv. Miami (P.A.A.)...............Ar. | 5:15 pm |
| 10:15 am | Ar. Havana (P.A.A.)..............Lv. | 3:00 pm |

a—S'eepers may be occupied until 7;00 am.
b—Sleepers placed for occupancy at 10:00 pm.

### Via Dixie Limited, Ponce de Leon and Flamingo

| The Flamingo | Ponce de Leon | Dixie Limited | | | Dixie Limited | Ponce de Leon | The Flamingo |
|---|---|---|---|---|---|---|---|
| 9.40 am | 10.40 am | 12.20 pm | Lv. Chicago.........Ar. | 4.00 pm | 4.30 pm | 4.40 pm | |
| 12.05 pm | 12.05 pm | | Lv. Detroit.........Ar. | | 4.29 pm | 4.28 pm | |
| 12.05 pm | 12.05 pm | | Lv. Cleveland.......Ar. | | 3.50 pm | 3.50 pm | |
| 8.30 pm | 8.15 pm | | Lv. Cincinnati......Ar. | | 8.35 am | 8.10 am | |
| 9.40 pm | 9.15 pm | 9.40 pm | Lv. Jacksonville....Ar. | 7.15 am | 7.15 am | 7.15 am | |
| 7.20 am | a6.30 am | 7.20 am | Ar. Miami (F.E.C.)..Lv. | 10.00 pm | 10.00 pm | 10.00 pm | |
| 9.00 am | 8.00 am | 9.00 am | Lv. Miami (P.A.A.)..Ar. | 5.15 pm | 5.15 pm | 5.15 pm | |
| 11.15 am | 10.15 am | 11.15 am | Ar. Miami (P.A.A.)..Lv. | 3.00 pm | 3.00 pm | 3.00 pm | |

| DAILY | Miami-Nassau, Bahamas | DAILY |
|---|---|---|
| 9:00 am | Lv. Miami.......................Ar. | 5:00 pm |
| 11:00 am | Ar. Nassau......................Lv. | 3:00 pm |

# PAN AMERICAN AIRWAYS
### IN CONNECTION WITH
## FLORIDA EAST COAST RAILWAY

obsolete equipment was considered and carried out during the year 1930 to the extent of the retirement of 69 locomotives, 25 passenger train cars, 1,003 freight train cars and 243 units of work train equipment.[142] Applications for abandonment of track would be shortly forthcoming.

By December of 1930, branch line train service had been noticeably reduced. Orange City service was down to one mixed train each way daily except Sunday, while East Palatka to Palatka service was down to two trips daily. Meanwhile San Mateo was served by the "Hastings—Bunnell Local," trains 45 and 46, and no longer had "its own" East Palatka service. Main line service was down to seven trains, with the "Havana Special" continuing on to Key West and an additional train, "The Oversea" operating on an all daylight schedule between Miami and Key West daily.

The debacle was about to begin.

Mayport branch service, which had seen five daily trains each way in the summer of 1930, was cut to one mixed train daily except Sunday for the summer of 1931. Through Miami—Jacksonville service was down to two trains, and from this point until the end of Key West service, only numbers 75 and 76, "The Havana Special," would carry passengers through to Key West.

Then, at 12:01 AM, Tuesday, September 1st, 1931, over the signature of Louie W. Strum, Federal District Judge, and at the request of the Standard Oil Co. of Kentucky, acting for itself and all other creditors, the Florida East Coast Railway, concurring on behalf of itself and its creditors, was placed under the control of W. R. Kenan, Jr., and former U. S. Senator Scott M. Loftin, as receivers.

With all that had been done, with total commitment to the creditors and stockholders, nothing, in the most trying economic depression the world had ever known, had been enough. The Florida East Coast Railway, unable to generate enough revenue to meet its outstanding equipment trust and accounts payable obligations, was bankrupt.[143]

128. Beebe, Lucius, "The Trains We Rode," Volume I, reprinted in "Trains" Magazine, October, 1965, pp. 29-30.
129. FEC 1923 Annual Report, p. 6
130. For information on the Okeechobee branch, particularly the portion from the Lake northward, see Chapter 6.
131. The FEC, from its inception in September, 1895, and with the singular exception of its operation by the USRA, when it bore the name "Railroad," has always been known by the surname title "Railway." Style book editors along the East Coast of Florida, and, most particularly in the Miami area, are strongly urged to take heed!
132. In later years, besides the continued operation of the diners by themselves, the ACL, and the IC, FEC diners on through trains were operated by the Pennsylvania, Louisville & Nashville and Chicago & Eastern Illinois Railroads, at various times.
133. FEC Ry. passenger timetable, January 1, 1924, p. 28.
134. When it became evident, in the 1930's, that Hialeah Yard was a surplus facility and that the Okeechobee branch would not be extended to Miami, the yard was withdrawn from service, not to be returned to service, in a much altered form, until 1963.
135. Letter dated October 14, 1925 from FEC to Miami Beach City Manager Claude Renshaw, author's collection.
136. FEC Annual Report, P. 30, 1925
137. Jacksonville Beach was formerly known as Pablo Beach, the name change having been made after April of 1924 and before April of 1926
138. FEC Passenger Timetable, July 20, 1926, p. 20
139. Correspondence between FEC vice president Rodenbaugh and Miami Beach City Manager Renshaw, February 16 and 18, 1926, author's collection.
140. Op cit, "The Railroad that Died at Sea," p. 32
141. FEC 1927 Annual Report, p. 5
142. FEC 1930 Annual Report, p. 5
143. For a detailed account of the direct actions causing the bankruptcy, and the placing of the railroad into receivership, see "FEC Railway Co. Receivership Record, Volume I," Documents 1 through 7.

The station at Atlantic Beach was conveniently adjacent to the Continental Hotel, a Flagler property.

UNION DEPOT, JACKSONVILLE, FLA.

Union Depot at Jacksonville, Florida. The depot was serviced by the electric streetcars of Jacksonville Traction Company which provided local transportation to much of Jacksonville. The depot was the central station for the Florida East Coast Railway, the Georgia Southern & Florida, Atlantic Coast Line, and Seaboard Airline Railway.

In June, 1892, the branch line from San Mateo Junction to San Mateo, a distance of 2.8 miles was constructed to serve the fruit and vegetable growers of that section who formerly used the St. Johns River Steamships. The FEC built an elegant Victorian type station to serve as the terminal of the branch and for many years thereafter offered daily except Sunday passenger train service utilizing one trip of the East Palatka—Palatka shuttle trains. Finally, however, time, tide and economics caught up to the branch and on September 8, 1942, the 2.8 miles originally built by the St. Johns and Halifax River Railway Company was abandoned.

Lemon City and Coconut Grove are now parts of Miami. But once, many, many years ago, they were separate, incorporated municipalities, connected to Miami by the steel threads of the Flagler System. This edifice, after removal of the agent by the railroad (due to the proximity of Little River and Buena Vista) was sold to the City of Miami, and for many years thereafter served, albeit much altered, as the Lemon City Branch of the Miami Public Library.

—(J. Nelson Collection)

How times change! The Philippine waiter shown in the interior view of the lounge car "Camaguey" of the Havana Special taken at Key West on February 28, 1930, has been replaced by a black waiter in this late 1940s FEC publicity shot made at Jacksonville Terminal. While there are no smoking materials in the 1930 view, the later view seems to feature passengers with unlit cigarettes in their hands.

FEC Mountain 432 blasts south out of Jacksonville with an express for Miami. Jacksonville Union Terminal is visible just to the left of the bridge girders. During the 1926-27 season there were 12 regularly scheduled passenger trains operating in each direction between Jacksonville and Miami, with two of those trains continuing on to Key West.

In 1923, for use on the Key West Extension, the FEC bought the "R. M. DeGarmo" for
$17,000.00. The proud little tug carried the Flagler System insignia, though in a somewhat
homestyle fashion, on its stack, while its own name appeared over the cabin and on both sides of
the bow. In 1937, following the complete abandonment of the fabled railroad that went to sea,
the FEC sold the DeGarmo for $7,000—a not inconsiderable sum considering the age of the boat,
it's original price, and the era—to DesRocher & Watkins towing, and at that point, track was lost
of the fine little ship.

*—(Charles & Richard Beall collection)*

It's the great Miami boom and lots were selling four times in one day. The County Causeway
(background) was under construction and Miami was a-building at a frantic pace. At the P. and
O. dock facilities along Biscayne Blvd. Pullman cars were being used to house convention
delegates. In addition to this facility and Buena Vista, the FEC had private car parking available at
the passenger station, the wye north of the passenger station and Southside just over the Miami
River Bridge. Of particular interest is the variety of "antique" automobiles parked in the
foreground and the vendor plying his trade at roadside. The private railway cars are equipped
with cloth skirting dropped below the car body encompassing the battery boxes, ice chests and
sanitary facilities enabling the cars to be maintained in the scorching heat.

It was the heyday of the Florida boom, and, as if to acknowledge the preeminence of the East Coast of Florida as the "American Riviera" the Shrine voted to hold their 1928 National Convention in the Magic City. The FEC, doing its part, published an elaborate booklet to commemorate the great event. In 1927 Mountain 439 was posed in front of the venerable Miami Station with all of the FEC officials who were Shriners present.

The hostesses are waving 'goodbye' and the band is plucking the strings as the second section of the aristocrat of winter trains prepares to depart Miami in early 1938.

Little River Station, January 27, 1961, complete with recently added second floor.

—(*Charles & Richard Beall collection*)

Engineer Turnipseed was the hogger on the second section of the Florida Special south from Fort Pierce on February 12, 1935. He had told the engineer of the first section that he would be "right on his tail." The first section crossed the Jupiter draw without incident, and the bridge tender, expecting a wait of at least 15 minutes for the second section, opened the bridge. Less than five minutes later Turnipseed roared through the red signal as the bridge tender frantically attempted to get the bridge reclosed. Turnipseed 'big-holed' (threw on the emergency brakes) in a desperate effort to stop the train. He almost did, but the locomotive itself, according to testimony by the fireman and the bridge tender, "just barely slid into the water." The tender, as can be seen in the photo, stayed on the track, but the 427 managed to tear up the bridge which had almost gotten closed. Shortly thereafter, engineer Turnipseed was seeking other employment.

# CHAPTER 8

# STRUGGLE AND RECOVERY

Though everything about the actual declaration of receivership was couched in the legal terminology required by such proceedings, it is not difficult to visualize the trauma, misgivings and heartbreak that accompanied the acceptance of the receivership as a necessity for the railroad's survival.

According to Harold K. North, former Assistant General Passenger Agent of the FEC, who had been with the railroad for seven years when the receivership was announced, there had been an air of gloom hanging over the railroad for some time. "Nobody," North related, "outside of Kenan's staff, knew what was in store, or even if we would continue operating. We were notified immediately that the Company would be in the hands of the receivers, but nobody knew anything about our future. The only gladdening news was that Mr. Kenan and Mr. Loftin, who had been with our legal department, were going to be our receivers."[144]

At the end of 1931, Kenan, as president of the Corporation, and Kenan and Loftin, as receivers, announced that, though operating expenses had declined from 1930 by over $1.75 million, revenues had declined by over $2.3 million. They went on to say that, "In view of the continued decline in our Gross Revenues since 1926, in which year the total Railway Operating Revenues amounted to $29,457,459, whereas the total Railway Operating Revenue for 1931 was $9,379,029, it was not possible for the Railway to earn a sufficient amount or obtain funds from outside sources in order to meet its fixed charges."[145]

If 1931 was bad, 1932 and 1933 were worse, with revenues falling to roughly $6.7 million in both 1932 and 1933. There wouldn't be an upturn until 1934.

Kenan and Loftin realized that, while the main line demanded as much passenger service as the region would support, drastic steps were needed to stop the drain being caused by barely breaking even or losing branch lines. Consequently, in 1932, bus-truck service was substituted for regular train service on the Orange City branch (which, itself, was abandoned and dismantled in 1934); the Mayport Branch, from Spring Glen to Mayport, 21.3 miles was abandoned; and the Ormond Branch, 1.7 miles was abandoned.

On February 1, 1932, wages on the railroad, with the agreement and acceptance by the labor unions, were lowered 10 per cent.

The general business conditions were such that there was practically no development in the railroad's territory, and because of that, only three new industrial side tracks were constructed during all of 1932.[146] For the 1932-33 winter season, five trains operated each way between Miami and Jacksonville. FEC passenger timetables were still glossy and large, and featured, in December of '32, full page ads for the FEC Hotel Co., Model Land Co., and Pan American Airways, in connection with the rail-air service to Havana via Miami.

The pit still appeared bottomless in 1933, and the FEC began to complain bitterly against subsidized competition from truckers. To help themselves in the fight against this competition, the FEC established pickup and delivery service, for less than carload shipments, in eight East Coast cities, but only one industrial siding was built during the entire year.

Meanwhile, the FEC was lowering ticket prices. Miamians could travel to Key West and Havana for $24.00. Key Westers could buy a round trip ticket to Miami at the daily excursion rate of $4.75 or wait until Sunday and get it for $2.50.[147]

1934 brought an improvement in business to the FEC, as the nation began to show a small increase in production and a slight decline in unemployment. 1934 showed Operating Revenues of $7.6 million while 1935 strengthened a fraction more, to $7.7 million. As in 1932, 1934 saw only three industrial sidings laid, while it appears that none were added in '35. In a two year program initiated in 1934, the receivers decided to retire 29 locomotives, 431 freight cars and 66 work train cars by December 31, 1935. 68 pieces of freight car equipment were, however, converted to work train equipment.

A petition by the receivers to abandon the branch from Palatka to East Palatka was denied by the ICC, but the railroad received permission from the Florida Railroad Commission to substitute bus-truck service for regular train service. It was likely that the vehicle formerly used on the Orange City branch would suffice, and the receivers claimed that savings would amount to $12,000 per year. The next-to-last abandonment prior to the ending of service on the line from East Palatka to Palatka came following ICC permission, on August 7, 1935, to abandon the Palm Beach branch.

For the 1934-35 season, another train was added, giving six each way between Jacksonville and Miami. The number remained the same for 1935-36, but, beginning with the 1936-37 season, began to grow.

It appeared that the downward trend was beginning to reverse. Even the wreck of 4-8-2 #427 at the Jupiter draw on February 12, 1935, which cost the railroad $174,583.00 did not dampen the feeling that things just might improve. They would, but not in 1935.

The coquettish Caribbean, mothering horrors that had struck hard at the Sunshine State since it was known to man, bred another demon. At 1:32 Saturday afternoon, August 31, 1935, the Jacksonville weather bureau advised of a tropical disturbance 60 miles east of Long Island in the Bahamas, moving west-northwest 300 miles southeast of the Florida Keys. On Sunday, the storm was reported travelling slowly, at eight miles an hour, generally west. Due warning was sent along the Keys and broadcast over the radio for two full days, but the men in charge of the camps, where U. S. veterans were based as they were building the Overseas Highway, appeared not to have taken the information too seriously.

The advisory of 1:43 PM on Labor Day placed the hurricane 200 miles east of Havana and 180 miles southwest of the Keys. It was still moving west and indications were that only gales would strike the Keys.

At 4:41 the first warning that the hurricane had swung northwest stated that it was advancing toward the Keys. F. B. Ghent, director of Veterans' camp work on the Keys, was in Jacksonville. His assistant, Ray Sheldon, was in Key West. They secured weather bureau reports every four hours, telephoning each other frequently. Sheldon reached the camp at 4:00 Sunday afternoon. Monday morning, deciding it was impractical to wait longer, he called Miami and asked the FEC offices how quickly a train could be made up and reach Lower Matecumbe.[148] He was told it could be done in three hours. The distance was 90 miles.

Shortly after the 1:43 PM Labor Day advisory, Ghent telephoned Sheldon and learned that the barometer was lower at Matecumbe than in Miami.[149] Ghent ordered the veterans to be evacuated to Hollywood, 18 miles north of Miami and called the FEC's main offices in St. Augustine. Because of the holiday, they were closed, but the message was put through to F. L. Atcheson, assistant to Superintendent A. I. Pooser, who was called in New Smyrna. Pooser had the order telephoned to Miami immediately.

The request for the train was received not later than 2:35 PM, but preparations had begun in the Miami (Buena Vista) yard shortly after 2:00. To call a crew on Labor Day was, in itself, no small task. To steam up a locomotive requires at least two hours and no switch engine was available until 3:00. J. J. Haycraft, engineer on the rescue train, remembered being called at 3:10 PM.[150] The switcher hurriedly went about its task of putting the 11 car train (6 baggage cars, 2 coaches and 3 box cars) together, but repairs on one car delayed the train until 4:25. This was 16 minutes before the weather bureau advised that the storm had changed course.

The train was delayed for another ten minutes at the Miami River drawbridge because of holiday traffic on the river. The sky was darkening rapidly and death lurked in the air as the relief train sped south to Homestead. There, Haycraft, trainmaster G. R. Branch, and conductor J. F. Gamble decided to reverse the engine, so that they could back down to the storm area and then pull out engine facing forward, thereby being able to utilize the headlight on the return trip.[151] It was now 5:15, and the gale was rising. At 6:50, near Camp No. 1, a derrick beside the track hooked into the engine cab and before it could be disengaged an hour and twenty minutes were lost. The train finally reached Islamorada at 8:20.

Hell was raging across the Keys. Haycraft could not see the little station and ran two or three cars beyond it. Meanwhile, Sheldon and thirteen veterans had driven up from Matecumbe. At 7:00, with the storm threatening the Islamorada depot, Sheldon and his men took refuge in a box car on the siding. The wind had attained a speed subsequently estimated at close to 200 miles per hour. Huge waves roared over the track, which was seven feet above sea level.

Five minutes later a fearful tidal wave drove in from the Atlantic just as Sheldon and his men scrambled into the engine cab. Some of the veterans didn't make it and were swept to their deaths. The wave, clutching at the rescue train, washed the cars from the track and turned them over. Only 4-8-2 #447 remained on the rails.

Almost 42 miles of devastated extension was obliterated or left tangled with skeleton timbers. Everywhere, homes were flattened and washed away. Men, women and children died without a chance of assistance. Over 577 people, veterans and civilians died that terrifying night.

An army of rescuers came next day to the dead ends of travelled ways in ambulances, trucks, motor cars and airplanes. The Red Cross was everywhere. Doctors, nurses and supplies were landed in requisitioned boats, and, to prevent looting, state and local authorities gave the order, "Shoot to Kill!"

Religious rites were held in front of funeral pyres built with salvaged timbers soaked in oil. The sun's heat made this an imperative. A number of people who could be identified were buried in Miami, and a beautiful monument was later erected in Matecumbe, which briefly records the bare facts of the disaster.

The death knell of "Flagler's Folly" had been trumpeted to a horrified world on the winds of one of the greatest natural disasters the nation would ever know.[152] An exhausted FEC, overworked, overburdened and overwrought, had no place left to turn. Never again would the deep, melodious whistles be heard on the keys. Never again would the "Havana Special" burnish the rails south of Miami. Never again would a ticket be sold at a depot south of Florida City. The dream had come to a terrible, anguished, brutal ending. The Key West Extension became "The Railroad that Died at Sea."[153]

This picture, made by an Associated Press staff photographer travelling through the Florida Hurricane Zone shortly after the 1935 hurricane, was the first close-up of the eleven car FEC train thrown from the tracks by the force of the winds and the tidal wave. The train had been dispatched to evacuate a rehabilitation camp of World War I veterans building highway bridges on the Florida Keys. The train got no further than Islamorada. At that point, the storm struck in all its fury and only the engine was left on the track.

Following World War II, the West India Fruit and Steamship Company opened operations by establishing a Steamship line for freight cars between the Port of Palm Beach, at Riviera Beach, and Havana. This brochure highlighted the advantages of the all rail route to Cuba.

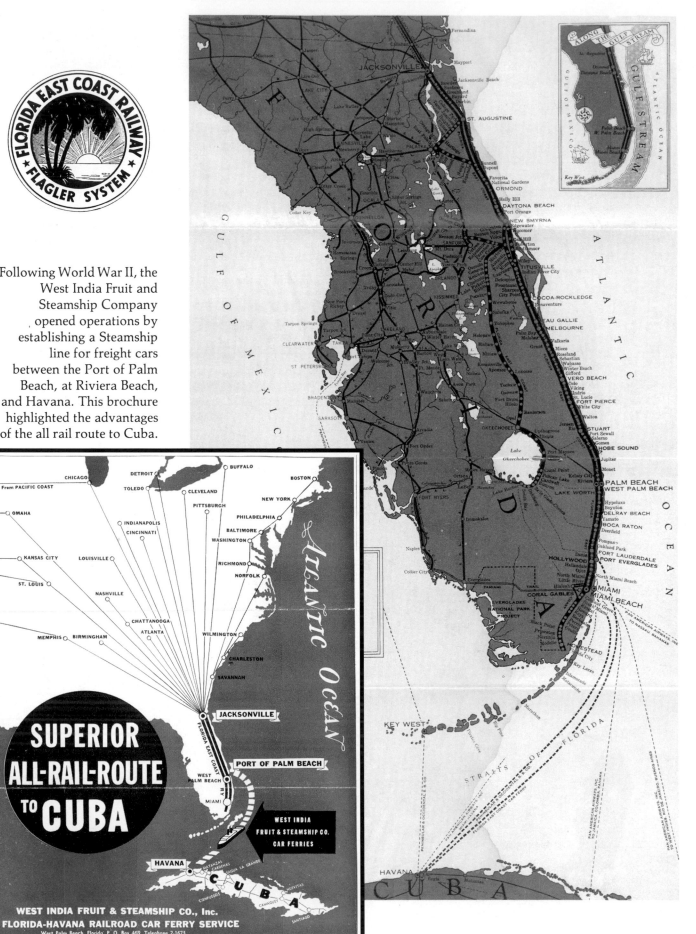

SUPERIOR ALL-RAIL-ROUTE TO CUBA

WEST INDIA FRUIT & STEAMSHIP CO. CAR FERRIES

WEST INDIA FRUIT & STEAMSHIP CO., Inc.
FLORIDA-HAVANA RAILROAD CAR FERRY SERVICE
West Palm Beach, Florida, P. O. Box 469, Telephone 2-1673

A stunned FEC, in the blink of an eye, had lost forty miles of line. Traffic was immediately embargoed south of Florida City, and the railroad began compiling figures on restoration costs. After submitting all figures, including traffic for years previous, projected traffic, costs of restoration and the like, the receivers petitioned the Court for authority to abandon. The Federal Court approved this petition on August 10, 1936, and the ICC entered an order authorizing the abandonment on September 26, 1936. The receivers, under authority of the Court, sold the right of way, embankments and bridge structures from Mile Post 397, just south of Florida City, to Mile Post 519, just north of Key West, to the Overseas Road and Toll Bridge District, Monroe County, the State Road Department of Florida and the City of Key West for $640,000.00. Savings above that included $160,000.00 of taxes cancelled and $100,000.00 as a result of not having to level the fills between the Keys.[154]

The FEC Car Ferry Co., several months after the storm, began operations to Havana from Port Everglades (moved to Port of Palm Beach following the Second World War) and the P&O Steamship Co. moved their operation from Key West to Miami and began offering service from there to Havana for passengers and LCL freight.[155]

As devastating as the loss of the Key West Extension was, the railroad had to continue to operate. Trains continued on schedule and business, as well as could be expected, went on as usual. Improvements, such as could be afforded, were made, and in 1935, 8 coaches and 3 dining cars were air-conditioned, with the first announcement of this revolutionary new improvement in passenger service being ballyhooed boldly on the inside cover of the May 18, 1935 passenger timetable.

It appears that no passenger timetable was issued between May 18, and December 13, 1935, and, if this was the case, the reason was that the FEC announced the publication, in the December 13 timetable, of "The Story of A Pioneer," which was a 32 page history of the railroad. Copies could be had for the asking, and they, along with the revised reprints of 1946, 1952 and 1956 have become collector's items.

Finally, to close the year 1935, the railroad added another Jacksonville-Miami round trip, making six for the 1935-36 season. The Hastings-Bunnell Local no longer existed, but numbers 29 and 30, the "Daylight Express," took eleven hours between the railroad's two largest cities and operated "via East Palatka."

As if to postscript the Key West Extension, the FEC continued to use the "Overseas" emblem until the July 1, 1936 timetable. Since the hurricane, the FEC's timetable maps had shown dots from Florida City to Key West, with a note below stating that the dots indicate "Service south of Florida City indefinitely Suspended." With the October 15, 1936 timetable, the FEC's new emblem, which was used until 1965, became a rising sun with three palms in the foreground. The line simply ended at Florida City. Service south of Miami was offered by Trains 41 and 42, mixed freight and passenger service, to Florida City.

1936 was a good passenger year. On February 29, Train 88, the renowned aristocrat of winter trains, the "Florida Special," operated north from Miami in seven complete sections. For years past, 87 and 88 had operated in multiple, as necessary, but in 1936, from January 3 to April 18, the "Florida Special" established a record in patronage. During its period in service it was operated in two sections on 44 days, in three sections on 23 days, in four sections on 12 days, in five sections on 2 days, in six sections on four days, and in seven sections on one day, each section complete with Recreation Car, Orchestra and Hostess.[156]

Moreover, this great train celebrated its 50th anniversary in the 1936-37 winter season, with all the publicity appropriate to such an occasion. Six other through trains operated between Jacksonville and Miami, one more than the previous year, for a total of seven. Unlike pre-depression times, though, only the "Florida Special" operated as an all Pullman train. All of the other trains carried coaches, almost as if to respect the depressed financial condition of the travelling public.

In 1937, four more coaches and seven diners received air-conditioning.

The Key West terminal property, the only part of the former Extension not included in the previous sale, was sold to the government for $164,000.00. Flagler's $49 million project was removed from the rolls, in finality, for a grand total of $804,000.00.

Revenues improved slightly to $9.3 million in '37, but the deficit of $2.18 million was still enormous. The once huge inventory of locomotives, cars and work equipment continued to shrink, and by the end of 1937, 121 locomotives, 165 passenger train cars, 500 freight cars including 69 cabooses and 236 pieces of work equipment were what remained. Additionally, a bus-truck (for East Palatka-Palatka-San Mateo service), a bus, and two trucks were on the roster. For 1937-38, seven through Jacksonville-Miami trains were again offered.

Business in 1938 improved slightly once again, being almost $300,000.00 more than in '37, but the deficit remained at almost $2 million. 1938 was a year "on hold," with the equipment roster remaining the same as in '37, and for the '38-'39 winter season, the same seven trains operating. 1939 would also, in terms of revenue, hold relatively steady, but '39 would be the year of major changes in passenger train operations. The streamliners were just over the horizon!

Though the nation was abuzz with the fanatical and maniacal doings of the German madman, Hitler, and his brutal escapades, war involving the United States did not appear likely, so that the improvement of business and the ending of the depresion were central topics of conversation. The New York World's Fair, offering great hope for the future, was planned for 1939/1940. And, in railroading, which was near the forefront of the American consciousness, as airlines are today, the names "Zephyr," and "Silver Streak," and "Rocket" and "Streamliners" were becoming household words. It became obvious to the FEC that streamlined, diesel-powered passenger train service was an imminent necessity, and to that end, following the preparation and gathering and collating of data, the receivers, on June 15, 1939, petitioned District Federal Judge Louie W. Strum[157] for authority to purchase two 2,000 horsepower diesel locomotives and two 7 car streamlined, lightweight passenger trains. After intense hearings, during which numerous witnesses were called to testify pro and con, Judge Strum, on June 22, approved the request and empowered the receivers to purchase the locomotives from Electro Motive Corporation at a total price not to exceed $354,804.80, and the two 7 car trains at a total price not to exceed $1,024,712.50. Additionally, the Judge approved expenditures not exceeding $54,000.00 for additional facilities at Buena Vista and Jacksonville for servicing the trains, and $25,000.00 for advertising their inauguration and operation.[158]

The approval came not a moment too soon. The rival of the ACL-FEC combine was the Seaboard, and *they* had wasted no time at all in putting in diesels or streamliners. The SAL's first diesels went into operation on the famous "Orange Blossom Special" in December of 1938, while the streamlined, stainless steel, diesel powered "Silver Meteor" began operating on February 2, 1939, as the first Miami-New York train operating electrically powered all the way.[159] The FEC and ACL were "behind the eight ball," and they would have to move fast to catch up.

Since the streamliners could not possibly be in service until December, the railroad installed air-conditioning equipment on 10 more coaches and equipped them with reclining seats, improved lights and updated toilet facilities. In addition, eight of the 800 class Mountain (4-8-2) type engines were converted to make them suitable for fast passenger train service.[160] 817 was tested with the modified equipment in September, proved a success, and the other seven engines that had been selected were also modified. With the use of the 800s in passenger service, double heading on long trains was almost eliminated.[161]

To build up national interest in the trains, one of which was to be for strictly local (Miami-Jacksonville) service and the other for New York-Miami through service, the FEC and the Atlantic Coast Line initiated a national "name the train" contest for the purpose of naming the New York-Miami streamliner.

The FEC, as soon as approval had been received to purchase the new trains, carried on a two month discussion by mail between the two receivers, L. C. Haines, Corporate treasurer, A. A. Jackson, assistant to the receivers, and J. D. Rahner, General Passenger Agent relating to the naming of the Jacksonville-Miami streamliner. Additionally, several lower echelon middle management types involved themselves and submitted names also.

In July, Rahner came up with a list of 16 names, including such as "Rapido" and "Speedking." Though these weren't used, several of his other suggestions, notably "South Wind" were used on other FEC trains. On July 28, Rahner added 13 names, among them "Eastcoaster," and "The Flagler." Then, on July 29, Kenan wrote to Loftin and told him that he (Kenan) liked Loftin's suggestion "Spirit of Florida." On August 1, Jackson wired Loftin that he (Jackson) liked the name "The Flagler" or "Osceola."[162] Between the 1st and the 9th, Jackson apparently spoke to Kenan and Loftin and advised Rahner that "Spirit of Florida" had been selected. As things were to further transpire, it hadn't, because on August 11, Loftin wrote to Kenan and advised him that the name "Henry M. Flagler" would be preferable. The Budd Company, builders of the train, and "the local committee" referred to in the August 11th letter, believed that the "Henry M. Flagler" name would be much better as far as advertising mileage was concerned. Kenan, on August 12th, though professing preference for "Spirit of Florida," concurred with Loftin and accepted "Henry M. Flagler" as the name for the train.[163]

Meanwhile, the plans for a contest to name the through train were also proceeding, and after a national contest under the supervision of Reuben H. Donnelly Corp., the first prize of $300.00 was awarded to one Betty Creighton of Pittsburgh for the name, "The Champion," with 27 other additional prizes awarded aggregating $650.00. Apparently Miss Creighton's entry arrived first, as seven other winners had also entered the name "The Champion." Notification was duly made in November and all that was left was the christening of the "Henry M. Flagler," and "The Champion."

The inaugural trip of the first FEC streamliner, the Henry M. Flagler, was a much-heralded event, which included the breaking of a bottle of champagne on the locomotive's pilot.

On December 2, 1939, the brand new streamliner "The Champion" left Jacksonville for Miami followed, on December 3, by the inaugural trip of the "Henry M. Flagler." Appropriate ceremonies were held in most of the communities through which the trains passed. While the FEC supplied its own equipment for the "Henry M. Flagler," "The Champion's" equipment consisted of the seven car FEC train and two identical ACL trains. As time progressed, the Pennsylvania and RF&P railroads became part of the equipment pool. In later years, with the train running between 16 and 21 cars, it was not uncommon to see three diesels totalling 6,500 horsepower pulling trains made up of cars from all four railroads, and, from time to time, New Haven Railroad cars, also.

The FEC numbered the two new diesels 1001 and 1002. They were designated "E3A" units by the builder; the 1001 had the words "Henry M. Flagler" painted on her sides, toward the front, and the 1002 was painted "The Champion." Later units would also be painted for specific trains but this practice was discontinued when it became apparent that that particular locomotive could not always be available for that train.

The two baggage-dormitory cars were named "New Smyrna" and "Stuart."[164] The diners were "Fort Lauderdale" and "Fort Pierce,"[165] and the eight coaches were named "Delray Beach," "Melbourne," "Hollywood," "Hobe Sound," "Vero Beach," "Pompano," "Boca Raton," and "Cocoa Rockledge."[166]

The trains were completed with the addition of two stunning, streamlined, rounded end, tavern-lounge-observation cars, decorated inside in a Florida motif.

"The Champion" and the "Henry M. Flagler" were about to lead the FEC into a new era.

The problem with the new era would be that during the "old era," intermittently during the 1930's, Edward Ball, Trustee for the Florida DuPont interests—the Estate of the late Alfred I. DuPont—had begun buying the FEC bonds at an average of 11 cents on the dollar. Since he had purchased 55 percent of the $45 million second mortgage ($26 million worth) he had apparently spent less than $4 million for the bonds.[167] Kenan, for several reasons, could not or would not purchase the bonds at this deflated level. According to Kenan's grand-nephew, Thomas S. Kenan, III, "There was every reason for the Flagler heirs[168] to keep control, but William Kenan, my great-uncle, was Executor and Trustee (of the Estate) as well as Co-receiver of the railroad and he was adamant against self dealing."[169] Kenan was at a disadvantage in two other ways.

First, he was one of the receivers, appointed by the federal court when the railroad was thrown into bankruptcy. This meant that he was obligated to serve the interest of the bondholders, who were as vociferous as they were despairing. Kenan probably would have been violating Federal law if he had gone into the market in competition with Ball.

Second, Kenan may not have had the ready cash to buy the FEC bonds even if he could have done so legally and morally. The combined holdings of he and his sisters were at their lowest value at the time Ball was buying FEC bonds at rock bottom prices.

It was at this point, in 1940, that the conflict began between the Estate (Kenan), the DuPont interests, and the Atlantic Coast Line, all of whom believed that they had the right, legally and/or otherwise, to control the FEC.

In 1941, realizing that the Florida East Coast Railway had slipped from his grasp, William R. Kenan, Jr., a man of honor, loyalty and perseverance, resigned as a receiver, taking no futher active part in the management of the Railroad, though remaining President of the corporate entity.

On January 25, 1941, the Bond Committee filed with the Court a petition requesting reorganization of the railway under Section 77 on the Bankruptcy Act., and on January 31, the petition was approved. Subsequently, the court appointed Trustees and their appointment was ratified by the ICC on April 21.

Though the ramifications would be numerous, for the instant only one momentous event had occurred: the railroad was no longer in receivership; rather it was in reorganization, under a trusteeship, and the Trustees were Scott M. Loftin and Edward W. Lane. When all was said and done, the railroad, from that time on, would not—other than in name—be part of the Flagler System.

## FOOTNOTES

144. Interview with Harold K. North, June 5, 1984
145. FEC 1931 Annual Report, pp 5 & 6
146. FEC 1932 Annual Report, p. 7
147. Op cit, "The Railroad that Died at Sea," p.34
148. It is unclear who Sheldon spoke to in Miami, but the great likelihood is that he would have been put through to the office of the Superintendent of Miami-Hialeah Terminals.

149. The barometer readings in the 1935 hurricane were the lowest that have ever been recorded.
150. "Engineer Tells of Train Wreck," article in the "Miami News," September 5, 1935.
151. Ibid
152. Op cit, "Hurricane Between . . . ." pp 19-21.
153. There are several other descriptions that present a more lurid, if not ghastly picture, but it is believed that the description offered herein is more than ample to portray the level of tragedy the September 2, 1935 hurricane wrought.
154. FEC 1936 Annual Report, pp 7-8
155. FEC 1935 Annual Report, p. 5
156. FEC Passenger Timetable, December 11, 1936, p. 41
157. Judge Strum was the Federal judicial authority over the FEC's receivership from its initiation in 1931 until 1948, when he was either transferred to another jurisdiction or retired.
158. FEC Rwy. Co. Receivership Record, Volume III, Documents 860 and 861, pp 29-136
159. From New York to Washington, DC, the train operated as a strictly electric train, under catenary belonging to the Pennsylvania RR. From Washington to Richmond, trackage belonged to the RF&P RR, and Seaboard used its own rails from Richmond to Miami. From Washington to Miami, the train was pulled by diesel-electric locomotives.
160. FEC 1939 Annual Report, p. 7
161. See also FEC Receivership Record, Volume VII, pp 397-401
162. Osceola was a great Seminole Indian chief, and is a common name today among the tribes still inhabiting the Florida Everglades.
163. Receivers File 610, various letters, as noted. Collection of the Author.
164. The "New Smyrna" (later "New Smyrna Beach") and "Stuart" were apparently changed to coaches later on, to conform with the naming system. Baggage dormitories on the FEC were named after rivers. Coaches were named after on-line cities.
165. The "Fort Pierce" was later destroyed in an accident and scrapped.
166. "FEC Railway Equipment Trust, Series I, Lease and Agreement Between the FEC and its Receivers and Girard Trust Company," November 1, 1939, p. 2, as shown in Volume VII of FEC Receivership Records
167. "How Kenans Lost FEC to Ed Ball," article in Miami Herald, 1965 (Exact date unknown)
168. Kenan was Flagler's brother-in-law
169. Letter from Thomas S. Kenan, III to the author, July 7, 1981

**Actual photograph of SEVEN COMPLETE SECTIONS of the Florida Special operated over the Florida East Coast Railway on February 29, 1936.**

# FLORIDA SPECIAL

## FOR FIFTY YEARS
### Leader of All Florida Trains in Speed and Luxury of Equipment

Beginning January 2, 1937

## 27 hrs. 40 mins. New York-Miami

## The Only Train in the World featuring

# RECREATION CAR

A section of fill is shown just south of Islamorada after the Labor Day 1935 hurricane.

In this scene of utter desolation, FEC 4-6-2 153 (now owned and operated by the Gold Coast Railroad) gingerly pushes the first survey train into the hurricane-ravaged area, south of Key Largo, following the Labor Day, 1935 hurricane.

The devastation following the Labor Day (September 2), 1935 hurricane was so immense, and so brutal, that mere words do not—cannot—convey the depth of the destruction. Winds of 200 MPH obliterated Long Key Fishing Camp, as well as 40 miles of railroad. This view, taken shortly after the storm subsided, does not include the remains of the Long Key depot, out of the picture to the left. Looking south, the last several hundred feet of trackage on the island, and, indeed, the bridge trackage itself, has been stripped from the roadbed. To the right of the embankment, by the boat dock, only a few feet of the narrow gauge trackage remain. The little tunnel for the narrow gauge is visible just beyond and to the left of the water tank, the base of which, being of concrete, is the only tangible evidence of the Fishing Camp or Railroad still in existence on the island.

—*(Historical Association of Southern Florida)*

500 was to the Atlantic Coast Line what 1001 was to the FEC—their first streamlined, diesel electric-powered piece of locomotive equipment. Coast Line enthusiasts swear allegiance to the interesting and unusual purple color scheme (devised by EMD in conjunction with the railroad's executive and operating departments in reverence to the long standing use of purple on Coast Line buildings and timetables) which remained standard diesel hue until W.T.Rice became president of the road in 1959 and promptly ordered all of the diesels repainted to a somber and colorless black.

For this photograph, on January 14, 1940, Wolfe posed "The Champion," powered by Coast Line's first diesel, at the Boca Raton Station while enroute to Miami. Though records are inexact, it appears that Coast Line diesels carried certain trips of joint FEC-ACL streamliners all the way through from Richmond to Miami.

The swing span on Seven Mile Bridge was originally intended for Bahia Honda, but the Federal Government mandated that a boat channel be made south of Pigeon Key. Bahia Honda was left as a 'closed channel' bridge, though boats could, of course, pass beneath the bridge itself. The operator's house, atop the drawer, must have been a fascinating place. Though trains were somewhat infrequent...two passenger trains and a regularly scheduled freight daily in each direction in the good years...there was something so awesome, so majestic about Seven Mile Bridge that one might have found it, in its solitude, to be a placid and peaceful haven from which to watch the fish, and the birds, and the coral reefs and the passing of the boats, and, oh, yes, perhaps even to ruminate over the various merits of the 100 series of 4-6-2s as opposed to the 400 series of 4-8-2s, and their relative appearances and abilities. Or even to think about the significance of this wondrous and incredible work, this thing called the Railroad that Goes to Sea. And what of that operator's house above the swing span? It survived the death of the railroad, and oversaw the concreting of this wonderful and marvelous structure, and served well and admirably until the early 1980s when the greatest terror of all, the automobile and gasoline truck collision, occurred right below the house. And then, in a horrific and tragic conflagration, which, worst of all, claimed several lives, this fine and venerable building, one of only two structures remaining from the railroad itself, fell victim to the horror of the fire, and perished in the blaze, leaving the former station at Key West as the last edifice in existence on what, even today, is called the 'eighth wonder of the world.'

—Romer photo: Florida Collection Miami-Dade Public Library.

FECs first diesel E3A 1001 was named the "Henry M. Flagler" and it pulled the train by the same name between Jacksonville and Miami for slightly over a year. The 1001 was a beautiful piece of motive power and is shown shortly after the inauguration of the train in this elegant portrait taken at the Miami Station.

In this 1942 photograph E6A 1004 is being cleaned after a trip.

# CHAPTER 9

# WAR AND (ALMOST) PROSPERITY

As the new decade dawned, the FEC, though still burdened by deficits of elephantine proportions, was, physically, a completely different railroad than it had been entering the 1930s.

858 miles of track had become 679. 248 steam locomotives had been reduced to 121 steam and 2 diesel; passenger cars, the only rolling stock that had remained even relatively stable, had been reduced from 198 units to 179, 14 of which were streamlined; freight cars had shown a precipitous decline, from 2,655 on January 1, 1930 to 458 on January 1, 1940. Non revenue and maintenance of way equipment, for which the FEC used the euphemism "Company Service Cars," had also dropped by more than half, from 587, including 6 office cars to 235, including 4 office cars.[170] A slimmed down FEC, though unaware of the coming demands that would be thrown upon it by World War II, was ready to meet the challenge.

As the pace of American business began to quicken in 1940, so too did the pace of the FEC. Though the deficit hung in the $2 million area, revenues increased in the first year of the new decade, to almost $10 and 3/4 million. By the end of 1941, with World War II engulfing the civilized world and the United States being pulled into it on December 7, revenues were $11.5 million, and the deficit had dropped to $1.3 million. An additional diesel-E6A 1003, arrived in 1941, while E6B 1051 along with E6As 1004 and 1005 were ready for service in 1942. Additionally 6 more streamlined passenger cars arrived in '41. In the way of stations, the railroad built a passenger stop at Camp Murphy, just below Hobe Sound.

But 1940 will likely stand as the most active year of the diesel era. Since the "Henry M. Flagler," with its 5 hour 59 minute Miami—Jacksonville schedule could not seem to generate the level of volume that had been projected, and since the FEC had been asked to be the partner in streamlined trains operating from the Midwest via three different railroads, and since the "Henry M. Flagler" equipment was available to be utilized in that manner, the "Henry M. Flagler," on December 13, 1940, made its last trip under that name. The equipment then became part of the pool of cars operating the "Dixie Flagler," which made its first southbound trip from Chicago on December 17, arriving Miami on December 18, and every third day thereafter. The "Dixie Flagler" alternated with the Illinois Central's "City of Miami," and the Pennsylvania's "South Wind." Each train had alternate routes, but each operated from Jacksonville to Miami on the same schedule as FEC Number 3, being Number 4 northbound.

Additionally, "The "Champion," on December 21, was doubled in size, becoming a 14 car coach streamliner, with two taverns (one in the center and one rounded end observation on the rear) and two dining cars. The "Vacationer" and the "Florida Special" were both dieselized in December, and all assigned equipment on all trains (except the mixed on the branches)[171] was air conditioned.

As noted above, 1940 and 1941 were still deficit years, but then, in 1942, for the first time since 1926, the FEC Railway, with revenue of 20.8 million, showed a net income of slightly over $5 million. The increased military traffic, both passenger and freight, was igniting a fire under the railroad.[172]

Because of the net income of 1942, and the fact that it was obvious during the year that there would be a net, the Deposit Committee of the First and Refunding 5% Mortgage Bonds petitioned the Court, on April 10, 1942 to pay one matured coupon aggregating $1,125,000. Hearings were held on the petition on June 11 and September 29th. At the latter hearing it was shown that the earnings would be sufficient to permit payment of the amount without impairing the cash position of the trustees and the Court made an Order, dated September 30, 1942, authorizing the payment of the coupon which became due on *September 1, 1931*, the coupons payable on presentation on or after October 22, 1942.

Passenger revenues for '42 were 40% of total revenue. But in 1943, with revenue jumping to over $32.5 million and net income at almost $5 million, passenger revenue reached almost 44% of total revenue. Because of the continued improvement in revenues and earnings, the First and Refunding 5% Mortgage coupons due March 1 and September 1 of 1932 were paid.

The battle for control of the FEC was being carried on in the courts, as it would be until 1958. The

ACL forces and the DuPont forces were so far apart that compromise appeared unreachable, and in fact, no compromise was ever made.[173]

From 1942 until the end of the War, train names and numbers changed rapidly each year. With almost every timetable change, new trains were being added and others removed. In May of 1942, "The Tiresaver," an all coach train between Miami and Jacksonville made its first appearance. Though the railroad had, for the winter of 1940-1941 carded 10 trains, and 9 for '41—'42, the Office of Defense Transportation ordered a limit of 8 scheduled trains, Miami—Jacksonville for the winter of 1942—43. They did not, however, limit special movements or additional sections, and FEC stations saw a daily parade of passenger and freight trains. It was common practice, during the Second World War, for most trains on the FEC to operate with at least two sections, so that, conceivably, as many as 32 passenger trains (or more) could pass any given station on any given day.

In 1944, Railway operating revenues dropped slightly, to $31.7 million, and in 1945 to $29.5 million. A $1.6 million surplus in '44 became a $76,325.00 deficit in '45.

Because of the War, new equipment was not available, and the FEC made do with a slight decrease in equipment from 1940. Locomotives were down to 108, including 6 diesels. Passenger cars tallied at 164, a decline of 15 units since 1940, and freight cars 458, down 17 from 1940.

Again in 1944 and 1945, the protagonists in the struggle for control of the railroad continued their pitched battles, without measurable success for either side.

The trustees, meanwhile, continued to operate the railroad, making every effort to increase efficiency and effect economies. To that end, and with the approval of the Court of June 7, 1944, an application was filed with the ICC for a certificate of Convenience and Necessity covering the abandonment of the portion of the Okeechobee Branch between Maytown and a point approximately 14 miles south of Okeechobee, a distance of 136 miles, and for the construction of a Cutoff, thirty miles in length, extending from Fort Pierce, on the main line, to the southern point of abandonment on the branch. Following hearings and ICC Examiner's favorable recommendation, the ICC approved the abandonment and new construction.[174]

In 1944, 50 all-steel box cars in the 21000 series and 50 box—express cars in the 600 series were received and in 1945 the railroad received 15 more diesel locomotives. In 1946, 11 streamlined passenger cars arrived and in 1947 the railroad received 8 more streamlined cars and five more passenger diesels. By January, 1946, the road was advertising that all principal passenger trains were diesel powered.

The winter seasons of 1946-47 through 1949-50 saw 10 Miami—Jacksonville round trips daily. On December 2, 1947, the FEC, to match their stunning diesel paint scheme of red, yellow and silver, issued the winter season timetable in the red and yellow format. From 1921 until the summer of 1939, the timetables had featured the Company's emblem on the covers. From November, 1939, until September, 1947, the timetable covers had either a streamliner rendering or the passenger traffic department's passenger train artwork with a map of the railroad superimposed on the State of Florida. While the previous covers were not unattractive, the new cover was colorful and eye-catching, and, with palm trees, soft clouds, and the diesels in red and yellow, they presented a beautiful and modern appearance. For the next 13 years, until replaced by the new regime's "blues," this cover held sway.

In 1946, revenues dropped to $26.5 million with a $109,494.00 net income. For 1947, revenues increased slightly to over $27 million, but the deficit for the year was over $2.6 million.

Operationally, two major events occurred in the 1946-47 period. The FEC, which had been without its Cuba connection since March of 1945, entered into an agreement with the West India Fruit and Steamship Co., and late in 1946, Florida-Havana Railroad Car Ferry service again operated, this time from the Port of Palm Beach. Then, on March 21, 1947, just before the opening of the new cutoff from Ft. Pierce to Lake Okeechobee, the Peavy-Wilson Lumber Co., owner of a large tract of timberland on the Kissimmee Valley line, reached agreement with the Trustees to lease the northerly 53.5 miles of the branch, from Maytown to Holopaw, until June 30, 1951.[175] From April 1, 1947, until June 30, 1951, the former FEC trackage reverberated to the sounds of Peavy-Wilson's logging engines busily moving lumber to the FEC connection at Maytown.

On April 1, 1947, train service began on the "New" Lake Okeechobee branch. Railroad buffs and historians have, since the building of the cutoff, questioned one facet of the new line: it appeared, from all indications, that the Town of Okeechobee, at the top of the Lake, furnished a good deal of traffic for the FEC, yet the line from Ft. Pierce bisected the old line almost 14 miles south of Okeechobee City. To this day, the question remains: why did the new line not meet the old at Okeechobee? Unless statements of carloadings originated and received clearly dictated otherwise (and it appears they did not) the line *should* have gone into Okeechobee. New information, which has surfaced in the last several years, has finally given us the answer to the "Why south of—and not into—Okeechobee City?" question. Interstate Commerce Commission reports on the abandonment and new construction clearly indicate that neither the Seaboard nor the ICC would oppose the abandonment and cutoff IF the FEC would agree to turn over carloadings in Okeechobee to the Seaboard. The savings in train miles and expenses of operating facilities such as bridges and stations on the entire line were certainly greater than the carloadings gleaned from Okeechobee, itself, so the FEC accepted the proviso and agreed to angle the new cutoff so that it would cross the Seaboard and connect with the existing line at Port Mayaca.

Interestingly enough, the branch did not die immediately. Peavy–Wilson Lumber Co., operating a fleet of wood burning steam engines, leased the FEC's tracks from Maytown (so they could connect with the FEC) south to a point below Holopaw, and that arrangement kept that part of the Kissimmee Valley Extension "alive" until 1951, when, with the lumber played out, and little left to cut, the agreement was ended, and the lonely and bucolic line, which had started with such great hopes and plans to serve as a second main line, finally saw it's last locomotive.

Today, from Okeechobee north, there is little that remains of the "K. V." line, and the current "K" branch, from Ft. Pierce to Lake Harbor, is under lease to the South Central Florida Railroad for 20 years. Even today, driving north from Okeechobee, there is almost no sign that the longest of the Florida East Coast's branch lines provided reliable service for 36 years in a region that, even today, remains one of the few relatively unspoiled areas of what is now America's fourth largest state.

The 1947 Annual Report states it succinctly: Branch Line Mileage Owned and Operated, 143.01. This compares to 250.24 at the end of 1946. The FEC had lost another 107 miles. 1948 was another deficit year for the railroad. On revenues of 28.6 million, over $1.6 million higher than in 1947, the railroad lost over $2.4 million.

1949s deficit was almost double 1948s, with the loss topping $4.4 million, and yet the ACL and the DuPont interests fought on, neither giving ground, neither willing to give up the fight. The FEC, as ordered by the Court, paid Interest Coupons Nos. 18, 19 and 20 on the 5% First and Refunding Mortgage, for maturation dates of September 1, 1933, March 1, 1934, and September 1, 1934, respectively, in amounts totalling $3.375 million.

Even with the hideous 1949 deficit, the railroad was able to continue to purchase new equipment through the instrument of conditional sale agreements, wherein banks and lending institutions furnished the funds and owned the equipment until it was paid for by the railroad. During the year, through the use of Equipment Trust Series "K," the FEC purchased F3As 501–508; F3Bs 551–554; BL2s 601–606 and 22 streamlined passenger cars: 14 all room sleeping cars, 2 six bedroom-bar-lounge cars, and 6 coaches.

On December 15, 1949, the "Florida Special" was inaugurated with all streamlined equipment for its 62nd season. And, on that same date, the New York Central and the Southern Railway, in conjunction with the FEC, inaugurated a new, winter-season only train to be known as the "New Royal Palm." This fine streamliner, carrying full diner and lounge facilities, featured Pullman sleeping car service from NYC origination points including Detroit, Chicago, Buffalo and Cleveland, with the Southern Railway adding a sleepers in Cinncinati and Atlanta. The train was "topped off" with a beautiful, new, round end, tavern-lounge-observation car.

To close the decade, the FEC, for the first time in the history of the railroad, departed from the previous somber Annual Report format, and, instead of the bland, colorless cover, which simply stated the name of the Company with the information that it was the Annual Report for such and such a year, and gave the names of the Trustees,[176] it suddenly burst forth with a marvelously executed full color painting, by commercial artist Leslie Ragan, of the last three cars of "The Champion" passing bushes and palm trees, with water and a beach in the background. The closest car to the reader was a round end, tavern-lounge-observation car, and the octagonal sign reading "The Champion" on the rear end is quite prominent.

It was a welcome change from the old format and a colorful way to start the new decade.

FEC's diesels have never been built by anyone other than General Motors. 1005 heads an A-B-A set, built especially to power the Florida Special. This photograph was made by Wolfe at La Grange, Illinois, just prior to the locomotive set being accepted by the Florida East Coast Railway.

If ever a station was well tended and looked after on the FEC, it was the gem-like beauty at Hobe Sound. In the September 7, 1959 issue of *Life* Magazine, this station, seen here from the cab of a southbound FEC streamliner in the early 1950s was the center piece of a Coca-Cola advertisement, name board and all!
—*(Charles Beall photograph)*

The first arrival in Miami of the then seven-car all-coach *City of Miami*. For this trip and for some time thereafter, I.C. diesels carried the streamliner thru to Miami. (December, 1940)

*FOOTNOTES*

170. FEC Annual Reports for 1929 and 1939.
171. The end of branch line passenger service was pre-ordained, both by economics and the inroads of the automobile. The last passenger timetable to list branch line passenger (mixed) service is the timetable dated June 1, 1941. However, the E. Palatka-San Mateo bus service lasted until early 1943, when the 2.8 mile branch was abandoned. The December 5, 1942 passenger timetable is the last to show this service. B. Palatka-Palatka bus service was shown for the last time in the May 21, 1944 passenger timetable. Interestingly enough, the Operating (Employee) timetables showed the Titusville–Benson Junction service as "Mixed" until 1951, while first New Smyrna-Lake Harbor then Ft. Pierce—Lake Harbor and Miami—Florida City service retained the "Mixed" designation until the April 25, 1954 issue. Apparently, the 3 branches retained express, baggage and/or Railway Mail Service after passenger service was discontinued. The New Smyrna & Lake Harbor RPO operated on that route until 1947, and the South Miami depot handled Railway Express shipments long after 1941, so it is likely the above hypothesis is correct.
172. FEC 1942 Annual Report, P. 7
173. For a complete and detailed discussion and analysis of the proposals, recommendations and objections of each party, the reader is referred to the Reorganization proceedings of the FEC Railway, most likely available, besides the few sets in private hands, through the Federal Archives, Atlanta, GA
174. FEC 1945 Annual Report pp 7 and 8.
175. FEC Railway Reorganization Proceedings, Volume 4, pp 468–513
176. It should be noted that Edward W. Lane died on March 23, 1942, and was replaced as Trustee by John W. Martin, former Governor of Florida, on April 10, 1942.

It was quite a diversion for the golfers as the FEC passenger trains sliced through the middle of the Miami Shores Country Club fairways. High speed freight trains, up to 12 a day in each direction still disturb the placidity of the course and its environs.

F3A 503 built by EMD in January 1949 is on the point of a long merchandise freight. Green signal flags indicate that this is a 'section' of a scheduled train: probably a 'fruit train' headed north.

During the forties, Atlantic Coast Line diesels operated through on certain name trains from Richmond to Miami. In this view ACL 503 leads the "Vacationer" into Stuart.

Though never known as a motive power innovator, the FEC, in an attempt to effect operating savings on the Lake Okeechobee Branch, purchased a group of six strange-looking locomotives known as BL-2s. These engines, of 1500 hp each, were bought in November and December of 1948 and operated until the early 1960s. FECs operating crews were never enthralled with the BL-2s and, consequently, no re-order was ever placed.

BL2 601 gleams in the red, yellow and silver striped livery of the FEC. The circular corporate logo can be seen adjacent to the steps leading into the cab. The BL2 leads GP7 652 as the pair draw a train of gravel-loaded gondolas south on the main line north of Jupiter in 1957.

The BL2s, as homely as they were, could be engagingly photogenic. 606 with engine compartment doors open idles at Buena Vista on December 20, 1959.

When the FEC reached Miami on April 15, 1896, and inaugurated passenger service on April 22nd of that same year, they boarded and detrained passengers at a thoroughly inadequate and obviously temporary box-like structure at what became the southeast corner of what is now Flagler Street and NW 1st Avenue. Rare indeed are the photos of that pitiful structure. But the FEC was not without its grandiose plans, and in either 1897 or 1898 (if not forever "lost," then the date is simply misplaced) a lovely station, with breezeways, open platforms and a two story structure complete with "widow's walk" opened its doors. This second station, located on the site of what eventually became the Freedom Tower, and what was built at the *Miami News* Building, soon became outmoded, with its two tracks and limited facilities.

*—(J. Nelson Collection)*

Eventually, the Seaboard and the Southern offered to purchase the FEC jointly and allow it to retain its independence in order to thwart the perceived monopoly that "Coast Line" might have on railroading in Florida.

Enter, at this point, the St. Joe Paper Company, a subsidiary of the Alfred I. DuPont Estate. Edward Ball, as Trustee of the Estate, had, interestingly enough, initially had the opportunity to ascend to his position of power and authority the same way that William R. Kenan did: the sister of each of them married the Boss!

The Estate had, under Ball's wise guidance, purchased 55% of the Second Mortgage Bonds of the railroad, giving them, in a sense, ipso facto control of the railroad. Part of the appeal of the DuPont—St. Joe Paper ownership was that it would keep the FEC a "Florida Industry and Institution," a catch phrase the FEC had used since the late 40s.

Edward Ball, though short in stature and almost Yoda-like[188] in appearance, was, when it came to the ability to size up situations and control them, a giant among men. Miami, the railroad's major terminal point, had, for some years, felt that the railroad paid it short shrift with its refusal to build a new passenger station to replace the less than loved 1912 model at which the Miami *Herald* and Miami *News* editorialists were forever taking potshots.[189] In addition to retaining control of the railroad within the State, Ed Ball promised Miami a new passenger station!

On April 18, 1958, the ICC Hearing Examiner recommended the denial of the merger proposed by the ACL, and approval, with modifications, of bondholders plans providing for internal reorganization. On June 26, 1958, all parties of record, with certain modifications not affecting capitalization and internal control, agreed to the plan recommended by the Examiner. Final approval was given by the ICC on January 12, 1959 and by the U.S. District Court on February 13, 1959.[190] The Atlantic Coast Line, late in 1958, accepted the decision and removed itself from further contention.

On November 3, 1960, the Court entered an Order setting final hearing, on Motion for Consummation, for November 25, 1960. After hearing on November 25, 1960, the Court entered its Final Order and Decree of Consummation which provided that the Reorganization should be consummated at 1:05 AM, January 1, 1961.

Under terms of the Reorganization, the old First Mortgage was paid and discharged, the holders of unsecured claims paid at a rate of 37.6% on the dollar and provisions made for the holder of each $1,000 5% First and Refunding Mortgage Bond to receive a $500.00 First Mortgage Bond in the Reorganized Company, a $500.00 Second Mortgage Bond in the Reorganized Company, 32 shares of common stock and $4.23 in cash.[191]

There was something "whole" about the "new" FEC station. It was big—but not too big. It was convenient—but not so that it caused traffic tie-ups. It was businesslike—but not spartan. On December 8, 1912, FEC 37, a 4-4-0 which was dismantled in 1925, had the honor of bringing the first of multi-thousands of FEC passenger trains into the Miami depot. Though agitation for a new depot began in 1919, the FEC was not easily pushed, and, while plans had finally been drawn for a new station at the Buena Vista Yard site, the 1912 version remained, solid and unyielding, until September 27, 1963, when demolition began. From late 1957 when he began photographing the FEC until the dark and dreary days of demolition, the author, who photographed this scene in 1962, felt a communion with the station. And now, over 20 years after its untimely demise, the Gold Coast Railroad Musuem, as part of their move to the Metrozoo area in South Dade County, plans to rebuild this building almost exactly as shown here, as a major part of their recreation of an earlier, more peaceful, more beautiful Miami.

The proposed Miami Station meant to replace the old passenger station in downtown Miami. This station, slated for the Buena Vista Yard site was on the drawing boards at the time the 1963 strike began. It was, of course, never built.

On February 21, 1961, the Board of Directors of the Florida East Coast Railway, *NOT* in Receivership or Reorganization, met for the first time since 1931.

The new management was faced with an immediate crisis. With Castro's takeover of Cuba in 1960, the lucrative car ferry business through the Port of Palm Beach began to suffer and by 1961, contributions to freight revenue from this source had vanished.

It was this situation that the FEC faced in September, 1961, when the 11 nonoperating[192] unions presented their wage demands on all United States railroads and negotiations were scheduled to get underway at the national level. FEC management at this point made what the unions would probably call a heretical move. They (the management) decided that their only hope of salvation lay in a settlement that dealt with their own special problems on a local basis. This could not be done by negotiation through the national group and the FEC, therefore, politely refused to join in negotiations on an industry-wide basis. The unions stuck to the accepted script and ignored the FEC until a settlement had been hammered out nationally.

They then came to the FEC and demanded that the FEC settle on the national basis. From July, 1962, until December of that year, the FEC and the unions met on a regular basis, with the FEC making 10 separate proposals to the unions. These proposals were designed to give the employees an increase but still permit the railroad to operate within the income it had available. One offer actually exceeded the national settlement of a 4.5% increase—the railroad proposed to give the unions on the FEC a 5 per cent wage increase, spread out over an 18 month period.[193]

But the unions said "no" to all of the FEC's proposals. They simply refused to consider any offer that deviated in any way from the national pattern.[194]

As may be expected, there were numerous charges and countercharges regarding who was "at fault" in the strike.[195] But the most curious written salvo in the war of words that sallied forth immediately after (and then for several years following) the strike's beginning was an 8½'' x 13'' "handout" issued over the signature of the FEC Employees' Strike Committee/J. H. Hadley, Chairman/Mayflower Hotel, Jacksonville/March 25, 1963. In this sheet, Hadley, apparently speaking for the entire striking group of employees listed reasons why the strike should end and railed at Ball and the FEC for prolonging the strike.

FEC non-operating employees set up picket lines at FEC facilities on January 23rd, 1963. Here, two employees walk the picket line at the NE 29th St. entrance to Buena Vista Yard in a futile effort to bring an early end to a debilitating and bitter labor dispute. In a settlement which was to change the face of Railroad Brotherhood labour negotiations for all time, the unions that had gone on strike voluntarily decertified and ceased to exist on the Florida East Coast.

Then, in the next-to-last paragraph, Hadley states, "Mr. Ball has a full legal right to follow his go-it-alone policy. *His employees and their representatives have never balked at negotiating separately with the FEC.*[196] But that doesn't mean we have to take less for our services than other railroads are paying."

In retrospect, there is something terribly empty and ironic about that statement. Many FEC employees, in conversations with the author following the start of the strike stated that they, as individuals, did not want to "go out," but, so they said, "the national unions forced us to." Hindsight, so the saying goes, is perfection compared to foresight. In hindsight, *IT APPEARS* that the statement of the Union was that they (the Union) would negotiate separately provided the settlement was the same as that of every other railroad. Might the outcome not have been different if the union's dogma was not so pervasive?

Speaking to the Transportation Club of Atlanta on October 24, 1963, W. L. Thornton, now (1984) Chairman of the Board of both the Railroad and its new parent, Florida East Coast Industries, said, " . . . . we have found . . . . there was an unbelievable amount of featherbedding . . . . we are now back into almost full freight operation with a little over 700 employees, compared to in excess of 2,000 before the strike. When we resume passenger service in addition to freight service, we do not anticipate that we will require more than 1,000 employees to perform the same work that was done before the strike by approximately 2,000 employees."[197]

A most interesting sidelight was a letter to all employees from Trustee John W. Martin, following settlement with the Nonoperating Unions. Martin, in the two page letter, advised all employees that the FEC, which would honor all parts of the contract, was in complete disagreement with the union shop principle and its inherent unfairness.[198] Martin concluded the letter by saying "The Trustee, after taking into consideration all of the elements of the problem, signed the Union Shop Agreement with the belief that the constitutionality of an enforced unionism agreement, which is so foreign to the American way of life, will be tested by employees, on this or some other railroad, and that such an agreement will fall. This expression of opinion on the part of the Trustee, however, does not modify the obligations which the Railway assumed in entering into the Union Shop Agreement and the Trustee and his officers will carry out all such obligations with their customary good faith in labor agreement matters as long as the Union Shop Agreement exists."[199] Martin, of course, did not know that the principles to which he was referring would be tested on his very own FEC. After all, how could he? The letter was written on November 12, 1953.

177. FEC Railway Annual Reports, 1950 through 1962
178. The 1955 FEC Annual Report notes that the South Miami station was built as a passenger station that year, with facilities for baggage and express. However, service ended (for passengers) south of Miami in 1941. The tariffs remained open in order to service special movements, and it may have been for this reason that the station was listed as a "passenger station." The station was demolished in 1980, following the sale of the right of way south of NW 9th Street in Miami to the Metro Dade Rapid Transit project.
179. Cocoa-Rockledge was opened in Dec. 1962, one month before the strike began.
180. Passenger service ended January 22, 1963, with the strike beginning the following day.
181. It is interesting to note that the Chicago streamliners operated on the same schedule for several years, and different schedules and train numbers when they worked two out of three days or two of them worked every other day and the third train operated every third day. Though ten trains are shown in the timetable, there were only nine operating on certain days.
182. See Number "D. 7." in the text for an explanation of the "Miamian's" operation. On days it was not running, there would be five trains each way each day.
183. According to recollections by several members of the passenger department of the FEC, the "New Royal Palm" was discontinued because the NYC and Southern could not agree on distribution of revenue, and not because the train was insufficiently patronized.
184. The "City of Miami" and the "South Wind" each operated every other day.
185. FEC 1953 Annual Report, p. 2
186. FEC 1957 Annual Report, p. 2
187. FEC 1961 Annual Report, p. 1
188. "Yoda", in the movie "Return of the Jedi" is the diminutive mentor of the virtuous Jedi Knights.
189. The potshots were frequent and often vitriolic. The author, a friend and defender of the FEC, had numerous letters printed in both papers to the effect that if Miami wanted a new station, the county or municipal government should build the station, just as they were doing for the airlines in building Miami International.
190. FEC 1958 Annual Report, p. 14
191. FEC 1960 Annual Report, p. 14
192. "Nonoperating" unions are those that do not actually operate the trains
193. The FEC offered a 12 cent per hour increase based on 4¢ per hour each 6 months over an 18 month period.
194. Thornton, W. L., "The Florida East Coast Story," in "Progressive Railroading," July-August, 1964
195. The strike, as noted previously, began on January 23, 1963. Last *ORIGINATING* runs for all trains began on January 22, with several trains reaching terminals after midnight without incident.
196. Italics are the authors.
197. "'Incredible Degree of Featherbedding' Said to be Revealed by Long FEC Strike," article in "Traffic World," November 2, 1963.
198. Florida is a "Right-to-Work" State. In simplest terms, no person may be denied employment because of his or her refusal to join a labor union. Each person, union member or not, has what many believe is an absolute constitutional right: the Right to Work.
199. Martin, John W., Trustee, FEC Railway. Mimeographed letter to all Employees, November 12, 1953, p. 2

Florida East Coast Railway's

**NEW STATION**
AT
**NORTH MIAMI**
FLORIDA

Makes Travel
**MORE CONVENIENT**
to and from the north Dade
County and Miami Beach areas

**FLORIDA EAST COAST RAILWAY**

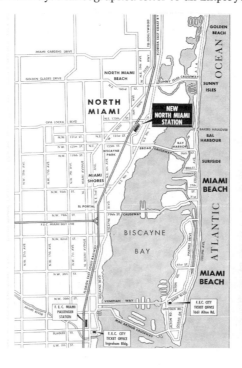

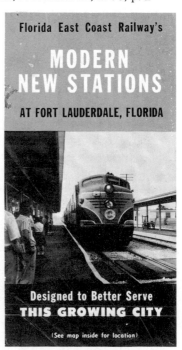

Florida East Coast Railway's

**MODERN NEW STATIONS**

**AT FORT LAUDERDALE, FLORIDA**

**Designed to Better Serve**
**THIS GROWING CITY**

(See map inside for location)

# CHAPTER 11

# "USE PREMISES AND RIDE TRAINS AT OWN RISK"

The strike began on January 23, 1963. For the first ten days after the strike started, nothing moved.[200] The eleven nonoperating unions had put up picket lines, and the five on-train unions and five other nonoperating unions, although not technically on strike, refused to cross the picket lines. The FEC continued to meet with the striking unions, but it became more and more obvious that the unions would not settle for anything other than the terms of the national settlement, and that the railroad was in for a lengthy work stoppage.

For several weeks prior to the strike, the main management team—then president William B. Thompson, Jr., then vice president and chief operating officer W. L. Thornton and others, including Gordie Stewart, assistant chief operating officer—met daily to assess the progress of the negotiations. Progress, as viewed almost twenty years later, was nil. The management had hoped to formulate some sort of contingency plan, but, since none of them had been through a total and complete work stoppage, nobody was certain in which direction to go.

When the strike started, management, in constant touch with Ed Ball, debated the options. Ball was adamant. The railroad could not, he believed, meet the union's demands on an immediate basis and continue to operate. Finally, Thompson, Thornton, Stewart and the others reached the decision that was to forever transform the FEC: Eleven days after the strike started, on February 3, 1963, supervisory personnel operated a freight train from Jacksonville to Miami and return. Union or no, the Florida East Coast Railway would operate.

While the union attempted various and sundry manuevers, both legal (in the courts) and political (in the state legislature and in Congress) a small group of misguided individuals, seeking to "punish" the railroad for operating, committed over 200 crimes against FEC property, including removal of rail, tampering with switches and gunshots into diesel cabs. Added to that, the Kennedy administration exerted enormous pressure on the railroad, mostly through the Florida DuPont interests, to settle the strike. The railroad simply would not back down, and it appeared that even the FBI was disinterested in the crimes, even though they affected interstate commerce.

There had been several wrecks, one in September of 1963 involving 37 cars and a larger one near Oak Hill on October 18, 1963 involving 52 cars. Then, on February 9, 1964, saboteurs blew up two trains, one in North Miami Beach and the other within 15 miles of where the President of the United States, Lyndon B. Johnson,was pressing a button to break ground for the new Cross Florida Barge Canal.[201] If there was any single incident that was to affect the final outcome of the strike, the decertification of the unions from the FEC many years later, this was unequivocally it. Johnson was livid with rage at what had happened, and furious with J. Edgar Hoover that such a thing *could* have happened within such close proximity.

Johnson ordered the FBI to throw its full manpower into the case, and within three weeks four men were arrested and charged with conspiracy to blow up a Florida East Coast freight train. All four were former FEC employees and members of the striking unions, or of unions honoring the picket lines, one being recording secretary of his local.

Following trials and appeals, all four were convicted and sentenced to prison.

From that point on, the violence abated, though nuisance complaints were reported on an almost regular basis. On April 8, 1966, near Boca Raton, somebody fired shots at the engine cab of a freight, with no injuries reported and no suspects arrested.

Once it was shown that the Federal Government would no longer condone acts of violence, and, the FEC had won, on grounds of full merit, each of the court challenges to its right to operate a railroad without union employees, the company was able to turn its complete attention to the business at hand. By late 1964, 700 people were back at work, including some union members who felt that the need to feed, clothe and house their families outweighed the union's demands.

As late as October 1963, it appeared that the FEC had every intention of resuming the passenger business, should the strike be settled. When Thornton spoke to the Transportation Club of Atlanta, he referred to the possible restoration of passenger service. A month earlier, however the railroad, to the jubilant exhortations of Miami's ever short-sighted politicians, had begun the demolition of the infamous downtown passenger station.

"Nothing to it," they chortled. "Hit it with the wrecker ball, and it'll come right down!" Right? Wrong! On Monday, September 26, 1963, with the press, television, radio and dozens of onlookers assembled, the wrecking ball *bounced* off the southwest corner of the *sturdy* old station. Five times the ball was lifted, and five times it bounced. The now forlorn depot, loved by only a very few (obviously including this writer), would not be taken without a determined struggle. Like most of the FEC's buildings in South Florida, the station was constructed of Dade County pine, one of the strongest woods known and totally impervious to termites. Since 1912, this building had withstood all that the tropics had to offer: hurricanes, blazing sun, blinding rainstorms, the threat of fire, termites, insects and whatever else could be thought of. From the day that demolition started, the building did not succumb until November 12, 1963, 47 days later.[202]

From that point on, many small stations were demolished, and it became evident that not only would the strike not end, but that the FEC, as long as there was a strike, would not return to the passenger business. Passenger department employees were furloughed or retired or, if they were able, transferred to other departments. Harold K. North, formerly Assistant General Passenger Agent, became bridge tender at Ft. Lauderdale, then watchman at Buena Vista before its demolition, and then joined the freight sales department before finally retiring. Bob Stroman, formerly a City Ticket Agent, now deceased, went to work in signal maintenance. Roger Barreto, now FEC's vice president in Miami, became a clerk in the freight traffic department.

Of all the people that a passenger-less FEC agitated, it agitated Miami Mayor Robert King High the most. High, as had politicians in muckraking days, used the FEC as a constant whipping boy, chastising it for everything from late trains, to discourteous staff, to the "old" Miami station. Since his immediate political goal was to attain the Governor's office, High felt that nothing in Florida could possibly attract the attention of the entire state as much as forcing the FEC to resume passenger service.

High was astute enough to realize that simple demands would not persuade or force the FEC to run passenger trains again, so he unleashed the Miami City Attorney's office. In checking through old records, and with the cooperation of the Florida Railroad and Public Utilities Commission (now the PSC) the Attorneys discovered that the FEC was operating illegally! The original charter of the Railroad, never updated, required that the railroad provide, daily except Sunday, passenger service between the points of Jacksonville and Miami. As far as the City of Miami was concerned, (and High lost no time in trumpeting it to the news media) the FEC Railway was in violation of its charter and unless passenger service was resumed immediately, High demanded that the railroad cease operating.

The FEC's attorneys, more annoyed than outraged, found, much to their consternation, that High was *possibly* correct, and that there was some language in the charter that *might* require passenger service. The FEC, on the grounds that it was unsafe to transport passengers on a railroad that had been subject to so many acts of vandalism and malicious damage, refused to institute passenger service and refused to stop running freight trains.

High and the City of Miami, keeping the news media well-informed every step of the way, presented their case to the RR&PUC. The Commission, siding with the City, found that it was the duty and obligation of the FEC to restore full passenger service "as immediately as same can be judiciously implemented." The FEC, in total disbelief at the order, appealed to the State Supreme Court.

The Supreme Court of Florida, although an elected body, saw the issue in a different light than the RR&PUC, which felt much more keenly that it was subject to the vagaries and temperament of the voters.

The Court partially overruled the PUC. The order was qualified to mean that the road must provide a train equal to the "public necessity." The Court further stipulated that both coach and first class service were to be provided and that the service must operate so as to be in conformance with the specifications of the Charter.

The FEC, after untold hours of consternation and rumination, accepted the decision, and announced, in mid-July of 1965, that they would, indeed, comply with the lawful order and re-instate passenger service, offering coach and first class accommodation, in each direction between Miami and Jacksonville, daily except Sunday. [203]

# Florida
## EAST COAST RAILWAY
### TIME TABLE

Effective August 2, 1965

# FLORIDA EAST COAST RAILWAY COMPANY

## PASSENGER TRAIN SCHEDULES

| SOUTHBOUND Read Down No. 1 | DAILY EXCEPT SUNDAY | NORTHBOUND Read Up No. 2 |
|---|---|---|
| 9:40 A.M. | Jacksonville | 4:20 P.M. |
| 10:30 | St. Augustine | 3:30 |
| 11:35 | Daytona Beach | 2:25 |
| 12:01 P.M. | New Smyrna Beach * | 2:05 |
| 12:40 | Titusville | 1:25 |
| 1:05 | Cocoa-Rockledge | 1:05 |
| 1:35 | Melbourne | 12:45 |
| 2:15 | Vero Beach | 12:01 P.M. |
| 2:35 | Fort Pierce * | 11:40 |
| 3:00 | Stuart * | 11:15 |
| 3:45 | West Palm Beach | 10:30 |
| 4:20 | Boca Raton | 9:55 |
| 4:30 | Pompano Beach * | 9:45 |
| 4:50 | Fort Lauderdale | 9:25 |
| 5:00 | Hollywood * | 9:15 |
| 5:15 P.M. | North Miami | 9:00 A.M. |

## RAIL FARES

| BETWEEN JACK-SONVILLE AND | One-way in Coach | One-way in Parlor Car |
|---|---|---|
| St. Augustine | $ 1.16 | $ 1.64 |
| Daytona Beach | 3.34 | 4.67 |
| New Smyrna Beach | 3.78 | 5.31 |
| Titusville | 4.69 | 6.58 |
| Cocoa-Rockledge | 5.30 | 7.43 |
| Melbourne | 5.91 | 8.28 |
| Vero Beach | 6.91 | 9.70 |
| Fort Pierce | 7.34 | 10.27 |
| Stuart | 7.95 | 11.11 |
| West Palm Beach | 9.09 | 12.74 |
| Boca Raton | 9.85 | 13.81 |
| Pompano Beach | 10.10 | 14.15 |
| Fort Lauderdale | 10.35 | 14.51 |
| Hollywood | 10.55 | 14.79 |
| North Miami | 10.86 | 15.23 |

\* — Conditional or flag stop.

1 — Connections to New York, Chicago and Cincinnati. Southbound train No. 1 is scheduled to depart from Jacksonville after arrival of ACL No. 1 from New York at 9:15 A.M., ACL No. 5 from Chicago at 9:25 A.M., SAL No. 21 from New York at 3:50 A.M., SAL No. 57 from New York at 8:50 A.M., and SOU No. 3 from Cincinnati at 6:55 A.M. Northbound train No. 2 is scheduled to arrive at Jacksonville before departure of ACL No. 2 at 6:00 P.M. enroute to New York, ACL No. 6 at 6:40 P.M. enroute to Chicago, SAL No. 22 at 8:10 P.M. enroute to New York, and SOU No. 4 at 10:00 P.M. enroute to Cincinnati. (Times shown for arrival and departure of ACL, SAL and SOU trains subject to change without notice.)

2 — Coach and parlor car accommodations are available. (First class tickets required for parlor car seats.)

3 — Tickets may be purchased from conductor upon boarding train, or from vendor in waiting rooms at regular stop stations. FEC waiting rooms will be opened 30 minutes prior to scheduled departure time.

### NOTICE TO THE PUBLIC
**FLORIDA EAST COAST RAILWAY COMPANY**
**IS OPERATED UNDER STRIKE CONDITIONS**

THE RAILWAY HAS TAKEN SECURITY MEASURES TO PROTECT ITS EMPLOYEES FROM SUSTAINED ACTS OF SABOTAGE AND VIOLENCE AGAINST THE RAILROAD SINCE THE STRIKE BEGAN JANUARY, 1963, BUT IT HAS NOT, AND IN FACT CANNOT PREVENT DELIBERATE AND PREMEDITATED CRIMINAL ACTS.

PASSENGERS ARE HEREBY NOTIFIED THAT ALTHOUGH THE TRACK AND EQUIPMENT ARE MAINTAINED IN GOOD CONDITION, AND FEC TRAINS ARE OPERATED IN ACCORDANCE WITH THE PRESCRIBED SAFETY REGULATIONS OF THE INTERSTATE COMMERCE COMMISSION, THE RAILWAY CANNOT, UNDER PREVAILING CIRCUMSTANCES, PROVIDE OR OFFER TRANSPORTATION FREE FROM THE DANGERS OF CRIMINAL ACTS OF SABOTAGE AND VANDALISM. ALL PASSENGERS USING FEC TRAINS DO SO WITH THE FULL KNOWLEDGE AND UNDERSTANDING OF THE CONDITIONS UNDER WHICH THEY ARE OPERATED, AND ASSUME ALL RISK FOR DEATH, INJURY OR LOSS OF PERSONAL PROPERTY RESULTING FROM ANY ACTS OF SABOTAGE AND VANDALISM.

Though the railroad had, since the beginning of 1964, been paring down the passenger fleet, 10 heavyweight coaches, 23 streamlined coaches, 1 streamlined combine, all 5 of the tavern-lounge-observations,[204] a bar lounge, 2 sleeper-bar-lounges, 5 streamlined diners, 2 streamlined baggage dormitories, and 17 sleeping cars, all streamlined, were still on the property, along with 104 heavy-weight baggage, mail and box express cars.[205]

The FEC, though determined to live up to the letter of the ruling, was equally determined to limit itself to the carriage of paying passengers only, and, consequently, it was decided that no checked baggage, remains, US Mail, Company Mail or Express would be carried, nor would any passes, either of the FEC or any other line be honored.[206]

A convenient and usable schedule was arranged: Number 1 left Jacksonville at 9:40 AM arriving in Miami at 5:15 PM; Number 2 left Miami at 9:00 AM, arriving Jacksonville at 4:20 PM. The train would carry a porter, on-board passenger service agent, conductor and flagman, and be operated on the front end by an engineer and a head end brakeman. Both trains would operate with coach service and first class accommodations available. First class was a seat in one of the tavern-lounge-observation cars, which were to be considered parlor car (first class) seats. Additionally, passengers in either section could order lunch, and the order would be transmitted to a restaurant enroute.[207] The passenger agent or porter would collect the funds and exchange them at the appropriate stop for the box lunches. Passengers could purchase soft drinks and coffee on board, but no alcoholic beverages would be available.

The date of August 2, 1965 was set as the initial day for the restored passenger service. And Robert King High was a hero. Except for one small detail.

There was no longer an acceptable passenger facility in the City of Miami itself. In their zeal to have the downtown station torn down, and in their glee at having it so done, not one of the politicos, in their shallow brilliance, gave one iota of thought to the fact that the FEC no longer had a downtown terminal.

The nearest station—and it had been mostly for freight and express prior to the strike—was at Little River, on NE 79th Street. The closest strictly passenger facility, and one that was relatively new, having been constructed in 1955, was in North Miami, at NE 16th Avenue and 129th Street. It was, the FEC decided, going to be their southernmost terminal.

High was astounded and fulminated furiously to all who would listen, but to no avail. The trains would, and did, for their entire operation, have their southern terminal at North Miami.

To initiate the operation, the FEC washed and cleaned coaches "Miami" and "St. Augustine," and tavern-lounge-observation "St. Lucie Sound" for the first northbound run (behind E9A 1032) and coaches "Boynton" and "Hollywood," and tavern-lounge-observation "Lake Okeechobee" (behind E9A 1035) for the first southbound run. The author, carrying a sign welcoming the FEC back into the passenger business, and accompanied by younger brother Bennett, (an inveterate train rider, though not a railroad buff) purchased the first ticket sold at the North Miami depot on that bright, sunshiny Monday.[208]

Amidst major press coverage, and national wire service interest, the two trains began their operations which lasted just short of three years.

When it was announced that the railroad would go back into the passenger business, they continually referred to the violence that had punctuated the strike. To the shock and surprise of almost all, the railroad posted large signs, 12½" x 17" that stated, below the words "Notice to the Public," that the "Florida East Coast Railway Company Is Operated Under Strike Conditions/Use Premises and Ride Trains at Own Risk."[209] The message was further underscored when the timetable issued August 2, 1965 carried the same warning. Interestingly enough, and for reasons now unknown, the two subsequent timetables, dated May 15, 1967 and December 16, 1967, respectively, did not carry or allude to the strike warning message.

Richard Beall, an FEC engineer and the son of an FEC engineer, knew steam only from his father's pictures and reminiscences. Unhappy at being too young to have photographed steam on the FEC, young Beall determined to shoot everything else FEC still extant. His superb collection of photographs of the FEC, both bought and taken, bears witness to that. When, in late 1978, Dade County's rapid transit authority announced the purchase of the FEC's right of way, from downtown Miami to the Dadeland-Kendall area for use by rapid transit, Richard determined that the event would not pass unrecorded, and proceeded to photograph the entire line, almost 11 miles, crossing by crossing. SW 8th Street, near the site of the former Southside passenger car holding tracks is particularly poignant. The large brick building is actually on the other side of the Miami River. It was torn down by the FEC in 1983. The entire scene has changed, of course, and now trains of Dade County's Metrorail cross the Miami River high above this same roadbed. Though the ballast, tracks and ties are gone, a good bet is that the ghost of the "Havana Special" still rolls slowly past this crossing on its phantom trips to and from Key West.

*—(Richard Beall photograph)*

The FEC, in adhering to the letter of the PUC's order, did operate a superior passenger service, with equipment fully maintained and in fine working order. Air conditioning on coaches and in the tavern-lounge-observations was always functioning, and the six diesel units used for the passenger service, E7A 1011 and E9As 1031 through 1035 were cleaned daily and kept in perfect condition. In addition to the cars listed on opening day, coaches "Titusville," "Homestead" and "Bunnell" filled out the active roster.

Within a few months of the inaugural, the train was shortened from two coaches and a tavern-lounge-observation in each direction to one coach and a tavern-lounge-observation. In either case, it was a beautiful train, and was, contrary to the jibes referring to it as the "Toonerville Trolley," America's shortest, full service streamliner.

Six days per week train passenger agents John Smart and M. H. Fields would greet passengers in North Miami and Jacksonville respectively. At a set point, the trains would meet, and the crews would "exchange trains," the Miami based crew returning to Miami, and the Jacksonville crew returning to the "Northern gateway." Six days per week, on time and without fanfare, Numbers 1 and 2 sped between Florida's two largest cities. Finally, with expenses far outweighing revenues,[210] the Railroad appealed to the Florida Public Service Commission (formerly the RR&PUC) for relief.

On July 23, 1968, the FEC posted, at the 16 stations that the train served, notice that, permission having been given by the PSC, Trains 1 and 2 would be discontinued following their completion of trips of July 31, 1968.[211]

To a railroad buff there is nothing sadder than a "last day." Be it the last day that a station is open or the last day of steam locomotive operation or the last trip of an RPO or an entire passenger train, railroad buffs are filled with a sadness at events like these that only other deeply committed historians can know or understand. July 31, 1968 was such a day.

All aboard tried their best to be cheerful, and, in the main, they succeeded, since the inevitability was never in doubt. None the less there was an emptiness, and a hurt feeling in the pit of the stomach. When the southbound train arrived at North Miami, and all passengers were detrained, and the crew had posed for the obligatory photographs, the train headed for Hialeah Yard for the last time, but a prophetic mood of sunset melancholy and impending dark as the cars neared their yard suggested the darkest of nights into which, at the end of day, all things must go.

### FOOTNOTES

200. It was the first time since May 23, 1913, the day of Memoriam for Henry M. Flagler, that the railroad was completely and totally stilled

201. If ever socialistic-thinking, anti free-enterprise quasi-liberals have stumbled on a hare-brained pork barrel of a scheme, it is the atrocity known as the Cross Florida Barge Canal. Aside from the enormous environmental destruction, the canal is simply unnecessary, the cost exhorbitant, and the benefits non-existent. If he had done nothing else beneficial, Richard M. Nixon will be remembered (and should be honored by Floridians) as the President who *STOPPED* the atrocity less than halfway to completion.

202. In the author's early railroad buff years, the Miami Station was almost like a second home to the young man who fancied this very special railroad. The polished woods, the old pictures, the brass ticket windows, and the generally friendly greetings received from such as William Wooten, depot ticket agent, ticket sellers L. C. Bugg and Eddie Apfelbaum, and, of course, Harold North and the passenger department in general, made the station a wonderful place to go, not only to photograph the building and trains but also the people that made the FEC what it was. To this day, the author's memories of the Miami Station are filled with warmth and gladness at having been fortunate enough to experience something that today's railfans can only read or hear about.

203. David P. Morgan in "Trains Magazine," February, 1975, article reprinted by FEC Railway

204. Although 5 tavern-lounge-observations were on the roster, the "Hobe Sound," having had its streamlined sides removed in preparation for smooth-siding in order to match the remainder of the cars on the "City of Miami" was still a sideless and roofless hulk, this once beautiful car would hardly be considered operational.

205. "Summary of Equipment," FEC Rwy., St. Augustine, July 1, 1965

206. "Circular 72," FEC Rwy., July 29, 1965

207. The restaurant, according to the author's recollection, was in Ft. Pierce, Vero Beach, or Melbourne.

208. Almost 3 years later, on July 31, 1968, the author purchased the last FEC Railway passenger ticket ever sold.

209. In addition to the warning, printed in large letters, the sign advises schedule times and times tickets are sold and advised passengers regarding their assumption of liability when using the train.

210. For the two days short of three years that the train ran, it averaged only 16.4 passengers per day, *TOTAL*, in each direction

211. Florida PSC Order Number 4394, in its Docket 9126-RR

10 miles south of St. Augustine, in 1964, a train was sabotaged. Note the hi-railer in front of the lead engine. From 1963 until 1968, every train on the FEC was preceded by an armed guard in a Chevrolet station wagon equipped with railroad wheels.

Within just a few days of the advent of the ill-timed and destined-to-doom 1963 strike the FEC was operating freight trains utilizing supervisory personnel. It was the first extensive use of highway vehicles equipped with flanged wheel attachments. All trains, including the passenger trains, were preceded by a Hi-railer. On December 27, 1966, Hi-railer 18 pauses in front of the Fort Pierce Station. The infamous warning to passengers advising them to "USE PREMISES AND RIDE TRAINS AT YOUR OWN RISK" is posted just to the left of the woman standing just behind the hood of the Hi-railer.

In mid-1963, strikers determined to sabotage FEC operations (since the FEC would not back down at the bargaining table and trains had been running since 11 days after the strike started on January 23 of that year) blew up a freight train by placing dynamite on the tracks. FP7A 572, F3B 553, GP9R 676 and GP7R 621 were the victims. The train crew escaped, with only minor injuries. The saboteurs were later apprehended and incarcerated.

—(Richard Beall collection)

Miami Station—20, 30s, 40s? Only the cars are different! The station could look like this on any given day in any winter season from the mid 20s to the late 40s and very early 50s.

—(J. Nelson Collection)

The inside of the Miami City Ticket Office was..."solid." It was massive, with high ceilings and huge wooden tables and chairs. And it was right on the corner of SE Second Avenue and SE First Street, the first—and largest—of the ticket offices on "Railroad Row." Behind the wall on the right were the Miami offices of the Passenger Traffic Department, and out the door, straight ahead, the lobby of the Ingraham Building. For a railroad where passengers furnished as much as 44% of gross revenue, nothing less could have been expected.

—*(FEC Official Negative: Historical Association of Southern Florida Collection)*

The steam engines have been bumped from main line passenger service in the circa 1950 view but they are still handling the switching chores at the Miami Station. The ubiquitous Dade County Courthouse looms in the background with the implication that IT is the FEC Miami Station, rather than the wooden building in front of it.

FEC passenger trains operated between Jacksonville and North Miami from August ??, 19?? until July 31, 1968. On August 2nd, 1965, the author photographed E9A 1032 and it's ??????? train, coaches "Miami" and "St. Augustine," and tavern-lounge-observation "St. Lucie.?

It's March 11th, 1967 and the FECs two car streamliner is providing six day a week service between Jacksonville and Miami. Number 1034, an E9A built in January, 1955 by EMD is southbound at Fort Pierce. (Photo by G. Votava)

It's August 2nd, 1965, and by Florida State Supreme Court Order, the FEC is back in the passenger business. In this photo the author is carrying a sign that said "Welcome back—we missed you." This picture, taken at the North Miami Station, was used on the front page of the "Miami Herald" and by wire services nationally.

A closeup of the 'sunrise' emblem which succeeded the Overseas Extension emblem and preceded the "Going Places in Florida" emblem. The emblem was used from 1936 until 1965 and its full-colored hues accented the beauty of the red, yellow and silver diesels.

# CHAPTER 12

# "CONFUSION TO THE ENEMY"

In 1968, the last year that passenger service was operated, revenues were $25.7 million. In 1983, operating revenues were over $115 million. The change in the FEC was startling and dramatic!

The "new" FEC is, in railroading, a brave new world. Asked to account for the extraordinary success of the FEC in keeping costs and rates down, and profits high, the average railroader is apt to reply with a single word: "Labor."

It is true that the FEC, which operates under its own, updated work rules (e.g., two man rather than three or five man train crews; an eight hour rather than a 100 mile day) has by far the lowest labor costs of any major railroad anywhere in the world. FEC spends only 30 cents out of every revenue dollar on labor costs, including fringes and payroll taxes. By comparison, the best labor ratio among carriers that operate under nationally negotiated work rules is the 42% posted by the Southern. The industry average is around 53% and some northeastern roads, including Conrail, are paying out between 60% and 65% of revenues in labor costs.

But that, insists FEC Chairman Winfred L. Thornton, tells only part of the story. "Certainly, labor has made it possible," observed Thornton, "but the real savings is in car utilization.

"The industry gets 59 miles per day per car. Southern railroads get about 53 miles. On the FEC we get 88 miles—and remember, this is a terminating railroad. Every car we handle, we terminate. You can appreciate that it would be an even better situation for a bridge carrier that just handled cars and did not have the delays of loading and unloading.

"The utilization of equipment—turning it around faster and getting it off the railroad—[212] is really where the savings is. That's the real money. And it comes from running short, frequent trains."[213]

From the effects of the strike, FEC emerged with a "new freedom-to-manage" that, says Thornton, has resulted in the creation of "the most modern and well-maintained railroad in the country. We have centralized traffic control and continuous welded rail from Jacksonville to Miami. We have almost 250 miles[214] of concrete crossties. We have hot box, dragging equipment, and loose wheel detectors at 20 mile intervals in addition to shifted-load detectors every 40 miles. We have achieved one of the finest safety records among railroads our size, having won either the first, second or third place Harriman Safety Awards 11 years out of the past 12.[215]

"Where we were operating three through freights in each direction before the strike, we are now operating eight or more in each direction. We have more than doubled our revenue ton-miles."[216]

All of this has been made possible, says Thornton, by sweeping rule changes in six major areas.

1. "We eliminated the 100 mile day and substituted an eight hour day with time and one-half for overtime, essentially the same basis as for a yard crew.

2. "We eliminated any restrictions concerning road crews running in and out of or through a terminal.

3. "We eliminated any restrictions limiting yard crews from performing road work or road crews from performing yard work.

4. "We eliminated any restrictions limiting starting time for yard engines—in other words, yard engines can be started whenever the service requires.

5. "We eliminated any restrictions on the number of men required on a yard or train crew; we use those men that the service requires.

6. "We provided a single seniority date for all train and engine service employees in both road and yard service, that is, the date of their original employment. In other words, a man may simultaneously qualify as a yard switchman, yard conductor, yard engineer, road conductor and road engineer, with his original seniority date in each class, and bid on any job he is qualified to hold that his seniority permits."[217]

It was the implementation of these rules that led to a strike being called by several of the operating unions that, though not technically on strike, had honored the nonoperating unions' picket lines. With the nonoperating unions' strike in its fourth year, three of the operating unions—the Order of Railway Conductors, the Brotherhood of Locomotive Firemen and Enginemen, and the Brotherhood of Railroad Trainmen struck on April 24, 1966. This occurred following the establishment, by management, of new work rules which eliminated a great deal of featherbedding and revised pay scales to provide eight hours pay for eight hours work in all classes of service. This action (the strike) was taken after negotiations and mediation had failed to achieve agreement and the procedures of the Railway Labor Act had been exhausted.[218]

As if to underscore the position of the railroad, the U. S. Supreme Court, on May 23, 1966, held that a carrier has the duty to make all reasonable efforts to continue its operations during a strike and may make such changes in working conditions as are essential to continue its operations.[219]

A fourth operating union, the Brotherhood of Locomotive Engineers, was added to the list of striking unions on March 12, 1967, as a result of the announcement that the management was putting new work rules into effect. "The new work rules for the Brotherhood of Locomotive Engineers not only gave the engineers the greatest job security but also increased their individual compensation so that they now receive the highest hourly rate of pay for eight hours work of any railroad in the nation. As in the case of the other three operating crafts, the new rules did away with 'make work' practices and provided for medical insurance and other benefits."[220]

FEC continued to operate more and more efficiently as the years wore on. Then in 1970, the first of the unions agreed to a settlement. Locomotive firemen and the FEC agreed to an $800,000 settlement in a suit filed by the union alleging the railroad violated collective bargaining agreements. The settlement was submitted to U.S. District Judge Charles R. Scott as a compromise to the $7.5 million suit filed in 1967 by 75 senior rated firemen.[221]

1970 proved to be an interesting year in another way. "A short nationwide strike began against most of the Eastern railroads as well as a majority of those in the South and West—but the FEC kept running! And when the others went "back to work," the FEC was still on strike! This twist developed when a nationwide rail strike that began at 12:01 AM on December 10 showed signs of a quick settlement. The FEC was sending freight on its regular runs and is serving points all along the Florida East Coast, but will probably be affected by what happens at the northern railheads."[222]

Since the strike started, the FEC had been making excellent use of their fleet of diesels. However, nothing could make the engines younger and the years were taking their toll. By the end of July of 1968, not including the 13 passenger units that were still on the property, the railroad was down to 75 locomotives, the newest of which were the 10 GP9Rs, numbers 667-676, built in 1957.[223]

The oldest, the three BL2s, build in 1948,[223] and the eight F3As and four F3Bs, built in 1949,[224] were running out their last miles. The BL2s, in fact, were stored out of service in New Smyrna Beach.[225] For over two and one-half more years, the FEC pushed their motive power to the limit. Finally, in the Spring of 1971, the railroad received its first new locomotives since 1957. EMD Builder Numbers 36,773 through 36,782, known as GP40s, with a fuel capacity of 3,000 gallons (compared to 1700 gallons for the GP9-Rs) and 3,000 horsepower (compared to 1,750 horsepower for the GP9s) carrying FEC numbers 401 through 410 arrived on the property and immediately went to work.

In June of that year (1971) news began leaking out that a settlement of the nonoperating unions' strike against the railroad was close to a settlement. Ten of 11 nonoperating unions tentatively agreed to return to work. Their return depended upon agreement by the 11th union, the signalmen, and approval of the settlement by a federal court handling a union suit against the railroad.

In addition to a financial settlement the railroad also agreed to reinstate all of the strikers, most of them over a "short period of time," sources said. "Many however are now dead, retired or employed elsewhere."

The report, dated June 2, 1971 went on to say that "An FEC spokesman in St. Augustine said that he had heard nothing of an impending settlement and could not comment. He referred all calls to the railroad's personnel office, which was closed."[226]

The next day, the FEC confirmed the possibility that the strike by the "nonops" was near a conclusion. "The status at this moment is inactive because all the unions must sign," he said. His reference was to the signalmen, who, for the time being, refused to sign, much to the annoyance of several other unions, among them the Brotherhood of Railway and Airline Clerks.[227]

Nothing further appeared to happen until August, when the "Miami Herald" reported that "The Nixon

Administration's request for an immediate end to all strikes and lockouts in the country could end the eight year old strike against the FEC Railway, an administration official said Thursday."[228]

Though this gave hope to the former employees, and the communities along the line, as far as the possibility of passenger service restoration went, that particular "problem" had been eliminated in finality when, on May 1, 1971, Amtrak took over all US rail passenger services, except for those on three railroads. If a railroad had no passenger service when Amtrak took it over, it could not be required to operate passenger trains over its lines, though it was not forbidden to do so. By this time, the FEC had no intention of returning to the passenger business.

Finally, on December 18, 1971, it was announced that a settlement had been reached and that both sides were in agreement. Over 900 former employees had already returned to work, and, of the remaining 1,100, all but 100 had taken other jobs.[229] One detail held up the return of the strikers.

"Union officials said they did not expect the strikers back on the job until Scott completed hearings on individual suits against the unions and determined new wages for the various crafts involved.

The officials said those hearings probably would not be completed until sometime in March."[230]

Unhappily, the unnamed union officials misjudged. The suits dragged on until December of 1974, and it wasn't until the settlement of $1.57 million was announced and signed on December 17, 1974, that the suit of the nonoperating unions came to an end.[231]

Unfortunately, the strike, in toto, was not over. The strikes that were called by the operating unions in 1966 and 1967 continued. It was not until 1975 and 1976 with the NLRB's decertification of the unions that the strike of the operating crafts would come to a final and sadly fruitless ending.

In 1972, the railroad bought 5 more 3,000 horsepower diesels, designated GP-40-2s. They were numbered 411 through 415 and were followed up by 416, 417 and 418 in 1974. With the arrival of these engines, the railroad had on hand four SW's, for limited yard switching, 15GP7Rs and 23 GP9-Rs for road use, and the 18 GP40s and GP40-2s.

Through the intervening years since the strike had started, the railroad had been demolishing unused stations up and down the line. Several met kinder fates. Princeton, south of Miami, was moved to Miami's Crandon Park for use as a railroad Museum and is now scheduled to be part of the Gold Coast Railroad complex at the Metrozoo. Homestead was moved to the Pioneer Museum at Florida City. Hobe Sound and Stuart were reportedly purchased and moved. Sebastian was moved south of the town and, for a short time was used as housing for migrant laborers. Gifford was moved west of the railroad and rebuilt, also for migrant housing. Unhappily, dozens of other stations, from 1964 through 1972 were simply bulldozed or otherwise demolished, and the only extant records of their existence are in historical files or collector photographs.

As the railroad became more and more of a point to point operation, those facilities that were unnecessary to the revitalized operation were altered or abandoned.

The same held true for branch lines (those few left) that were no longer "pulling their weight." As soon as the strike began, the FEC had moved all Miami area operations to Hialeah Yard, west of the City on the Miami Belt Line. Trains from the north crossed northeast 79th Street in Miami and then swung west on the Miami Belt. Use of the trackage from Little River south to Kendall Jct., the point at which the line from Hialeah Yard met the old main line, passing through Lemon City, Buena Vista, downtown Miami, Southside, Coconut Grove, and South Miami, dwindled to strictly switcher trips. In late 1970 or early 1971, the bridge across the Miami River saw the passage of an FEC train for the last time, and on January 21, 1972, it was announced that the trestle would be removed.[232] Once this was done, early in the spring, the historic line utilized by passenger trains until 1941 and by freights operating from Buena Vista thereafter, was severed.

During 1974, the FEC received authority from the ICC to abandon 31 miles of branch line between Aurantia (near Titusville) and Benson Junction and completed the removal of the line in 1975.[233] The miles of road operated at the close of 1974 became 499.[234]

Next to go was the line from East Palatka to Bunnell Junction, originally built as the St. Johns & Halifax Railroad. The FEC now consisted of the Jacksonville-Miami main line, the short branch to the Kennedy Space Center, the Ft. Pierce-Lake Harbor branch, and the Hialeah Yard-Florida City branch, as well as the line from St. Augustine through Spuds and Hastings to East Palatka. Each and every operating mile of the "new" FEC is a revenue producer.

From 1974 until 1976, no new locomotives were bought, but between 1977 and 1980, the railroad

W. L. Thornton, Chairman of the Board of the Florida East Coast Railway.
—*Photograph Courtesy FEC Railway)*

Raymond W. Wyckoff became the FEC's President on May 30, 1984.
—*(Photograph Courtesy FEC Railway)*

"Confusion to the Enemy!" was his long time toast, and when, on June 24, 1981, Edward Ball died, a giant of Florida's history passed from the scene. In tribute to Ball's memory, the Edward Ball Building, at the foot of Miami's majestic Biscayne Boulevard, adjacent to the former site of the Royal Palm Hotel, overlooks the New World Center of the South.
—*(Photograph Courtesy FEC Railway)*

added 11 GP38-2s numbered 501-511 and rated at 2,000 horsepower and 11 more GP40-2s, 419 through 429. The railroad now has four SW switchers, 28 GP40s and GP40-2s,[235] 11 GP 38-2s and 23 GP9-Rs, for a total of 66 units.

What is so amazing about the number of units (compared with over 200 in 1926) is the volume of business that has developed on the railroad since 1968. Operating revenues of $30 million in 1969 and 1970 became almost $35 million in 1971, $39.5 million in 1972 and $47.6 million in 1973. Though dropping slightly in 1974 and then to just over $42 million in 1975, they have climbed steadily since, touching $100 million for the first time in 1980.[236]

In 1979, in what was termed a friendly condemnation proceeding, Metropolitan Dade County (Miami) purchased 9.2 miles of the FEC track along U.S. 1 from just northof Dadeland Shopping Center area to the Miami River. The strip of land is from 70 to 100 feet wide.[237] With other properties sold through condemnation, revenues of $28.3 million were included in 1979's income statement, and $4.8 million in 1980's income statement.

In 1980, the "unthinkable" happened. With net income over $28 million, something that had never before occurred on the Florida East Coast Railway took place. The FEC declared a cash dividend! After never having paid its shareholders a cent, the FEC directors voted an initial payout of 10 cents per share to stockholders of record on March 21, 1980. The decision killed one of FEC (then) Chairman Edward Ball's favorite boasts.

"We have an unbroken dividend record," the 91 year old industrialist-financier was fond of saying. "We've never paid a dividend."[238]

Revenues continued to rise and in 1981 were over $106 million. But the year was marked with sadness, as it had been in years past when great leaders of the FEC had passed away. After sustaining a fall several months previously, Edward Ball, the brilliant Trustee of the Alfred I. DuPont Estate, Chairman of the Board of the St. Joe Paper Company and the FEC Railway, succumbed on June 24, 1981. Though a different man in a different era, Ball had a reputation akin to that of Flagler's. In his own way, in his own time, Edward Ball, was, if not an Empire Builder, than surely an empire developer. He would have his Bourbon and Branch Water before dinner, and raise his glass to make his famous toast: "Confusion to the enemy!"

Overseeing the paper company and the railroad were only part of what he did. He was also chairman of the Florida National Group of Banks (which the Courts forced him to divest in the late 70's) and had been, among other things, Chairman of the Florida Exhibits at the 1939-1940 New York World's Fair, and Guarantor of the 1947 Bond Issue that enabled Dade County to connect Key Biscayne with the mainland.[239] Though he had developed the reputation of tight-fisted toughness that, apparently, all men of his level of wealth and power develop, he was charitable to those he deemed worthy and headed the Nemours Foundation, a large part of whose proceeds go to aiding crippled and handicapped children. A painting of him graced the cover of the 1979 FEC Annual Report.[240]

Following an appropriate period of mourning, the Board of Directors of the Railroad named Winfred L. Thornton as Chairman, continuing as President. At the same time, Raymond W. Wyckoff was named Executive vice president. Wyckoff joined the FEC in 1948, and in 1963 became director of personnel, becoming vice president and director of personnel in 1964. In 1967, he was named vice president in charge of transportation, personnel, claims, legal and property protection. In 1972, he became senior vice president with jurisdiction over all departments. His new position would continue his previous authority and add to that, the responsibility of assisting President Thornton.[241]

With Thornton and Wyckoff in command, operating revenues reached $115.3 million in 1983. With condemnations and other sales of various properties, total revenues topped $157 million. Net income of over $43.5 million was over $14 million more than the total revenue of the railroad in the great Florida boom year of 1926![242]

At the 1984 Annual Meeting, held in St. Augustine on May 23, stockholders ratified, by a huge majority, a proposal to turn Florida East Coast Industries, then a subsidiary of the railroad, into a holding company, with the railroad and Commercial Realty and Development Company, another railroad subsidiary, into subsidiaries of the Holding Company, which would be FEC Industries. It was the belief of the Board of Directors that "the establishment of this holding company structure is desirable because it should provide increased operational flexibility and would permit clearer delineation of organizational responsibilities and performance."[243]

## FOOTNOTES

212. Per diem refers to the rate each railroad pays for having another railroad's freight cars on its property. In effect, a rental figure.
213. "FEC: Florida's Productivity Showcase," in "Railway Age," May 8, 1978, p. 40.
214. Concrete crossties are now in place in over 300 miles of FEC trackage.
215. The article being quoted from is dated 1979. (See Footnote 217). Since then the railroad has received the award 16 out the past 17 years.
216. Ton-miles is a measurement used to determine the number of tons moving one mile.
217. "FEC: We Dared to be Different," in "Railway Age," November 26, 1979, pp 28—29
218. FEC 1966 Annual Report, p. 5
219. Ibid, p. 6
220. Ibid, pp. 5—6
221. Miami Herald, January 1, 1970
222. "FEC Twist: On Strike, but Running," in Miami Herald, December 10, 1970.
223. FEC Summary of Equipment, July 1, 1968
224. Ibid
225. Three of the six BL-2s had already been sold and were off of the property
226. "Longest Rail Strike Appears Near End," in Miami Herald, June 2, 1971
227. "FEC Confirms Strike Near Settlement," in Miami Herald, June 3, 1971
228. "End Near for FEC Walkout?", in Miami Herald, August 20, 1971
229. "$1.5 million settlement reached in 9 year FEC railway strike" in "Miami News," December 18, 1971
230. Ibid
231. "$1.57 million ends FEC strike" in Miami News, December 18, 1974
232. "FEC to raze old trestle at last . . . . " in Miami News, January 21, 1972
233. FEC 1974 Annual Report, p. 2
234. Ibid, p. 2
235. GP-40 402 was destroyed in the accident caused by vandalism at Oakland Park, near Ft. Lauderdale on February 12, 1979
236. Source: FEC Railway Annual Reports
237. "Rapid Transit Land Purchased," in Miami Herald, November 10, 1978
238. "Perfect FEC Dividend Record Falls" in Miami Herald, January 11, 1980.
239. Key Biscayne, now a heavily populated suburban area, was the vacation White House for Richard Nixon during his terms in office.
240. Not since Henry M. Flagler appeared on the cover of the 1912 booklet, "Florida East Coast" had an FEC chief executive been so honored.
241. "FEC Bulletin," Summer-Fall, 1972, p. 1
242. FEC Railway Annual Reports, 1983 and 1926
243. FEC Railway Cover Letter to Notice of Annual Meeting and Proxy Statement/Prospectus, April 13, 1984.
244. The ICC delineates railroads by earnings, with Class I being the largest gross, Class II the next largest and so forth.

## SPEEDWAY TO SUNSHINE

Florida East Coast Railway is the modern double track speedway to all points on the Florida East Coast, colorful land of palms and sunshine.

Its finely equipped, Diesel-powered trains will speed you south in utmost comfort and safety over a roadbed noted for its riding smoothness.

More fine through trains are available over the Florida East Coast Railway than any other Florida route. They conveniently serve the entire coast, including its smaller towns and resorts as well as its larger cities.

Skirting the ocean shore this is the only railroad through historic old St. Augustine, Ormond, Daytona Beach, the interesting citrus groves and pretty towns along the beautiful Indian River.

When you purchase your tickets to Florida, be sure that they are routed via this modern Speedway to Sunshine.

The above photo is the back page of FECs descriptive booklet entitled "Florida East Coast" for the year 1950.
                    —*(Florida Collection, Miami-Dade Public Library)*

Dania, 1916.

A pristine model of perfection in station architecture, Dania basks in the warm winter sun, February 3, 1961.

In the 1920s (and, in fact, until the mid 1950s) Florida City looked like this.

—(J. Nelson Collection)

The FEC station at South Miami (formerly known as Larkins) was replaced in the late 50s with a concrete block structure.

—(Photo by W. Moneypenny)

Perrine Depot in South Dade County, ca. 1906. This station burned to the ground in July 1984.

Princeton Station was preserved by the Junior Women's Club of Miami and moved to Crandon Park on Key Biscayne as part of the short-lived Dade County Railroad Museum. With the moving of the Zoo to higher ground in the vicinity of the old Richmond NAS (orginal site of the Gold Coast Steam Railroad and Museum) the narrow gauge tourist line at the park, along with the Atlantic Coast Line caboose and Princeton Station were left to their fate. But, lo and behold, along came one Roger Schmorr (he of the bringer of steam to Miami fame) and the knights of the Gold Coast Railroad to move (an absurd scheme!) the Gold Coast back to its original home with a massive project including the rebuilding of the Miami Station. "Fools," it was thought! "This can never be!" But, somehow, it is, in 1984, occurring, with the Gold Coast having received lands and funds for moving to the Metrozoo site. And Schmorr (he of the taker on of impossible tasks fame) is ready to begin the removal of the forlorn railroad museum on Key Biscayne to its place in the sun as part of the Gold Coast Railroad Museum complex—at Metrozoo!

An early view of Delray Beach.                    —(J. Nelson Collection)

Military Junction Station. This is a complete mystery as far as FEC stations go. It was apparently built in the 40s in the center of the wye between 62nd and 71st Streets in Miami and was meant to serve the military. However, the station appears in only two FEC employee timetables in the 1940s and to the best of available knowledge never was a station stop for a passenger train.

On February 12, 1979, three late teenaged boys threw a main line switch at Oakland Park, near Ft. Lauderdale. Southbound 98, a first class train rolling south at almost 45 miles per hour, suddenly shunted off the main line, and, before the crew could react, piled up at the end of the short siding. Again, nobody was killed, and the junior gangsters were apprehended and sentenced to jail, but the 402, with frame bent, was declared a total loss and retired. 505 was repaired and returned to service.                                        —(Richard Beall Photographs)

**What if you had to call the president of your company every time you were 15 minutes late?**

**What if a railroad had to set in concrete its promise to modernize?**

FEC

**HIGHWAY DISPATCH COMPANY**

we believe in the American way

RAIL

Under the management of Raymond W. Wyckoff, the FEC (as it is today) was totally customer service oriented. These three brochures feature various facets of FEC's service, from demanding on-time operation to modernizing the railroad to the over-the-road subsidiary's partnership with the rail service.

# CHAPTER 13

# DIVERSIFICATION

As noted previously, in 1984, shortly before the original edition of *Speedway to Sunshine* went to press, the FEC reorganized into a holding company structure in which Florida East Coast Industries, Inc. was created and become the parent company of Florida East Coast Railway and of Gran Central Corporation, a real estate development company.

The reorganization was designed to allow Gran Central to develop surplus properties formerly owned by the railroad. It was at this point that W. L. Thornton assumed the chairmanship and presidency of Industries. (Mr. Thornton had been chairman and president of the railroad since shortly after the death of Edward Ball, in 1981.) Mr. Thornton named Raymond W. Wyckoff president of the railroad and Carl F. Zellers president of Gran Central.[145]

In June of 1992, after 44 years with the railroad, R. W. Wyckoff retired, having served in executive capacities for much of his career with the FEC. Ray Wyckoff was a hands-on manager, and his micro-management style was somewhat unique in the manner in which he was made aware of every aspect of the railroad's operation. His hands-on approach included overseeing almost every facet of the FEC, from sales and marketing to operations. He was not without his detractors, but the results from operations indicate, in retrospect, that, as Mr. Thornton would later comment, "He was the right person for the job at the time."[146]

Mr. Wyckoff's shipper-directed advertising was somewhat unique in the railroad business at that time, and one of the most famous of the ads asked, "What if you had to call the president of your company every time you were 15 minutes late?" with a hand holding a pocketwatch below the question. The brochure stated that every time a train was more than 15 minutes late, Mr. Wyckoff's office was advised of the reason or reasons. Engineers and conductors whose trains ran late for a certain number of trips would be instructed to meet with "RWW" to discuss the problem.

During Ray Wyckoff's tenure, the railroad acheived record profits and continued its remarkable safety record of being first in its class and winning the coveted Harriman Award for Railroad Safety for 16 straight years. Early in 1992, Mr. Wyckoff

### Gran Central Corporation

Gran Central Corporation was formed by Florida East Coast Industries as a wholly owned real estate development company to build, own and manage its real estate projects. Since 1984 approximately 4,200,000 square feet of office, rail-served warehouse buildings and office/showroom/warehouse buildings have been completed or are under construction.

| Project | Building Type | Gross Square Feet |
|---|---|---|
| Jacksonville: | | |
| Barnett Plaza | Office Building | 80,000 |
| duPont Center | Office Buildings | 164,000 |
| Gran Park at Interstate South | Office/Showroom/Warehouse | 276,000 |
| Gran Park at The Avenues | Office Buildings | 240,000 |
| | Office/ Showroom/Warehouse | 105,000 |
| | Office/Warehouse | 137,000 |
| Melbourne: | | |
| Melbourne Business Center | Office/Showroom/Warehouse | 28,000 |
| Riviera Beach: | | |
| Gran Park at Lewis Terminals | Office/Showroom/Warehouse | 61,900 |
| | Rail Warehouse | 175,500 |
| | Cross Docks/Warehouse | 75,000 |
| Pompano Beach: | | |
| Build to Suit | Rail Warehouse | 54,000 |
| Miami: | | |
| McCahill Tract | Warehouse | 300,000 |
| Gran Park at Miami | O/S/W & Warehouses | 1,510,016 |
| Total Completed | | 3,206,416 |

Current Buildings Under Construction:

| Project | Building Type | Gross Square Feet |
|---|---|---|
| Jacksonville: | | |
| Gran Park at The Avenues | Office Warehouse | 154,000 |
| Gran Park at Deerwood | Office Building | 140,000 |
| Gran Park at Deerwood | Office Building | 130,000 |
| Miami: | | |
| Gran Park at Miami | Front Load Warehouse | 138,000 |
| | O/SIW & Warehouse | 313,500 |
| Total Under Construction | | 955,500 |

All of the above facilities have been constructed from Cash Flow and are not burdened by any debt financing.

Prior to the change of name to Flagler Development, Gran Central published this fact sheet, telling about the company and it's extensive holdings. Since this piece was printed, the property owned and under construction has greatly expanded, and Flagler Development has become one of the largest and most successful industrial/warehouse property developers in Florida.

The worst horror facing a locomotive engineer is the threat of a collision, particularly one involving a fuel tanker. At Atlantic Boulevard and Dixie Highway, in January of 1981, that specter almost came to pass when the Gulf Oil truck shown here barely stopped in time for the on-coming FEC train and wound up with the southwest crossing arm on its back.

—*(The Author )*

noted that the railroad was approaching its 100th anniversary and began to think about the coming Centennial, the celebration of which could occur in 1995 or 1996, depending on certain other factors. It would, however, be for his successor to carry out the plans and bring to reality the FEC's Centennial celebration.

In 1992, after serving 11 years as president of the railroad, Mr. Wyckoff retired. Mr. Zellers assumed the presidency of the railroad following Wyckoff's retirement, while Mr. Thornton retained the position as chairman of Industries.

Carl Zellers was a different kind of leader than Mr. Wyckoff had been. Under his management style, employees had greater decision-making power. While Mr. Zellers was president of Gran Central, it had been vested with approximately 23,000 acres of land following the 1984 reorganization and proceeded to move toward development of infrastructure and other improvements necessary for the construction of office buildings, rail warehouses, dock-high front loading warehouses and flex-use office-showroom-warehouse-type buildings.

During Mr. Zellers' early FEC career in accounting, he had made numerous decisions that resulted in extraordinary savings to the railroad. This experience would serve him in good stead in his management of the new land development company.

Between 1984 and approximately 1996, Gran Central constructed or leased approximately 4,500,000 square feet of building space in Gran Parks, in Jacksonville, Riviera Beach, and Miami and was considered a major developer along the entire east coast of Florida.[147] One of Mr. Zellers' fondest recollections was of his fellow president, Ray Wyckoff, sometimes less than good naturedly complaining to Mr. Thornton that too much of the railroad's assets were being diverted to Gran Central, with Mr. Thornton patiently explaining to "RWW" that it was necessary to do so in order for the land department to be able to make its contributions to the success of Industries over the long term. As Mr. Zellers related, "I had to smile because Ray, even though he didn't want to acknowledge it, certainly understood!"[148]

In 1994, after operating as the nation's only non-national union railroad since the job actions of 1963, the Florida East Coast operating employees were once again organized and many of them joined the United Transportation Union, which represents operating department employees today. While Mr. Zellers was not overjoyed by these events, his unique personality and management style made the process and subsequent contract negotiations acceptable to both sides, and he should be credited with creating an atmosphere of fairness and stability for all.

Under Mr. Zellers' leadership, the railroad would strike out into uncharted territory, and for the first time in its history, prepare to operate rail service outside the State of Florida.

145. Bramson, Seth H. *Centennial Edition: The Story of a Pioneer*, 5th ed., Florida East Coast Railway, 1996, p. 39.
146. Interview with W. L. Thornton, July 27, 1996.
147. Op Cit, *Centennial Edition: The Story of a Pioneer*, p. 39
148. Interview with Carl F. Zellers, Jr., July 14, 1996.

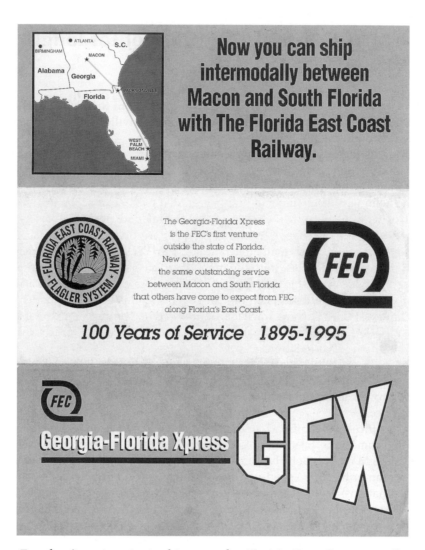

For the first time in its history, the Florida East Coast actually operated its own trains outside of Florida. In a historic arrangement with Norfolk Southern Corp., the FEC began through service to Macon, Georgia, and called it the GFX, for Georgia–Florida Xpress.

in the service. Appropriate announcements were made, labor negotiations and agreements were completed, and the new service, using Florida East Coast locomotives, began as scheduled on March 1, 1995. FEC GP40-2 "Centennial" locomotives 444 and 446, painted appropriately to celebrate the railroad's upcoming Centennial year were chosen for the inaugural and performed flawlessly, allowing the opening to come off without a hitch.

Although highly successful, the service was terminated on February 29, 1996. Incredibly, one of the major reasons for the termination was the fact that given the cut-off times (the times when shipments were guaranteed to move provided they were at the terminal by that time), the train was often fully loaded, with no more flat cars on which to place waiting trailers. Those trailers would then have to be hauled via highway using FEC tractors owned by ITI, the railroad's highway-intermodal subsidiary, to Jacksonville, and the cost of that transportation, given the number of trailers involved, was simply prohibitive.

Though the cessation has been a lengthy one, I have no doubt that there will be a resumption of this service, perhaps not to Macon, but certainly somewhere well north of Jacksonville. Florida East Coast locomotives will, in the not too distant future, once again lead freight trains across the St. John's River, to CSX or NS trackage and on to as yet undetermined terminals. In a nation where state lines are mostly mere formalities, the FEC's speed and service will once again cross Florida's border into Georgia and possibly beyond. And I believe that day is coming sooner rather than later.

149. The term "trackage rights" refers to one railroad leasing or granting operating rights to another railroad over the first railroad's track. In some cases the granting railroad operates the trains for the grantee; in other cases the grantee operates its own trains. Trackage rights can range in length from several hundred feet to many miles.

On Saturday, July 27, 1996, the FEC's Centennial train, with Presidential car *Ferdinand Magellan* on the rear, backed down the historic trackage toward the display area at the Port of Miami lead track. The Miami Coast Guard and various student ROTC units provided the color guard for ceremonies involving various local dignitaries and railroad officials. In shirt sleeves on the rear platform is then Miami commissioner J. L. Plummer, while just barely visible in the *Magellan*'s doorway is then FEC Industries Chairman W. L. Thornton.

# CHAPTER 15

# CENTENNIAL!

It is (almost) hard to believe that 142 years after the very first of the FEC's predecessors turned a wheel for the first time, and 106 years after the name of the J. St. A. & I. R. Railway was changed to Florida East Coast Railway, there are only a handful of either AAR Class One railroads or railroads that are more than short lines but not quite Class One (a class determined solely by yearly revenue) in existence in the U. S. today.

Short of the massive Norfolk Southern, BNSF, Union Pacific and CSXT (along with what is now called CNIC, which incorporates the Canadian National's takeover of the Illinois Central, the Wisconsin Central and the group of railroads operating in northern New England), about the only two large independent railroads in existence are the Kansas City Southern and the incredible Florida East Coast Railway. It is as hard to believe as it is logical.

Raymond W. Wyckoff called me in 1992 to discuss the railroad's 100th anniversary. In the most technical sense, the predecessor line's name was changed to Florida East Coast in September 1895. The FEC's first predecessor operated its mule-drawn vehicle in 1859. Mr. Flagler made his first railroad purchase on December 31, 1885, but Mr. Wyckoff believed that 1995 should be considered the Centennial date, given the date the railroad was named. Obviously, since the other dates were at least, at that time, seven years past, I quickly agreed.

When Mr. Wyckoff retired just a few months later, nothing further had been done. Carl Zellers was appointed to take Mr. Wyckoff's place, but I did not want to appear presumptuous by rushing him on the Centennial issue, as I knew he had other problems and concerns, so I held off on the Centennial discussions for some time. Finally, in mid-1993, I broached the question with him. He was gracious but not yet ready to get into the details. I called again in March of 1994 to remind him that, while I understood that he had other things on his mind, we were only a year and a half from the great date. In the meantime, plans were proceeding apace on many fronts for the Miami Centennial, to be celebrated through a series of events beginning in early 1996 and culminating with the Centennial weekend of July 27 and 28, 1996. Little did anyone know at the time that the FEC would steal the Centennial show!

During the March 1994 call CFZ asked me to become involved in preparations for the celebration. Fortunately, unbeknownst to me at the time, we had "inside" help!

The FEC's Vice President of Engineering, Bill Stokeley, was a warm man whose wife, by coincidence, has the same first name as my wife. In this way, we were "connected." Better still, the FEC's number-two corporate attorney, a young man by the name of Kenneth Charron, was not only determined to see that there would be a Centennial but was also well liked by Mr. Zellers while at the same time "having Mr. Thornton's ear." Out of the blue, in mid-'94, I received a call from Mr. Charron, whom I had not yet met but with whom I would become close friends. Ken had already approached Mr. Thornton, and both had agreed that we needed to do something to get the Centennial arrangements moving. Since I had been actively involved in the planning for the Miami Centennial, I was ready and eager to begin planning with the FEC.

Although Ken and I talked over the next several months, it was an announcement at a Miami Centennial marketing committee meeting that served as the catalyst for the railroad to bring itself up to speed. In this meeting, held at the offices of the Downtown Development Authority, one of the members said, loudly and with certainty, "We're going to run a steam-pulled passenger train over the FEC from Jacksonville to Miami to celebrate the Centennial, and we're going to have the President of the United States aboard for part of the trip." He went on to elaborate all that they would do with this imaginary train, and when he finished his huffing and puffing I raised my hand and when called on said, very quietly, "I don't want you to think me a naysayer, and it all sounds wonderful, but I wonder if anybody has discussed this with the Florida East Coast Railway." His response was that the committee didn't have to discuss it with anybody, that "if this group wants it done, it will get done." I suggested that nothing was going to happen on the Florida East Coast unless the Florida East Coast's management wanted it to happen, and that I did not think it would be a good idea to act like tough guys with the FEC. I was told I was being negative.

Following the meeting, I called first Mr. Zellers and then Mr. Charron, related the discussion noted above, and recommended that it was time for the railroad to take action and begin to move in a concrete way toward the Centennial. A few days later, I was asked to participate in a conference call with Mr. Zellers, Mr. Charron, Transportation Superintendent Deputy and Engineering Vice President Bill Stokeley. The decision was made to schedule the FEC Centennial to coincide with the Miami Centennial, and at that point I was asked to serve as liaison to the Miami Centennial committee on behalf of the railroad; to advise the committee that the railroad would enthusiastically participate in the joint Centennial celebration; and to put into writing a plan for what the railroad could and should do in order to assure that the Centennial would be a success.

Plans could now begin in earnest, and Mr. Thornton and Mr. Zellers in effect turned the program over to Ken and me. It should be noted, though, that in order to keep Mr. Zellers apprised I would call every so often and speak to the woman who had first served as Mr. Wyckoff's secretary and who would eventually do the same for Mr. Anestis, but who, in the interim period, was Executive Secretary to Mr. Zellers. Francis Mueller was nothing short of "a peach." Her warmth and encouragement were there from the beginning, and it became clear that she was very much with us in working toward making the railroad's Centennial nothing short of a once-in-a-lifetime celebration.

Shortly after the conference call, Ken asked me to prepare a written proposal of what we should do. We were running short of time, with the end of 1995 fast approaching, but since I had created a proposal earlier for Mr. Wyckoff, little revision was required. My plan was as follows:

A tie-in with the City of Miami so that the Centennial celebration would be a joint FEC-City of Miami event. (As things would turn out, the City of Miami part became little more than a concert in Bayfront Park with some ancillary celebrations, while the FEC train would become the "heart and soul" of the joint centennial.)

A display train was to be brought to downtown Miami to serve as the centerpiece of the celebration. This display train would feature FEC diesel locomotives, one of the dormant steam engines at the Gold Coast Railroad, several different types of FEC freight cars, and former FEC passenger cars, both heavyweight and streamlined, which were also at the Gold Coast. Along with all of that, both Mr. Thornton and Mr. Zellers felt that the former U. S. Presidential car, the *Ferdinand Magellan*, a centerpiece of the displays at the Gold Coast, should be part of the Centennial exhibit. I heartily concurred.

A reprint of the company's historical booklet, *The Story of a Pioneer*. This glossy, 40-page, 6" x 9" booklet had originally been published offset style during the 1935-36 season, when J. D. Rahner was the General Passenger Agent. It was republished in 1946 to reflect the changes, including dieselization and the soon to be operating Lake Okeechobee cutoff, then was reprinted again in 1952 and 1956, each time with minor changes. It had not been reprinted since '56. It was time to publish a completely updated edition of *The Story of a Pioneer*.

Employee involvement. Without the wholehearted interest and cooperation of the employees of the FEC, Centennial could not be a success. All concerned agreed, and, happily, Bill Stokeley, Vice President of Engineering, was one of those who had been pushing for a celebration event. Fortunately for all of us, Bill assigned Larry DaRosa, senior car foreman, to the task of overseeing the conversion of one of the "gang" cars,[150] which was being used as a bunk car for the maintenance crews that were still going out on the road in what are still called work trains. At the same time, Hialeah diesel mechanical foreman Rudy Dolentina was asked to assist in the project and he enthusiastically accepted. Rudy had been with the Chicago & Northwestern and, like Larry DaRosa, had a great interest in both the railroad as an occupation and the railroad as a historical entity.

Volunteer service performed by Florida's railroad buff community to act as both hosts and safety observers to assist with any safety related problems or issues that could possibly arise.

A repainting of one of the smaller diesels (at that time several of the SW 1200 yard switchers were still on the property) into the glorious red and yellow paint scheme for display purposes.

With the exception of the repainting of the diesel (see Chapter 16), everything proposed would come to pass.

*Centennial Edition*

*The Story of a*

# PIONEER

*A brief history of the Florida East Coast Railway and its part in the remarkable development of the Florida East Coast*

## FLORIDA EAST COAST RAILWAY

*A Florida Industry and Institution*

During the 1935-36 season the FEC published, for the first time, a history of the railroad. Subsequent editions followed, in 1946, for the Company's 50th Anniversary, then in 1952 and in 1956. Forty years later, with the support of FEC vice president Bill Stokeley and corporate attorney Kenneth Charron, Chairman Thornton and President Zellers approved the publication of an updated Centennial edition of *The Story of a Pioneer*, with almost all new photographs, historical background and information about the railroad, FEC Industries and Gran Central Corporation, the land, warehousing, building construction and management arm of FEC Industries now known as "Flagler Development."

Things were coming down to the proverbial wire. Once Ken Charron and Larry DaRosa had selected the best of the gang cars from the lineup at New Smyrna, that car was pulled out and brought to Bowden Yard, New Smyrna shop, Ft. Pierce terminal, and Hialeah in order to give the employees the opportunity to look it over and suggest ideas to make the car usable as a display car. That car would become the centerpiece of the FEC display train.

The railroad donated the material and furnishings, and hundreds of FEC employees donated time and effort in preparing the car. It was my job to pick out the images and decide how and where in the car to display them. Superintendent of Property Protection Jim Keeley lent his FEC models, and the Historical Association of Southern Florida donated two showcases for the exit end of the car. Refurbishing proceeded under Larry DaRosa's watchful eye.

Because I was serving as a member of most of the City of Miami Centennial committees, it was my privilege to report to them that the FEC would celebrate its centennial not in 1995, but along with the City of Miami in July 1996. The reaction was one of pure delight. The people at the Gold Coast Railroad were delighted to be asked to participate, and the FEC, in a magnanimous gesture of good will, announced that once the Centennial festivities concluded, the display car, with number changed to 1996 would be donated to the Gold Coast.

Various historic organizations were also preparing for displays commemorating Miami's first century. In September of '95 I approached Marcia Zerevitz, Director of the Sanford L. Ziff Jewish Museum of Florida, and suggested to her that, for the Centennial, the Museum should feature the works of legendary FEC company photographer Harry M. Wolfe. On April 23, 1996, the great exhibit opened: "By Train to America's Playground: Florida East Coast Railway, photographer Harry M. Wolfe and his images of Flagler's Florida 1926-1958," co-sponsored by the Florida East Coast Railway. The exhibit remained in place until September 1 and, along with FEC Exhibit Car 1996, it was considered one of the centerpieces of both the Miami Centennial and the grand FEC event.

It is difficult to find enough superlatives to describe the work of Harry Wolfe. Certainly there have been other great photographers along the east coast of Florida, and others whose work involving Miami is superb, but nobody else combined the subjects of trains with the landscape and people of Florida's east coast to create lasting photographic art. Because Wolfe was an in-house or company photographer his work had previously gone unremarked, yet during his career Harry Wolfe's pictures depicted the Florida East Coast, at work, at play, and in turmoil, from the great Florida boom of the 1920's, through the "bust" that followed, the destruction of the Key West Extension, dieselization, World War II and in to the 50's.

For the FEC–City of Miami Centennial in 1996, the Florida East Coast was the primary sponsor of an exhibit honoring its long-time photographer, the beloved Harry M. Wolfe.

Harry Wolfe's family: Mr. and Mrs. Wolfe and son Jimmy to Harry's left. Seated are Ruth and Leonard. Jimmy passed away in the 1970s. Ruth was unable to attend the event honoring her father, but Leonard and wife Gene had the pleasure of seeing tribute paid to a man whose work had, for so long, gone unrecognized.

I was fortunate enough to locate Harry's younger son, Leonard, and his beautiful wife, Gene, who had served as one of Harry's best models while she and Leonard were dating. Gene and Leonard were the honored guests at the opening of the exhibit, and FEC Vice President Roger Baretto represented the railroad at an event attended by hundreds of Miami's social elite, people from all races, nationalities and religions, who came to honor the man I consider to be Florida's greatest photographer. Using Wolfe's negatives to present, for the first time, the work of the man who had preserved the history of the east coast on film, the author, as guest curator, memorialized the great photographer.

Because of work involved in readying the exhibit train, I knew it would be necessary to enlist the services of Florida's railroad buff community. A request for volunteers was sent out through the various chapters of the National Railway Historical Society, to the Gold Coast Railroad, and to several model railroad clubs. A volunteer chairman was appointed and, with the assistance of Chief Keeley and the FEC's Special Service (Police) Department, three safety meetings were conducted at Hialeah Yard. Volunteers were required to attend all three meetings in order to be participants. We wound up with close to 70 volunteers!

The FEC announced that on Friday afternoon, July 26, they would sponsor a large luncheon at Hialeah Yard for invited guests, including major shippers, company officers, and various political leaders. The 1996 was to be painted and completely finished inside so that I could give tours to the assembled guests. Bill Stokeley, Larry DaRosa, Rudy Dolentina, and the hundreds of employees turned a somewhat rundown gang car into a magnificent 85-foot display car, painted on the outside in blue, with the "Speedway to America's Playground" slogan, and sporting three of the FEC's emblems: the Oversea Railway, the Sunrise, and the current "Going Places in Florida" emblem.

With only a few days to go, the last picture was put in place and the two showcases filled with the display items. A sign at the entrance said: "The Management and Employees of the Florida East Coast Railway Welcome You Aboard." Stepping from the entrance and turning right to go into the main display area of the car, the first picture guests saw was of Henry M. Flagler, and from there, in chronological order, were photographs of the east coast and the railroad's role in developing it, with views of Jacksonville and St. Augustine in the 1880s, through to the FEC's modern diesel units. Rudy and his son had spent days preparing the captions that I had given them for each picture. Photographs of FEC employees were featured throughout. Visitors then passed the two display cases before reaching the exit.

Major shippers, members of the Board, and other invited guests clambered aboard to enjoy the walk through history and, on July 26, were the first of tens of thousands who over that weekend would see and walk through the exhibit car, the FEC heavyweight and streamlined coaches, and the *Ferdinand Magellan*. Although I had known Mr. Thornton for close to 36 years, I had the opportunity to thank him for all he had done, not only in making the Centennial a reality but also in allowing me on the property during the difficult times. "We always thought of you as a member of the family," he replied. Roger Baretto took particular delight in telling guests that he had got me started, elaborating on the fact that I had started coming in to the FEC's Ingraham Building passenger department office as a little kid in 1958. A fine and genteel man, Roger Baretto, who had come to work for the railroad in the late 1940s as a clerk in the then-thriving passenger traffic department, had reached the rank of Vice President and would retire from the FEC with 50 years service. I enjoyed telling his son, Rodney, a political mover and shaker in Miami, that I was one of the few people in Miami who had known his dad longer than he had!

The big day had at last arrived, and the display train was assembled, with several different freight cars, the display car, two Gold Coast Railroad-owned former FEC coaches, and the *Ferdinand Magellan*. Volunteers were asked to be at their appointed posts on Saturday morning as early as 7:30 A.M. Some were to meet the display train in downtown Miami, and others would ride in from Hialeah Yard with the train.

About a week before the train was to move from Hialeah to downtown, I received an unexpected call from Mr. Zellers. "Would you," he asked, "be willing to serve as the conductor for what might be our last passenger train? And will you wear your FEC uniform?" He further agreed to allow my wife, Myrna, to serve as uniformed on-board passenger agent. Thus, at 7:30 A.M., Saturday, July 27, the train was ready to roll from Hialeah Yard, Myrna and Seth were aboard in full regalia, and the train was magnificent. The railroad had prepared the display car perfectly, and at the entrance end, the former restroom had been turned in to a private office for me, complete with air-conditioning, so that I would be able to take a break, since I was expected to serve as host and guide for the car and the train in my capacity as company historian.[151]

Chief Keeley had arranged for the various police departments along the route (Hialeah, Miami-Dade, and Miami) to escort the train from the yard into downtown Miami, where it would be parked—including locomotives—on the original FEC track, adjacent to the Miami News/Freedom Tower building and leading to the Port of Miami. I use the term "original" because Miami's second station was at 6th Street (now NE 6th Street) and "the Boulevard" (now Biscayne Boulevard). That station served from a few months after the first train arrived (the first station was in place for just a few months, on what would become the main line at about 12th —now Flagler—Street). When construction was completed, the "new station" opened and would serve until mid-1912, when the "newer" Miami station opened on Avenue E (later NW First Avenue). The station on 6th Street was partially dismantled and moved to a site just north of the "newer" station, where it served for many years as part of the Railway Express Agency facility. The Miami News/Freedom Tower site is, to any FEC enthusiast, hallowed ground, as it was on that spot that Miami's first full-service FEC station stood for 16 years.

FEC Miami-Hialeah Terminals Superintendent Wayne Blaylock was responsible for the setup and movement of the train. What a magnificent job he did that day! Mr. Blaylock is now Director of Operations for the entire south half of the railroad. The Special Service Department had police cars positioned strategically throughout the route, which was to follow the Miami Belt to its junction with the old main line, pull forward on the north leg of the wye at 71st Street and NE 4th Court, and then travel back down the former main line to "Arena Station" (so named because the train would stop at the Miami Arena). Here, civic and business leaders—who had been furnished with tickets based on FEC tickets in my collection— would board the train for the short trip to Biscayne Boulevard. The train would be there for two days, Biscayne would be closed, and the freight display cars, parked next to the Miami News/Freedom Tower building, would block the west side of the Boulevard.

On the morning of Saturday, July 27, 1996, the FEC's *Centennial Special* departs Hialeah Yard enroute to "Arena Station" and the joint FEC–City of Miami 100th Anniversary display on the historic Port of Miami lead trackage, once the original Miami passenger station trackage and the P & O Steamship Co. dock track.

The author and wife Myrna, enjoy the view from the *Magellan*'s observation platform.

Enjoying a glorious day and an even more glorious event, Mr. and Mrs. Roger Barreto and three of their children take in the sights from the rear platform of the *Ferdinand Magellan* after the train was temporarily parked for the opening ceremonies of the Centennial. Mr. Barreto had just retired as Vice-President of the railroad after a 50-year career which began in the Miami office of the Passenger Traffic Department in 1945.

At approximately 9:00 A.M., Superintendent Blaylock gave the highball, and the two Centennial engines began to pull. Dozens of FEC employees came in on their day off to see the train depart. First Hialeah police, then Miami-Dade County police, and then Miami police, all with lights flashing and sirens blasting, escorted the train as it rolled east over the Belt. FEC's police stayed with the train for its entire route, and FEC Lt. Nelson Berrios, using the FEC's marked police car, stayed with or ahead of the train. Finally, we slowed for the wye and Berrios pulled his car into the middle of NE 79th Street to block traffic while Superintendent Blaylock dropped off the train to give backing instructions.

Backing in to the "Arena Station" was a joyful event for this writer, for I had not ridden an FEC train in to downtown Miami since late in 1962, just before the strike began. It was a wonderful feeling as I described my FEC passenger train riding days to my beloved bride (at that time, of 20 years!) As we rolled south toward the station, I, being the conductor, had the privilege of riding in the vestibule, and familiar faces came into view including old friends Mitchell "Flash" Greene and Phyllis and Steve Strunk, of Key West, who had come up to see the train. Upon boarding the guests at the Arena, Myrna and I happily went through the train announcing to all that they should keep their tickets as a souvenir of this great day. We gave the highball and proceeded to Biscayne Boulevard, where the train was stopped with the Ferdinand Magellan's open end observation platform facing the Boulevard. It was at that point that the Centennial festivities were put into high gear.

It was my honor to introduce to the crowd Florida Senator Bob Graham and various Miami City and Miami-Dade County dignitaries. Perhaps the greatest honor, though, was the opportunity to introduce, first, Carl F. Zellers, and then, W. L. Thornton, each of whom briefly addressed the crowd and welcomed them to the joint Centennial. Following the speeches, the train was moved across the Boulevard, with the passenger cars on the east side and the freight display cars and engines blocking the west side (southbound lanes).

My old friend Leonard Certain and his wife ,Susan, had come down for the weekend, and Leonard worked the car with me. In the two days, literally thousands of people passed through the car. Each person received an annotated written history of the company and had the opportunity to learn about the glorious history of America's most unique railroad by walking through the car and enjoying the various displays. On Sunday evening, the 28th, close to sundown, the train returned to Hialeah Yard. Geoffrey Tomb, writing in the *Miami Herald* on July 30, penned the following words: "The only thing that tied 1896 Miami to the 1996 Centennial event was the Florida East Coast train and its wonderful display car." Tomb added that it was "fortunate for this city that the Florida East Coast Railway committed its resources to this event."

For the railroad and its employees, however, Centennial would not be over until November. Mr. Zellers and Mr. Charron realized that the employees of the company, who had done so much to make it all "happen," were entitled to enjoy the fruits of their labors, and it was decided to move the car to each of the railroad's yards or terminals so that the employees would have the opportunity to see and understand the history of the railroad. Ken called me on behalf of Messrs. Thornton and Zellers and asked if I would mind accompanying the car to the various terminals and serving as the host for the railroad. Suffice to say, it was another great honor accorded me by the FEC.

Arrangements were made for the car's first trip to be to Bowden. I would ride in the display car, directly behind the engine, and we would leave Hialeah on an early train, arriving in Bowden Yard late in the afternoon. The car would be parked there for the weekend. When I got to Hialeah, Chief Keeley had "bad news" for me: the generator car, which provided the air-conditioning for the display car, was not working properly, and he wondered if I would mind riding in the engine. Were there words to express my glee? I think not!

Train handling on the FEC is an art, and the men and women who run the FEC's trains are nothing short of artists. On the morning of September 6, 1996, engineer Jerry Monecue took that train, with four units and 131 car-lengths, all 11,455 feet of it, and handled it as if it were a passenger train. With Ron Cooley serving as conductor, the trip went by all too quickly. When we stopped in Ft. Pierce to drop off one unit and several cars, all of the Ft. Pierce yard employees took a quick look at the car and were already aware we would be back in several weeks to spend time with them. Passing through New Smyrna Beach, several of the men from the diesel shop came out to greet the passing train.

The display car would spend time in Bowden, St. Augustine, New Smyrna Beach, Ft. Pierce and Hialeah, completing its duties late in October. Following closing cleanups, the car was transferred to CSX for delivery to the Gold Coast Railroad, where it maintains a place of honor and brings back joyous memories to the many who participated in Miami's and the FEC's glorious Centennial.

Though Ken Charron is no longer with the railroad, and CFZ has retired, a special note of thanks is due to them and to all of the employees of the various FEC departments who helped to make the company's Centennial one of the greatest events in Miami's or the railroad's history. I don't know what can be done to top it in 2096!

*FOOTNOTES*

150. On some railroads, what are referred to as "track gangs" still live for days—and sometimes weeks—at a time on board work trains, which carry equipment cars, bunk cars, kitchen/dining cars and, usually, tank cars for fresh water for the crews. The living accommodation cars are often called "gang cars."

151. Because of my work on the FEC's Centennial, as well as my authorship of this book, Mr. Charron suggested to Mr. Thornton and Mr. Zellers that I be given an official company title as Historian of the Railroad. Both agreed, and today I am one of only two people in the United States who hold that title with a railroad, the other being the historian of the Union Pacific. Shortly after becoming Chairman and President of Industries, Robert Anestis reconfirmed that appointment.

Well-known railroad enthusiast Bill Folsom shot a "ghost from the past" that has come back to life! FEC then Vice President and now President John D. McPherson quietly ordered the repainting of GP-40 type engine 406 into the glorious red and yellow paint scheme of a by-gone era. Mr. McPherson felt that with the coming of the Millennium the FEC's history should be vividly noted, and decided to honor both that history and the future and had 406 repainted as the 2000. The New Smyrna Beach shop forces, under the direction of Bryan Hathaway, faithfully re-created the most magnificent color scheme on or by any American railroad. More than two years later, both railfans and company employees are thrilled to see this stunning reminder of the greatest American railroad story ever told.

194

# CHAPTER 16

## 2000—AND THE 2000!

The Centennial wound down, the year came to an end and the more humdrum daily railroad operations continued on the Florida East Coast. However, change was on the horizon.

The FEC's parent company, St. Joe Paper, was about to go from a closely held private company to a publicly held corporation. Almost concurrently with this action, the decision was made that, over a period of time, St. Joe would give up its control of FEC Industries and allow its longtime subsidiary to set out on a course of its own.

In early 1998, a seminal event not related to the St. Joe-FEC situation, occurred: a young south Florida man by the name of Steve Spreckelmeier located an FEC steam engine in Texarkana, Texas. This engine, 0-8-0 253, had been "sold down the river" by the FEC during the Depression (see steam locomotive roster) and had served its remaining operative years on the Louisiana & Arkansas Railroad, working the station and yards in Texarkana. Upon retirement, the 253 had been donated to a local park, where it sat on display, partially exposed to the elements and slowly deteriorating. Mr. Spreckelmeier, with assistance from several partners and his father, purchased the engine and arranged to have it moved to south Florida.

Through the generosity of FEC Vice President of Operations Marshall Deputy and President Zellers, the Florida East Coast moved the long out-of-service former FEC engine from Jacksonville to Hialeah yard at no charge. It was a generous and thoughtful contribution to the preservation of the line's grand heritage.

Under the direction of Steve Spreckelmeier, 253 is nearing operating condition, and plans call for the engine to be put into regular service on trackage in south Dade County, either for excursion or dinner train operations. Since the operational demise of the 113 and 153 at the Gold Coast Railroad in south Miami-Dade County, the storage of FEC 98 (Savannah & Atlanta 750), and the lengthy but temporary dismantling of 4-6-2 148 (which is being restored as these words are being written), there have been no active FEC steam locomotives. Engine 253 will bring steam back to Florida, and no small debt of gratitude is due to Steve Spreckelmeier and his associates.

After a more than six-year presidency, Carl Zellers announced that he would retire at the end of 1998. The Board, noting changes in the economy, as well as the huge stockpile of cash that the FEC had built up through the careful shepherding of resources by Messrs. Thornton, Wyckoff, and Zellers, made a major decision: FEC Industries would finally begin to use that cash to expand, and in no small way!

In mid-1998, after lengthy discussions, the Board decided that the new President and Chairman of FEC Industries would be a different kind of person, a man with a solid background in not only railroading but also in the financial world. In addition, that person would be able to bring with him a diverse group of talented individuals who could not only operate the railroad at the high levels of efficiency and re-investment that it had become famous for, but who could also chart a course for a future that would combine railroading with land development and the most modern forms of communication, both microwave and computer.

Robert W. Anestis was the perfect choice to serve as the new Chairman, President and CEO of FEC Industries. He had been president of Guilford Industries and had created a Class I

Robert W. Anestis, Chairman, President and CEO of Florida East Coast Industries

It became a near obsession for FEC buffs to photograph the 2000. Here, just south of North Miami Beach's 163rd Street crossing, the author was fortunate enough to catch the engine "on the point" of a fast- moving southbound freight.

railroad holding company with more than $300 million in annual revenue. He graduated from Harvard University in 1971 as part of the first Harvard class to receive a joint Master of Business Administration and Law degree and had served two years as a Captain in the U.S. Air Force. His love of railroading was reflected in the fact that he had been a five-percent owner of the Seminole Gulf Railroad, a Florida tourist shortline and common carrier, and maintained a great interest in both railroading and railroad memorabilia.

Mr. Anestis did not rush in and take over, however. He worked diligently with outgoing President Zellers for almost six months in order to absorb the FEC culture and learn about the uniqueness of the railroad and its people. That action would stand him in good stead when, on December 31, 1998, Carl Zellers retired. Mr. Anestis formally assumed his office on January 1, 1999.

Joining him was longtime colleague Bob McSwain. Mr. McSwain's experience, both as President of his own company and as Executive Vice President of Guilford Industries, facilitated his move to FECI. He was initially named Executive Vice President for Special Projects for FECI and President of the Flagler Development Company. However, on December 1, 2000, Mr. McSwain was named Vice Chairman of the Board of FECI. He retains jurisdiction over special projects and initiatives as directed by Mr. Anestis.

On July 7, 2000, the name of Industries' land ownership and development subsidiary, Gran Central Corporation, was changed to Flagler Development Company. As Mr. Anestis explained, "This name change will not only reflect the historic roots of this company, but will allow the public to immediately identify with a company whose founder is the single most recognized name in the business, historic and public communities of Florida." On December 23, 1999, G. John Carey had been named Executive Vice President and Chief Operating Officer of Gran Central Corporation. On December 1, 2000, he became President of Flagler Development, and under his leadership the company continues to expand its strong presence in the ownership of both land and warehouse space along the east coast.

For the railroad, another very special talent was enlisted. Vice President of the Railway John McPherson would, with the retirement of the beloved Marshall Deputy, longtime assistant to Mr. Zellers and Vice President of Transportation, be named President and Chief Operating Officer of the Railway, with Mr. Anestis retaining the executive positions of Industries.

Great events were unfolding as the FEC prepared to enter the new Millennium, and one of them was the discovery by Ft. Lauderdale steam and FEC buff Steve Spreckelmeier that an FEC 0-8-0 switcher which had been sold to the Louisiana & Arkansas Railway during the Depression and had spent its entire remaining life both working and on display in Texarkana, Texas, might be available for purchase. Spreckelmeier and several associates pulled off the steam engine coup of the decade: with approval by then FEC Vice President Marshall Deputy and President Carl Zellers, the FEC graciously moved the engine at no charge from Jacksonville to Miami using special heavy duty flatcars.

Former FEC 0-8-0 #253 is shown enroute to Miami. This view was taken by Gibbons Robichaux in September 1998 at CSX's East Bridge Yard, New Orleans, en route to Jacksonville, Florida, and interchange with the FEC.

—(*Steve Spreckelmeier photo*)

FEC's 150-ton American Brownhoist wrecking crane 3377 remains extant today thanks to Chairman Robert W. Anestis and President John McPherson, who donated the crane and it's accompanying work car to a steam-operated historic railroad. With the assistance of 25-year FEC employee Ray ("Mac") McCall, the 253 Project Restoration Crew has put this venerable and irreplaceable machine back into operating condition.

A native of Missouri, John D. McPherson earned his Masters degree in Management from MIT. With a railroad career stretching back to 1966 and encompassing an ever-widening range of jobs and responsibilities, Mr. McPherson was named President of the Illinois Central in 1998 after having served for five years as that railroad's Senior Vice President of Operations. While leaving the Illinois Central was not easy for him, the excitement and challenge of joining Bob Anestis and the Florida East Coast as President and Chief Operating Officer of Railway was irresistible. He has proven, in two years on the job, to be exactly what the doctor ordered, and he is highly regarded by employees, customers and the public at large.

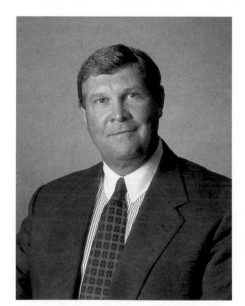

John McPherson, President,
Florida East Coast Railway

Though his predecessors had long grappled with the question of whether or not to deal with Amtrak and the return of passenger train service to the east coast, Mr. McPherson finally decided that Amtrak was simply another customer, and if the right arrangements in regard to operations, track rebuilding, and scheduling could be made, Amtrak would be welcome as an FEC customer. To that end, and after lengthy discussion and negotiations (and the running of two short Amtrak test trains on the east coast), a contract was signed.

To encourage governmental, political and media support, Amtrak, with trains under the direction of that company's Jeff Barker, arranged with the Florida East Coast to operate a round-trip on Monday, June 18, 2001, from Jacksonville to Hialeah Yard, with return the following day. With five-minute station stops in each direction at the proposed "station" cities of St. Augustine,

On June 18 and 19, 2001, Amtrak and the FEC operated a special passenger train to garner support for a re-institution of passenger service over the FEC from Jacksonville to West Palm Beach. Under the direction of Amtrak's Jeff Barker the train stopped in each of the cities slated for stations. Onboard guests included Amtrak and FEC management, personnel and media and political figures at the state and local level whose input and support would be vital in winning approval for the service. Operating Jacksonville-Miami on the 18th, the train, with FEC 442 on the head end (or "point" in railroad jargon), led an Amtrak engine and six cars on the round trip, returning to Jacksonville the following day. In January of 2002, Florida Governor Jeb Bush announced unequivocal state support for the new service, with two trains daily proposed to operate on the route by sometime late in 2004, although construction and infrastructure improvements could delay the service up to two years.

—*(Robert W. Schmorr photo)*

Daytona Beach, Titusville, Melbourne, Cocoa, Vero Beach, Ft. Pierce, and Stuart, the train proved to be nothing short of a smashing success. Political figures from each of the cities were aboard, as well as FEC Vice President of Transportation Charles Lynch and other FEC executives. Amtrak marketing and communications personnel saw to it that all was well, and Mr. Barker did a splendid job discussing the train operation and the route's possibilities. (I served as color commentator and provided historical background along the route.)

Currently, Daytona Beach is the largest U.S. city without rail passenger service, and these trains would remedy that deficiency. If Amtrak is able to convince Congress that passenger service is a necessary and an important part of the overall transportation picture in the greatest country in the world, I am certain we will see passenger trains again operating on the FEC, after an absence dating from July 30, 1968.

Of course, much more has occurred on the FEC: the elimination of work trains; the exchange of crews midway on the 350-mile route so that all engineers and conductors can return to their home terminals daily; the repainting of diesel 406 in the magnificent red and yellow paint scheme, and its renumbering as 2000 to celebrate the millennium. Other FEC engines have received "Operation Life Saver" paint jobs, and of course the four "Centennial" engines celebrating the railroad's first 100 years operate daily, but nothing is as magnificent and as exciting as seeing the 2000 leading a brace of locomotives and a long, fast freight train in the glorious paint scheme of the past.

As I wrote in the original edition of this book, the story of the FEC is now current and must come to a temporary halt. But knowing her the way I do, having come to Miami in 1946, when the railroad was celebrating its 50th Anniversary, and having lived with her and loved her for now 54 years (from the time my dear father, may he rest in peace, began bringing me to Buena Vista Yard, in 1947), I also know that there will, very soon, be more to tell.

Though the FEC will always be the builder, and the backbone, and the freight lifeline of Florida's East Coast—without which both I-95 and US 1 would operate in rush hour traffic condition 24 hours per day, seven days a week—so will she also be, in our hearts as well as in our minds, America's *Speedway to Sunshine*.

HOTEL PONCE DE LEON.
ST. AUGUSTINE FLA.
O·D·SEAVEY ·MANAGER·

"Just arrived at St. Augustine"

St. Augustine
Station in 1905.
The old yards
are on the right,
Flagler Park (not
yet named) is on
the left and the
offices are center.

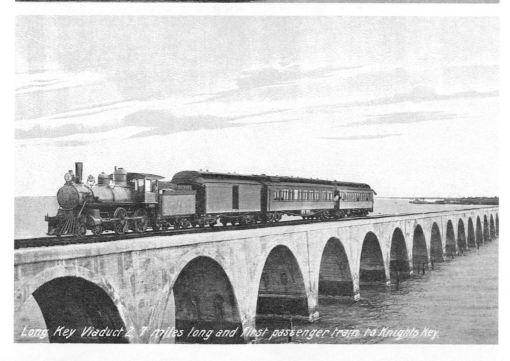

Long Key Viaduct 2.7 miles long and first passenger train to Knights Key.

First passenger
train to Knights
Key, reputed to
be carrying
Flagler.

A standard publicity photograph at Miami.

In 1955 the FEC bought five E9A type locomotives from Electro Motive Division. They were known as 'Cadillacs' by their crews because they were so smooth running and so powerful and they were the 'Queens' of the FEC fleet. In this view taken by Bill Volkmer, 1035 is awaiting the highball at West Palm Beach on July 16, 1960.

#652, a 1750 H.P. road switcher sits at New Smyrna Beach in this Jan. 1961 photo by C.G. Parsons.

SW1200 228 is shown in the transitional color scheme on April 4, 1962, at Jacksonville.

During the strike the FEC operated their passenger train between Jacksonville and Miami, using E7A 1011 and the five E9s. E9A 1034 is shown at New Smyrna Beach, October 8, 1966.

In a transitional view, E7A 1014 is at the Buena Vista roundhouse on September 25, 1960.
—*(Volkmer photo; author's collection)*

FEC SW 233 switches the Rovac Corporation at Rockledge on April 12, 1978.
—*(Bob Selle photo)*

FEC 3377 is a longtime veteran of wrecker service on the railroad and has been assigned to both Hialeah and Buena Vista Yards since the mid 1930s.
—(R. Schmorr)

FEC caboose 812 had been converted from a ventilated express box car. This photograph by the author was taken on December 13, 1969, at Hallandale.

FEC GP40 404 about to leave the Electro Motive Plant at LaGrange, Illinois, in 1971 for delivery to the Florida East Coast. The 400s and the 500s which were GP40s and GP30s, were the first of the 'New Breed' of diesels on the FEC.

#609 in a fresh coat of blue with the yellow nose decoration poses for the photographer in the bright Florida sunshine.

One of the great ironies in the preservation of the steam locomotive by American railroad buffs is that the railroad that saved no steam locomotives itself has had saved by other parties the largest number of steam locomotives of any single engine type of any single railroad. FEC 4-6-2 Pacific type locomotives are now in operation in several parts of the United States. This photo of FEC 80, which was sold to the Savannah and Atlanta and became their 750, was taken at Flowers Branch, Georgia.

For as long as the Florida East Coast had been in existence the Annual Report was printed in the most somber business tones.

Suddenly, for reasons that have long since faded from memory the years 1949-1952 brought a stunning series of full color covers featuring FEC scenes. With the 1953 report came an enlarged format but a black and white photo on the cover, a format which then continued until 1957. To this day no one on the railroad can explain the sudden burst of verdant, tropical color.

**1949 ANNUAL REPORT**
FLORIDA EAST COAST RAILWAY COMPANY

## In Conclusion

In what the author refers to as his most poignant photograph, the memories of early railroad-buffing, the Miami station, the FEC, and the famed passenger train, "City of Miami", spring forth like water from a deep well. "There is something," he recalls, "in the configuration of the brick, the open door, and the time-worn Pullman porter standing loyally at his post in front of two Pullmans painted in Illinois Central colors, but owned by the New York Central and the Chicago and Northwestern respectively, that brings forth memories of my favorite railroad, my favorite station and my favorite passenger train. No other photograph captures the mood so perfectly."

Buena Vista Yard, 1942. Railbuff David P. Morgan is now Editor of Trains Magazine.

# ROMANTIC REMINISCENCES

There are two Florida East Coast Railways, one for the romantic and one for the realist. The former FEC lingers in fading passenger timetables, 8 x 10 publicity glossies, and worn diaries; the latter is a "special situation" within the industry, a Dunkirk for organized labor, and a joy to its customers. The old FEC created an American Riviera, built the "Railroad That Went to Sea," metamorphosed during 1924 and 1925, entered receivership in 1931, and thereafter operated in unreal tranquility as an insolvent super railroad. The new FEC dates from 6 a.m. on January 23, 1963, when organized non-operating employees struck the carrier over its unwillingness to abide by a national settlement on a pay increase of 10.48 cents an hour. From that incident stemmed a single track, streamlinerless, no caboose, two man crew maverick of a railroad with an operating ratio more than 20 points below that of the Class I average.

The old FEC appeals to the heart; the new FEC appeals to the head. Both are recommended for your consideration...

...For the outlander, the central question about Florida East Coast in 1975 is what implication, what lesson, FEC offers to the rest of railroading. Mr. Flagler's FEC—that resort-building, seagoing, boom riding romantic of a railroad—was indigenous to the shore and the state it served. But this new creature is an embarrassment to its industry unless the contention can be proved that FEC is a "special situation"—a special situation which through Brotherhood miscalculation and legal fluke managed to discard 100 mile days, craft divisional lines, and national pay settlements (FEC paid an average wage of $9996 in 1973 vs. a national rail average of $13,627) and in the process turn a hopeless insolvent into one of the safest, most service minded, and best maintained components of the national rail system.

There is no magic in the FEC miracle, no patent on its positives. There is a lot of gut-grinding intestinal fortitude, a lot of loneliness. Finally, conversation with Winfred Thornton brings out a revealing comment on the trials and tribulations dating from 6 a.m., January 23, 1963. He says, without rancor but for the record, that support and sympathy for FEC came not so much from other railroads as from the customers.

...David P. Morgan in February, 1975 "TRAINS" Magazine, Copyright 1975 by Kalmbach Publishing Co., and used with permission.

FEC's Miller Shops were considered the most modern in the south. The steam locomotive craftsmen who plied their trade within these walls were indeed from another era. Miller was capable of doing everything from building freight and passenger cars to rebuilding steam engines. 320, 810, and 809 are all in various stages of repair.

—(Wolfe photo)

Another view of the interior of Miller Shop locomotive erecting building with 818 hoisted to reveal 4-6-2 131 over a repair pit.

—(H. Wolfe)

At Miller Shops, crews built up years and years of service. While the names of the individuals are unknown to us at this time, the scene at the front of the massive locomotive shop depicts a presentation ceremony to a long-time employee. The photograph was taken from the transfer table and shows locomotive 425 with her nose poking out of stall 110.

SW 1200 type switcher 230 is shown at Bowden Roundhouse, sometime in the late 1950s.

The immenseness of Miller Shops is shown in this view of the transfer table and the Locomotive Erecting Shops, though by this time, 1965, this facility had been completely abandoned and only engine 1002 was still being housed at Miller. It was evident that in their heyday, the shops were a beehive of men and machinery and the repair and servicing of the steam power of the FEC made the shops the center of the maintenance activities of the railroad.

FEC officials and train crew pose on the platform at Jacksonville Terminal.

It took a crew of forty-four to operate the "Henry M. Flagler." Add to this the fact that the operating crews (engineer, fireman, brakeman, conductor and trainman) changed staffs three times between Miami and Jacksonville and one has an idea of the cost of operating the seven car streamliner. A total of fifty-four salaries between Miami and Jacksonville.    —(Wolfe photo)

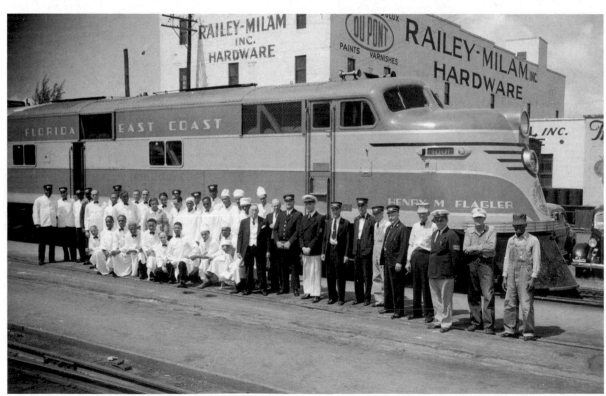

Wolfe never failed to get a smile from the operating crews and he never failed to see to it that they each got a copy of the picture that he took of them following the performance of their duties in setting up a train or an engine for a publicity photo. FEC engineer 'Chuck' Beall is shown on the far left in front of BL2 604.

Former FEC engineer W.H. Howell studies the valve gear and boosters of 4-6-2 153 now in use on the Gold Coast Railroad in South Miami.

Buena Vista Yard was a sprawling yard, shop, repair and storage facility in the heart of Miami. Bounded on the north by N.E. 36th St., the south by N.E. 29th St., the west by North Miami Ave., and the east by N.E. 2nd Ave., the Yard was a throbbing, vital setting for the FECs southern divisions. Laird climbed on one of the towers to photograph Buena Vista during the steam to diesel and heavyweight to lightweight passenger car transition. This view looks southeast with the towers of downtown Miami barely visible in the background.

"Whoops!" The hostler had a little too much steam up and dropped 0-8-0 259 into the turntable pit at Buena Vista Yard in 1947. 259 was soon back on the tracks.

–*(Scotty Laird photo)*

Scotty Laird had a fondness for his 35mm. cameras and during his years with the FEC took 63 black and white photographs recording life as it was at Buena Vista Yard. Through a series of chance meetings, the author was able to purchase the entire collection from Laird, along with several of his slides. Laird committed to film scenes of day-to-day activity at Buena Vista such as no one else apparently thought to do. In the time-honored railroad tradition, a group of railroad shop and engine men pose with their mascot aboard 0-8-0 256.

It was a tradition at Buena Vista Yard for each group of employees to have their picture taken.

By the automobiles, we know it's the late teens or early 20's. By the number on the locomotive (28, sold in 1930) we have almost conclusive proof of the date. But the location. Were that it appeared even near this way today! NE 2nd Avenue and 36th Street looking south today is a cacophony of urban waste, ugly buildings and misproportioned signs.

Standing across the tracks (about 35 years later) and facing in the opposite direction, we are now looking north as two FEC E7A's enter the NE 36th Street — NE 2nd Avenue intersection. Immediately after crossing the street, Buena Vista's throat tracks begin. On the left side of the photograph, the Shell service station, though in a different form, still exists today but the Penton building (historic in its own right) was torn down in 1983.                    *(J. Nelson Collection)*

From its construction in 1912 until the dark day that the FEC strike started in January 1963, the Miami Station saw millions of travellers pass through its venerable portals. Essentially unchanged for the 51 years of its existence, the only additions made were a concrete waiting room, a baggage room and dining car commissary and the Railway Express facilities north of the station. The station itself generated controversy continuously through the years from the 1940s until the end of service, as Miami's civic leaders agitated for a new station. (During the height of the controversy in the late 1950s and early 1960s, the author wrote numerous letters to the two local newspapers—The Miami *Herald* and the Miami *News*—decrying *their* shortsightedness in demanding that private funds from a corporation in trusteeship be spent to construct a new passenger station while tens of millions in public funds were being used to build Miami's new airport.) On August 2nd, 1965, following a decision by the State Supreme Court, the FEC found itself back in the passenger business, and until July 31, 1968, operated America's shortest full service streamliner. (A two car train.) The irony of this resurrection was that, since the FEC had torn down the Miami Station in Sept., Oct. & Nov. 1963, there were no passenger facilities in the city of Miami itself, and the six day a week train originated and terminated at the North Miami depot.

It's any winters' day in the 30s or early 40s and the station is thronged with travellers and well-wishers. The "Gulfstream Express," train 34, was an FEC 'pickup' train. It carried an FEC diner as far as Jacksonville as well as coaches for local points, but the bulk of the train was made up of Pullman cars for numerous points on connecting lines that went as far west as Kansas City and as far north as Grand Rapids, Michigan.

## "FLORIDA EAST COAST"

If from the ice and snow you'd flee
Consult a "guide" for the F.E.C.
Just pack your trunk with summer clothes
And leave the North to storms and snows.

At Jacksonville, you are sure to see
The best looking train marked F.E.C.
You'll find it strictly up to date.
Running "on time;" seldom late.

The scenery? Fine as it can be
All along the line of the F.E.C.
You'll enjoy the trip all the way
From Jacksonville to Biscayne Bay.

And when the Bay at last you see,
Close to the track of the F.E.C.
You'll think of the North so icy cold
Compared to our groves with our fruit of gold.

You'll think right then, with mirthful glee,
"I'm glad I took the F.E.C.
I've missed the snow, the freeze, the sleet,
Nor do I suffer from chilly feet."

And next winter you are sure to be
On some train of the F.E.C.,
Coming down, to weather fine,
To balmy air and bright sunshine.

And then again, one year maybe,
This first-class road, the F.E.C.,
Will to Key West extended be,
When you ride above the sea.

The rails will reach from Key to Key
And travelling on the F.E.C.
Will be in pleasure; best of all,
You'll then come down in early Fall.

Catch fish and sail or hunt maybe,
Along the line of the F.E.C.,
With fine Hotels, all kinds of boats,
Yes, everything that swims or floats.

You'll tell your friends, each one you see,
of the grandest of routes, the F.E.C.
Whose trains are fine and service best,
Between Jacksonville and old Key West.

.... *FEC 1908-09 "EAST COAST OF FLORIDA"*

OUT OF THE SHADOWS INTO THE SUN

Again the

# TROPICS CALL

In its 49th consecutive winter season (1936-37), the "Florida Special," here led by 4-8-2 438 is marking its 5000th trip over the FEC railway. Though the exact Dade County location is unknown due to a dearth of landmarks, the likelihood is that the train is between what is now N.E. 163rd St. and N.E. 183rd St.

# APPENDICES

The first car to Key West. Claude Nolan in a nationally publicized event drove this 1927 LaSalle from Homestead to Key West on the FEC right of way in December, 1926. Nolan, behind the wheel, and his driving partner both wore life preservers for the whole trip.

—(H. Wolfe)

Welcome aboard! What railway crewman would close the doors on such good looking visitors. Miss Florida Special 1963 in her one-piece swimsuit is followed up the steps of FEC 1034 by Miss Florida Special of 1888. The young ladies are two of the hostesses assigned to the 1963 "Florida Special."

# APPENDIX la

ALL TIME LISTING OF PASSENGER TRAIN NAMES USED
ON THE
FLORIDA EAST COAST RAILWAY

Advence East Coast Champion
Advance Florida Special (Note 1)
Advance Havana Special (Note 1)
A.C.L. New York & Florida Special
Biscayne Local
Biscayne, The
Caribbean Mail
Champion, The
Chicago and Florida Limited
Chicago and Florida Special
City of Miami
Daylight Express
Day Local
Dixie Flagler
Dixie Flyer
Dixieland
Dixie Limited
Dixie Palm
East Coast Champion
East Coast Express
East Coast Limited
East Coast Special
Everglades

Everglades Limited
F.E.C. Limited
Flagler Limited
Florida Limited
Florida Special
Floridan (Note 2)
Gulf Stream (Note 3)
Gulf Stream Express
Hastings-Bunnell Local
Havana Mail
Havana Special
Henry M. Flagler
Homestead Local
Homestead Accomodation
Key West Special
Key West Express
Local Express
Miami Accommodation, The
Miami Local
Miami & Nassau Special
Miamian
Miami Express
New Royal Palm

New Smyrna Express
New York & Florida Mail
New York & Florida Special
Night Local
Ormond Special
Oversea Limited
Oversea, The
Palm Beach Limited
Palm Beach & Miami Express
Palm Beach & Miami Limited
Palm Beach & Miami Special
Palm Dixie
Ponce de Leon
Royal Palm
Royal Poinciana (Note 3)
Seaboard Florida Limited
Tamiami Champion
Tamiami, The
Tiresaver, The
Tropical Limited
Vacationer
Weekend Champion
West Indian Limited

Notes:

1. Though the Advance Havana Special has been listed as a separate train, this was not done for the Fast Coast Champion when it operated with "All Coach Section" and "Coach~Pullman Section," nor was it done for the Florida Special when it operated with a "New York Section" and a "Boston Washington Section." For the purposes of this tabulation, individual names ONLY were considered.

2. The first trip of the Floridan was carried in the FEC's December 23, ~923 timetable as "Floridian." The January 1, t924 timetable spelled the name correctly, that is, without the second "I."

3. The Gulf Stream and Royal Poinciana were composite trains; that is, though they may have carried an FEC coach and/or diner, their primary function was the forwarding of through sleepers and/or other equipment from one or more connecting trains. In various years, the Gulf Stream and Royal Poinciana acted as the composite train for the Dixieland (C&EI), Sunchaser (IC) and Jacksonian (later the Florida Arrow on the PRR). Though the four trains were featured in the section of the timetable (for the appropriate year) listing equipment, they were not carried in the schedule portion of the timetable with their own names, with the singular exception of the "Dixieland," after the name was changed from "Dixie Flagler."

Every publicity shot the FEC did—almost to the very end of passenger service— bespoke the refinement and tradition of the Flagler System. The step box is lettered "The Champion!"

—*(Charles & Richard Beall collection)*

The Miami Station is a hubbub of activity just prior to the departure of the "Dixieland" in 1952.

The "Dixie Flagler," successor to the "Henry M. Flagler," a through train in conjunction with the Atlantic Coast Line, Nashville, Chattanooga and St. Louis, Louisville and Nashville and Chicago and Eastern Illinois is northbound over FEC bridge 360.27, six miles north of the downtown Miami passenger station.

An FEC SW type diesel switcher is coupled to the rear of I.C. owned "City of Miami" observation 3300 or 3305. The train was often so long that it had to be loaded on two adjacent tracks and the switcher would couple the rear cars to the forward section of the train.

In the 1920s and 30s Miami was an exciting place to be. The hustle and bustle of a just barely past adolescent metropolis are highly visible in this late 1930s scene looking west on Flagler Street in downtown Miami.

Charles Beall, a longtime FEC engineer, stands at left as "Bay Biscayne" is being readied for "The Tiresaver," a World War II era train. The man on the right is Ed Pelliser.

Below is the special anniversary celebration taking place in 1937 marking the 50th year of the "Florida Special".

230

**APPENDIX 1-b**
**LIST OF TERMINAL CITIES WHICH COULD BE REACHED VIA SLEEPING CAR FROM FEC RAILWAY POINTS SOUTH OF JACKSONVILLE**
**(See Note 1)**

| | | |
|---|---|---|
| Asheville | Colorado Springs | New York |
| Atlanta | Columbus (OH) | Philadelphia |
| Augusta | Denver | Pittsburgh |
| Boston | Detroit | Quebec |
| Buffalo | Grand Rapids | St. Louis |
| Chattanooga | Indianapolis | Springfield (MA) |
| Chicago | Kansas City | Toledo |
| Cincinnati | Louisville | Washington, DC |
| Cleveland | Murray Bay (ONT) | |

Note 1:    Intrastate FEC sleeping car lines are not listed.

# INDIVIDUAL
## VACATION TRIP "B"
### NEW YORK, N. Y. ◆
AND RETURN

I.V.T. No.
B

**ESSENTIAL EXPENSES INCLUDED**

Stamp

Here

When officially stamped the coupons as originally bound into this cover will be honored for the service and accommodations as called for.

General Passenger Agent.

---

**INDIVIDUAL VACATION TRIPS**
Essential Expenses Included
## ONE PERSON

**AUDITOR'S STUB—No Value**
To be forwarded to Auditor of Passenger Accounts in accordance with instructions.
Sold in Connection with Railroad Ticket

I.V.T. No. B

| Form | No. | Expires |
|------|-----|---------|

Amount Collected $

### FLORIDA EAST COAST RAILWAY COMPANY
W. R. Kenan, Jr. and S. M. Loftin, Receivers

---

**INDIVIDUAL VACATION TRIPS**
Essential Expenses Included
## ONE PERSON

**AGENT'S STUB**
To be retained by Agent
Sold in Connection with Railroad Ticket

I.V.T. No. B

| Form | No. | Expires |
|------|-----|---------|

Amount Collected $

### FLORIDA EAST COAST RAILWAY COMPANY
W. R. Kenan, Jr. and S. M. Loftin, Receivers

---

**INDIVIDUAL VACATION TRIPS**
Essential Expenses Included
## ONE PERSON

### NEW YORK CITY
Terminal System, Inc.

**TAXICAB TRANSFER**
PENNSYLVANIA STATION
to
HOTEL LINCOLN

I.V.T. No. B

When honored to the satisfaction of the original purchaser and mailed with monthly statement, this coupon is redeemable by
### FLORIDA EAST COAST RAILWAY COMPANY
W. R. Kenan, Jr. and S. M. Loftin, Receivers

---

**INDIVIDUAL VACATION TRIPS**
Essential Expenses Included
## ONE PERSON

### NEW YORK CITY
Hotel Accommodations—5 Nights
**HOTEL LINCOLN**
(Present this Coupon when you register)
Value of this coupon is based on the reduction in price for two (2) persons to a room. For single occupancy the rate is $1.00 per day, additional to be paid when registering.

I.V.T. No. B

When honored to the satisfaction of the original purchaser and mailed with monthly statement, this coupon is redeemable by
### FLORIDA EAST COAST RAILWAY COMPANY
W. R. Kenan, Jr. and S. M. Loftin, Receivers

---

**INDIVIDUAL VACATION TRIPS**
Essential Expenses Included
## ONE PERSON

### NEW YORK CITY
Rockefeller Center, Inc.

**Observation Roofs—Rockefeller Center**
*Inquire at Hotel Desk*

I.V.T. No. B

When honored to the satisfaction of the original purchaser and mailed with monthly statement, this coupon is redeemable by
### FLORIDA EAST COAST RAILWAY COMPANY
W. R. Kenan, Jr. and S. M. Loftin, Receivers

---

**INDIVIDUAL VACATION TRIPS**
Essential Expenses Included
## ONE PERSON

### NEW YORK CITY
Gray Line Motor Tours, Inc.

**TOUR NO. 1**
"Seeing Greater New York"
*Make reservation at Hotel Desk*

I.V.T. No. B

When honored to the satisfaction of the original purchaser and mailed with monthly statement, this coupon is redeemable by
### FLORIDA EAST COAST RAILWAY COMPANY
W. R. Kenan, Jr., and S. M. Loftin, Receivers

---

**INDIVIDUAL VACATION TRIPS**
Essential Expenses Included
## ONE PERSON

### NEW YORK CITY
National Broadcasting Company, Inc.

**Radio City N. B. C. Studio Tour**
*Inquire at Hotel Desk*

I.V.T. No. B

When honored to the satisfaction of the original purchaser and mailed with monthly statement, this coupon is redeemable by
### FLORIDA EAST COAST RAILWAY COMPANY
W. R. Kenan, Jr. and S. M. Loftin, Receivers

---

**INDIVIDUAL VACATION TRIPS**
Essential Expenses Included
## ONE PERSON

### NEW YORK CITY
Terminal System, Inc.

**TAXICAB TRANSFER**
HOTEL LINCOLN
to
PENNSYLVANIA STATION

I.V.T. No. B

When honored to the satisfaction of the original purchaser and mailed with monthly statement, this coupon is redeemable by
### FLORIDA EAST COAST RAILWAY COMPANY
W. R. Kenan, Jr. and S. M. Loftin, Receivers

---

Any uncertainty as to accommodations embraced will be clarified by referring to the Folder advertising these Vacation Trips. Reference should be made to information shown in connection with Trip of corresponding number.

When days, or parts of days are not assigned, suggestions as to interesting places to visit are mentioned in the Folder.

This combination trip is planned as a convenience to our patrons and is offered at a reduction from the regular charges in consideration of which the purchaser agrees to make use of the service and accommodations in the order provided by the coupons as incorporated and within the time limit of the Railroad Ticket in connection with which it is sold.

Purchaser _____

Permanent
Address _____

| Form | Number | Expires |
|------|--------|---------|

Sold in Connection
With Railroad Ticket _____

## APPENDIX 1-c
## FEC RAILWAY GENERAL PASSENGER AGENTS
### 1895—1963

*Joseph Richardson* From September, 1895 until sometime between January 7, 1896 and February 22, 1897. Richardson was with the predecessor(s) including the JStA&IR but due to dearth of early records, little is known of his age or the reasons for his leaving the FEC.

*J. D. Rahner* Rahner's name appears for the first time on the February 22, 1897 timetable as Assistant G.P.A., but with no G.P.A. listed, so it can reasonably be assumed he was "head man" in the passenger department from then until just before January of 1909. Rahner is then listed as G.P.A. from January 5, 1909 until November 1, 1939.

Rahner was a "Southern gentleman," ramrod straight, highly respected by all he dealt with. According to H.K. North, Rahner never joked or smiled, but was totally honest and scrupulouly fair with all. He retired after the inauguration of the streamliners on December 2 and 3, 1939.

*George L. Oliver* Oliver was Assistant G.P.A. and was listed as G.P.A. for the first time on December 16, 1939. Oliver was later made Passenger Traffic Manager and his name appears in FEC timetables for the final time on March 1, 1960. He retired April 1, 1960.

Like Rahner, Oliver was highly thought of by his associates, both superiors and subordinates. Correspondence in the author's files tends to bear out this assessment. He retired nine months before the Trusteeship ended.

*R.L. Baker* Baker's name is listed as G.P.A. from April 25, 1960 until the last pre-strike FEC timetable, January 12, 1962.

Baker had been the chief clerk in the passenger department for many years, and knew the workings of the department "as well as anyone," according to several sources.

A NOTE ON FEC PASSENGER TRAIN ON-BOARD SERVICE:
As with almost all other railroads, passenger trainmen were under the jurisdiction of the operating department, rather than the passenger department, as they should have been. Most instances of rudeness, discourtesy to passengers and aberrant behavior by passenger trainmen can be linked to the belief of many (not most) of the passenger trainmen that their union could protect them from even minimal discipline. Had the passenger department been responsibile for the training and discipline of the operating crews, it is likely that the attitudes of passenger trainmen would have been much different.

# APPENDIX 2

## COMPLETE LIST OF FLORIDA EAST COAST RAILWAY COMPANY LOCOMOTIVES SINCE THE RAILWAY WAS BUILT

## STEAM LOCOMOTIVES

| Loco. Nº (Name) | Wheel Arrangement | Date Acquired | Builder | Builder's Nº | Date of Disposition | Information |
|---|---|---|---|---|---|---|
| SERGEANT | 4-4-0 | 1883 | Unknown | Unknown | 1898 | Given Number #1, date not known, sold to Florida Southern Railroad |
| #1 | 4-4-0 | 11-1886 | Unknown | Unknown | 9-1918 | Sold to E.T. Roux and Sons |
| ASTOR | 4-4-0 | Unknown | Unknown | Unknown | 1892 | Given Number #2, date not known; changed to #10 in 1894, sold to L.W. Johnson |
| #2 | 4-4-0 | Unknown | Unknown | Unknown | 1889 | Sold to Florida Southern Railway |
| #2 | 4-4-0 | 11-1888 | Unknown | Unknown | 12-1918 | Sold to Getman Commercial Company |
| ? | 4-4-0 | Unknown | Unknown | Unknown | 1894 | Sold to S.V. White |
| TOMOKA | 4-4-0 | Unknown | Unknown | Unknown | 1890 | Sold to Allen Works |
| LANCIER | 4-4-0 | Unknown | Unknown | Unknown | 1892 | Given Number #3, date not known; changed to #11, sold to L.W. Johnson |
| #3 | 4-4-0 | 11-1888 | Unknown | Unknown | 9-1916 | Sold to Ackerman and Ellis. |
| #4 | 4-4-0 | 1894 | Unknown | Unknown | 1899 | Changed to #18, sold to J.T. & R. Boone |
| #4 | 4-4-0 | 1886 | Baldwin (BLW) | Unknown | 1889 | Sold to Florida Southern Railway |
| #4 | 4-4-0 | 1887 | Unknown | Unknown | 1889 | Sold to Florida Southern Railway |
| #4 | 4-4-0 | 11-1888 | Unknown | Unknown | 4-1918 | Sold to R.T. Roux and Sons |
| #5 | 4-4-0 | 1887 | Baldwin (BLW) | Unknown | 1889 | Sold to Florida Southern Railway |
| #5 | 4-4-0 | 1889 | Unknown | Unknown | 7-1903 | Changed to #9, sold to Cashen and McGuire |
| #5 | 4-4-0 | 12-1889 | Unknown | Unknown | 2-1918 | Sold to E.W. Bond Company |
| #6 | 4-4-0 | Unknown | Unknown | Unknown | 3-1889 | Scrapped |
| #6 | 4-4-0 | 1-1889 | Schdy | Unknown | 1-1924 | Sold to E.W. Bond Company |
| #7 | 4-4-0 | 3-1889 | Unknown | Unknown | 3-1889 | Second hand from Pennsylvania Railroad |
| #7 | 4-4-0 | 1-1889 | Schdy | Unknown | 1-1924 | Sold to Ojus Rock Company. Note: A Secondary source indicates that this locomotive was sold in 1918 to a small sawmill company in South Florida, later to Naranga Rock Co. It was retired in 1924 and put on display at Naranga. It was built as a coal burner, changed to oil in 1916, then to wood in 1918 and back to oil in 1920. |
| #8 | 4-4-0 | 12-1894 | Unknown | Unknown | 8-1914 | Sold to D.J. Coughlin. |
| #9 | – | – | – | – | – | See #5 |
| #10 | 4-4-0 | 1-1892 | Unknown | Unknown | 8-1916 | Sold to K.W. Extension sub-contractor for $3000 and then sold to Munson Steamship Line |
| #11 | 4-4-0 | 1-1892 | Unknown | Unknown | 8-1916 | Sold to K.W. Extension sub-contractor for $3000 and then sold to Domindo Nazabal |
| #12 | 4-4-0 | 1-1892 | Unknown | Unknown | 5-1914 | Sold to K.W. Extension sub-contractor for $3000 and then sold to Drake Lumber Company |
| #13 | 4-4-0 | Unknown | Unknown | Unknown | Unknown | Sold |
| #13 | 4-4-0 | 1892 | Unknown | Unknown | 12-1924 | Changed to #16; Dismantled |
| #14 | 4-4-0 | 11-1892 | Unknown | Unknown | 6-1920 | Sold to Savannah Creosoting Company |
| #15 | 4-4-0 | 11-1892 | Unknown | Unknown | 2-1925 | Dismantled |
| #16 | – | – | – | – | – | See #13 |
| #16 | 4-4-0 | 1-1893 | Unknown | Unknown | 1-1916 | Changed to #18 |
| #17 | 4-4-0 | 1-1893 | Unknown | Unknown | 1-1916 | Sold to South Georgia Railway |
| #18 | – | 1892 | – | – | – | Changed to #19 after original #19 was sold |
| #18 | – | – | – | – | – | See #4 |
| #18 | – | – | – | – | – | See #16 |

| Loco. N° (Name) | Wheel Arrangement | Date Acquired | Builder | Builder's N° | Date of Disposition | Information |
|---|---|---|---|---|---|---|
| #19 | 4-4-0 | 1-1893 | Unknown | Unknown | 2-1906 | Sold to R.H. Haney |
| #19 | 4-4-0 | 1892 | Unknown | Unknown | 7-1917 | Sold to Warner Sugar Refining Co., Cuba |
| #19 | – | – | – | – | – | See #17 |
| #20 | 4-4-0 | 1-1893 | Unknown | Unknown | 7-1917 | Sold to Warner Sugar Refining Co., Cuba |
| #21 | 4-4-0 | 11-1893 | Unknown | Unknown | 5-1920 | Sold to Southern Phosphate Company |
| #22 | 4-4-0 | 11-1893 | Unknown | Unknown | 1-1925 | Dismantled |
| #23 | 4-4-0 | 11-1893 | Unknown | Unknown | 7-1917 | Sold to Warner Sugar Refining Co., Cuba |
| #24 | 4-4-0 | 11-1893 | Unknown | Unknown | 8-1917 | Sold to American Trading Company |
| #25 | 4-4-0 | 11-1893 | Unknown | Unknown | 2-1913 | Destroyed in wreck Feb. 16, 1913 and written out of accounts |
| #26 | 4-4-0 | 11-1893 | Unknown | Unknown | 11-1919 | Sold to Export Phosphate Company |
| #27 | 4-4-0 | 11-1893 | Unknown | Unknown | 5-1918 | Sold to Taylor County Lumber Co. |
| #28 | 4-6-0 | 11-1897 | Unknown | Unknown | 9-1930 | Sold to Walter-Wallingford Co. for Scrap |
| #29 | 4-6-0 | 11-1897 | Unknown | Unknown | 1-1930 | Sold to Walter-Wallingford Co. for Scrap |
| #30 | 4-6-0 | 11-1897 | Unknown | Unknown | 1-1930 | Sold to Florida Iron and Metal Co. |
| #31 | 4-6-0 | 11-1897 | Unknown | Unknown | 5-1926 | Sold to Kershaw Construction Co. |
| #32 | 4-6-0 | 11-1897 | Unknown | Unknown | 5-1927 | Dismantled |
| #33 | 4-6-0 | 1-1900 | Unknown | Unknown | 5-1926 | Sold to Kershaw Construction Co. |
| #34 | 4-6-0 | 1-1900 | Unknown | Unknown | 6-1926 | Sold to Kershaw Construction Co. |
| #35 | 4-6-0 | 1-1900 | Unknown | Unknown | 9-1930 | Sold to Walter-Wallingford Co. for Scrap |
| #36 | 4-6-0 | 1-1900 | Unknown | Unknown | 11-1925 | Dismantled |
| #37 | 4-6-0 | 1-1900 | Unknown | Unknown | 8-1925 | Dismantled |
| #38 | 4-6-0 | 1-1900 | Unknown | Unknown | 3-1925 | Sold to Walter-Wallingford Co. for Scrap |
| #39 | 4-6-0 | 1-1900 | Unknown | Unknown | 8-1934 | Sold to Osceola Cypress Co. |
| #40 | 4-6-0 | 5-1902 | Baldwin (BLW) | Unknown | 2-1925 | Sold to Drake Lumber Co. |
| #41 | 4-6-0 | 5-1902 | Baldwin (BLW) | Unknown | 9-1930 | Sold to Walter-Wallingford Co. for Scrap |
| #42 | 4-6-0 | 5-1902 | Baldwin (BLW) | Unknown | 2-1925 | Sold to Sutton Bros. |
| #43 | 4-6-0 | 5-1902 | Baldwin (BLW) | Unknown | 9-1930 | Sold to Walter-Wallingford Co. for Scrap |
| #44 | 4-6-0 | 5-1902 | Baldwin (BLW) | Unknown | 4-1925 | Sold to Donohoo Construction Co. |
| #45 | 4-4-2 | 1-1904 | Schdy | 28412 | 9-1930 | Sold to Walter-Wallingford Co. for Scrap |
| #46 | 4-4-2 | 1-1904 | Schdy | 28413 | 9-1930 | Sold to Walter-Wallingford Co. for Scrap |
| #47 | 4-4-2 | 1-1904 | Schdy | 28414 | 11-1925 | Dismantled |
| #48 | 4-4-2 | 1-1904 | Schdy | 28415 | 11-1925 | Dismantled |
| #49 | 4-4-2 | 1-1904 | Schdy | 28416 | 11-1925 | Dismantled |
| #50 | 4-4-2 | 1-1904 | Schdy | 28417 | 11-1925 | Dismantled |
| #51 | 4-4-2 | 1-1904 | Schdy | 28418 | 9-1930 | Sold to Walter-Wallingford Co. for Scrap |
| #52 | 4-4-2 | 1-1904 | Schdy | 28419 | 11-1925 | Dismantled |
| #53 | 4-4-2 | 1-1904 | Schdy | 28420 | 11-1925 | Dismantled |
| #54 | 4-4-2 | 1-1904 | Schdy | 28421 | 7-1923 | Destroyed by Explosion |
| #55 | 4-4-2 | 3-1905 | Schdy | 31240 | 11-1925 | Dismantled |
| #56 | 4-4-2 | 3-1905 | Schdy | 31241 | 9-1930 | Sold to Walter-Wallingford Co. for Scrap |
| #57 | 4-4-2 | 3-1905 | Schdy | 31242 | 11-1925 | Dismantled |
| #58 | 4-4-2 | 3-1905 | Schdy | 31243 | 9-1930 | Sold to Walter-Wallingford Co. for Scrap |
| #59 | 4-4-2 | 3-1905 | Schdy | 31244 | 9-1930 | Sold to Walter-Wallingford Co. for Scrap |

| Loco. N° (Name) | Wheel Arrangement | Date Acquired | Builder | Builder's N° | Date of Disposition | Information |
|---|---|---|---|---|---|---|
| #60 | 4-4-2 | 12-1905 | Schdy | 39047 | 11-1925 | Dismantled |
| #61 | 4-4-2 | 12-1905 | Schdy | 39048 | 9-1930 | Sold to Walter-Wallingford Co. for Scrap |
| #62 | 4-4-2 | 12-1905 | Schdy | 39049 | 9-1930 | Sold to Walter-Wallingford Co. for Scrap |
| #63 | 4-4-2 | 12-1905 | Schdy | 39050 | 9-1930 | Sold to Walter-Wallingford Co. for Scrap |
| #64 | 4-4-2 | 12-1905 | Schdy | 39051 | 6-1925 | Sold to Kershaw Construction Co. |
| #65 | 4-6-2 | 12-1907 | Schdy | 44605 | 6-1929 | Sold to Bond-Booker Lumber Co (9/30), recovered and sold to Southern Sugar Co 1938 their #65 |
| #66 | 4-6-2 | 12-1907 | Schdy | 44606 | 9-1930 | Sold to Walter-Wallingford Co. for Scrap |
| #67 | 4-6-2 | 12-1907 | Schdy | 44607 | 9-1930 | Sold to Walter-Wallingford Co. for Scrap |
| #68 | 4-6-2 | 12-1907 | Schdy | 44608 | 9-1930 | Sold to Walter-Wallingford Co. for Scrap |
| #69 | 4-6-2 | 12-1907 | Schdy | 44609 | 8-1930 | Sold to Walter-Wallingford Co., delivered to Georgia Northern Railway |
| #70 | 4-6-2 | 12-1907 | Schdy | 44610 | 9-1930 | Sold to Walter-Wallingford Co. for Scrap |
| #71 | 4-6-2 | 12-1907 | Schdy | 44611 | 9-1930 | Sold to Walter-Wallingford Co. for Scrap |
| #72 | 4-6-2 | 12-1907 | Schdy | 44612 | 9-1930 | Sold to Walter-Wallingford Co. for Scrap |
| #73 | 4-6-2 | 12-1907 | Schdy | 44613 | 9-1930 | Sold to Walter-Wallingford Co. for Scrap |
| #74 | 4-6-2 | 12-1907 | Schdy | 44614 | 9-1930 | Sold to Walter-Wallingford Co. for Scrap |
| #75 | 0-6-0 | 12-1907 | Schdy | 44615 | — | Changed to #201 |
| #76 | 0-6-0 | 12-1907 | Schdy | 44616 | — | Changed to #202 |
| #77 | 4-6-2 | 1-1910 | Schdy | 46564 | 9-1930 | Sold to Walter-Wallingford Co. for Scrap |
| #78 | 4-6-2 | 1-1910 | Schdy | 46565 | 9-1930 | Sold to Walter-Wallingford Co. for Scrap |
| #79 | 4-6-2 | 1-1910 | Schdy | 46566 | 6-1925 | Sold to Walter-Wallingford Co. for Scrap |
| #80 | 4-6-2 | 1-1910 | Schdy | 46567 | 10-1935 | Sold to Savannah and Atlanta Railway #750, then National Railroad Historical Society, 1962 |
| #81 | 4-6-2 | 1-1910 | Schdy | 46568 | 9-1930 | Sold to Walter-Wallingford Co. for Scrap |
| #82 | 4-6-2 | 1-1910 | Schdy | 46569 | 9-1930 | Sold to Walter-Wallingford Co. for Scrap |
| #83 | 4-6-2 | 3-1911 | Schdy | 49921 | 9-1930 | Sold to Walter-Wallingford Co. for Scrap |
| #84 | 4-6-2 | 3-1911 | Schdy | 49922 | 9-1930 | Sold to Walter-Wallingford Co. for Scrap |
| #85 | 4-6-2 | 3-1911 | Schdy | 49923 | 11-1925 | Destroyed by explosion |
| #86 | 4-6-2 | 3-1911 | Schdy | 49924 | 9-1930 | Sold to Walter-Wallingford Co. for Scrap |
| #87 | 4-6-2 | 3-1911 | Schdy | 49925 | 9-1930 | Sold to Walter-Wallingford Co. for Scrap |
| #88 | 4-6-2 | 5-1911 | Schdy | 50133 | 9-1930 | Sold to Walter-Wallingford Co. for Scrap |
| #89 | 4-6-2 | 5-1911 | Schdy | 50134 | 9-1930 | Sold to Walter-Wallingford Co. for Scrap |
| #90 | 4-6-2 | 5-1911 | Schdy | 50135 | 9-1930 | Sold to Walter-Wallingford Co. for Scrap |
| #91 | 4-6-2 | 5-1911 | Schdy | 50136 | 9-1930 | Sold to Walter-Wallingford Co. for Scrap |
| #92 | 4-6-2 | 5-1911 | Schdy | 50137 | 9-1930 | Sold to Walter-Wallingford Co. for Scrap |
| #93 | 4-6-2 | 9-1911 | Schdy | 50138 | 9-1930 | Sold to Walter-Wallingford Co. for Scrap |
| #94 | 4-6-2 | 9-1911 | Schdy | 50139 | 9-1930 | Sold to Walter-Wallingford Co. for Scrap |
| #95 | 4-6-2 | 9-1911 | Schdy | 50140 | 9-1930 | Sold to Walter-Wallingford Co. for Scrap |
| #96 | 4-6-2 | 9-1911 | Schdy | 50141 | 7-1941 | Sold to Georgia and Florida Railroad #500; retired 10/51 |
| #97 | 4-6-2 | 9-1911 | Schdy | 50142 | 9-1930 | Sold to Walter-Wallingford Co. for Scrap |
| #98 | 4-6-2 | 9-1911 | Schdy | 50143 | 2-1931 | Sold to Southern Sugar Co. |
| #99 | 4-6-2 | 9-1911 | Schdy | 50144 | 9-1930 | Sold to Walter-Wallingford Co. for Scrap |
| #100 | 4-6-2 | 9-1911 | Schdy | 50145 | 9-1930 | Sold to Walter-Wallingford Co. for Scrap |
| #101 | 4-6-2 | 9-1911 | Schdy | 50146 | 6-1930 | Sold to Atlanta, Birmingham and Coast Railroad #71; then to Atlantic Coast Line 7071, scrapped 8/51 |
| #102 | 4-6-2 | 9-1911 | Schdy | 50147 | 9-1930 | Sold to Walter-Wallingford Co. for Scrap |

| Loco. N° (Name) | Wheel Arrangement | Date Acquired | Builder | Builder's N° | Date of Disposition | Information |
|---|---|---|---|---|---|---|
| #103 | 4-6-2 | 8-1913 | Schdy | 53892 | 6-1930 | Sold to Atlanta, Birmingham and Coast Railroad #72; then to Atlantic Coast Line 7072, Scrapped 11/55 |
| #104 | 4-6-2 | 8-1913 | Schdy | 53893 | 9-1930 | Sold to Walter-Wallingford Co. for Scrap |
| #105 | 4-6-2 | 8-1913 | Schdy | 53894 | 6-1930 | Sold to Atlanta , Birmingham and Coast Railroad #73; then to Atlantic Coast Line 7073, Scrapped 6/52 |
| #106 | 4-6-2 | 8-1913 | Schdy | 53895 | 6-1930 | Sold to Walter-Wallingford Co. for Scrap |
| #107 | 4-6-2 | 8-1913 | Schdy | 53896 | 6-1930 | Sold to Walter-Wallingford Co. for Scrap |
| #108 | 4-6-2 | 8-1913 | Schdy | 53897 | 6-1930 | Sold to Atlanta, Birmingham and Coast Railroad #74 — scrapped 1946 |
| #109 | 4-6-2 | 8-1913 | Schdy | 53898 | 9-1930 | Sold to Louisiana and Arkansas #309, scrapped 1/39 |
| #110 | 4-6-2 | 8-1913 | Schdy | 53890 | 6-1930 | Sold to Atlanta, Birmingham and Coast Railroad #75, then to Atlantic Coast Line 7075, scrapped 1/50 |
| #111 | 4-6-2 | 8-1913 | Schdy | 53891 | 6-1930 | Sold to Atlanta, Birmingham and Coast Railroad #76, then Ap. Nor. #301 |
| #112 | 4-6-2 | 8-1913 | Schdy | 53892 | 6-1930 | Sold to Atlanta, Birmingham and Coast Railroad #77, then Atlantic Coast Line 7077, scrapped 8/46 |
| #113 | 4-6-2 | 8-1913 | Schdy | 53902 | 9-1930 | Sold to Walter-Wallingford Co. for scrap; sold to U.S. Sugar Corp. #113 in 1938 |
| #114 | 4-6-2 | 8-1913 | Schdy | 53903 | 9-1930 | Sold to Walter-Wallingford Co. for Scrap |
| #115 | 4-6-2 | 1-1914 | Schdy | 53904 | 6-1930 | Sold to Atlanta, Birmingham and Coast Railroad #78, then to Ap. Nor. #300, then GC&L 10/39 |
| #116 | 4-6-2 | 1-1914 | Schdy | 53905 | 9-1930 | Sold to Promoters for staged collision at Hialeah (2/31) |
| #117 | 4-6-2 | 1-1914 | Schdy | 53906 | 6-1930 | Sold to Atlanta, Birmingham and Coast Railroad #79 — Used on Dixie Flyer — rebuilt streamlined |
| #118 | 4-6-2 | 1-1914 | Schdy | 53907 | 6-1930 | Sold to Atlanta, Birmingham and Coast Railroad #80, then to Atlantic Coast Line 7080, scrapped 12/51 |
| #119 | 4-6-2 | 1-1914 | Schdy | 53908 | 6-1930 | Sold to Atlanta, Birmingham and Coast Railroad #81, then to Atlantic Coast Line 7081, scrapped 12/54 |
| #120 | 4-6-2 | 1-1914 | Schdy | 53909 | 6-1930 | Sold to Atlanta, Birmingham and Coast Railroad #82, then to Atlantic Coast Line 7082, scrapped 9/46 |
| #121 | 4-6-2 | 1-1914 | Schdy | 53910 | 6-1930 | Sold to Atlanta, Birmingham and Coast Railroad #83, then to Atlantic Coast Line 7083, scrapped 1/50 |
| #122 | 4-6-2 | 1-1914 | Schdy | 53911 | 6-1930 | Sold to Atlanta, Birmingham and Coast Railroad #84, then to Atlantic Coast Line 7084, scrapped 6/50 |
| #123 | 4-6-2 | 1-1914 | Schdy | 53912 | 6-1930 | Sold to Atlanta, Birmingham and Coast Railroad #85, then to Atlantic Coast Line 7085, scrapped 5/48 |
| #124 | 4-6-2 | 1-1914 | Schdy | 53913 | 9-1930 | Sold to promoters for staged collision at Hialeah (2/31) |
| #125 | 4-6-2 | 1-1914 | Schdy | 53914 | 6-1930 | Sold to Atlanta, Birmingham and Coast Railroad #86, then to Atlantic Coast Line 7086, scrapped 7/50 |
| #126 | 4-6-2 | 1-1914 | Schdy | 53915 | 9-1930 | Sold to Walter-Wallingford Co. for Scrap |
| #127 | 4-6-2 | 10-1917 | Schdy | 57541 | 7-1934 | Sold to Georgia and Florida Railway #501, Retired 10/51 |
| #128 | 4-6-2 | 10-1917 | Schdy | 57542 | 7-1934 | Sold to Georgia and Florida Railway #502, Retired 10/51 |
| #129 | 4-6-2 | 10-1917 | Schdy | 57543 | 5-1935 | Sold to Georgia and Florida Railway #503, Retired 10/51 |
| #130 | 4-6-2 | 10-1917 | Schdy | 57544 | 10-1936 | Sold to Georgia Northern #130 |
| #131 | 4-6-2 | 10-1917 | Schdy | 57545 | 10-1935 | Sold to Atlantic and St. Andrews Bay Railway #131, scrapped 5/48 |
| #132 | 4-6-2 | 10-1917 | Schdy | 57546 | 2-1935 | Sold to Georgia and Florida Railway #504, Retired 10/51 |
| #133 | 4-6-2 | 10-1917 | Schdy | 57547 | 9-1934 | Sold to Georgia and Florida Railway #505, Retired 10/51 |
| #134 | 4-6-2 | 10-1917 | Schdy | 57548 | 2-1935 | Sold to Georgia and Florida Railway #506, Retired 10/51 |
| #135 | 4-6-2 | 10-1917 | Schdy | 57549 | 1-1937 | Sold to Georgia and Florida Railway #507, Retired 5/55 |
| #136 | 4-6-2 | 10-1917 | Schdy | 57550 | 10-1936 | Sold to Savannah and Atlantic Railway (#752) |
| #137 | 0-6-0 | 10-1918 | Schdy | 57551 | — | Renumbered 203 |
| #138 | 0-6-0 | 10-1918 | Schdy | 57552 | — | Renumbered 204 |
| #139 | 0-6-0 | 6-1920 | Schdy | 61022 | — | Renumbered 205 |
| #140 | 0-6-0 | 6-1920 | Schdy | 61023 | — | Renumbered 206 |
| #141 | 4-6-2 | 5-1920 | Richmond | 61762 | 10-1935 | Sold to Savannah and Atlantic Railway #751 |
| #142 | 4-6-2 | 5-1920 | Richmond | 61763 | 5-1934 | Sold to Atlanta and St. Andrews Bay Railway #142, scrapped 5/48 |
| #143 | 4-6-2 | 5-1920 | Richmond | 61764 | 5-1934 | Sold to Atlanta and St. Andrews Bay Railway #143, then to Columbia, Newberry and Laurens Railroad |
| #144 | 4-6-2 | 5-1920 | Richmond | 61765 | 12-1934 | Sold to Georgia & Florida Railway #508, Retired 10/55 |
| #145 | 4-6-2 | 5-1920 | Richmond | 61766 | 2-1935 | Sold to Atlanta & St. Andrews Bay Railway |

| Loco. N° (Name) | Wheel Arrangement | Date Acquired | Builder | Builder's N° | Date of Disposition | Information |
|---|---|---|---|---|---|---|
| #146 | 4-6-2 | 5-1920 | Richmond | 61767 | 5-1934 | Sold to Atlanta & St. Andrews Bay Railway |
| #147 | 4-6-2 | 6-1920 | Richmond | 61768 | 6-1952 | Sold to Bailes-Sty Construction Co. |
| #148 | 4-6-2 | 6-1920 | Richmond | 61769 | 6-1952 | Sold to U.S. Sugar Co. |
| #149 | 4-6-2 | 6-1920 | Richmond | 61770 | 7-1941 | Sold to Georgia and Florida Railway |
| #150 | 4-6-2 | 6-1920 | Richmond | 61771 | 11-1942 | Sold to Apalachicola Northern Railroad |
| #151 | 4-6-2 | 7-1922 | Schdy | 63260 | 7-1941 | Sold to Apalachicola Northern Railroad |
| #152 | 4-6-2 | 7-1922 | Schdy | 63261 | 7-1941 | Sold to Apalachicola Northern Railroad |
| #153 | 4-6-2 | 7-1922 | Schdy | 63262 | 1-1940 | Sold to U.S. Sugar Co. |
| #154 | 4-6-2 | 7-1922 | Schdy | 63263 | 1-1935 | Sold to Atlanta and St. Andrews Bay Railway |
| #155 | 4-6-2 | 7-1922 | Schdy | 63264 | 11-1942 | Sold to Apalachicola Northern Railroad |
| #156 | 4-6-2 | 7-1922 | Schdy | 63265 | 7-1941 | Sold to Georgia and Florida Railway |
| #157 | 4-6-2 | 7-1922 | Schdy | 63266 | 12-1941 | Sold to Columbia, Newberry and Laurens Railroad |
| #201 | 0-6-0 | 12-1907 | Schdy | 44615 | 4-1916 | Sold to E.P. Maule, Sold to Georgia Car & Loco Co. 12/36 |
| #202 | 0-6-0 | 12-1907 | Schdy | 44616 | 4-1916 | Sold to E.P. Maule, Sold to Georgia Car & Loco Co. 12/36 |
| #203 | 0-6-0 | 10-1918 | Schdy | 57551 | 5-1923 | Sold to Georgia and Florida Railway #501, Retired 10/51 |
| #204 | 0-6-0 | 10-1918 | Schdy | 57552 | 5-1923 | Sold to U.S. Sugar Co. #502 |
| #205 | 0-6-0 | 6-1920 | Schdy | 61022 | 5-1923 | Sold to Birmingham Rail and Loco Co. |
| #206 | 0-6-0 | 6-1920 | Schdy | 61023 | 9-1934 | Sold to City of Jacksonville (Docks) |
| #207 | 0-6-0 | 7-1922 | Schdy | Unknown | 7-1934 | Sold to Georgia and Florida Railway #28, Scrapped 1/46 |
| #208 | 0-6-0 | 7-1922 | Schdy | Unknown | 5-1934 | Sold to Atlanta and St. Andrews Bay Railway #208, Scrapped 1/39 |
| #209 | 0-6-0 | 7-1922 | Schdy | Unknown | 6-1934 | Sold to Birmingham Rail and Loco Co. |
| #210 | 0-6-0 | 2-1924 | Richmond | 65174 | 12-1952 | Sold to West India Fruit and Steamship Co. |
| #211 | 0-6-0 | 2-1924 | Richmond | 65175 | 7-1941 | Sold to Georgia and Florida Railway |
| #212 | 0-6-0 | 2-1924 | Richmond | 65176 | 7-1941 | Sold to Georgia and Florida Railway |
| #213 | 0-6-0 | 2-1924 | Richmond | 65177 | 7-1941 | Sold to Georgia and Florida Railway |
| #214 | 0-6-0 | 2-1924 | Richmond | 65178 | 7-1941 | Sold to Georgia and Florida Railway |
| #158 | 0-6-0 | 6-1922 | Schdy | 63267 | — | Renumbered 207 |
| #159 | 0-6-0 | 6-1922 | Schdy | 63268 | — | Renumbered 208 |
| #160 | 0-6-0 | 6-1922 | Schdy | 63269 | — | Renumbered 209 |
| #251 | 0-8-0 | 8-1924 | Richmond | 65768 | 5-1936 | Sold to Louisiana and Arkansas Railway #251 then to Louisiana Eastern Railway #18 |
| #252 | 0-8-0 | 8-1924 | Richmond | 65769 | 5-1936 | Sold to Louisiana and Arkansas Railway |
| #253 | 0-8-0 | 8-1924 | Richmond | 65770 | 5-1936 | Sold to Louisiana and Arkansas Railway |
| #254 | 0-8-0 | 8-1924 | Richmond | 65771 | 5-1936 | Sold to Illinois Terminal Company #36 |
| #255 | 0-8-0 | 8-1924 | Richmond | 65772 | 5-1936 | Sold to Illinois Terminal Company #37 |
| #256 | 0-8-0 | 5-1925 | Richmond | 66182 | 3-1955 | Sold to Southeastern Rail and Steel Co. for Scrap |
| #257 | 0-8-0 | 5-1925 | Richmond | 66183 | 2-1955 | Sold to Southeastern Rail and Steel Co. for Scrap |
| #258 | 0-8-0 | 5-1925 | Richmond | 66184 | 4-1955 | Sold to Florida Iron and Metal Co. for Scrap |
| #259 | 0-8-0 | 5-1925 | Richmond | 66185 | 2-1955 | Sold to Southeastern Rail and Steel Co. for Scrap |
| #260 | 0-8-0 | 5-1925 | Richmond | 66186 | 3-1955 | Sold to Southeastern Rail and Steel Co. for Scrap |
| #261 | 0-8-0 | 5-1925 | Richmond | 66187 | 3-1955 | Sold to Southeastern Rail and Steel Co. for Scrap |
| #262 | 0-8-0 | 5-1925 | Richmond | 66370 | 12-1954 | Sold to Florida Iron and Metal Co. for Scrap |
| #263 | 0-8-0 | 5-1925 | Richmond | 66371 | 12-1954 | Sold to Florida Iron and Metal Co. for Scrap |
| #264 | 0-8-0 | 9-1925 | Richmond | 66372 | 4-1930 | Sold to Illinois Terminal Company #34 |

AMERICAN LOCOMOTIVE COMPANY
65769
RICHMOND WORKS
JULY 1924

| Loco. N° (Name) | Wheel Arrangement | Date Acquired | Builder | Builder's N° | Date of Disposition | Information |
|---|---|---|---|---|---|---|
| #265 | 0-8-0 | 9-1925 | Richmond | 66373 | 4-1930 | Sold to Illinois Terminal Company #33 |
| #266 | 0-8-0 | 9-1925 | Richmond | 66374 | 3-1955 | Sold to Southeastern Rail and Steel Co. for Scrap |
| #267 | 0-8-0 | 9-1925 | Richmond | 66375 | 4-1930 | Sold to Illinois Terminal Company #35 |
| #268 | 0-8-0 | 5-1926 | Richmond | 66758 | Unknown | Unknown |
| #269 | 0-8-0 | 5-1926 | Richmond | 66759 | Unknown | Unknown |
| #270 | 0-8-0 | 5-1926 | Richmond | 66760 | 3-1955 | Sold to Southeastern Rail and Steel Co. for Scrap |
| #271 | 0-8-0 | 5-1926 | Richmond | 66761 | Unknown | Unknown |
| #272 | 0-8-0 | 5-1926 | Richmond | 66762 | 3-1955 | Sold to Southeastern Rail and Steel Co. for Scrap |
| #273 | 0-8-0 | 5-1926 | Richmond | 66763 | 2-1955 | Sold to Southeastern Rail and Steel Co. for Scrap |
| #274 | 0-8-0 | 5-1926 | Richmond | 66764 | Unknown | Unknown |
| #275 | 0-8-0 | 5-1926 | Richmond | 66765 | Unknown | Unknown |
| #276 | 0-8-0 | 5-1926 | Richmond | 66766 | Unknown | Unknown |
| #277 | 0-8-0 | 5-1926 | Richmond | 66767 | Unknown | Unknown |
| #278 | 0-8-0 | 5-1926 | Richmond | 66768 | Unknown | Unknown |
| #279 | 0-8-0 | 5-1926 | Richmond | 66769 | Unknown | Unknown |
| #301 | 4-8-2 | 12-1923 | Richmond | 65159 | 10-1954 | Sold to Florida Iron and Metal Co. |
| #302 | 4-8-2 | 12-1923 | Richmond | 65160 | 10-1954 | Sold to Florida Iron and Metal Co. |
| #303 | 4-8-2 | 12-1923 | Richmond | 65161 | 10-1954 | Sold to Florida Iron and Metal Co. |
| #304 | 4-8-2 | 12-1923 | Richmond | 65162 | 12-1941 | Sold to National Railways of Mexico #3200 |
| #305 | 4-8-2 | 12-1923 | Richmond | 65163 | 12-1941 | Sold to National Railways of Mexico #3201 |
| #306 | 4-8-2 | 12-1923 | Richmond | 65164 | 10-1954 | Sold to Florida Iron and Metal Co. |
| #307 | 4-8-2 | 12-1923 | Richmond | 65165 | 10-1948 | Sold to National Railways of Mexico #3206 |
| #308 | 4-8-2 | 12-1923 | Richmond | 65166 | 12-1941 | Sold to National Railways of Mexico #3202 |
| #309 | 4-8-2 | 12-1923 | Richmond | 65167 | 12-1941 | Sold to National Railways of Mexico #3207 |
| #310 | 4-8-2 | 12-1923 | Richmond | 65168 | 2-1945 | Destroyed in accident — Wewahotee |
| #311 | 4-8-2 | 12-1923 | Richmond | 65169 | 12-1941 | Sold to National Railways of Mexico #3208 |
| #312 | 4-8-2 | 12-1923 | Richmond | 65170 | 12-1941 | Sold to National Railways of Mexico #3203 |
| #313 | 4-8-2 | 12-1923 | Richmond | 65171 | 12-1941 | Sold to National Railways of Mexico #3204 |
| #314 | 4-8-2 | 12-1923 | Richmond | 65172 | 12-1941 | Sold to National Railways of Mexico #3209 |
| #315 | 4-8-2 | 12-1923 | Richmond | 65173 | 12-1941 | Sold to National Railways of Mexico #3205 |
| #401 | 4-8-2 | 11-1924 | Schdy | 65748 | 7-1936 | Sold to St. Louis Southwestern Railway #675 |
| #402 | 4-8-2 | 11-1924 | Schdy | 65749 | 6-1936 | Sold to Western Railway of Alabama #185, retired 7/54 |
| #403 | 4-8-2 | 11-1924 | Schdy | 65750 | 8-1936 | Sold to Western Pacific Railway #171, scrapped 1951 |
| #404 | 4-8-2 | 11-1924 | Schdy | 65751 | 8-1936 | Sold to Western Pacific Railway #172, scrapped 1951 |
| #405 | 4-8-2 | 11-1924 | Schdy | 65752 | 8-1936 | Sold to Western Pacific Railway #173, scrapped 1952 |
| #406 | 4-8-2 | 11-1924 | Schdy | 65753 | 8-1936 | Sold to Western Pacific Railway #174, scrapped 1950 |
| #407 | 4-8-2 | 11-1924 | Schdy | 65754 | 8-1936 | Sold to Western Pacific Railway #175, scrapped 1950 |
| #408 | 4-8-2 | 11-1924 | Schdy | 65755 | 8-1936 | Sold to Western Pacific Railway #176, scrapped 1952 |
| #409 | 4-8-2 | 11-1924 | Schdy | 65756 | 7-1936 | Sold to St Louis Southwestern Railway |
| #410 | 4-8-2 | 11-1924 | Schdy | 65757 | 8-1936 | Sold to Western Pacific Railway |
| #411 | 4-8-2 | 11-1924 | Schdy | 65758 | 7-1936 | Sold to St. Louis Southwestern Railway |
| #412 | 4-8-2 | 11-1924 | Schdy | 65759 | 8-1936 | Sold to Western Pacific Railway |
| #413 | 4-8-2 | 11-1924 | Schdy | 65760 | 7-1936 | Sold to St. Louis Southwestern Railway |

| Loco. Nº (Name) | Wheel Arrangement | Date Acquired | Builder | Builder's Nº | Date of Disposition | Information |
|---|---|---|---|---|---|---|
| #414 | 4-8-2 | 11-1924 | Schdy | 65761 | 8-1936 | Sold to Western Pacific Railway |
| #415 | 4-8-2 | 11-1924 | Schdy | 65762 | 8-1936 | Sold to Western Pacific Railway |
| #416 | 4-8-2 | 11-1924 | Schdy | 65763 | 7-1936 | Sold to St. Louis Southwestern Railway |
| #417 | 4-8-2 | 11-1924 | Schdy | 65764 | 7-1936 | Sold to Atlanta, Birmingham and Coast Railroad |
| #418 | 4-8-2 | 11-1924 | Schdy | 65765 | 7-1936 | Sold to Western Railway of Alabama |
| #419 | 4-8-2 | 11-1924 | Schdy | 65766 | 6-1936 | Sold to Western Railway of Alabama |
| #420 | 4-8-2 | 11-1924 | Schdy | 65767 | 6-1936 | Sold to Western Railway of Alabama |
| #421 | 4-8-2 | 5-1925 | Schdy | 66170 | 10-1948 | Sold to National Railways of Mexico #3314 |
| #422 | 4-8-2 | 5-1925 | Schdy | 66171 | 10-1948 | Sold to National Railways of Mexico #3315 |
| #423 | 4-8-2 | 5-1925 | Schdy | 66172 | 12-1954 | Sold to Florida Iron and Metal Co. for Scrap |
| #424 | 4-8-2 | 5-1925 | Schdy | 66173 | 1-1955 | Sold to Florida Iron and Metal Co. for Scrap |
| #425 | 4-8-2 | 5-1925 | Schdy | 66174 | 10-1948 | Sold to National Railways of Mexico #3316 |
| #426 | 4-8-2 | 5-1925 | Schdy | 66175 | 10-1948 | Sold to National Railways of Mexico #3317 |
| #427 | 4-8-2 | 5-1925 | Schdy | 66176 | 10-1948 | Sold to National Railways of Mexico #3318 |
| #428 | 4-8-2 | 5-1925 | Schdy | 66177 | 2-1955 | Sold to Southeastern Rail and Steel Co. for Scrap |
| #429 | 4-8-2 | 5-1925 | Schdy | 66178 | 10-1948 | Sold to National Railways of Mexico #3319 |
| #430 | 4-8-2 | 5-1925 | Schdy | 66179 | 2-1955 | Sold to Southeastern Rail and Steel Co. for Scrap |
| #431 | 4-8-2 | 5-1925 | Schdy | 66180 | 12-1947 | Destroyed in Accident at M.P. 358 |
| #432 | 4-8-2 | 5-1925 | Schdy | 66181 | 10-1949 | Destroyed in Accident on Seaboard Air Line Railway |
| #433 | 4-8-2 | 11-1925 | Schdy | 66451 | 9-1945 | Sold to National Railways of Mexico #3300 |
| #434 | 4-8-2 | 11-1925 | Schdy | 66452 | 9-1945 | Sold to National Railways of Mexico #3301 |
| #435 | 4-8-2 | 11-1925 | Schdy | 66453 | 12-1954 | Sold to Florida Iron and Metal Co. |
| #436 | 4-8-2 | 11-1925 | Schdy | 66454 | 4-1955 | Sold to Florida Iron and Metal Co. |
| #437 | 4-8-2 | 11-1925 | Schdy | 66455 | 1-1955 | Sold to Florida Iron and Metal Co. |
| #438 | 4-8-2 | 11-1925 | Schdy | 66456 | 1-1955 | Sold to Florida Iron and Metal Co. |
| #439 | 4-8-2 | 11-1925 | Schdy | 66457 | 4-1955 | Sold to Florida Iron and Metal Co. |
| #440 | 4-8-2 | 11-1925 | Schdy | 66458 | 12-1954 | Sold to Florida Iron and Metal Co. |
| #441 | 4-8-2 | 11-1925 | Schdy | 66459 | 10-1945 | Sold to National Railways of Mexico #3302 |
| #442 | 4-8-2 | 11-1925 | Schdy | 66460 | 10-1945 | Sold to National Railways of Mexico #3303 |
| #443 | 4-8-2 | 5-1926 | Schdy | 66716 | 10-1945 | Sold to National Railways of Mexico #3304 |
| #444 | 4-8-2 | 5-1926 | Schdy | 66717 | 10-1945 | Sold to National Railways of Mexico #3305 |
| #445 | 4-8-2 | 5-1926 | Schdy | 66718 | 10-1945 | Sold to National Railways of Mexico #3306 |
| #446 | 4-8-2 | 5-1926 | Schdy | 66719 | 10-1945 | Sold to National Railways of Mexico #3307 |
| #447 | 4-8-2 | 5-1926 | Schdy | 66720 | 10-1945 | Sold to National Railways of Mexico #3308 |
| #448 | 4-8-2 | 5-1926 | Schdy | 66721 | 10-1945 | Sold to National Railways of Mexico #3309 |
| #449 | 4-8-2 | 5-1926 | Schdy | 66722 | 10-1945 | Sold to National Railways of Mexico #3310 |
| #450 | 4-8-2 | 5-1926 | Schdy | 66723 | 10-1945 | Sold to National Railways of Mexico #3311 |
| #451 | 4-8-2 | 5-1926 | Schdy | 66724 | 10-1945 | Sold to National Railways of Mexico #3312 |
| #452 | 4-8-2 | 5-1926 | Schdy | 66725 | 10-1945 | Sold to National Railways of Mexico #3313 |
| #701 | 2-8-2 | 9-1925 | Schdy | Unknown | 1-1955 | Sold to Southeastern Rail and Steel Co. for Scrap |
| #702 | 2-8-2 | 9-1925 | Schdy | Unknown | 2-1955 | Sold to Florida Iron and Metal Co. for Scrap |
| #703 | 2-8-2 | 9-1925 | Schdy | Unknown | 1-1955 | Sold to Southeastern Rail and Steel Co. for Scrap |
| #704 | 2-8-2 | 9-1925 | Schdy | Unknown | 12-1954 | Sold to Florida Iron and Metal Co. for Scrap |

| Loco. N° (Name) | Wheel Arrangement | Date Acquired | Builder | Builder's N° | Date of Disposition | Information |
|---|---|---|---|---|---|---|
| #705 | 2-8-2 | 9-1925 | Schdy | Unknown | 1-1955 | Sold to Southeastern Rail and Steel Co. for Scrap |
| #706 | 2-8-2 | 9-1925 | Schdy | Unknown | 1-1955 | Sold to Southeastern Rail and Steel Co. for Scrap |
| #707 | 2-8-2 | 9-1925 | Schdy | Unknown | 1-1955 | Sold to Southeastern Rail and Steel Co. for Scrap |
| #708 | 2-8-2 | 9-1925 | Schdy | Unknown | 1-1955 | Sold to Southeastern Rail and Steel Co. for Scrap |
| #709 | 2-8-2 | 9-1925 | Schdy | Unknown | 2-1955 | Sold to Florida Iron and Metal Co. |
| #710 | 2-8-2 | 9-1925 | Schdy | Unknown | 1-1955 | Sold to Florida Iron and Metal Co. |
| #711 | 2-8-2 | 9-1925 | Schdy | Unknown | 1-1955 | Sold to Southeastern Rail and Steel Co. for Scrap |
| #712 | 2-8-2 | 9-1925 | Schdy | Unknown | 1-1955 | Sold to Southeastern Rail and Steel Co. for Scrap |
| #713 | 2-8-2 | 9-1925 | Schdy | Unknown | 1-1955 | Sold to Southeastern Rail and Steel Co. for Scrap |
| #714 | 2-8-2 | 9-1925 | Schdy | Unknown | 1-1955 | Sold to Florida Iron and Metal Co. |
| #715 | 2-8-2 | 9-1925 | Schdy | Unknown | 1-1955 | Sold to Southeastern Rail and Steel Co. for Scrap |
| #801 | 4-8-2 | 7-1926 | Schdy | Unknown | 11-1954 | Sold to Southeastern Rail and Steel Co. for Scrap |
| #802 | 4-8-2 | 7-1926 | Schdy | Unknown | 10-1940 | Destroyed by Explosion |
| #803 | 4-8-2 | 7-1926 | Schdy | Unknown | 12-1954 | Sold to Southeastern Rail and Steel Co. for Scrap |
| #804 | 4-8-2 | 7-1926 | Schdy | Unknown | 12-1954 | Sold to Southeastern Rail and Steel Co. for Scrap |
| #805 | 4-8-2 | 7-1926 | Schdy | Unknown | 11-1954 | Sold to Southeastern Rail and Steel Co. for Scrap |
| #806 | 4-8-2 | 7-1926 | Schdy | Unknown | 12-1954 | Sold to Southeastern Rail and Steel Co. for Scrap |
| #807 | 4-8-2 | 7-1926 | Schdy | Unknown | 12-1954 | Sold to Southeastern Rail and Steel Co. for Scrap |
| #808 | 4-8-2 | 7-1926 | Schdy | Unknown | 12-1954 | Sold to Southeastern Rail and Steel Co. for Scrap |
| #809 | 4-8-2 | 7-1926 | Schdy | Unknown | 12-1954 | Sold to Southeastern Rail and Steel Co. for Scrap |
| #810 | 4-8-2 | 7-1926 | Schdy | Unknown | 12-1954 | Sold to Florida Iron and Metal Co. for Scrap |
| #811 | 4-8-2 | 7-1926 | Schdy | Unknown | 1-1955 | Sold to Florida Iron and Metal Co. for Scrap |
| #812 | 4-8-2 | 7-1926 | Schdy | Unknown | 12-1954 | Sold to Southeastern Rail and Steel Co. for Scrap |
| #813 | 4-8-2 | 7-1926 | Schdy | Unknown | 5-1952 | Destroyed in rear end collision |
| #814 | 4-8-2 | 7-1926 | Schdy | Unknown | 11-1954 | Sold to Southeastern Rail and Steel Co. for Scrap |
| #815 | 4-8-2 | 7-1925 | Schdy | Unknown | 4-1951 | Destroyed by explosion at Delray |
| #816 | 4-8-2 | 7-1926 | Schdy | Unknown | 12-1954 | Sold to Southeastern Rail and Steel Co. for Scrap |
| #817 | 4-8-2 | 7-1926 | Schdy | Unknown | 12-1954 | Sold to Southeastern Rail and Steel Co. for Scrap |
| #818 | 4-8-2 | 7-1926 | Schdy | Unknown | 11-1954 | Sold to Southeastern Rail and Steel Co. for Scrap |
| #819 | 4-8-2 | 7-1926 | Schdy | Unknown | 12-1954 | Sold to Florida Iron and Metal Co. for Scrap |
| #820 | 4-8-2 | 7-1926 | Schdy | Unknown | 11-1954 | Sold to Southeastern Rail and Steel Co. for Scrap |
| #821 | 4-8-2 | 7-1926 | Schdy | Unknown | 11-1954 | Sold to Florida Iron and Metal Co. for Scrap |
| #822 | 4-8-2 | 7-1926 | Schdy | Unknown | 12-1954 | Sold to Southeastern Rail and Steel Co. for Scrap |
| #823 | 4-8-2 | 7-1926 | Schdy | Unknown | 11-1954 | Sold to Florida Iron and Metal Co. for Scrap |

FEC Atlantic type engine 61, a 4-4-2 wheel arrangement, poses on the site of the old St. Augustine Yards. In 1926 and 1927 when the FEC moved to Miller Shops, north of St. Augustine, the facilities in the old yard were abandoned, and the property gradually sold. U.S. Highway 1 now slices through the middle of the former yard area.

—(H. Wolfe)

FEC 4-6-2 68 was built, as were almost all FEC steam engines, by the American Locomotive Company. Number 68 came off the line in December, 1907, with nine other engines of the same wheel arrangement. She served in fast passenger service for most of her operating life on the FEC and in 1930 was sold to the United States Sugar Company.

4-6-2 80 has just come off the Jacksonville Beach branch and is inbound to Union Station with a four car passenger train.

—(H. Wolfe)

In 1937, F.A. Bonke, a railway buff living in New Jersey, photographed the cab of FEC 4-6-2 148 at Buena Vista Yard.

FEC 113 became United States Sugar 113 and is shown in August, 1961 at Bryant, Florida awaiting the call to the winter harvest. Sister 153 was already at the Gold Coast Railroad.

After the start of the depression, and the subsequent September, 1931 plunge into receivership, the FEC began selling its surplus steam engines to roads as widely scattered as the Cotton Belt, Western Railway of Alabama, Western Pacific, Illinois Terminal, Georgia & Florida, National of Mexico, and "The Bay Line," more properly known as the Atlanta & St. Andrews Bay, a short line operating from Panama City, Florida, on the state's panhandle to Dothan, Alabama, and a connection with the Central of Georgia. The Bay Line bought a number of the FEC's stable, though, unlike most of the other buying roads (not all of them are listed above) did not change the FEC numbers. 4-6-2's 131 and 143, and 0-6-0 206 (which was first FEC 140, then became FEC 206) sport their original tenders, headlights, builder's and number plates. All three are in Panama City, Florida, the 131 on April 20, 1939; the 143 on September 8, 1940, and the 206 on September 28, 1940.

*—(J. Nelson Collection)*

244

Following the Feb 12, 1935 accident and subsequent plunge into the river at Jupiter, 427 was salvaged and repaired. It would have been a shame to discard such a beautiful and useful piece of equipment and Wolfe photographed her in all her glory at Miller Shops after repairs.

FEC 4-8-2 431 stands for the station stop at Long Key. It's 1932 and three years later the destruction wrought by the Labor Day hurricane will forever change both the railroad and the Keys themselves. Note the fresh water tank cars on the siding to the right.

432, with the Jacksonville-Miami local. The FEC, as a Florida industry and institution (and, perhaps, with a touch of nostalgia?) continued to operate, until 1961, one train per day via East Palatka following the completion of the Moultrie Cutoff between St. Augustine and Bunnell in 1926. Prior to that all trains operated via the circuitous route through such Metropoli as Spuds, Yelvington, Espanola and Roy. Since 29 and 30 (known at various points in their illustrious history as the *Daylight Express*, *The East Coast Express*, or the *locals*) operated without either streamlined cars or connections at Jacksonville, it was unnecessary to equip them with diesels until steam operation was no longer economical due to its sparseness. On April 20, 1948, the Daylight Express is pulling out of New Smyrna.

—*(DeGolyer photograph, J. Nelson Collection)*

FEC steam double-headers on their long, high speed passenger trains were not an uncommon sight along the East Coast. Though the location is unknown the drama of big time steam Railroading is entirely evident.

4-8-2 436 pulls into Hollywood northbound in the spring of 1938.

We're in New Smyrna Beach and it's mid-afternoon as 4-8-2 435 backs past the passenger station while 443 brings its long heavyweight passenger train to a stop.

Almost every great, passenger-carrying railroad has, among its aficionados, a group who will swear that, among all others, one particular type of engine, on that buff's particular railroad, was the finest ever produced. The Erie, the NYC, the Santa Fe...they all have their fervent fans... and yet, for sheer strength, for sheer power, for sheer beauty in motion, the 400 series of the East Coast Line had few equals. Built by American Locomotive from November, 1924 through May of 1926, 401 through 452 were the archtype of magnificence in steam passenger power. By 1948, there was little need for steam power in passenger service on the FEC, and so, sadly but faithfully, the remaining 400's performed their duties as road switchers and freight engines, much to the unhappiness of the (then) rare railroad buff along the St. Augustine Route. Though 440 would not be sold to Florida Iron and Metal Co. for scrap until 1954, there is something depressing about seeing her downgraded, as she dolefully switches a local freight at Jacksonville on April 17, 1948.

—*(DeGolyer photo, J. Nelson Collection)*

The occasion is lost somewhere in the annals of history, but fortunately Harry Wolfe recorded the Jacksonville Police Band in front of 4-8-2 441. The terminal itself is now abandoned, the steam engine is scrapped and the Jacksonville Police no longer sponsor their own band.

4-8-2 442 was caught by FEC photographer Harry Wolfe as she stepped gingerly past the New Smyrna Roundhouse just after leaving the Passenger Station.

Was Boca Raton simply a photogenic location, or did 442 with the Miamian, on January 14, 1940, enhance the locale with a surreal beauty?
—(J. Nelson Collection)

443, with a 14 car extra, thunders through St. Augustine in the late 1920's.
—(DeGolyer photograph, J. Nelson Collection)

4-8-2 445 is on the northbound Tamiami. It's five o'clock in the afternoon of July 26th, 1939, and Frank Siefert photographed this scene from the platform at Daytona Beach.

At MP 105.8, near Ormond Beach, Wolfe caught one of the magnificent Mountain type engines — in this case, 447 — with 10 cars. Despite a complete lack of reference points, it appears that the train is headed south.

—(J. Nelson Collection)

FEC 4-8-2 was one of the swift Mountain type passenger speedsters that powered FECs fleet of fine passenger trains from 1927 until the early 1940s and brought to reality the slogan "Speedway to America's Playground."

FEC 4-8-2 451 is on the turntable at Bowden Roundhouse at South Jacksonville, in 1935.

FEC low drivered 2-8-2 702 is shown at Buena Vista Yard on April 2, 1944.

2-8-2 709 is working a peddler freight and we are standing behind the tender getting an excellent view of the "doghouse" that the FEC used for its head-end brakemen.

Main line steam left Miami for the final time in 1954. 2-8-2 709 pulled the boneyard special north. Scotty Laird, an FEC employee at Buena Vista Yard from 1944 until 1963 made this photograph and the lower photo on page 241.

We are standing between tracks 5 and 6 on the Miami passenger station platform on December 2nd, 1939, and 2-8-2 711 has coupled to the observation car of the brand new "Champion" preparatory to moving her back to Buena Vista Yard for servicing.

In retrospect, it is only through Providence that many of Wolfe's negatives survived. When he was on assignment, Wolfe had 'carte blanche' access to the Railroad and he was always delighted to photograph the crews as well as the scenes to which he had been assigned. In the pine woods, just south of St. Augustine, freight-hauling 802 pulled up so that Wolfe coud get a shot of "the boys".

During the winter season the FEC hauled thousands of carloads of potatoes to Northern markets from the area northeast of Palatka. One of the station stops on the line was actually known as "Spuds." 4-8-2 806 is shown here in front of the picturesque depot at Hastings, Florida, awaiting the hi-ball with a train of early potatoes. FEC publicity referred to these trains as the "Potato Specials."

—(H. Wolfe)

4-8-2 813 with a 12,000 gallon tender poses beautifully with a white plume bursting from her stack. A clearing in the piney woods behind Miller Shops was made to order for Wolfe's wide angle lens.

For anyone who has ever been to the New World Center of the South, the changes that have been wrought to the once sleepy little village of Miami defy description. The city today exceeds even the wildest imaginings of both Henry Flagler and Julia Tuttle. The time—1937—has been frozen, in what Wolfe meant to be simply a shot of two FEC passenger trains preparing to depart Miami. Instead, he has given us a moment of history such as has rarely been done in Miami's photo annals. The entire skyline, with the exception of the County Courthouse (which the FEC, by inference, showed as their Station in many publicity photos), has been obliterated. Who is that young boy walking across 5th St. in the lower right of the photo? What was the man in the cap in the foreground thinking as he looked at 4-8-2- 812? And the speck to the left of the Courthouse as well as to the left of the utility pole is actually a plane pulling a banner that says, "On your way home see Silver Springs." Miami's Rapid Transit now runs where the FEC once originated America's premier winter passenger trains, and with the exception of the Courthouse itself the only hearkening back to those glorious days of great passenger train service are the planes that still carry the banners exhorting the tourists to "See Silver Springs."

The 800 series of Mountain type engines was built for the FEC in 1926. Though primarily for freight service, the 800s were occasionally called upon to handle passenger trains. They were massive, heavily built and exuded pure strength. This view of 815 personifies all of this even as she sits idle and 'cold'.

South of Jacksonville, FECs connections were limited (with only a few exceptions) to logging roads, sugar railroads, a shortline common carrier and a group of terminal or dock railways at West Palm Beach, Fort Lauderdale (Port Everglades) and Miami.

West Palm Beach Terminal Company was closely allied with the West India Fruit & Steamship Company, and until the late 1950s employed several 0-6-0 switchers in their yard and car ferry loading operation.

Here is WPB Terminal Company #9 in repose on company tracks at the Port of Palm Beach, which is actually located in Riviera Beach, just north of West Palm Beach.

Number 427 with a heavy express and mail train bound for Miami has just come off the St. Johns River bridge. The signal bridge, in the foreground, with signal heads over both tracks is indicative that the FEC utilized both tracks in both directions at this congested point. Note also the 'wig wag' road protection at the right of the photo.

ACL 1403, one of that road's stable of fast passenger engines, was of the same wheel arrangement—4-8-2—as the FEC's racehorses. She was bought by the Coast Line in 1943, from the Road of Phoebe Snow—the DL&W—and immediately began hauling "name" passenger trains between Jacksonville and Florence, SC, although she was noted in Coast Line territory in Central and West Coast Florida from time to time. "But," you say, "there is something odd looking sticking out from the beauty's tender!" And the answer of course is that that is nothing to worry about, as 1403 is turned at the Jacksonville Terminal Co., roundhouse. It's just the angle of the shot, and it's only one of those new Illinois Central diesels that they use on that "City of Miami" job. No need to worry 'bout them! They're just an experiment—can't hold a candle to a fast steamer!

# FLORIDA EAST COAST RAILWAY COMPANY
## DIESEL LOCOMOTIVES NOT IN SERVICE IN 1984

| Locomotive Number | Builders No. | Type | Wheel Classification | Date Purchased | Horsepower | Disposition |
|---|---|---|---|---|---|---|
| 222 | 17360 | SW-1200 | B/B | 1/53 | 1200 HP | Sold to Woodward Iron Co., Woodward, AL, 8/31/68 |
| 223 | 17361 | SW-1200 | B/B | 1/53 | 1200 HP | Sold to Dominion Foundry & Steel Ltd., 4/30/69 |
| 224 | 17362 | SW-1200 | B/B | 1/53 | 1200 HP | Sold to Woodward Iron Co., Woodward, AL, 8/31/68 |
| 225 | 17363 | SW-1200 | B/B | 1/53 | 1200 HP | Sold to Woodward Iron Co., Woodward, AL, 8/31/68 |
| 227 | 17365 | SW-1200 | B/B | 1/53 | 1200 HP | Sold to Precision Engineering Co. 11/30/68 |
| 228 | 17366 | SW-1200 | B/B | 1/53 | 1200 HP | Sold to Precision Engineering Co. 11/30/68 |
| 230 | 20089 | SW-1200 | B/B | 12/54 | 1200 HP | Sold to Newberg & Southshore RR 12/22/72 |
| 231 | 20090 | SW-1200 | B/B | 12/54 | 1200 HP | Sold to Union Railroad Co. 12/22/72 |
| 232 | 20091 | SW-1200 | B/B | 12/54 | 1200 HP | Sold to Union Railroad Co. 12/22/72 |
| 234 | 20093 | SW-1200 | B/B | 12/54 | 1200 HP | Destroyed in accident, Jacksonville, 6/10/60 |
| 235 | 20094 | SW-1200 | B/B | 12/54 | 1200 HP | Sold to Newberg & Southshore RR 12/22/72 |
| 402 | 36774 | GP 40 | B/B | 1971 | 3000 HP | Destroyed in derailment MP 336.4 2/12/79—sold to Electro-Motive Division. |
| 501 | 5516 | F3-A | B/B | | 1500 HP | |
| 502 | 5517 | F3-A | B/B | | 1500 HP | |
| 503 | 5518 | F3-A | B/B | | 1500 HP | |
| 504 | 5519 | F3-A | B/B | | 1500 HP | |
| 505 | 5520 | F3-A | B/B | 1/49 | 1500 HP | Sold to Precision Engineering Company 1/31/71 |
| 506 | 5521 | F3-A | B/B | | 1500 HP | |
| 507 | 5522 | F3-A | B/B | | 1500 HP | |
| 508 | 5523 | F3-A | B/B | | 1500 HP | |
| 551 | 5524 | F3-B | B/B | | 1500 HP | |
| 552 | 5525 | F3-B | B/B | 1/49 | 1500 HP | Traded to Electro-Motive Division 1/31/71 |
| 553 | 5526 | F3-B | B/B | | 1500 HP | |
| 554 | 5527 | F3-B | B/B | | 1500 HP | |
| 571 | 15568 | FP7-A | B/B | | 1500 HP | |
| 572 | 15569 | FP7-A | B/B | | 1500 HP | |
| 573 | 15570 | FP7-A | B/B | 12/51 | 1500 HP | Sold to Precision Engineering Company 1/31/71 |
| 574 | 15571 | FP7-A | B/B | | 1500 HP | |
| 575 | 15572 | FP7-A | B/B | | 1500 HP | |
| 601 | 5528 | BL-2 | B/B | 11/48 | 1500 HP | Traded to Electro-Motive Division 1/31/71 |
| 602 | 5529 | BL-2 | B/B | 11/48 | 1500 HP | Dismantled for serviceable parts 9/11/61 |
| 603 | 5530 | BL-2 | B/B | 11/48 | 1500 HP | Dismantled for serviceable parts 8/10/60 |
| 604 | 5531 | BL-2 | B/B | 11/48 | 1500 HP | Dismantled for serviceable parts 3/31/61 |
| 605 | 5532 | BL-2 | B/B | 12/48 | 1500 HP | Traded to Electro-Motive Division 1/31/71 |
| 606 | 5533 | BL-2 | B/B | 12/48 | 1500 HP | Traded to Electro-Motive Division 1/31/71 |
| 607 | 17344 | GP-7R | B/B | 10/52 | 1500 HP | Sold to Precision National Corp. 11/4/74 |
| 608 | 17345 | GP-7R | B/B | 10/52 | 1500 HP | Sold to Southwestern Railway Co. 5/15/78 |
| 609 | 17346 | GP-7R | B/B | 10/52 | 1500 HP | Sold to Diesel Electric Service 2/15/80 |
| 610 | 17347 | GP-7R | B/B | 10/52 | 1500 HP | Sold to Diesel Electric Service 2/15/80 |
| 611 | 17348 | GP-7R | B/B | 10/52 | 1500 HP | Traded to Electro-Motive Division 5/15/78 |
| 612 | 17349 | GP-7R | B/B | 10/52 | 1500 HP | Sold to Diesel Electric Service 2/15/80 |
| 613 | 17350 | GP-7R | B/B | 10/52 | 1500 HP | Sold to Precision National Corp. 11/4/74 |
| 614 | 17351 | GP-7R | B/B | 10/52 | 1500 HP | Sold to Southwestern Railway Co., 5/15/78 |
| 615 | 17352 | GP-7R | B/B | 10/52 | 1500 HP | Sold to Southwestern Railway Co., 5/15/78 |
| 616 | 17353 | GP-7R | B/B | 10/52 | 1500 HP | Sold to Precision National Corp. 11/4/74 |

| Locomotive Number | Builders No. | Type | Wheel Classification | Date Purchased | Horsepower | Disposition |
|---|---|---|---|---|---|---|
| 617 | 17354 | GP-7R | B/B | 10/52 | 1500 HP | Sold to Diesel Electric Service 2/15/80 |
| 618 | 17355 | GP-7R | B/B | 10/52 | 1500 HP | Sold to Southwestern Railway Co., 5/15/78 |
| 619 | 17356 | GP-7R | B/B | 10/52 | 1500 HP | Sold to Southwestern Railway Co., 5/15/78 |
| 620 | 17357 | GP-7R | B/B | 10/52 | 1500 HP | Sold to Diesel Electric Service 2/15/80 |
| 621 | 17358 | GP-7R | B/B | 10/52 | 1500 HP | Sold to Southwestern Railway Co. 5/15/78 |
| 653 | 19764 | GP-9R | B/B | 12/54 | 1750 HP | Sold to Precision National Corp. 2/28/72 |
| 665 | 20006 | GP-9R | B/B | 12/54 | 1750 HP | Sold to Precision National Corp. 2/28/72 |
| 671 | 23133 | GP-9R | B/B | 12/54 | 1750 HP | Sold to Precision National Corp. 2/28/72 |

# DIESEL-ELECTRIC (PASSENGER) LOCOMOTIVES NOT IN SERVICE IN 1984

**Built by Electro-Motive Division, General Motors Corporation**

| Locomotive Number | Builders No. | Type | Wheel Classification | Date Purchased | Horsepower | Disposition |
|---|---|---|---|---|---|---|
| 1001 | 956 | E3A | A1A-A1A | 11/30/39 | 2000 HP | Retired 4/30/60 – dismantled at Miller Shops for parts |
| 1002 | 957 | E3A | A1A-A1A | 11/30/39 | 2000 HP | Sold to Precision Engineering Company 11/30/68 |
| 1003 | 1196 | E6A | A1A-A1A | 12/14/40 | 2000 HP | Retired 12/31/62 – dismantled for parts |
| 1004 | 1567 | E6A | A1A-A1A | 3/1/42 | 2000 HP | Retired 5/25/62 – dismantled for parts |
| 1005 | 1568 | E6A | A1A-A1A | 3/1/42 | 2000 HP | Retired 11/30/68 – sold to Precision Engineering Co. |
| 1006 | 2293 | E7A | A1A-A1A | 4/45 | 2000 HP | Retired 11/30/68 – sold to Precision Engineering Co. |
| 1007 | 2294 | E7A | A1A-A1A | 4/45 | 2000 HP | Sold to Precision Engineering Co. 7/16/66 |
| 1008 | 2521 | E7A | A1A-A1A | 5/45 | 2000 HP | Sold to Precision Engineering Co. 11/30/68 |
| 1009 | 2522 | E7A | A1A-A1A | 4/45 | 2000 HP | Sold to Precision Engineering Co. 7/16/66 |
| 1010 | 2523 | E7A | A1A-A1A | 4/45 | 2000 HP | Sold to Precision Engineering Co. 7/16/66 |
| 1011 | 2524 | E7A | A1A-A1A | 4/45 | 2000 HP | Sold to Precision Engineering Co. 11/30/68 |
| 1012 | 2525 | E7A | A1A-A1A | 4/45 | 2000 HP | Sold to Precision Engineering Co. 7/16/66 |
| 1013 | 2526 | E7A | A1A-A1A | 4/45 | 2000 HP | Sold to Precision Engineering Co. 11/30/68 |
| 1014 | 2527 | E7A | A1A-A1A | 4/45 | 2000 HP | Sold to Precision Engineering Co. 7/16/66 |
| 1015 | 2528 | E7A | A1A-A1A | 4/45 | 2000 HP | Sold to Precision Engineering Co. 7/16/66 |
| 1016 | 2529 | E7A | A1A-A1A | 4/45 | 2000 HP | Sold to Precision Engineering Co. 11/30/68 |
| 1017 | 2530 | E7A | A1A-A1A | 4/45 | 2000 HP | Sold to U.S. Steel Corp. 9/2/66 |
| 1018 | 4390 | E7A | A1A-A1A | 9/47 | 2000 HP | Sold to U.S. Steel Corp. 4/13/67 |
| 1019 | 4391 | E7A | A1A-A1A | 9/47 | 2000 HP | Sold to U.S. Steel Corp. 9/2/66 |
| 1020 | 4392 | E7A | A1A-A1A | 9/47 | 2000 HP | Sold to Precision Engineering Co. 11/30/68 |
| 1021 | 4393 | E7A | A1A-A1A | 9/47 | 2000 HP | Sold to U.S. Steel Corp. 4/13/67 |
| 1022 | 4394 | E7A | A1A-A1A | 9/47 | 2000 HP | Sold to Precision Engineering Co. 11/30/68 |
| 1031 | 20083 | E9A | A1A-A1A | 1/55 | 2250 HP | Sold to Precision Engineering Co. 11/30/68 |
| 1032 | 20084 | E9A | A1A-A1A | 1/55 | 2250 HP | Sold to Precision Engineering Co. 11/30/68 |
| 1033 | 20085 | E9A | A1A-A1A | 1/55 | 2250 HP | Sold to Precision Engineering Co. 11/30/68 |
| 1034 | 20086 | E9A | A1A-A1A | 1/55 | 2250 HP | Sold to Precision Engineering Co. 11/30/68 |
| 1035 | 20087 | E9A | A1A-A1A | 1/55 | 2250 HP | Sold to Precision Engineering Co. 11/30/68 |
| 1051 | 1569 | E6B | A1A-A1A | 3/1/42 | 2000 HP | Sold to Precision Engineering Co. 7/16/66 |
| 1052 | 2295 | E7B | A1A-A1A | 5/45 | 2000 HP | Sold to Precision Engineering Co. 7/16/66 |
| 1053 | 2531 | E7B | A1A-A1A | 5/45 | 2000 HP | Sold to Precision Engineering Co. 7/16/66 |
| 1054 | 2532 | E7B | A1A-A1A | 5/45 | 2000 HP | Sold to Atlantic Coast Line Railroad 4/30/66 |

# DIESEL LOCOMOTIVES IN SERVICE IN 1984

## SWITCHING LOCOMOTIVES

### SW UNITS—1200 HP (Units 221 & 226, Model SW-9; Units 229 & 233, Model SW-1200)

| Unit No. | Builder and No. | Date Built | Wt. Working Order & Wt. on Drivers | Driver Dia. | No. | Tractive Power | Tank Capacity Fuel Oil |
|---|---|---|---|---|---|---|---|
| 221 | EMD 17359 | 1953 | 246,010 | 40" | 8 | 60470 | 600 gallons |
| 226 | EMD 17364 | 1953 | 246,150 | 40" | 8 | 60750 | 600 gallons |
| 229 | EMD 20088 | 1954 | 247,250 | 40" | 8 | 61000 | 600 gallons |
| 233 | EMD 20092 | 1954 | 246,270 | 40" | 8 | 60970 | 600 gallons |
| TOTAL 4 | | | | | | | |

## ROAD LOCOMOTIVES—GENERAL PURPOSE

### GP UNITS—3000 HP (Units 401-410, GP-40; Units 411-429, Model GP 40-2)

| Unit No. | Builder and No. | Date Built | Wt. Working Order & Wt. on Drivers | Driver Dia. | No. | Tractive Power | Tank Capacity Fuel Oil |
|---|---|---|---|---|---|---|---|
| 401 | EMD 36773 | 1971 | 264,510 | 40" | 8 | 62976 | 3,000 gallons |
| 403 | EMD 36775 | 1971 | 264,310 | 40" | 8 | 62926 | 3,000 gallons |
| 404 | EMD 36776 | 1971 | 264,670 | 40" | 8 | 62016 | 3,000 gallons |
| 405 | EMD 36777 | 1971 | 264,970 | 40" | 8 | 63091 | 3,000 gallons |
| 406 | EMD 36778 | 1971 | 266,920 | 40" | 8 | 63578 | 3,000 gallons |
| 407 | EMD 36779 | 1971 | 264,710 | 40" | 8 | 63026 | 3,000 gallons |
| 408 | EMD 36780 | 1971 | 265,170 | 40" | 8 | 63141 | 3,000 gallons |
| 409 | EMD 36781 | 1971 | 265,270 | 40" | 8 | 63166 | 3,000 gallons |
| 410 | EMD 36782 | 1971 | 264,930 | 40" | 8 | 63081 | 3,000 gallons |
| 411 | EMD 5813-1 | 1972 | 263,950 | 40" | 8 | 62589 | 3,000 gallons |
| 412 | EMD 5813-2 | 1972 | 265,088 | 40" | 8 | 62873 | 3,000 gallons |
| 413 | EMD 5813-3 | 1972 | 264,788 | 40" | 8 | 62798 | 3,000 gallons |
| 414 | EMD 5813-4 | 1972 | 264,058 | 40" | 8 | 62616 | 3,000 gallons |
| 415 | EMD 5813-5 | 1972 | 263,846 | 40" | 8 | 62563 | 3,000 gallons |
| 416 | EMD 74650-1 | 1974 | 264,992 | 40" | 8 | 62839 | 3,000 gallons |
| 417 | EMD 74650-2 | 1974 | 263,342 | 40" | 8 | 62427 | 3,000 gallons |
| 418 | EMD 74650-3 | 1974 | 264,498 | 40" | 8 | 62716 | 3,000 gallons |
| 419 | EMD 786169-1 | 1979 | 266,118 | 40" | 8 | 63121 | 3,000 gallons |
| 420 | EMD 786169-2 | 1979 | 265,318 | 40" | 8 | 62921 | 3,000 gallons |
| 421 | EMD 786169-3 | 1979 | 263,626 | 40" | 8 | 62493 | 3,000 gallons |
| 422 | EMD 786169-4 | 1979 | 262,768 | 40" | 8 | 62284 | 3,000 gallons |
| 423 | EMD 786169-5 | 1979 | 262,876 | 40" | 8 | 62294 | 3,000 gallons |
| 424 | EMD 797320-1 | 1980 | 266,318 | 40" | 8 | 63171 | 3,000 gallons |
| 425 | EMD 796325-1 | 1980 | 264,636 | 40" | 8 | 62751 | 3,000 gallons |
| 426 | EMD 796325-2 | 1980 | 264,376 | 40" | 8 | 62686 | 3,000 gallons |
| 427 | EMD 796325-3 | 1980 | 267,968 | 40" | 8 | 63584 | 3,000 gallons |
| 428 | EMD 796325-4 | 1980 | 263,706 | 40" | 8 | 62518 | 3,000 gallons |
| 429 | EMD 796325-5 | 1980 | 264,688 | 40" | 8 | 62764 | 3,000 gallons |
| TOTAL 28 | | | | | | | |

# ROAD LOCOMOTIVES—GENERAL PURPOSE

## GP UNITS—Model GP 38-2 2000 HP

| | | | | | | | |
|---|---|---|---|---|---|---|---|
| 501 | EMD 776040-1 | 1977 | 40" | 8 | 264,150 | 62458 | 3,200 gallons |
| 502 | EMD 776040-2 | 1977 | 40" | 8 | 262,502 | 62046 | 3,200 gallons |
| 503 | EMD 776040-3 | 1977 | 40" | 8 | 262,902 | 62146 | 3,200 gallons |
| 504 | EMD 776040-4 | 1977 | 40" | 8 | 263,302 | 67246 | 3,200 gallons |
| 505 | EMD 776110-1 | 1978 | 40" | 8 | 263,332 | 62219 | 3,200 gallons |
| 506 | EMD 776110-2 | 1978 | 40" | 8 | 263,372 | 62319 | 3,200 gallons |
| 507 | EMD 776110-3 | 1978 | 40" | 8 | 260,032 | 61394 | 3,200 gallons |
| 508 | EMD 776110-4 | 1978 | 40" | 8 | 263,732 | 62319 | 3,200 gallons |
| 509 | EMD 776110-5 | 1978 | 40" | 8 | 263,932 | 62369 | 3,200 gallons |
| 510 | EMD 776110-6 | 1978 | 40" | 8 | 263,782 | 62331 | 3,200 gallons |
| 511 | EMD 777041-1 | 1978 | 40" | 8 | 260,332 | 61469 | 3,200 gallons |

TOTAL  11

## GP UNITS—1,750 HP MODEL GP-9R

| | | | | | | | |
|---|---|---|---|---|---|---|---|
| 651 | EMD 19762 | 1954 | 40' | 8 | 237,730 | 59430 | 1,600 gallons |
| 652 | EMD 19763 | 1954 | 40' | 8 | 237,990 | 59500 | 1,600 gallons |
| 654 | EMD 19765 | 1954 | 40' | 8 | 237,930 | 59480 | 1,600 gallons |
| 655 | EMD 19766 | 1954 | 40' | 8 | 237,870 | 59470 | 1,600 gallons |
| 656 | EMD 19767 | 1954 | 40" | 8 | 237,930 | 59480 | 1,600 gallons |
| 657 | EMD 19998 | 1954 | 40" | 8 | 237,830 | 59460 | 1,600 gallons |
| 658 | EMD 19999 | 1954 | 40" | 8 | 237,990 | 59500 | 1,600 gallons |
| 659 | EMD 20000 | 1954 | 40" | 8 | 237,990 | 59500 | 1,600 gallons |
| 660 | EMD 20001 | 1954 | 40" | 8 | 238,050 | 59510 | 1,600 gallons |
| 661 | EMD 20002 | 1954 | 40" | 8 | 237,630 | 59410 | 1,600 gallons |
| 662 | EMD 20003 | 1954 | 40" | 8 | 237,770 | 59440 | 1,600 gallons |
| 663 | EMD 20004 | 1954 | 40" | 8 | 238,690 | 59670 | 1,600 gallons |
| 664 | EMD 20005 | 1954 | 40" | 8 | 237,990 | 59500 | 1,600 gallons |
| 666 | EMD 20007 | 1954 | 40" | 8 | 238,150 | 59540 | 1,600 gallons |
| 667 | EMD 23129 | 1957 | 40" | 8 | 244,200 | 59290 | 1,700 gallons |
| 668 | EMD 23130 | 1957 | 40" | 8 | 244,100 | 59260 | 1,700 gallons |
| 669 | EMD 23131 | 1957 | 40" | 8 | 244,320 | 59320 | 1,700 gallons |
| 670 | EMD 23132 | 1957 | 40" | 8 | 244,160 | 59280 | 1,700 gallons |
| 672 | EMD 23134 | 1957 | 40" | 8 | 244,120 | 59270 | 1,700 gallons |
| 673 | EMD 23135 | 1957 | 40" | 8 | 244,640 | 59400 | 1,700 gallons |
| 674 | EMD 23136 | 1957 | 40" | 8 | 244,400 | 59340 | 1,700 gallons |
| 675 | EMD 23137 | 1957 | 40" | 8 | 244,760 | 59430 | 1,700 gallons |
| 676 | EMD 23138 | 1957 | 40" | 8 | 244,400 | 59340 | 1,700 gallons |

TOTAL  23

SWITCHING LOCOMOTIVES ............................................. 4
ROAD LOCOMOTIVES—GENERAL PURPOSE ............................. 62

TOTAL  66

Does the cop want him to "pull over" or is he just admiring the sleek beauty of E7A 1008?

SW 228 was so fresh from the factory that the horns and stacks were still capped when Scotty Laird took this photo in late January or early February 1953.

The steam engines have been bumped from main line passenger service in the circa 1950 view but they are still handling the switching chores at the Miami Station. The ubiquitous Dade County Courthouse looms in the background with the implication that *IT* is the FEC Miami Station, rather than the wooden building in front of it.

Following the takeover by Castro the ferries were sold and WPB Terminal Co. survived by eking out a subsistence earned switching cars locally. The steam engines were disposed of and SW type switcher 238 (origins unknown), sans lettering, was the sole replacement for the entire group of steamers.

551 through 554 were built by EMD in 1949 as F3B's so that E3A's 501 through 508 could run in 3 unit (A-B-A) sets. 551 is at Buena Vista, shortly after delivery.

—(Charles & Richard Beall collection)

The traffic towers (one is shown here at N.W. 5th St.) in downtown Miami were a familiar sight to Miamians for many years.

In order to turn the FECs passenger trains at Miami, (since there was no loop at Buena Vista Yard until 1961) the FEC switchers would couple to the rear of the train; pull the train north past 71st Street (which was the entrance to the Miami Belt) and then push the train onto the Belt. At that point they would reverse direction and come forward on the other leg of the wye, completing the turn. They then headed south to Buena Vista Yard. This view taken at the Little River Station shows SW1200 224 just prior to reversing one of the streamliners.

Two diesel streamliners pass on the famous double iron, 1.4 miles south of the New Smyrna Beach passenger station.

—(J. Nelson Collection)

E6A 1005 sweeps past Buena Vista Yard with a fourteen car passenger train.

It's early in the morning of March 11, 1959 and E7A 1014 is drifting south past Buena Vista Yard with train 76, the Havana Special.

276

Following the emergence from receivership in 1961 the new ownership proceeded to eliminate the stunning red, yellow and silver paint scheme in favor of a much muted blue. GP7R 613, F3A 508, and FP7A 572 lead a high-speed piggyback train through Fort Lauderdale on September 8, 1967.

—(Photo by George Votava)

E7A 1008 thunders across Jupiter Inlet with the "City of Miami."

E6A 1003, a 2000 horsepower Electro Motive product built in the summer of 1940, lasted until the end of FEC passenger service. Shown in this photo #9 is approaching the St. Lucie Sound drawbridge.

When the FEC inaugurated streamliner service they called the seven car train "Henry M. Flagler" in honor of the founder of the road. E3A 1001 made the Jacksonville-Miami round trip every day from December 1939 until December 1940 in 12 hours and 59 minutes. The train would leave Jacksonville at 8 a.m., arrive Miami 1:59 p.m., be serviced in one hour, depart Miami at 3 p.m. and arrive back in Jacksonville at 8:59 p.m. The 1001 did this seven days a week, except when being serviced. In December, 1940, the Illinois Central, Pennsylvania and Chicago and Eastern Illinois, in conjunction with other connecting roads, inaugurated through Miami-Chicago stream-lined service. On December 17, 1940, the "Henry M. Flagler" became the "Dixie Flagler" and operated through to Chicago on an every third day schedule.

Unfortunately the 'cabins' in the upper right do not belie the location of the photo, but it is 1939 or 1940 and E3A 1001, in its original "from the factory" paint scheme is about to pass observation car "Bay Biscayne" on what must be the "Champion." The original photograph from the FEC files says "Stuart" and we can therefore surmise that the paved road on the right, with it's white, solid centerline is "U.S. Highway 1" and both trains are southbound.

E7B 1052 at the Miami Station.

—(Charles & Richard Beall collection)

FEC E7A 1021, with northbound train 3, slides into the old Fort Lauderdale depot.

SW9 226 is shown on August 29th, 1969, at New Smyrna Beach in the "terminal blues" paint scheme.

Wolfe was as artful with diesels as he was with steam. Here, E7A 1016 'drifts' the 1948-49 "New Royal Palm" to a gentle stop northbound at Fort Pierce. A sign hanging from the station eaves over the platform extolls the produce of the area…Indian River Fruit…Pure Juice…while the inevitable extra baggage of the returning tourists heading home to the north lies against the wheels of the baggage cart.

The FEC roundhouse at Buena Vista was a rickety-looking wooden structure, but it was built of Dade County Pine and was impervious to termites and weather. "Nighttime," said Laird, "was my favorite time to work, because we worked in the open year round and in the spring, summer and fall it was always much more livable after dark." Scotty took this photo of E7s 1014, 1022, 1021 and 1013 on the night of October 11,1954.

It's twilight in downtown Miami as GP7R 616, in blue paint scheme, idles near the passenger station in December 1961.

One of the great thrills of American Railroading was a ride on the Overseas Extension. This view, taken about 1927 shows a group of passengers on the "Havana Special" standing on the rear platform of the observation car as they cross the Long Key Viaduct.

## APPENDIX 3-a
## CONSTRUCTION MATERIALS USED IN BUILDING KEY WEST EXTENSION

Structural steel . . . . . . . . . . . . . . . . . . . . . . . . . . . . . . .38 million pounds
Concrete . . . . . . . . . . . . . . . . . . . . . . . . . .461,000 cubic yards (800,000 barrels)
Gravel . . . . . . . . . . . . . . . . . . . . . . . . . . . . . . . . . . . . .96,000 tons
Native corallime rock . . . . . . . . . . . . . . . . . . . . . . . .300,000 cubic yards
Reinforcing steel . . . . . . . . . . . . . . . . . . . . . .2,000 tons (4 million pounds)
Pine piles . . . . . . . . . . . . . . . . . . . . . . . . . . . . . . . . . . . .70,000
Jucone piles . . . . . . . . . . . . . . . . . . . .400, aggregating 77,927 cubic yards of rock
Sand . . . . . . . . . . . . . . . . . . . . . . . . . . . . . . . . .25,000 cubic yards
Trestle piles . . . . . . . . . . . . . . . . . . . . . . . . . . . . . . . . . . . .78,000

## APPENDIX 3-b
## FLOATING EQUIPMENT USED IN CONSTRUCTION OF KEY WEST EXTENSION

Launches . . . . . . . . . . . . . . . . . . . . . . . . . . .27 (5 to 50 horsepower)
Stern wheel steamers . . . . . . . . . . . . . . . . . . . .8 (from Mississippi River)
Tugs . . . . . . . . . . . . . . . . . . . . . . . . . . . . . . . . . . . . . . . . .3
Dredges . . . . . . . . . . . . . . . . . . . . . . . . . . . . . . . . . . . . . .12
Concrete mixers . . . . . . . . . . . . . . . . . . .10 (8 for water work, 2 for land use)
Pile drivers . . . . . . . . . . . . . . . . . . . . .12 (9 for water work 3 for land use)
Power Excavators . . . . . . . . . . . . . . . . . . . . . . . . . . . . . . . . .10
Catamaran . . . . . . . . . . . . . . . . . . . . . . . . . . . . . .1 (for coffer dams)
Derrick Barges . . . . . . . . . . . . . . . . . . . . . . . . .8 (10 to 30 ton capacity)
Lighters . . . . . . . . . . . . . . . . . . . . . . . . . . . . . . . . . . . . . .150
Steel barges . . . . . . . . . . . . . . . . . . . . . . . .2 (each 36 feet x 156 feet)
Locomotive cranes . . . . . . . . . . . . . . . . . . . . . . . . . . . . . . . . . . .6
Seagoing steamers . . . . . . . . . . . . . . . . . . . .2 (for handling cement in bulk)

All floating equipment was equipped with dynamos to generate electric light in order that work could continue on 24 hour basis, as necessary.

## APPENDIX 3-c
## LIST OF BRIDGES, KEY WEST EXTENSION

Jewfish Draw Bridge—223 feet
Key Largo Cut Bridge—360 feet
Tavernier Creek Bridge—133 feet
Snake Creek Bridge—192 feet
Whale Harbor Bridge—616 feet
Tea Table Relief Bridge—22 feet
Indian Key Bridge—2,004 feet
Tea Table Bridge—614 feet
Lignum Vitae Bridge—790 feet
Channel #2 Bridge—1,720 feet
Channel #5 Bridge—4,516 feet
Long Key Bridge—11,960 feet
Tom's Harbor Bridge 3—1,209 feet
Tom's Harbor Bridge 4—1,395 feet
Vaca Cut Bridge—120 feet
7-mile Bridge—35,716 feet
Little Duck-Missouri Bridge—800 feet
Missouri-Ohio Bridge—1,394 feet
Ohio-Bahia Honda Bridge—1,005 feet
Bahia Honda Bridge—5,356 feet
Spanish Harbor Bridge—3,311 feet

North Pine Bridge—620 feet
South Pine Bridge—806 feet
Torch Key Viaduct—779 feet
Torch-Ramrod Bridge—615 feet
Nile Channel Bridge—4,433 feet
Bow Channel Bridge—1,302 feet
Kemp's Channel Bridge—992 feet
Park Bridge—779 feet
North Harris Bridge—390 feet
Harris Gap—37 feet
Harris Bridge—390 feet
Lower Sugarloaf Bridge—1,210 feet
Saddle Bunch Bridge 2—554 feet
Saddle Bunch Bridge 3—656 feet
Saddle Bunch Bridge 4—800 feet
Saddle Bunch Bridge 5—800 feet
Shark Channel Bridge—1,989 feet
Rockland Channel Bridge—1,230 feet
Boca Chica Bridge—2,573 feet
Stock Island Bridge—360 feet
Key West Bridge—159 feet

# APPENDIX 4
## RAILWAY MAIL SERVICE (RAILWAY POST OFFICES) OPERATED ON THE FEC

| | | | |
|---|---|---|---|
| Jacksonville (Jack) & Titusville (note 1) | 1886-87 | | 159 Miles |
| Jack & Rockledge | 1893 | | 173.5 '' |
| Jack & Eau Gallie | 1893 | | 189.8 '' |
| Jack & Sebastian | 1893-94 | | 214.5 '' |
| Jack & Ft. Pierce | 1894 | | 241.6 '' |
| Jack & West Palm Beach | 1894-96 | | 299.0 '' |
| Jack & Miami | 1896-1912 | | 365.9 '' |
| | 1944-1963 | | |
| Miami & Key West (note 2) | 1909-1912 | | 156.0 '' |
| Jack & Key West (note 3) | 1912-1913 | | 522.0 '' |
| Jack & Ft. Pierce/Ft. Pierce & Key West (note 3) | 1913-1926 | | |
| Jack & Key West | 1926-1944 | | 522.0 '' |
| St. Augustine & Bunnell | 1930-1935 | | 50.0 '' |

**BRANCH LINES** (note 4)

| | | | |
|---|---|---|---|
| Titusville & Sanford (note 1) | 1887-1898 | 1899-1911 | 47.0 '' |
| Titusville & Enterprise | 1913-1917 | | 40.0 '' |
| New Smyrna & Okeechobee | 1921-1935 | | 141.1 '' |
| New Smyrna & Lake Harbor | 1935-1947 | | 196.6 '' |

Note 1: Jack & Titusville and Titusville & Sanford (1887-1898) were operated by the JT & KW Railroad

Note 2: Miami & Key West RPO operated by rail to Knight's Key and by steamship to Key West.

Note 3: In 1913 Jack & Key West became Jack & Ft. Pierce/Ft. Pierce & Key West, with crews changing at Ft. Pierce. In 1926 the line was retitled Jack & Key West Northern Division and Jack & Key West Southern Division (ND and SD were the abbreviations) but the crews continued to change at Ft. Pierce.

Note 4: While it appears that Jack & Mayport; New Smyrna Beach & Orange City; and Ft. Pierce & Lake Harbor did not have RPO service, all three lines carried mail in baggage or express cars in what was known as Closed Pouch (CP) service. No mail is sorted or cancelled in CP service.

3719 enhanced with air conditioners and logoed with the "Going Places in Florida" emblem shows its obvious Railway Post Office ancestry.

## APPENDIX 5
## FREIGHT EQUIPMENT AND COMPANY SERVICE EQUIPMENT

The 1962 Summary of Equipment, prepared by the Office of Vice-President and Chief Mechanical Officer, St. Augustine, Florida, is as follows:

### COMPANY SERVICE EQUIPMENT

| Type: | Capacity | Number Owned |
|---|---|---|
| Instruction Car | #3605 | 1 |
| Business Cars | #95 & Randleigh | 2 |
| Wrecking Cranes— | Steam 150 ton | 3 |
| Locomotive Cranes— | Diesel 25 ton | 2 |
| Wrecking Outfit Cars | | 18 |
| Fuel Oil Cars | (3300 & 18000 Series) | 16 |
| Water Cars | (900, 3300, 3400, 3500, and 18000 Series) | 19 |
| Wheelcars | | 14 |
| Tool Cars | | 16 |
| Cook, Dining, etc. | | 19 |
| Tie Unloading Cars | (3686-3688) | 3 |
| Misc. Cars | | 77 |
| | TOTAL | 210 |

### LEASED EQUIPMENT

| Type | Series | Number Leased | Length | Capacity |
|---|---|---|---|---|
| Tri-Level | TTX 476629 | 1 | 85 | 130 000 |
| | TTX 200280 | 1 | 87 | 120 000 |
| | 200287 | 1 | 87 | 120 000 |
| | 200309 | 1 | | |
| | 200335 | 1 | | |
| | 200345 | 1 | | |
| | 200348 | 1 | | |
| | 200352 | 1 | | |
| | 200353 | 1 | | |
| Flat—steel-gypsum Bd Series | 1301-1310 | 10 | 53 | 140 000 |
| Chassis 5515 (Auto) | 6601-6612 | 12 | — | — |

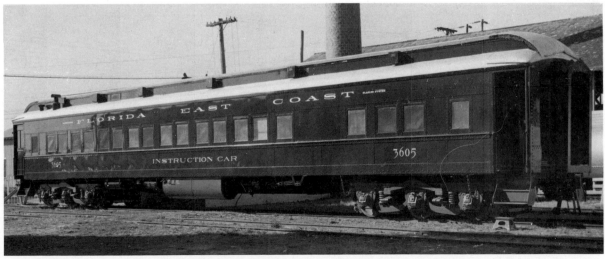

In order to properly train employees located north and south of St. Augustine, instruction car 3605 was a regular visitor to the FECs 'hinterlands.'

## FREIGHT EQUIPMENT

| Type | Series | Number owned | Year Built | Nominal Inside Length | Door Opening | Capacity |
|------|--------|-------------|-----------|----------------------|-------------|----------|
| Box-Steel Underframe | 20502-20679 | 35 | 1924 | 40' | 6'0 | 80 000 |
| Box-Steel | 21001-21061 | 49 | 1945 | 40' | 6'0 | 100 000 |
| | TOTAL | 84 | | | | |
| Flat-Steel-Gypsum Bd service | 1451-1458 | 7 | 1940 | 46' | | 100 000 |
| Flat-Steel Gypsum Bd service | 1465-1467 | 3 | 1926 | 48' | | 100 000 |
| Flat-Steel Gypsum Bd service | 1469-1479 | 11 | 1957-1958 | 46' | | 100 000 |
| Flat-Steel wheel cars | 1501-1503 | 3 | 1923 | 42' | | 80 000 |
| Flat-Steel | 2001-2020 | 20 | 1959 | 85' | | 130 000 |
| Flat-Steel | 2101-2122 | 22 | 1961 | 89' | | 95 000 |
| Flat-Steel | 7001-7192 | 25 | 1923 | 42' | | 80 000 |
| | TOTAL | 91 | | | | |
| Gondolas-Steel | 12001-12030 | 30 | 1942 | 42' | | 100 000 |
| Gondolas-Steel | 12101-12200 | 98 | 1953 | 42' | | 100 000 |
| Gondolas-Steel | 12201-12550 | 347 | 1957-1958 | 42' | | 140 000 |
| | TOTAL | 475 | | | | |
| Hoppers-Steel-Open Top | 13001-13030 | 30 | 1942 | 33' | | 100 000 |
| | 13501-13550 | 50 | 1957 | 40' | | 140 000 |
| | TOTAL | 80 | | | | |
| Covered Hopper-Steel | 14001-14200* | 197 | 1952-1957 | 29' | | 140 000 |
| | TOTAL | 197 | | | | |
| Caboose | | | | | | |
| Steel Underframe (38 radio) | 702-760 | 45 | 1926 | — | — | — |
| | TOTAL | 45 | | | | |
| | GRAND TOTAL | 972 | | | | |

*84 Hoppers are leased to North American Car Corporation.


## LEASED EQUIPMENT

| Type | Series | Number Leased | Length | Capacity |
|------|--------|--------------|--------|----------|
| Tri-Level | TTX 476629 | 1 | 85 | 130 000 |
| | TTX 200280 | 1 | 87 | 120 000 |
| | 200287 | 1 | 87 | 120 000 |
| | 200309 | 1 | | |
| | 200335 | 1 | | |
| | 200345 | 1 | | |
| | 200348 | 1 | | |
| | 200352 | 1 | | |
| | 200353 | 1 | | |
| Flat—steel-gypsum Bd Series | 1301-1310 | 10 | 53 | 140 000 |
| Chassis (Auto) | 6601-6612 | 12 | — | — |

One of the FECs ventilated boxcars of the 17000 series, built in 1920. Note the overseas emblem on the side of the car.

Duress breeds ingenuity, and as the ventilated express box cars became obsolete in the late 1960s they were converted to everything from tool cars to this strange-looking weed sprayer unit.

As befitted a railroad baron (not to mention Flagler's brother-in-law) the FEC's President, and later its Receiver, W. R. Kenan, travelled in the "Randleigh," which, though lettered for the Flagler System's railroad, he personally owned. As of this writing, the car is still in use on the Chesapeake & Ohio.
—*(Wolfe photo, J. Nelson Collection)*

FEC box car 609 at "Ol'Hoss" Warehouse in Miami on May 20, 1959.

21019 proudly boosts the Speedway to America's Playground.
—*(J. Nelson Collection)*

The FEC, like most other American railroads was judicious as well as thrifty in its use of wornout revenue equipment. 3443 shown in this photo as foreman-bunk-cook car had been converted from a 17000 series box car.

The classic little red caboose. This view, taken at Mount Vernon Car Manufacturing Company in Mount Vernon, Illinois, shows an FEC side door passenger-carrying caboose in all its glory. For some time, the branch line utilized these cabooses to carry passengers on their mixed trains as well as using combination mail-baggage-express cars at the end of the short freights.

It's sixty years later and FEC 817 has been converted to a road caboose from a ventilated express box car. Today (1984) only one of these cabooses (used by the Property Protection Department) still exists on "The railroad that is going places in Florida."

291

After 610 hit a semi at South Bay, 3377 was brought up
from Miami to rerail the GP7R. ("And you shoulda seen
the semi!")

—(Charles & Richard Beall collection)

# APPENDIX 6
## FEC PASSENGER EQUIPMENT (Early cars and Heavyweight)

| CAR TYPE | Series | FEC Name/Nº | Date Built or Acquired | Builder or Acquisition From | Date Rebuilt or Retired | Converted to | Conversion Date | New Number | Disposition | Notes |
|---|---|---|---|---|---|---|---|---|---|---|
| PRIVATE CAR | | 90 | June 1899 | Jackson and Sharp | | | | | Scrap 1924 | |
| PRIVATE CAR | | 91 | June 1914 | Jackson and Sharp | | | | | Scrap 1924 | |
| PRIVATE CAR | | 92 | July 1893 | Jackson and Sharp | | | | | Scrap 1925 | |
| OBSERVATION CAR | | 1 | July 1887 | Jackson and Sharp | 1909 | | | | Scrap 1925 | |
| OBSERVATION CAR | | 2 | July 1887 | Jackson and Sharp | 1909 | | | | Sold 1928 | |
| COACH-BAGGAGE | | 24 | Mar 1887 | Billinger and Small | | | | | Scrap 1926 | |
| COACH | | 25 | Feb 1889 | Jackson and Sharp | 1895 | | | | Scrap 1926 | |
| COACH | | 26 | Feb 1889 | Jackson and Sharp | 1895 | | | | Scrap 1926 | |
| COACH-BAGGAGE | | 28 | Mar 1887 | Billinger and Small | | (originally #4 from St. A. & H.R. Rly. Co.) | | | Scrap 1926 | |
| COACH-BAGGAGE | | 29 | Mar 1887 | Billinger and Small | | (originally #6 from St. A. & H.R. Rly. Co.) | | | Scrap 1926 | |
| COACH | | 30 | Jan 1893 | Jackson and Sharp | | | | | Scrap 1926 | |
| COACH | | 31 | Jan 1893 | Jackson and Sharp | | | | | Scrap 1924 | |
| COACH | | 32 | Jan 1893 | Jackson and Sharp | | | | | Scrap 1926 | |
| COACH | | 33 | Jan 1893 | Jackson and Sharp | | | | | Scrap 1926 | |
| COACH | | 34 | Jan 1893 | Jackson and Sharp | | | | | Scrap 1926 | |
| COACH | | 35 | Jan 1894 | Jackson and Sharp | | | | | Retired 1934 | |
| COACH | | 36 | Jan 1894 | Jackson and Sharp | 1926 | Bunk | 1926 | 3397 | Scrap 1929 | |
| COACH | | 37 | Jan 1894 | Jackson and Sharp | | | | | Scrap 1924 | |
| BAGGAGE-MAIL | | 38 | 1887 | Blain & Co. | | (originally #8 from St. A. & H.R. Rly. Co.) | | | Scrap 1926 | |
| COACH | | 40 | Feb 1887 | Jackson and Sharp | 1895 | (originally #9 from St. A. & H.R. Rly. Co.) | | | Scrap 1926 | |
| COACH | | 41 | Feb 1887 | Jackson and Sharp | 1895 | | | | Sold 1926 | |
| COACH | | 42 | Feb 1889 | Jackson and Sharp | 1895 | | | | Sold 1928 | |
| COACH | | 43 | Feb 1889 | Jackson and Sharp | 1895 | | | | Sold 1928 | |
| COACH | | 44 | Feb 1889 | Jackson & Sharp | 1895 | | | | Sold 1926 | |
| COACH | | 45 | Feb 1889 | Jackson & Sharp | 1895 | | | | Scrap 1943 | |
| COACH | | 46 | Feb 1889 | Jackson & Sharp | | | | | Sold 1926 | |
| COACH | | 47 | Jan 1893 | Jackson & Sharp | 1926 | Cook & Diner | 1926 | 3408 | Scrap 1942 | |
| COACH | | 48 | Jan 1893 | Jackson & Sharp | | | | | Scrap 1929 | |
| COACH | | 49 | Jan 1893 | Jackson & Sharp | 1926 | Bunk | 1926 | 3409 | Sold 1926 | |
| COACH | | 50 | Jan 1893 | Jackson & Sharp | | | | | Scrap 1926 | |
| COACH | | 51 | Jan 1893 | Jackson & Sharp | | | | | Scrap 1926 | |
| COACH | | 52 | Oct 1893 | Jackson & Sharp | 1894 | | | | Scrap 1927 | |
| COACH | | 53 | 1894 | Jackson & Sharp | | | | | Scrap 1929 | |
| COACH | | 54 | 1894 | Jackson & Sharp | | | | | Sold 1928 | |
| COACH | | 55 | 1894 | Jackson & Sharp | | | | | Sold 1926 | |
| COACH | | 56 | 1894 | Jackson & Sharp | | | | | Scrap 1926 | |
| COACH | | 57 | 1894 | Jackson & Sharp | | | | | Scrap 1927 | |
| COACH | | 58 | 1894 | Jackson & Sharp | | | | | Scrap 1927 | |
| COACH | | 59 | 1894 | Jackson & Sharp | | (originally #49 from St. J. & H.R. Rly. Co.) | | | Scrap 1927 | |
| COACH | | 60 | 1894 | Jackson & Sharp | | (originally #50 from St. J. & H.R. Rly. Co.) | | | Scrap 1927 | |
| COACH | | 61 | 1894 | Jackson & Sharp | | | | | Scrap 1927 | |
| COACH (Vestibule) | | 62 | Feb 1902 | American Car & Foundry Co. | | | | | Scrap 1927 | |
| COACH (Vestibule) | | 63 | Feb 1902 | American Car & Foundry Co. | | | | | Destroyed 1925 | |
| COACH (Open end) | | 64 | Feb 1902 | American Car & Foundry Co. | | | | | Scrap 1929 | |
| COACH (Open end) | | 65 | Feb 1902 | American Car & Foundry Co. | | | | | Scrap 1929 | |
| COACH (Platform end) | | 66 | Feb 1902 | American Car & Foundry Co. | | | | | Destroyed 1925 | |
| COACH (Platform end) | | 67 | Feb 1902 | American Car & Foundry Co. | | | | | Scrap 1929 | |
| COACH (Platform end) | | 68 | Feb 1902 | American Car & Foundry Co. | | | | | Scrap 1929 | |
| COACH (Platform end) | | 69 | Feb 1902 | American Car & Foundry Co. | | | | | Scrap 1926 | |
| COACH (Platform end) | | 70 | Feb 1902 | American Car & Foundry Co. | | | | | Dismantled 1930 | |
| COACH (Platform end) | | 71 | Feb 1902 | American Car & Foundry Co. | | | | | Sold 1927 | |

| CAR TYPE | Series | FEC Name/N° | Date Built or Acquired | Builder or Acquisition From | Date Rebuilt or Retired | Converted to | Conversion Date | New Number | Disposition | Notes |
|---|---|---|---|---|---|---|---|---|---|---|
| COACH | Mahogany Finish | 72 | Mar 1906 | Pullman Co. | | | | | Dismantled 1930 | |
| COACH | Oak Finish | 73 | Mar 1906 | Pullman Co. | | Work Car | | 3416 | Dismantled 1930 | |
| COACH | Mahogany Finish | 74 | Mar 1906 | Pullman Co. | | | | | Dismantled 1930 | |
| COACH | Mahogany Finish | 75 | Mar 1906 | Pullman Co. | | | | | Dismantled 1930 | |
| COACH | Mahogany Finish | 76 | Mar 1906 | Pullman Co. | | | | | Destroyed 1918 | |
| COACH | Oak Finish | 77 | Mar 1906 | Pullman Co. | | | | | Dismantled 1930 | |
| COACH | Mahogany Finish | 78 | Mar 1906 | Pullman Co. | | | | | Dismantled 1930 | |
| COACH | Oak Finish | 79 | Mar 1906 | Pullman Co. | | | | | Dismantled 1930 | |
| COACH | Oak Finish | 80 | Mar 1906 | Pullman Co. | | | | | Destroyed 1918 | |
| COACH | Oak Finish | 81 | Mar 1906 | Pullman Co. | | | | | Destroyed 1918 | |
| COACH | | 82 | Sept 1888 | Jackson and Sharp | (originally Parlor Car #102) | | | | Dismantled 1930 | |
| COACH | | 83 | Sept 1888 | | (originally Parlor Car #103) | | | | | |
| | | 100 | Jan 1912 | Pullman Co. | 1947 | Wrecker, Cook & Dining | 1947 | 3612 | | |
| | | 101 | Jan 1912 | Pullman Co. | 1947 | Instruction Car | 1948 | 3605 | | |
| | | 102 | Jan 1912 | Pullman Co. | 1947 | Wrecker, Tool Car | 1947 | 3607 | | |
| | | 103 | Jan 1912 | Pullman Co. | 1947 | | | | | |
| | | 104 | Jan 1912 | Pullman Co. | 1947 | Wrecker, Foreman & Sleeper | 1947 | 3608 | | |
| | | 105 | Jan 1912 | Pullman Co. | 1947 | Wrecker, Foreman & Sleeper | 1947 | 3610 | | |
| | | 106 | Jan 1912 | Pullman Co. | 1947 | Wrecker, Foreman & Sleeper | 1947 | 3611 | | |
| | | 107 | 1921 | | | | | | | |
| | | 108 | 1921 | | 1948 | Foreman & Dining | 1951 | 3631 | | |
| | | 109 | 1921 | | 1948 | Bunk | 1948 | 3617 | | |
| | | 110 | 1921 | | 1947 | Cook & Dining | 1947 | 3609 | | |
| | | 111 | 1921 | | 1947 | Cook & Dining | 1947 | 3613 | | |
| | | 112 | 1921 | | | | | | | |
| | | 113 | 1921 | | 1948 | Foreman & Dining | 1948 | 3618 | | |
| | | 114 | 1921 | | 1948 | Foreman & Dining | 1951 | 3632 | | |
| | | 115 | 1921 | | | | | | | |
| COACH | | 116 | 1921 | | 1957 | Foreman & Bunk | 1958 | 3673 | | |
| COACH | | 117 | 1921 | | 1957 | Cook & Dining | 1958 | 3674 | | |
| COACH | | 118 | 1921 | | | | | | | |
| COACH | | 119 to 150 | 1925 | | | | | | | |
| | | 151 | | | 1948 | Cook & Dining | 1948 | 3619 | Dismantled 1959 | |
| | | 152 | | | | | | | | |
| | | 153 | | | | | | | | |
| | | 154 | | | | | | | | |
| | | 155 | | | 1948 | Bunk | 1948 | 3620 | Scrap 1958 | |
| | | 156 | | | | | | | | |
| | | 157 | | | | | | | | |
| | | 158 | | | | | | | | |
| | | 159 | | | | | | | | |
| | | 160 | | | | | | | | |
| | | 161 | | | 1948 | Foreman & Cook | 1948 | 3621 | | |
| | | 162 | | | | | | | | |
| | | 163 | | | | | | | | |
| | | 164 | | | | | | | | |
| | | 165 | | | 1947 | Camp | 1947 | 3614 | | Converted to Bunk Car 1948 |
| | | 166 | | | | | | | | |
| | | 167 | | | 1946 | Foreman & Bunk | 1946 | 3602 | | |
| | | 168 | | | | | | | | |
| | | 169 | | | | | | | | |
| | | 170 | | | | | | | | |

| CAR TYPE | Series | FEC Name/N° | Date Built or Acquired | Builder or Acquisition From | Date Rebuilt or Retired | Converted to | Conversion Date | New Number | Disposition | Notes |
|---|---|---|---|---|---|---|---|---|---|---|
| COACH | | 204 | | | 1948 | Cook & Dining | 1948 | 3622 | | |
| COACH | | 205 | | | 1947 | Camp | 1947 | 3615 | Converted to Bunk 1948 | |
| COACH | | 206 | | | 1948 | Bunk | 1948 | 3623 | | |
| COACH | | 207 | | | 1948 | Foreman & Bunk | 1948 | 3616 | | |
| COACH | | 208 | | | 1948 | Foreman & Dining | 1948 | 3624 | Scrapped 1955 | |
| COACH | | 209 | | | 1948 | Foreman & Dining | 1948 | 3629 | | |
| COACH | | 210 | | | 1948 | Foreman & Bunk | 1948 | 3627 | | |
| COACH | | 211 | | | 1948 | Foreman & Dining | 1948 | 3628 | | |
| COACH | | 212 | | | 1948 | Foreman & Dining | 1948 | 3630 | Retired 1956 Sold 1957 | |
| MAIL | | 300 | Feb 1889 | Jackson & Sharp | | | | | Sold 1930 | |
| MAIL | | 302 | Feb 1893 | Jackson & Sharp | | | | | Sold 1930 | |
| MAIL | | 305 | Jan 1902 | American Car & Foundry Co. | | | | | Sold 1925 | |
| MAIL | | 306 | Jan 1902 | American Car & Foundry Co | | | | | Sold 1925 | |
| BAGGAGE-MAIL | | 308 | Jan 1894 | Jackson & Sharp | | | | | | |
| MAIL | | 309 | Jan 1912 | Pullman Co. | | | | | | |
| MAIL | | 310 | Jan 1912 | Pullman Co. | | | | | Note: Cars to 323 | |
| MAIL | | 311 | Jan 1912 | Pullman Co. | | | | | are shown on the | |
| MAIL | | 312 | Feb 1914 | Pullman Co. | | | | | 1937 inventory as still | |
| MAIL | | 313 | Feb 1914 | Pullman Co. | | | | | in service. | |
| MAIL | | 314 | Feb 1914 | Pullman Co. | | | | | | |
| MAIL-BAGGAGE | | 315 | Feb 1914 | Pullman Co. | | | | | | |
| MAIL-BAGGAGE | | 316 | Feb 1914 | Pullman Co. | | | | | | |
| MAIL-BAGGAGE | | 317 | | | | | | | | |
| | | 318 | | | | | | | | |
| RAILWAY POSTAL CARS | | 319 | | | | | | | | |
| | | 320 | | | | | | | | |
| | | 321 | | | | | | | | |
| | | 322 | | | | | | | | |
| | | 323 | | | | | | | | |
| BAGGAGE EXPRESS | | 402 | Jan 1899 | Barney, Smith & Co | | | | | Dismantled 1930 | |
| | | 403 | Jan 1899 | Barney, Smith & Co | | | | | Dismantled 1930 | |
| | | 404 | Jan 1899 | Barney, Smith & Co. | | | | | Dismantled 1930 | |
| | | 405 | 1895 | Jackson & Sharp | | | | | Dismantled 1930 | |
| | | 406 | 1895 | Jackson & Sharp | | | | | Dismantled 1930 | |
| | | 407 | 1895 | Jackson & Sharp | | | | | Dismantled 1930 | |
| | | 408 | 1895 | Jackson & Sharp | | | | | Scrap 1929 | |
| | | 409 | 1895 | Jackson & Sharp | | | | | Scrap 1929 | |
| BAGGAGE | | 411 | July 1887 | Jackson & Sharp | | | | | Sold 1930 | |
| BAGGAGE | | 412 | Jan 1888 | | | | | | Scrap 1924 | |
| BAGGAGE | | 413 | Jan 1889 | | | | | | Scrap 1920 | |
| BAGGAGE | | 415 | 1887 | Billinger & Small | | | | | Dismantled 1920 | |
| BAGGAGE | | 420 | Jan 1894 | Jackson & Sharp | | | | | Scrap 1925 | |
| BAGGAGE | | 421 | Jan 1894 | Jackson & Sharp | | | | | Scrap 1925 | |
| BAGGAGE EXPRESS | | 424 | Jan 1891 | American Car & Foundry Co. | | | | | Dismantled 1924 | |
| | | 425 | Jan 1891 | American Car & Foundry Co. | | | | | Scrap 1925 | |
| | | 426 | Jan 1891 | American Car & Foundry Co. | | | | | Scrap 1925 | |
| | | 427 | Jan 1891 | American Car & Foundry Co. | | | | | Dismantled 1930 | |
| | | 428 | Jan 1891 | American Car & Foundry Co. | | | | | Scrap 1924 | |
| | | 429 | Jan 1891 | American Car & Foundry Co. | | | | | Dismantled 1930 | |
| | | 430 | Mar 1906 | Pullman Co. | | | | | Dismantled 1930 | |
| | | 431 | Mar 1906 | Pullman Co. | | | | | Dismantled 1930 | |
| | | 432 | Mar 1906 | Pullman Co. | | | | | Dismantled 1930 | |
| | | 433 | Mar 1906 | Pullman Co. | | | | | Destroyed 1925 | |
| | | 434 | Mar 1906 | Pullman Co. | | | | | Dismantled 1930 | |

| CAR TYPE | Series | FEC Name/Nº | Date Built or Acquired | Builder or Acquisition From | Date Rebuilt or Retired | Converted to | Conversion Date | New Number | Disposition | Notes |
|---|---|---|---|---|---|---|---|---|---|---|
| BAGGAGE EXPRESS | | 435 | Mar 1906 | Pullman Co. | | | | | Dismantled 1930 | |
| | | 436 | Jan 1912 | Pullman Co. | | | | | Destroyed 1953 | |
| | | 437 | Jan 1912 | Pullman Co. | | | | | Unknown | |
| | | 438 | Jan 1912 | Pullman Co. | | | | | Destroyed 1953 | |
| | | 439 | Jan 1912 | Pullman Co. | | | | | Unknown | |
| | | 440 to 499 | 1926 | | | | | | | |
| DINER | | Royal Poinciana | Jan 3 1915 | ACL Ry. Co. | | | | | | |
| | | Ponce de Leon | Jan 3 1915 | ACL Ry. Co. | | | | | | |
| (Special) Ganz Motor Car | | | 1906 | Ganz Motor Car Co. (Vienna, Austria) | | | | | Sold Mar 31, 1921 | |

Note: 1935 inventory shows cars 436 to 461 as still in service. All others scrapped.

Note: Company year end reports indicate cars purchased, retired or sold but in most cases there are no names given or car numbers recorded. Where mentioned in the report, they are noted herein:

1. 1920 — Purchase 2 Diners; Ormond and Alcazar (purchased 2nd hand) also 2 all steel mail cars and 6 baggage express cars.
2. 1921 — Purchase 6 steel coaches—
3. 1922 — Purchase 10 baggage cars—
4. 1923 — Purchase 1 steel Diner (Breakers)
5. 1924 — Purchase 15 baggage cars; 2 mail cars
6. 1925 — Purchase 27 coaches and 20 rebuilt Pullman coaches; 3 Diners (Royal Palm, Casa Marina, St. Augustine)
7. 1926 — Purchase 15 coaches, 2 mail cars; 8 baggage cars, 2 Diners (Daytona and Key West) and Official Cars 93, 94, 95
8. No purchases for 1927, 1928 and 1929
9. 1930 — Retired 10 coaches, 16 baggage-express and 2 mail cars
10. No purchases for 1931, 1932, 1933, 1934, 1935 and 1936.

The scarcity of company records for early passenger equipment is evident by the above as well as the blanks in the preceeding passenger heavyweight chart.

# FEC PASSENGER EQUIPMENT (Heavyweight)

| CAR TYPE | Series | FEC Name/Nº | Date Built or Acquired | Builder or Acquisition From | Date Rebuilt or Retired | Converted to | Conversion Date | New Number | Disposition | Notes |
|---|---|---|---|---|---|---|---|---|---|---|
| SLEEPER | 10 Sect-1 Drawing Room | Fort Amador | 1949 | Pullman Co. | 1957 | Foreman & Bunk Car | 1957 | 3671 | | |
| | | Manchuria | 1949 | Pullman Co. | 1957 | Bunk Car | 1957 | 3668 | | |
| | | Streator | 1949 | Pullman Co. | 1957 | Bunk Car | 1957 | 3669 | | |
| | | Lindley | 1949 | Pullman Co. | 1957 | Bunk Car | 1957 | 3670 | | |
| | | Lake Goodwin | 1949 | Pullman Co. | — | — | — | — | Retired 1960 | |
| | | Lake Michigan | 1949 | Pullman Co. | — | — | — | — | Retired 1960 | |
| | 10 Sect-2 double bedroom | | | | | | | | | |
| | 10 Section-Observation | Piedmont College | 1949 | Pullman Co. | — | — | — | — | | |
| | | Mountain Side | 1949 | Pullman Co. | 1952 | Foreman & Bunk Car | 1954 | 3639 | | |
| | | Mountain Queen | 1949 | Pullman Co. | 1952 | Foreman & Bunk Car | 1954 | 3638 | | |

| CAR TYPE | Series | FEC Name/N° | Date Built or Acquired | Builder or Acquisition From | Date Rebuilt or Retired | Converted to | Conversion Date | New Number | Disposition | Notes |
|---|---|---|---|---|---|---|---|---|---|---|
| Baggage-Express | | #501 | 1950 | | | | | | Sold to SAL; numbered #6070 | This car is the only lightweight car bearing a number. |
| Baggage-Dormitory | | Halifax River | | | | | | | Sold to SAL; numbered #6057 | |
| | | St. Johns River | | | | | | | Sold to SAL; numbered #6058 | |
| Coach Baggage-Dormitory | | Indian River | 1939 | | | | | | Sold to SAL; numbered #6006 | |
| Coach-Baggage | | Banana River | 1939 | | | | | | Destroyed in 1953 accident | |
| Coach-Lounge | | Port Everglades | 1948 | | | | | | Destroyed in 1953 accident | |
| Coach | | Delray Beach | 1939 | | | | | | Sold to SAL; numbered #6252 | |
| | | New Smyrna Beach | 1939 | | | | | | Sold to SAL; numbered #6253 | |
| | | Melbourne | 1939 | | | | | | Sold to SAL; numbered #6254 | |
| | | Vero Beach | 1939 | | | | | | Sold to SAL; numbered #6255 | |
| | | Pompano | 1939 | | | | | | Sold to SAL; numbered #6256 | |
| | | Boca Raton | 1939 | | | | | | Sold to SAL; numbered #6257 | |
| | | Dania | 1946 | | | | | | Sold to SAL; numbered #6258 | |
| | | Eau Gallie | 1946 | | | | | | Sold to SAL; numbered #6259 | |
| | | Ormond | 1946 | | | | | | Sold to SAL; numbered #6260 | |
| | | Wabasso | 1946 | | | | | | Sold to SAL; numbered #6261 | |
| | | Belle Glade | 1946 | | | | | | Sold to SAL; numbered #6262 | |
| | | Jacksonville | 1946 | | | | | | Sold to SAL; numbered #6263 | |
| | | Stuart | 1946 | | | | | | Sold to SAL; numbered #6264 | |
| | | Pahokee | 1950 | | | | | | Sold to SAL; numbered #6265 | |
| | | Sebastian | 1950 | | | | | | Sold to SAL; numbered #6266 | |
| | | Canal Point | 1950 | | | | | | Sold to SAL; numbered #6267 | |
| | | Salerno | 1950 | | | | | | Sold to SAL; numbered #6268 | |
| | | Lantana | 1950 | | | | | | Sold to SAL; numbered #6269 | |
| | | Hypoluxo | 1950 | | | | | | Sold to SAL; numbered #6270 | |
| | | St. Augustine | 1954 | | | | | | Sold to SAL; numbered #6271 | |
| | | Miami | 1954 | | | | | | Sold to SAL; numbered #6272 | |
| | | Hollywood | 1954 | | | | | | Sold to SAL; numbered #6273 | |
| | | Cocoa-Rockledge | 1954 | | | | | | Sold to SAL; numbered #6274 | |
| | | Boynton | 1946 | | | | | | Sold to Long Island Railroad | |
| | | Bunnell | 1946 | | | | | | Sold to Long Island Railroad | |
| | | Homestead | 1946 | | | | | | Sold to Long Island Railroad | |
| | | Titusville | 1946 | | | | | | Sold to Long Island Railroad | |
| Diner | | Ft. Lauderdale | 1939 | | | | | | Sold to SAL; numbered #6115 | |
| | | Ft. Dallas | 1946 | | | | | | Sold to SAL; numbered #6116 | |
| | | Ft. Crum | 1950 | | | | | | Sold to SAL; numbered #6120 | |
| | | Ft. Pierce | 1939 | | | | | | Destroyed in 1953 accident | |
| | | Ft. San Marco | 1946 | | | | | | Sold to SAL; numbered #6118 | |
| | | Ft. Ribault | 1950 | | | | | | Sold to SAL; numbered #6119 | |
| | | Ft. Matanzas | 1946 | | | | | | Sold to SAL; numbered #6117 | |

| CAR TYPE | Series | FEC Name/N° | Date Built or Acquired | Builder or Acquisition From | Date Rebuilt or Retired | Converted to | Conversion Date | New Number | Disposition | Notes |
|---|---|---|---|---|---|---|---|---|---|---|
| Diner-Bar-Lounge | | South Bay | 1950 | | | | | | Unknown | |
| Sleeper | | Scott M. Loftin | 1954 | (4 Section - 4 Roomette-5 Double Bedroom) | | | | | Sold to CNR renumbered #1700; named Wirdigo | |
| | | Jamaica | 1954 | | | | | | Sold to CNR renumbered #1701; named Manitou | |
| | | Guatemala | 1949 | (10 Roomette - 6 Bedroom) | | | | | Sold to CNR renumbered #2130; named Terra Nova River | |
| | | Argentina | 1949 | (10 Roomette - 6 Bedroom) | | | | | Sold to CNR renumbered #2136; named Grand Codmy River | |
| | | Venezuela | 1949 | (10 Roomette - 6 Bedroom) | | | | | Sold to CNR renumbered #2132; named Moose River | |
| | | Brazil | 1949 | (10 Roomette - 6 Bedroom) | | | | | Sold to CNR renumbered #2133; named Ecum Secum River | |
| | | Chile | 1949 | (10 Roomette - 6 Bedroom) | | | | | Sold to CNR renumbered #2134; named Nashwaak River | |
| | | Oriente | 1949 | (10 Roomette - 6 Bedroom) | | | | | Sold to CNR renumbered #2135; named Grand Rivière | |
| | | Caparra | 1949 | (10 Roomette - 6 Bedroom) | | | | | Sold to CNR renumbered #2136; named Rivière Cloche | |
| | | Cuba | 1949 | (10 Roomette - 6 Bedroom) | | | | | Sold to CNR renumbered #2137; named Rivière St. Francais | |
| | | Columbia | 1949 | (10 Roomette - 6 Bedroom) | | | | | Sold to CNR renumbered #2138; named Belle River | |
| | | Bahamian | 1949 | (10 Roomette - 6 Bedroom) | | | | | Sold to CNR renumbered #2139; named Deep River | |
| | | Havana | 1949 | (10 Roomette - 6 Bedroom) | | | | | Sold to CNR renumbered #2140; named Petowawa River | |
| | | Honduras | 1949 | (10 Roomette - 6 Bedroom) | | | | | Sold to CNR renumbered #2141; named Naiscoot River | |
| | | Panama | 1950 | (14 Roomette - 2 Drawing Room) | | | | | Unknown | |
| | | Salvador | 1949 | (21 Roomette) | | | | | Unknown | |
| | | Uruguay | 1949 | (21 Roomette) | | | | | Unknown | |
| Sleeping-Bar-Lounge | | Magnolia | 1949 | (6 Bedroom-Bar-Lounge) | | | | | Sold to CNR renumbered #1095; named North Star | |
| | | Oleander | 1949 | (6 Bedroom-Bar-Lounge) | | | | | Sold to CNR renumbered #1096; named North Wind | |
| Bar-Lounge | | South Bay | 1950 | | | | | | Sold to SAL; renumbered #6620; originally built as a Diner-Lounge; Converted 1956 | |
| Tavern-Observation | | Lake Worth | 1939 | | | | | | Sold to SAL; renumbered #6606 | |
| | | Bay Biscayne | 1939 | | | | | | Sold to SAL; renumbered #6607 | |
| | | Hobe Sound | 1946 | | | | | | Scrapped by FEC, 1966 or 67. | |
| | | St. Lucie Sound | 1946 | | | | | | Sold to Private owners; later resold | |
| | | Lake Okeechobee | 1946 | | | | | | Sold to Long Island Railroad | |
| Business Car | | Azalea | 1950 | (5 Double Bed Rm-Bar Lounge-Observation) | | | | | | |

FEC coach 100 was the first of a series of heavy-duty, heavyweight all steel long distance coaches. All were numbered in the 100 series and all had reversible seats which could be arranged so that the passengers would be facing in the direction of travel regardless of which way the car was travelling.

FEC 90, Flagler's office car, is on display at the Flagler Museum in Palm Beach, Florida. However, a careful analysis of these three photos indicates that the car known as 90 at the Flagler Museum may not be the original office car. The earliest view of 90, shows it with wood sheathing and open windows. This view was taken at Wilmington, Delaware in 1898. The second view is shown at the Jackson and Sharp plant in Wilmington following rebuilding, February 1924. Both platforms have been enclosed and the ends have been sheathed in steel. The third view shows the final disposition of FEC 90; the car now belonging to a Mr. Darby of Darby Woodworking Products co., in Hagerstown, Maryland. This final photo came from the files of the L & N Railroad.

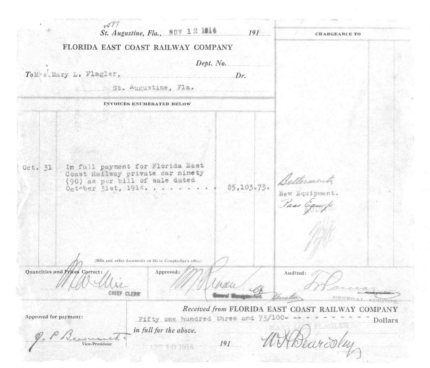

According to this bill of sale, FEC car 90 was sold to Mrs. Flagler, and this document adds confusion to the history of Flagler's private car. At the Flagler Museum in Palm Beach is the car "Rambler" bearing the number '90' on its side and the Museum brochure tells the story of the recovery of this car and its rebuilding and refurbishing. Unfortunately there is no reference in the brochure of the above sale from the FEC to Mrs. Flagler. The full history and disposition of the original car '90' after its purchase by Mrs. Flagler remains a mystery.

Early FEC cars contained the word "Railway" on the letterboard. By the 1920s, this designation had been removed. The words "Florida East Coast" were spread out and utilized the entire area instead. However, by that time the words "Flagler System" in smaller letters were on either side of the Florida East Coast name. Parlor Car 106 is shown shortly after its construction in 1895 at the Jackson and Sharp plant in Wilmington, Delaware.

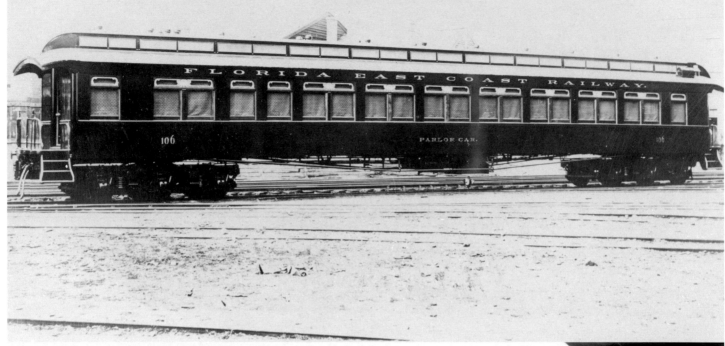

Heavyweight coach 114 at Jacksonville Terminal.

*—Wolfe photograph.*

Early FEC sleeping car 207 was built in Wilmington, Delaware, by the Jackson and Sharp Company in 1898. It was used on FEC trains within Florida.

Sixty foot baggage—RPO 318 at St. Augustine.

—(J. Nelson Collection)

Wolfe photographed full-length Railway Post Office 322 just after emerging from the Miller Yard car shops in 1940. By 1962 #322 was showing the ravages of use and age as loading was completed prior to leaving Miami as "Jack. & Miami R.P.O." northbound in train 6.

For special occasions the FEC co-operated with local civic associations by honoring their prowess. Baggage car 461 is shown at Buena Vista Yard.

467 is an example of the heavyweight, heavy duty, baggage cars used by the FEC. Photographed at Miller Shops, St. Augustine. (ca. 1939)

FECs dining car sevices were an anomaly over the years. At different times, they would be operated by the FEC, then by the Atlantic Coast Line and then be taken over again by the Florida East Coast. In the late 1940s and early 1950s, the FEC operated the cars themselves using a head steward as manager of the dining car department and utilizing crews who were employed by both the Atlantic Coast Line and themselves. FEC heavyweight diners were named after on-line cities as well as Flagler System Hotels. Dining car "Key West" is shown on a through New York to Florida train with the location being North Philadelphia, Pennsylvania, on January 2, 1938. "Royal Poinciana" is shown after being "stream-styled" at Miller Shops. Diner "St. Augustine" was photographed at Miller Shops in its namesake city. Both "Key West" and "St. Augustine" are seen with clerestory roof while "Royal Poinciana" is in full roof design (air-conditioned). FECs streamlined lightweight diners were all named after on-line cities with the prefix "Fort." They included Fort Dallas, Fort Drum, Fort Lauderdale, Fort Pierce, Fort Matanzas, Fort Ribault, and Fort San Marco.

Florida East Coast sleeping cars were named after various South American countries and Cuban cities and provinces. "Panama" was a two drawing room—14 roomette sleeper purchased in 1950 and "Salvador" was a 21 roomette sleeper car, purchased in 1949.

The only exception to the naming scheme as indicated above was "Scott M. Loftin"—a 6 bedroom—10 roomette sleeping car named for the FEC trustee shortly after his death.

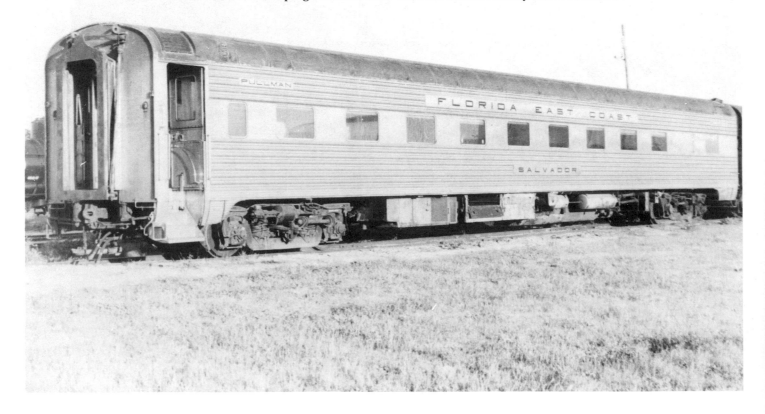

FEC Pullman "Scott M. Loftin" poses at the end of train 5, "The Southwind" on January 6, 1962 prior to departure from downtown Miami.

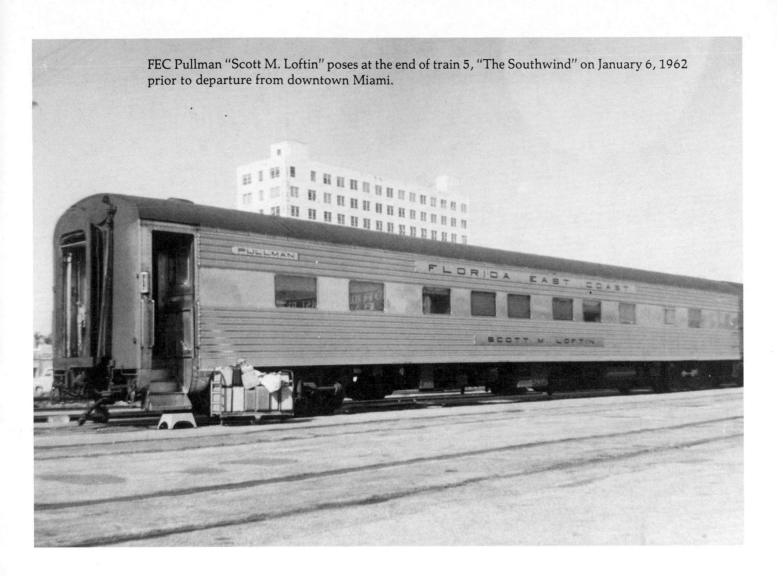

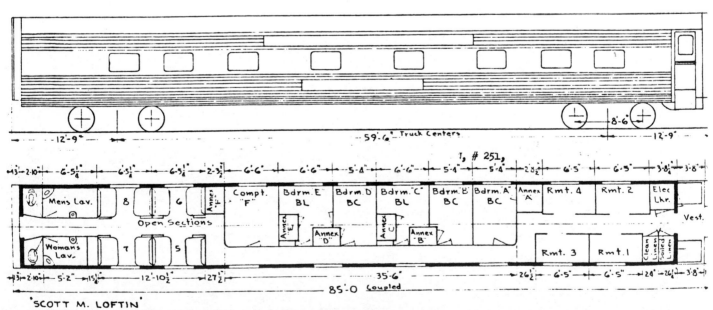

'SCOTT M. LOFTIN'

Sleepers "Scott M. Loftin" and "Jamaica" were built by Pullman Standard in 1954. The "Scott M. Loftin," named for a deceased FEC trustee and former Senator, was a 4 section, 4 roomette, 5 double bedroom, 1 compartment car, able to accommodate almost any budget or necessity for those wishing to utilize Pullman service.

Florida East Coast "South Bay" was one of a kind. It was a diner-bar-lounge, purchased in 1950. There were other 'one of a kind' cars operated on the FEC, such as 501, the road's only stream-lined lightweight baggage car. In this photo, "South Bay" reposes in front of Jacksonville Terminal on July 14, 1965, during the period that it was leased to the Southern Railway for use on its Jacksonville to Cincinnati trains.

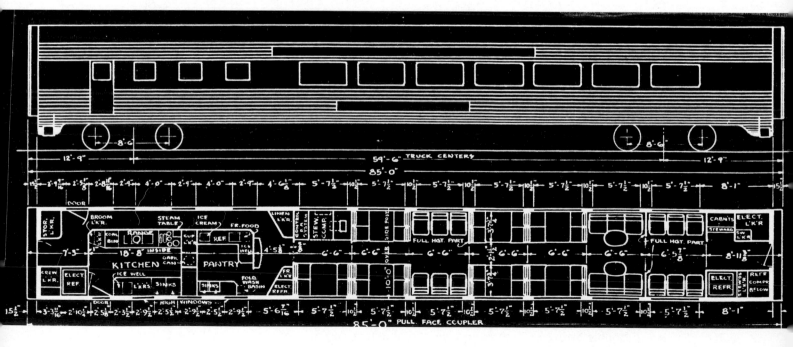

310

FEC diner "Fort Matanzas" at Buena Vista Yard, Miami on February 14, 1960.

Diners Fort Drum and Fort Ribault were built by Pullman Standard in 1949. Other streamlined diners, all in the "Fort" series (named after Florida Forts) were Fort Lauderdale, Fort Pierce, (1939); Fort Dallas, Fort Matanzas, and Fort San Marco, all built in 1946.

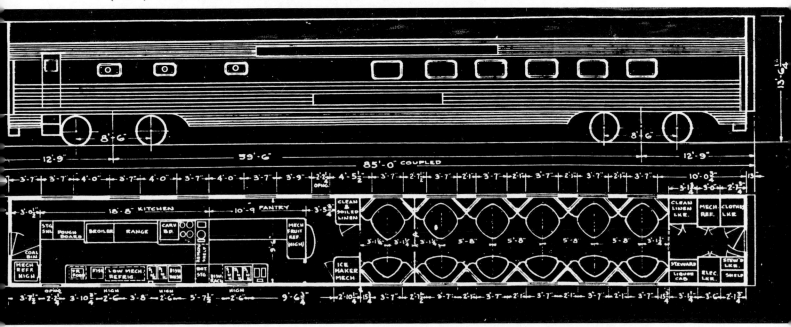

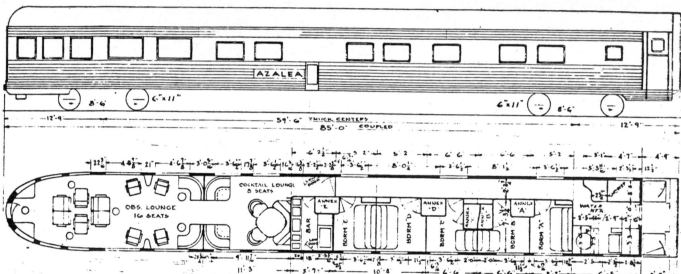

"Azalea" was another "one-of-a-kind" on the FEC. Built originally as the FEC's contribution to the observation car pool on "the New Royal Palm," the car eventually became the sole piece of in-use passenger equipment on the railroad, serving as the only office car on the system.

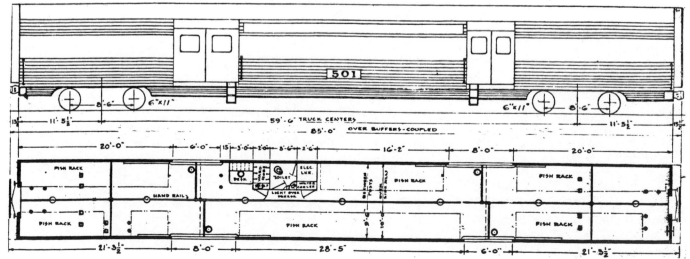

The 85 foot streamlined baggage car 501 built in 1950 by ACF, was the only one the FEC ever had.

# FLOOR PLANS OF THE "HENRY M. FLAGLER"

## DIESEL-ELECTRIC POWERED, STAINLESS STEEL CHAIR CAR TRAIN

### Between Jacksonville and Miami

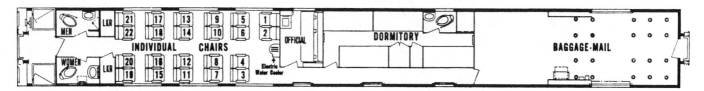

Car "F"—22 Seats—Passenger, Baggage and Crew Dormitory Coach

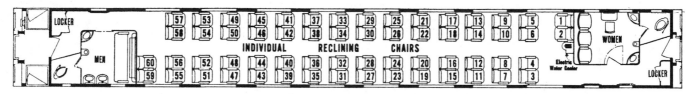

Cars "L", "O" and "I"—60 Seat Coaches

Car "R"—Dining Car

Car "D"—52 Seat Coach

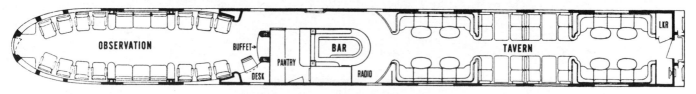

Car "A"—Tavern Lounge Observation

# FLORIDA EAST COAST RAILWAY

"Hobe Sound" was a strikingly beautiful streamlined rounded-end tavern-lounge-observation car that at various times bore the markers for the "Dixie Flagler" and the "Champion."

When the FEC strike started "Hobe Sound" had been torn down to the superstructure and all of the streamlined steel sheathing removed so that the car could be smooth sided, painted in Illinois Central colors, and added to the "City of Miami" passenger pool. For months, following the beginning of the strike, the frame rusted away like a forgotten hulk, at the Buena Vista Car Shops. Finally, almost three years later, it was carted away and dismantled.

After Wolfe photographed the various scenes, he would meet with J.T. Van Campen, for many years the railroad's advertising manager. It was "Van's" responsibility to handle the touchup work, such as that done in this view. In all liklihood, the train sitting on the southbound track at the beautiful, mission-style Hollywood Station was actually the "Champion," yet the retouched photo shows "Dixie Flagler." For the railfan the picture is important as it includes the station and shows the divider fence used to stop passengers from moving around the end of the stopped train and into the path of danger on the adjacent track.

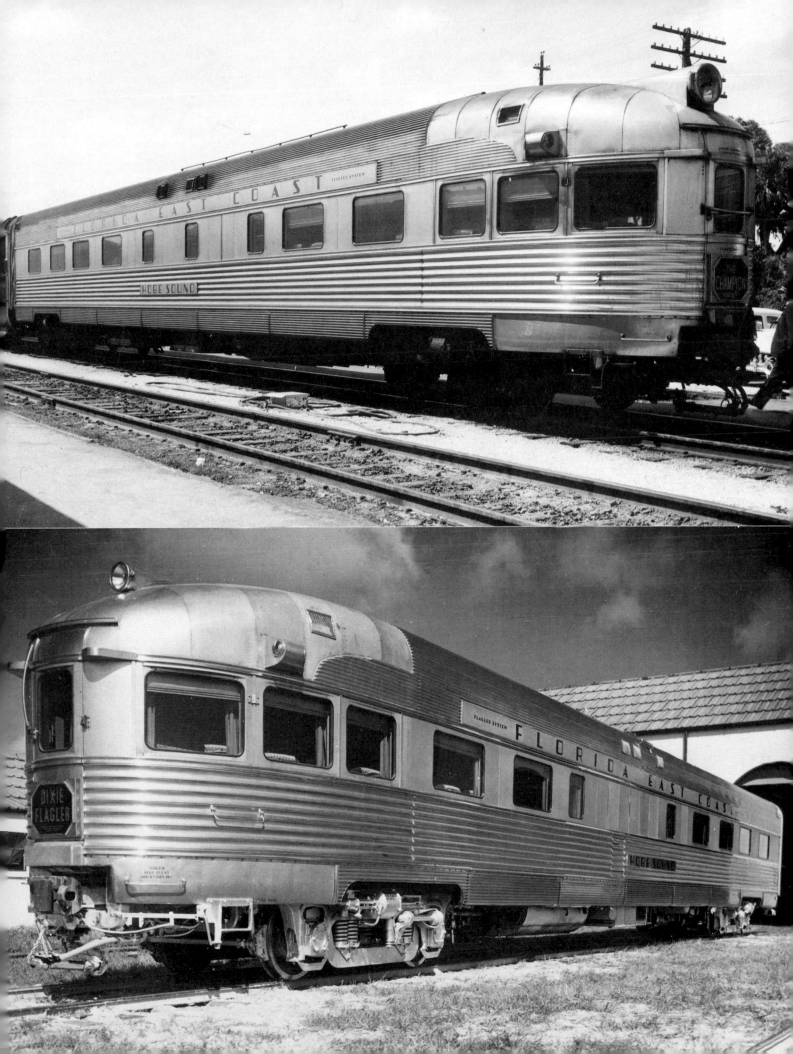

America's shortest full service streamliner pauses briefly at Vero Beach on its daily except Sunday southbound run between Jacksonville and Miami. We are looking at St. Lucie Sound as the train begins to roll slowly south.

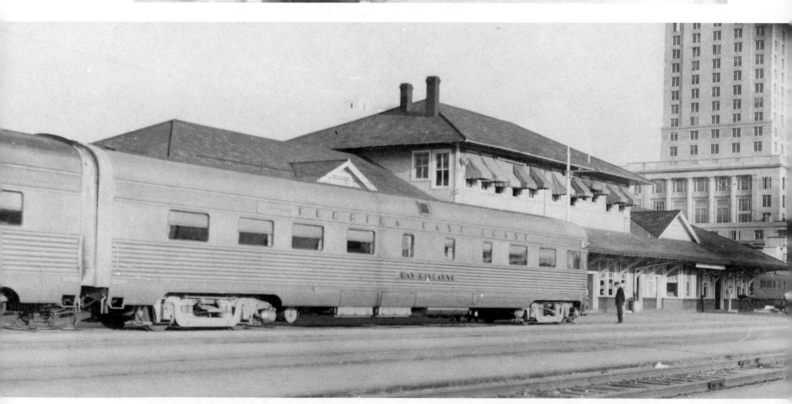

An FEC streamliner with tavern-lounge-observation "Bay Biscayne" on the tail rolls past the center of the Miami Station.

FEC coach "Eau Gallie" shown shortly after construction by the Edward G. Budd Co.

Coach "Delray Beach," and dining car "Fort Lauderdale" are the two names visible to the camera as the southbound Champion receives a wave from a Florida beauty in the late 40s—early 50's version of cheesecake.

—(J. Nelson Collection)

In a unique experiment, the Illinois Central and the Pennsylvania added dome cars to the "City of Miami" and "The Southwind" during the winter seasons from 1959. While the "Pennsy" left the cars in their Northern Pacific Railroad two toned green paint scheme, the Illinois Central, true to its traditions and high standards, repainted the cars each season for Florida service. In this October 16, 1959, view by the author, N.P. dome 307 is the car assigned to the "City of Miami."

One of the country's premier passenger trains in the streamliner era was the "City of Miami." Originated in 1940 as an every third day coach streamliner between Chicago, St. Louis and Miami, the train was immensely popular and alternated its trips with the "Dixie Flagler" (later "The Dixieland") and "The Southwind." Though the three trains originated in Chicago with different proprietary roads, and the routes were different, the trains were turned over to the FEC at Jacksonville. Originally numberd 3 and 4 on the FEC, the designations were later changed to 5 and 6. The train, in its brown, orange and yellow striped livery, with "City of Miami" painted above the windows, and finished off with a rounded-end observation car (invariably I.C. 3300, 3305 or 3320) was a sight to behold, averaging 14 to 21 cars depending on the season.

The FEC had a number of trains which carried Pullman cars for numerous points, with through Pullman service being offered to points as distant as Colorado Springs, Kansas City, Grand Rapids, Buffalo and Detroit. In this January 2, 1955 view, the "Frisco" Pullman (left center) will become part of the "Kansas City—Florida Special" in Jacksonville.

# APPENDIX 7
# FEC INTRASTATE CONNECTIONS

Due to its unique layout, and its topographical situation, the FEC, until the Seaboard arrived in Miami in January of 1927, had no competition on its lines. Connections were made at Jacksonville with the ACL, Seaboard and Southern; at Palatka with the ACL and GS&F; at Orange City Junction with the ACL; at Benson Junction with the ACL; at Okeechobee with the Seaboard; at Marcy below Okeechobee with the Seaboard; at West Palm Beach with the Seaboard and at several locations in the Miami area as well as a connection in Homestead (although this track connection is out of service).

The FEC also had terminal and port railway connections as follows:

(1) Jacksonville Port Area—the Atlantic and East Coast Terminal Railway.

(2) Palm Beach Port Area—the Port of Palm Beach Railway.

(3) Port Everglades Area—the Broward County Port Authority Railway.

(4) Miami Port Area—the Miami Municipal Railway.

There has been so little done in the way of research on the history of Florida's short lines and logging-industrial railroads that it is difficult to be able to compile a list, let alone provide a history of the roads with which the FEC connected. The Peavy-Wilson Lumber Company connected at Holopaw; the Union Cypress Company connected at Hopkins, south of Melbourne; the Naranja Rock Company operated gravel pits and their own railway in the area south of Kendal connecting with the FEC at Naranja, and the Trans Florida Central connected with the FEC at Sebastian and provided service to Fellsmere (15 miles) until 1952.

## THE JUPITER AND LAKE WORTH RAILWAY:

Though the Florida East Coast never connected with the Jupiter and Lake Worth Railway (for reasons noted below) it deserves mention in a book dealing with the FEC. State of Florida records indicate the J&LW, also known as the "Celestial Railroad" because it served the towns of Jupiter, Juno, Venus and Mars (the latter two being totally devoid of humanity) was incorporated in 1888, with stock authorized in the amount of $50,000.00. Work began, and was apparently completed, in 1889. The line was 7½ miles long.

Supposedly, the JStA&IR, building down the East Coast, attempted to buy the J&LW in order to absorb, and operate on, the right of way. For whatever reason, the J&LW people would not sell to Flagler. The JStA&IR simply built around the J&LW, leaving the little railroad without a rail connection. It may not have mattered previously, when connections were made with the Indian River Steamboat Co., which was under the same ownership as the J&LW but now, with through service available from Jacksonville to West Palm Beach without transfer, the steamship-railroad connection was redundant.

Because of the J&LW's previous refusal to sell to the Flagler interests, the JStA&IR refused to allow a track connection, and the Celestial Railroad withered away completely and died, apparently unnoticed and unlamented, in 1895. Venus and Mars immediately ceased to exist, and Juno, which was the County seat, became a nonentity, when in 1899, same was voted back to Miami.

Though the copious files of the Florida State Photographic Archives, after a thorough search by their Director and long time doyenne, Joan Morris, yielded only three photographs of FEC predecessors, they also contained what may be the only two known photographs of the geographic-but-not-corporate-predecessor of the FEC: the Jupiter and Lake Worth, aka, the "Celestial Railroad." Built "in the middle of nowhere," and serving the unlikely locales of Jupiter, Juno, Venus and Mars, the J&LW, without rail connections on either end, managed to avoid being taken over by the Flagler interests as they built toward West Palm Beach, and, in consequence, remained a 7½ mile isolated line of railroad that connected nothing with nothing. Shortly after the FEC (at that time the JSTA&IR) passed them by, the "Celestial Railroad," (represented here by what is believed to be their only equipment) passed, akin to a comet, through the Florida railroad scene, becoming a footnote to, but not a part of, the history of the FEC.

*—Florida State Archives: Author's Collection*

Connecting with the FEC at Holopaw, the Peavy-Wilson Lumber Co. leased a portion of the former Kissimmee Valley branch from the railroad following its abandonment for common carrier use. From 1947 until 1951 wood burning steamers such as the 104 (shown here) bustled through the Central Florida pine woods with trainloads of lumber for the FEC connection at Maytown.                                    —(Florida State Archives: Author's Collection).

In its last days in the early 30's, maintenance had become so poor on Union Cypress Co's Railroad that "unsafe" became mild terminology to describe the condition of the roadbed. #3, apparently a 2-6-0 type, literally fell through the trestle at Jane Green Creek. (Photographs of this operation are so rare that of the 10 or so unearthed by the author during research, this one alone was suitable for publication.)                                    —(Florida State Archives: Author's Collection)

# APPENDIX 8
# FLORIDA EAST COAST TRACK LAYOUT

*Office of Principal Assistant Engineer*
*St. Augustine, Florida — Nov. 10, 1931*
*Scale: 1 Mile = 2 Inches*

*Traced from map in Henry Morrison Flagler Museum*
*Palm Beach, Florida by J.F. Filby, Apr. 28, 1983*

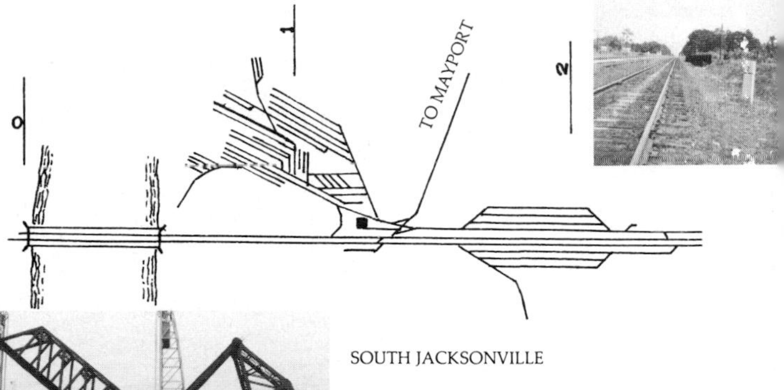

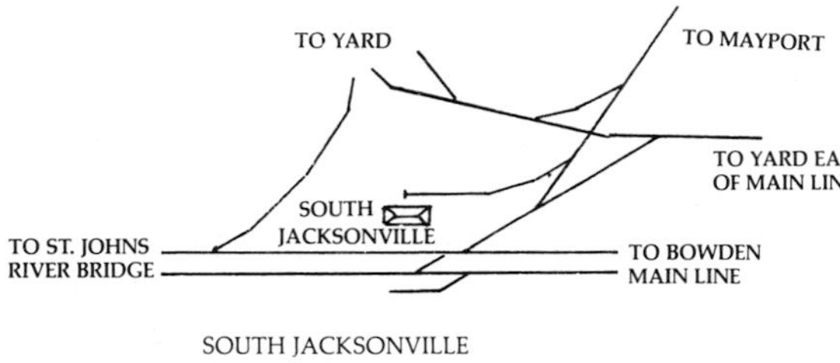

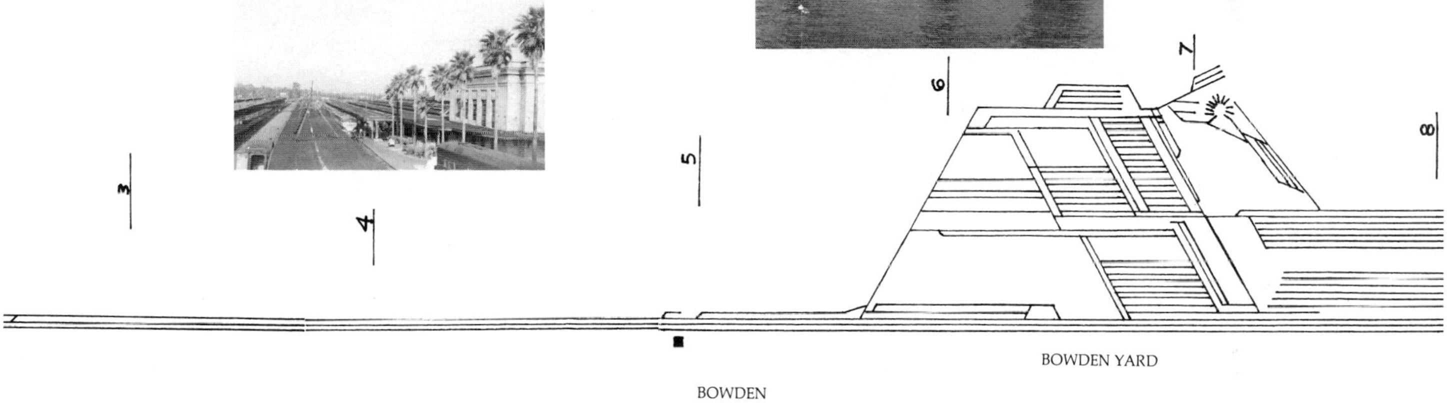

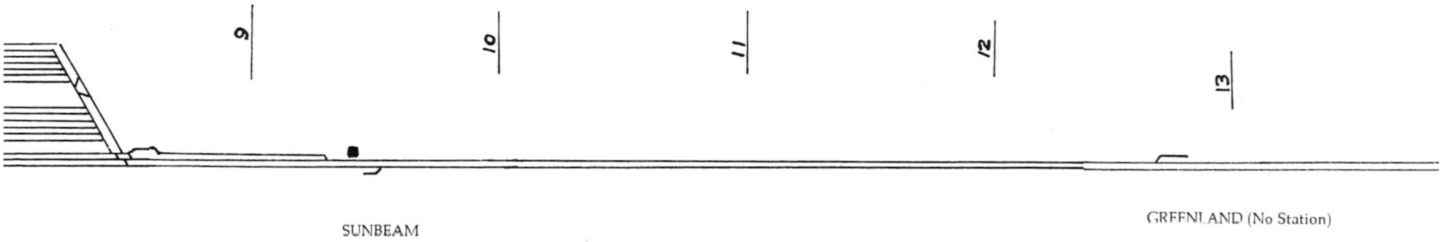

SOUTH JACKSONVILLE

TO MAYPORT

2

1

0

TO YARD

TO MAYPORT

TO YARD EAST
OF MAIN LINE

SOUTH
JACKSONVILLE

TO ST. JOHNS
RIVER BRIDGE

TO BOWDEN
MAIN LINE

SOUTH JACKSONVILLE

3

4

5

6

7

8

BOWDEN

BOWDEN YARD

9

10

11

12

13

SUNBEAM

GREENLAND (No Station)

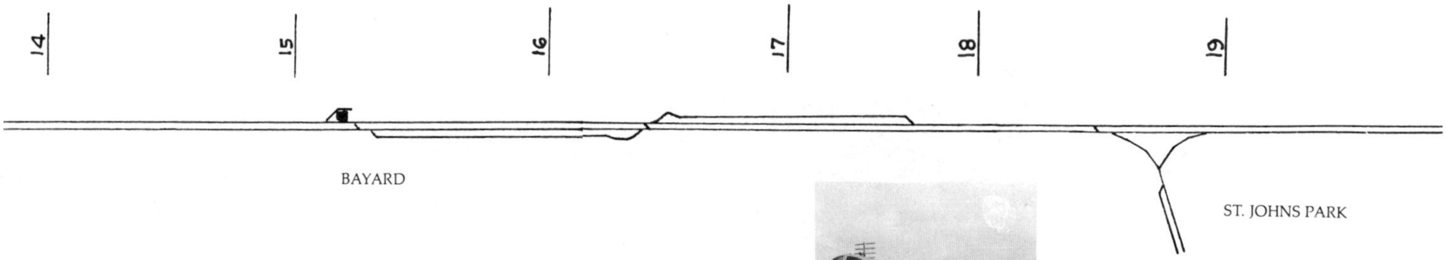

14

15

16

17

18

19

BAYARD

ST. JOHNS PARK

20    21    22    23    24    25

DURBIN

32    33    34    35    36    37    MJ-0

MILLER SHOPS

ST. AUGUSTINE

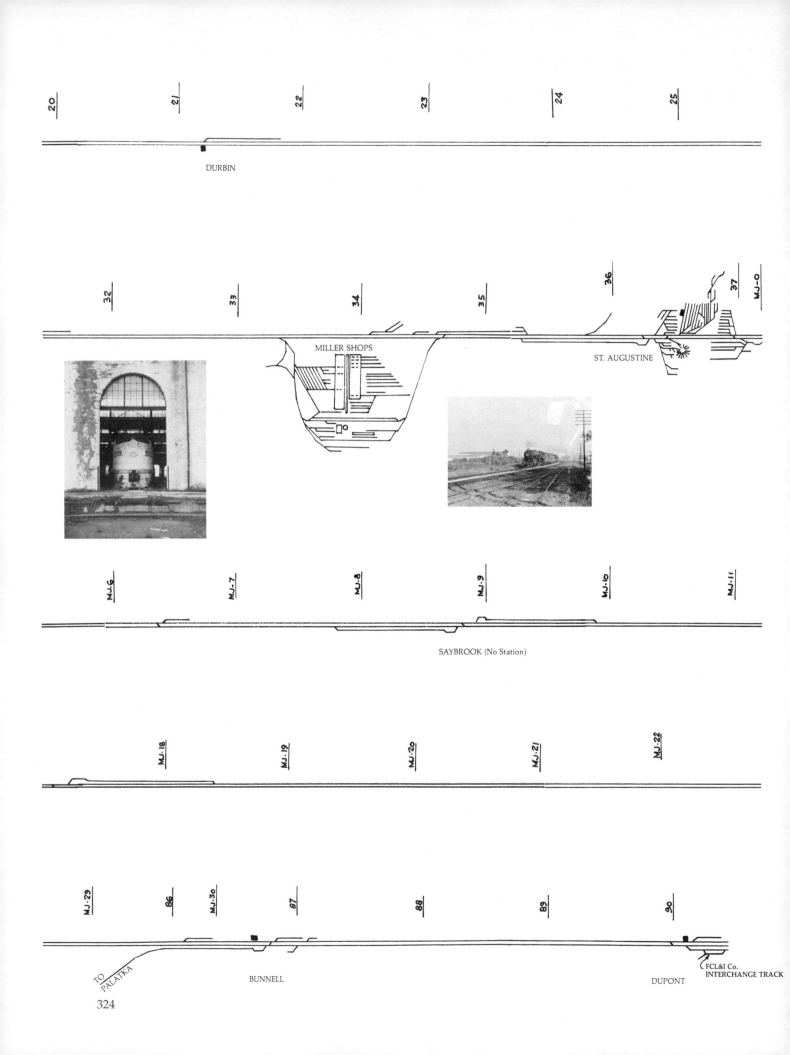

MJ-6    MJ-7    MJ-8    MJ-9    MJ-10    MJ-11

SAYBROOK (No Station)

MJ-18    MJ-19    MJ-20    MJ-21    MJ-22

MJ-29    86    MJ-30    87    88    89    90

TO PALATKA

BUNNELL

DUPONT

FCL&I Co.
INTERCHANGE TRACK

324

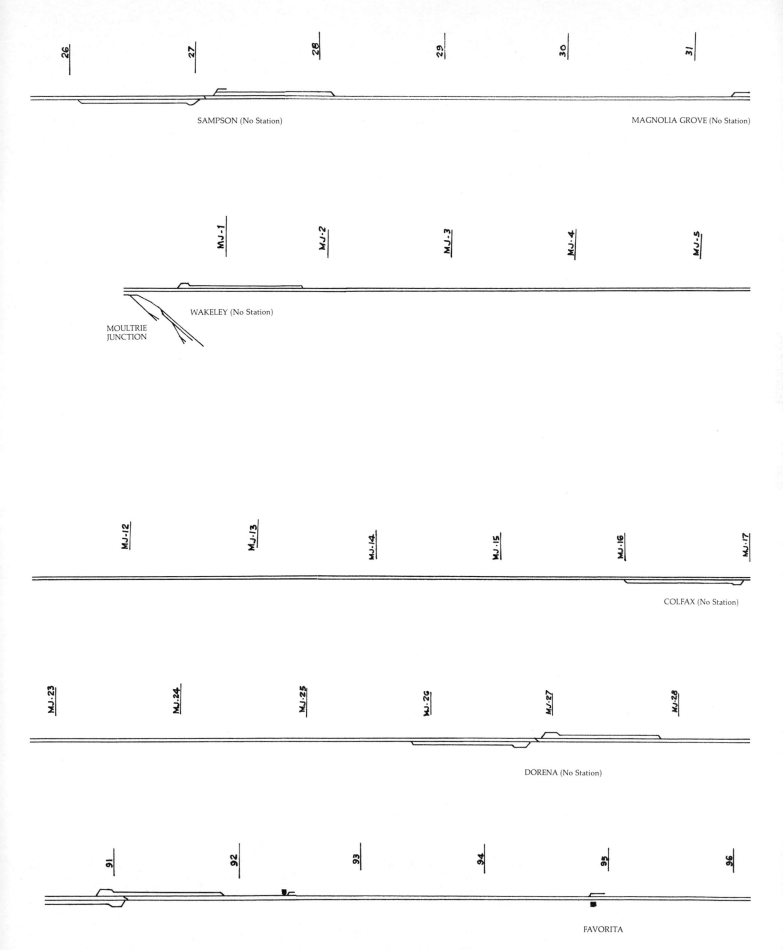

26    27    28    29    30    31

SAMPSON (No Station)

MAGNOLIA GROVE (No Station)

MJ-1    MJ-2    MJ-3    MJ-4    MJ-5

WAKELEY (No Station)

MOULTRIE
JUNCTION

MJ-12    MJ-13    MJ-14    MJ-15    MJ-16    MJ-17

COLFAX (No Station)

MJ-23    MJ-24    MJ-25    MJ-26    MJ-27    MJ-28

DORENA (No Station)

91    92    93    94    95    96

FAVORITA

325

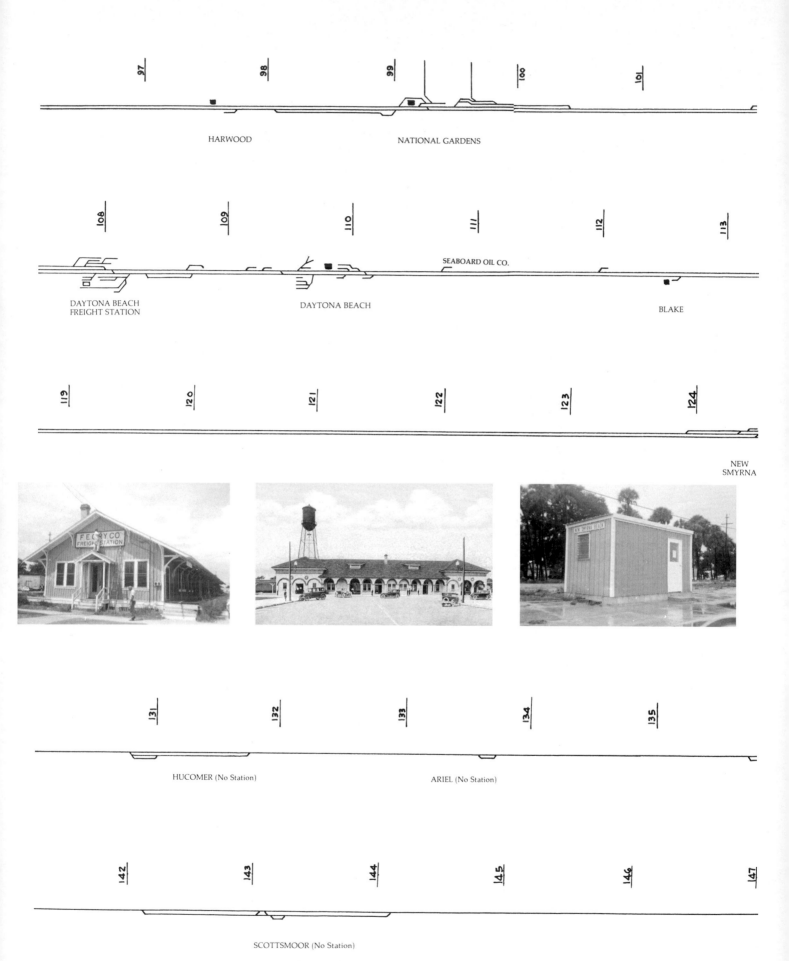

97     98     99     100     101

HARWOOD            NATIONAL GARDENS

108     109     110     111     112     113

SEABOARD OIL CO.

DAYTONA BEACH
FREIGHT STATION          DAYTONA BEACH          BLAKE

119     120     121     122     123     124

NEW
SMYRNA

131     132     133     134     135

HUCOMER (No Station)          ARIEL (No Station)

142     143     144     145     146     147

SCOTTSMOOR (No Station)

326

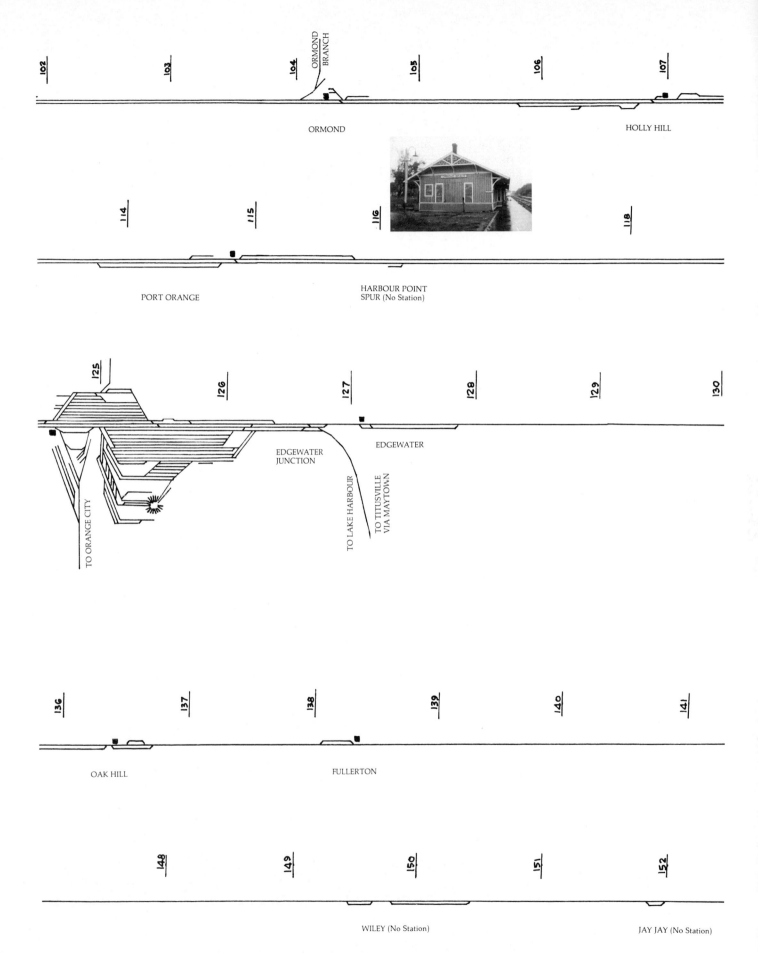

102    103    104    ORMOND BRANCH    105    106    107

ORMOND    HOLLY HILL

114    115    116    118

PORT ORANGE    HARBOUR POINT SPUR (No Station)

125    126    127    128    129    130

EDGEWATER JUNCTION    EDGEWATER

TO ORANGE CITY    TO LAKE HARBOUR    TO TITUSVILLE VIA MAYTOWN

136    137    138    139    140    141

OAK HILL    FULLERTON

148    149    150    151    152

WILEY (No Station)    JAY JAY (No Station)

327

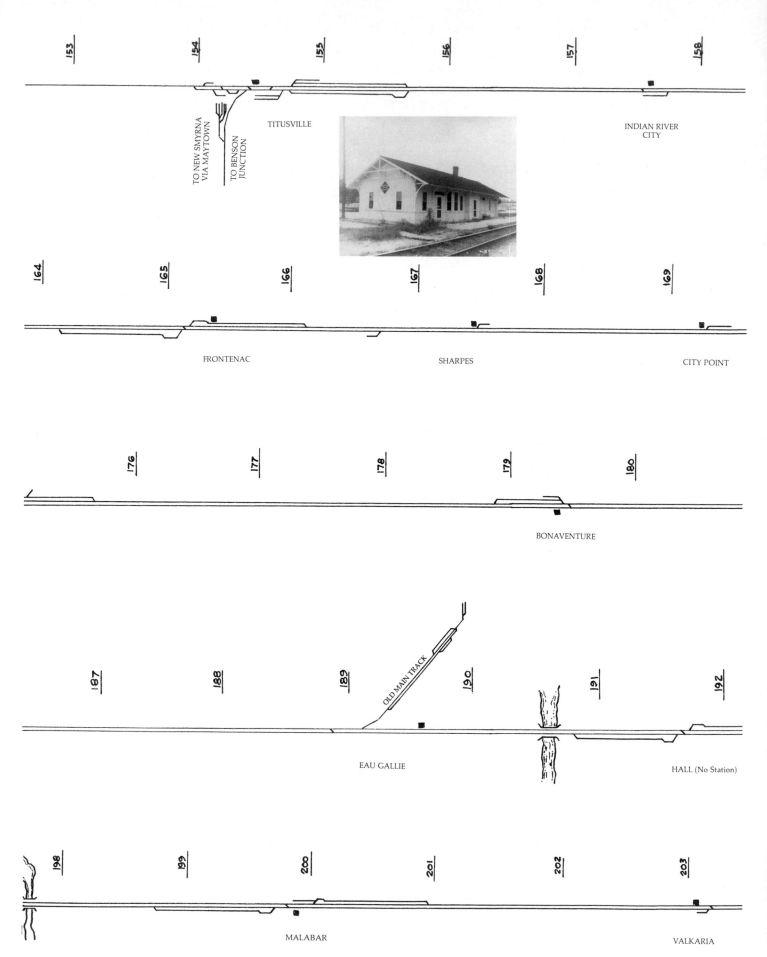

153    154    155    156    157    158

TO NEW SMYRNA VIA MAYTOWN

TO BENSON JUNCTION

TITUSVILLE

INDIAN RIVER CITY

164    165    166    167    168    169

FRONTENAC

SHARPES

CITY POINT

176    177    178    179    180

BONAVENTURE

187    188    189    190    191    192

OLD MAIN TRACK

EAU GALLIE

HALL (No Station)

198    199    200    201    202    203

MALABAR

VALKARIA

328

159 160 161 162 163

DELESDINE

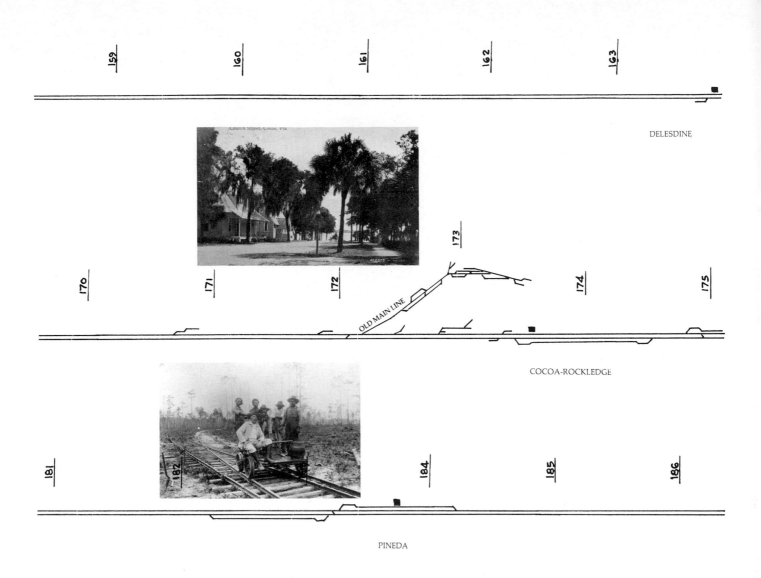

170 171 172 173 174 175

OLD MAIN LINE

COCOA-ROCKLEDGE

181 182 184 185 186

PINEDA

193 194 195 196 197

CRANE CREEK

MELBOURNE

PALM BAY

204 205 206 207 208

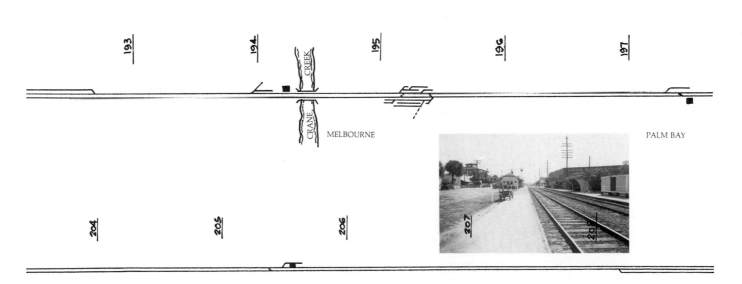

GRANT

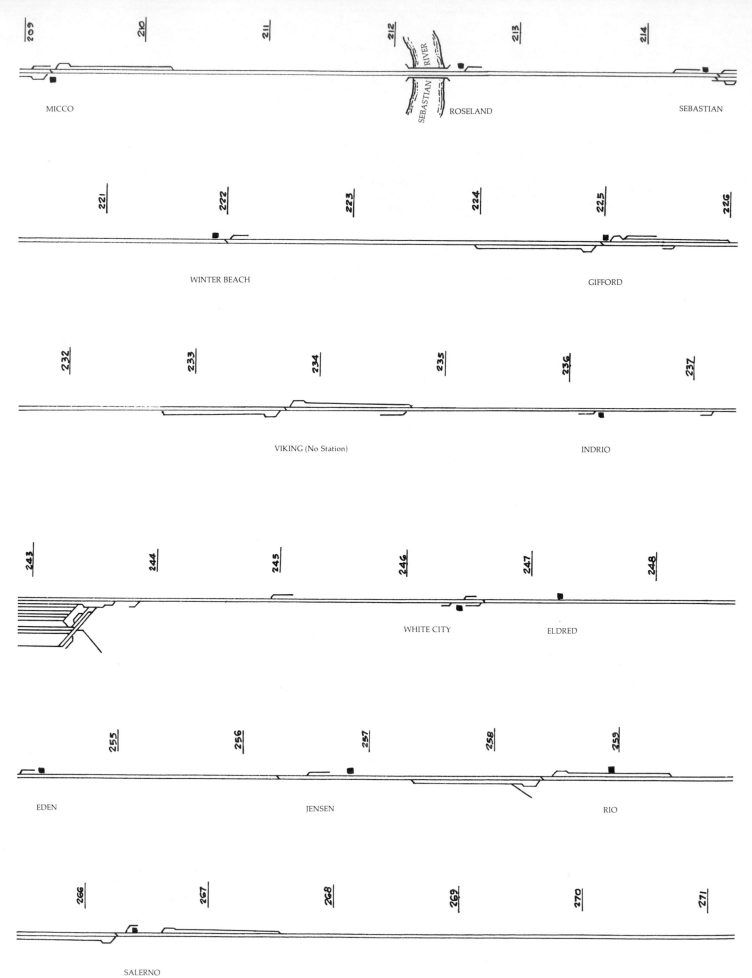

209
210
211
212
213
214

SEBASTIAN RIVER

MICCO

SEBASTIAN
ROSELAND

SEBASTIAN

221
222
223
224
225
226

WINTER BEACH

GIFFORD

232
233
234
235
236
237

VIKING (No Station)

INDRIO

243
244
245
246
247
248

WHITE CITY

ELDRED

255
256
257
258
259

EDEN

JENSEN

RIO

266
267
268
269
270
271

SALERNO

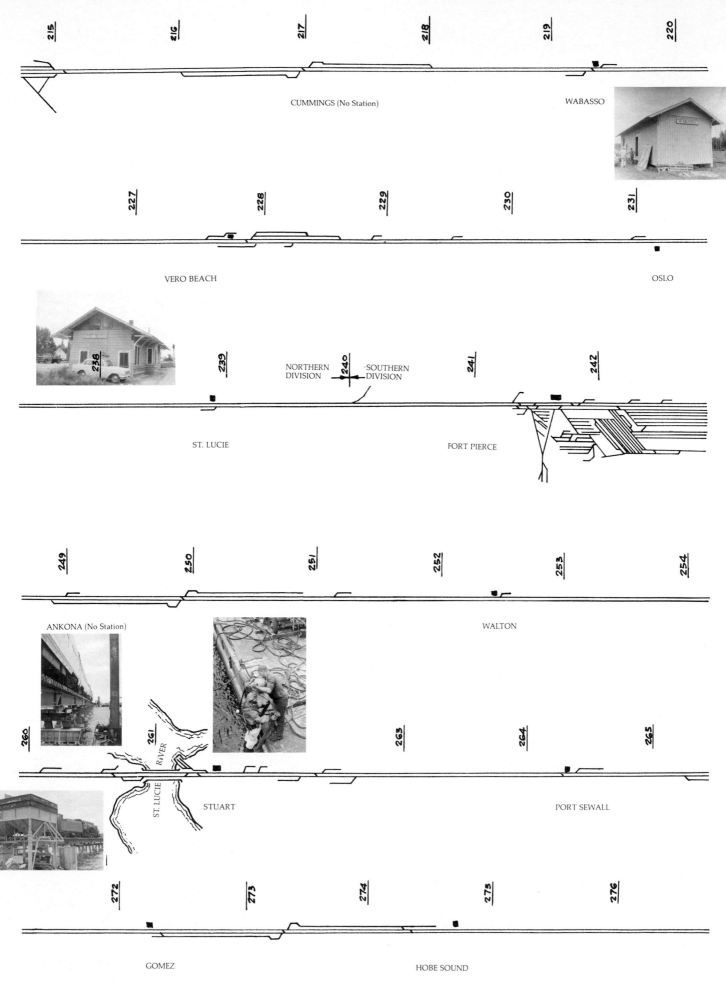

215 216 217 218 219 220

CUMMINGS (No Station)

WABASSO

227 228 229 230 231

VERO BEACH

OSLO

238

239 240 241 242

NORTHERN DIVISION    SOUTHERN DIVISION

ST. LUCIE

FORT PIERCE

249 250 251 252 253 254

ANKONA (No Station)

WALTON

260 261 263 264 265

ST. LUCIE RIVER

STUART

PORT SEWALL

272 273 274 275 276

GOMEZ

HOBE SOUND

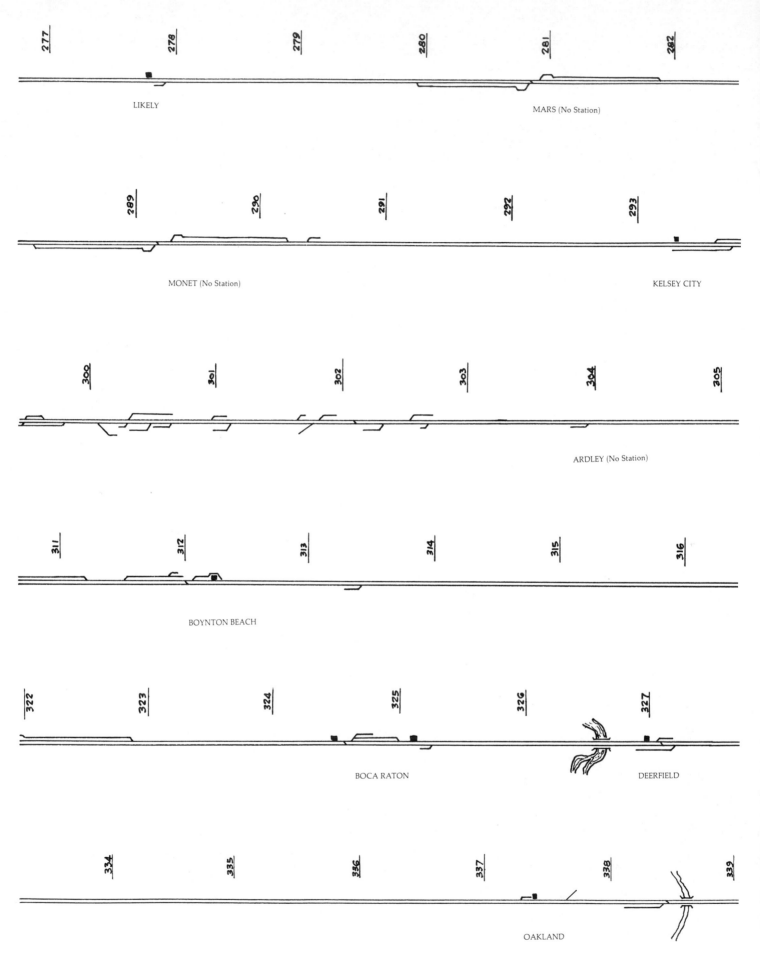

277    278    279    280    281    282

LIKELY                      MARS (No Station)

289    290    291    292    293

MONET (No Station)              KELSEY CITY

300    301    302    303    304    305

ARDLEY (No Station)

311    312    313    314    315    316

BOYNTON BEACH

322    323    324    325    326    327

BOCA RATON                  DEERFIELD

334    335    336    337    338    339

OAKLAND

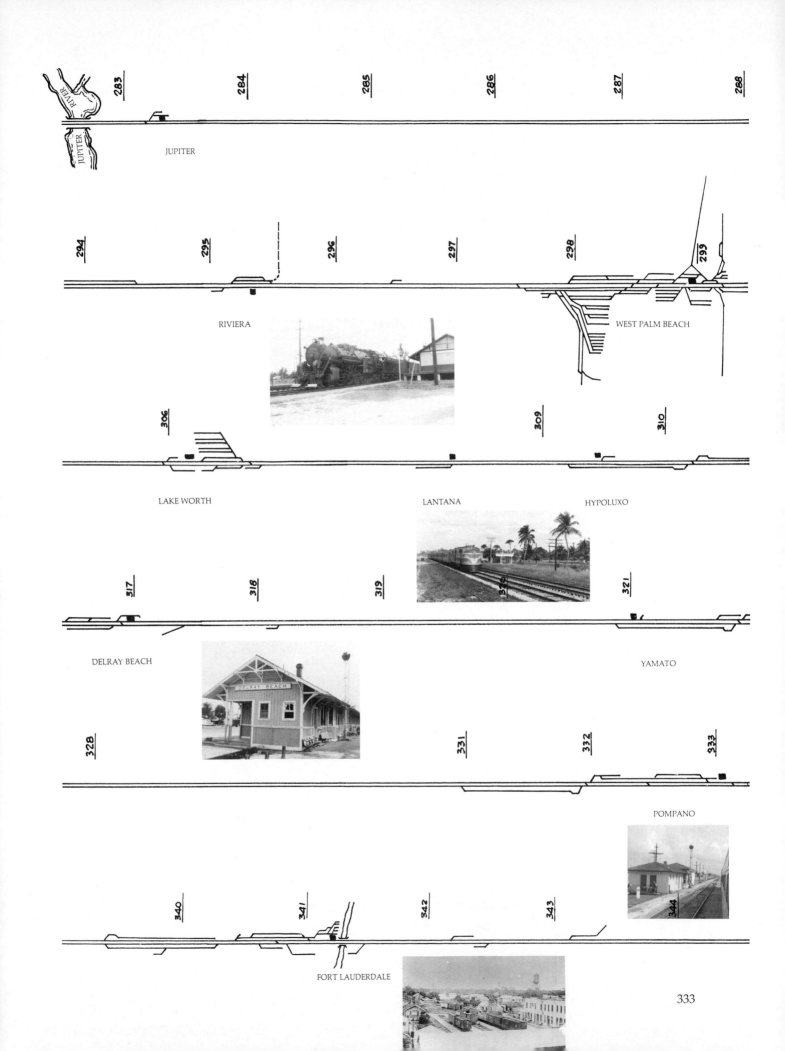

283 284 285 286 287 288

RIVER

JUPITER

JUPITER

294 295 296 297 298 299

RIVIERA WEST PALM BEACH

306 309 310

LAKE WORTH LANTANA HYPOLUXO

317 318 319 320 321

DELRAY BEACH YAMATO

328 331 332 333

POMPANO

340 341 342 343 344

FORT LAUDERDALE

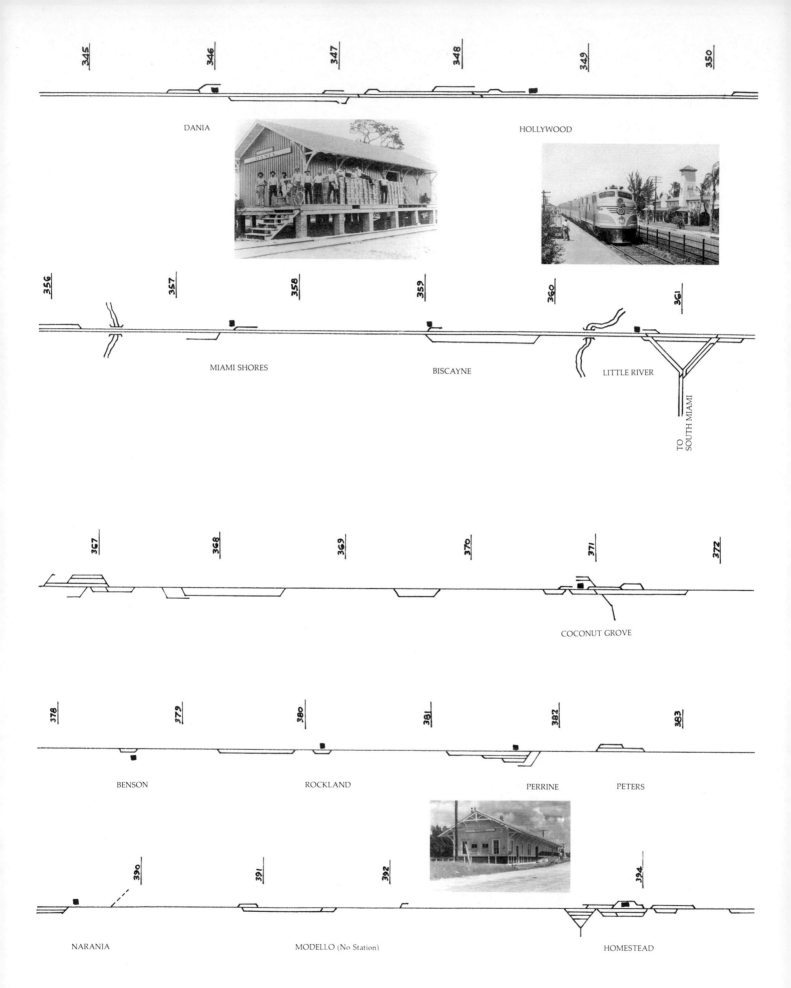

345 346 347 348 349 350

DANIA      HOLLYWOOD

356 357 358 359 360 361

MIAMI SHORES   BISCAYNE   LITTLE RIVER

TO
SOUTH MIAMI

367 368 369 370 371 372

COCONUT GROVE

378 379 380 381 382 383

BENSON   ROCKLAND   PERRINE  PETERS

390 391 392 394

NARANJA   MODELLO (No Station)   HOMESTEAD

334

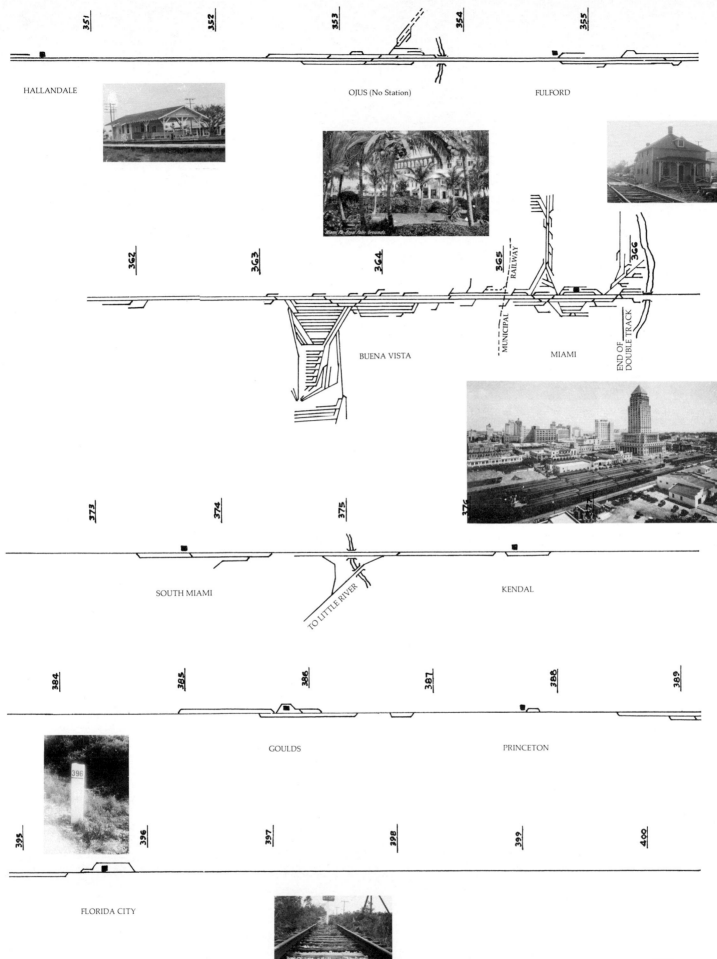

351  352  353  354  355

HALLANDALE

OJUS (No Station)

FULFORD

362  363  364  365  366

MUNICIPAL RAILWAY

BUENA VISTA

MIAMI

END OF DOUBLE TRACK

373  374  375  376

SOUTH MIAMI

TO LITTLE RIVER

KENDAL

384  385  386  387  388  389

GOULDS

PRINCETON

395  396  397  398  399  400

FLORIDA CITY

335

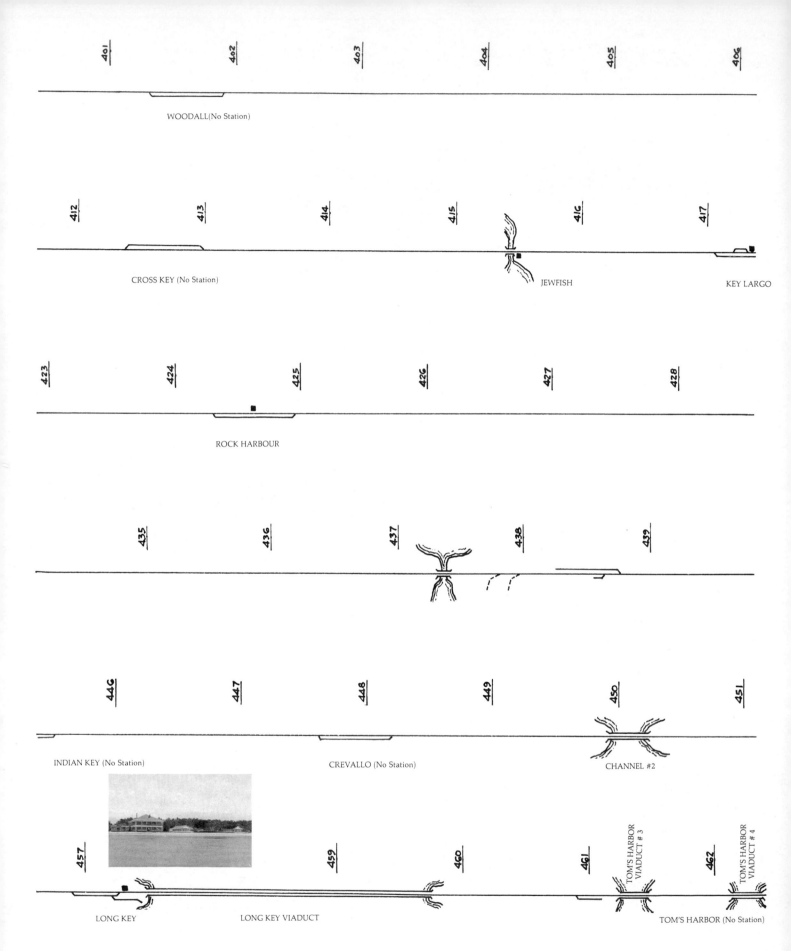

401　402　403　404　405　406

WOODALL(No Station)

412　413　414　415　416　417

CROSS KEY (No Station)　　　JEWFISH　　　KEY LARGO

423　424　425　426　427　428

ROCK HARBOUR

435　436　437　438　439

446　447　448　449　450　451

INDIAN KEY (No Station)　　CREVALLO (No Station)　　CHANNEL #2

457　459　460　461　462

TOM'S HARBOR VIADUCT # 3　　TOM'S HARBOR VIADUCT # 4

LONG KEY　　LONG KEY VIADUCT　　TOM'S HARBOR (No Station)

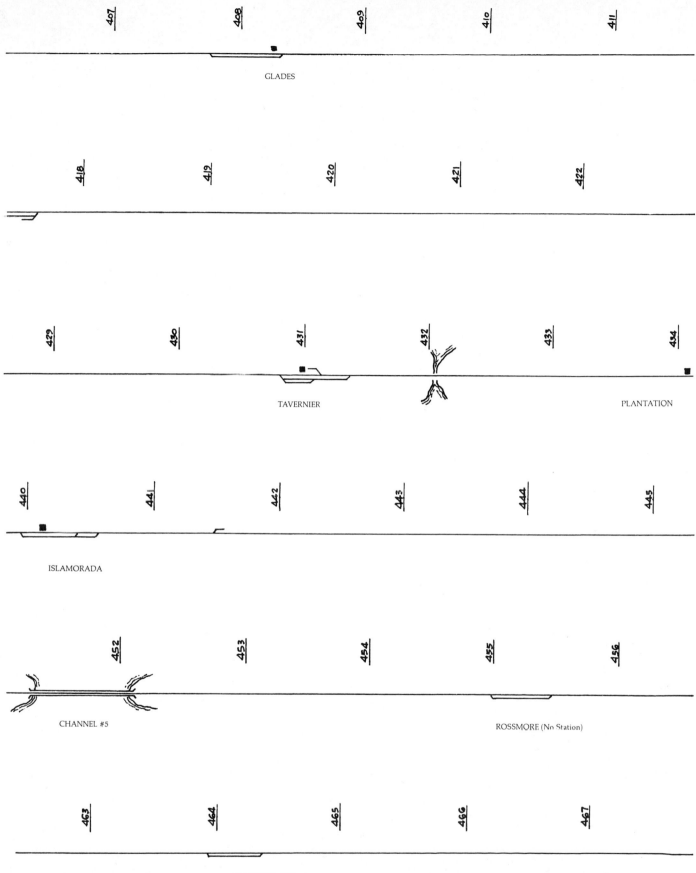

407 408 409 410 411

GLADES

418 419 420 421 422

429 430 431 432 433 434

TAVERNIER

PLANTATION

440 441 442 443 444 445

ISLAMORADA

452 453 454 455 456

CHANNEL #5

ROSSMORE (No Station)

463 464 465 466 467

GRASSY (No Station)

468 469 470 471 472 473

VACA (No Station)

480 481 482 483 484

MOSER CHANNEL VIADUCT PACET CHANNEL VIADUCT

LITTLE DUCK-
-MISSOURI
VIADUCT

MISSOURI-
-OHIO
VIADUCT

OHIO-
BAHIA HONDA
VIADUCT

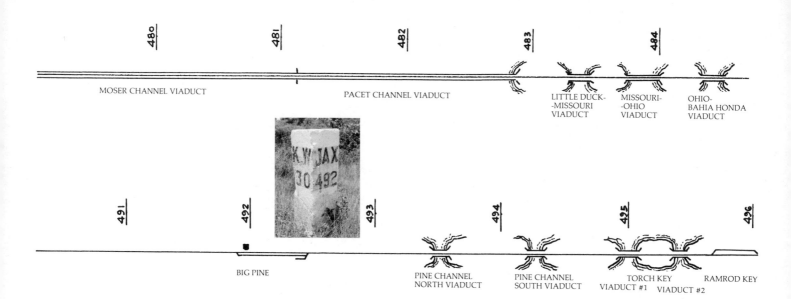

491 492 493 494 495 496

BIG PINE

PINE CHANNEL
NORTH VIADUCT

PINE CHANNEL
SOUTH VIADUCT

TORCH KEY
VIADUCT #1

VIADUCT #2

RAMROD KEY

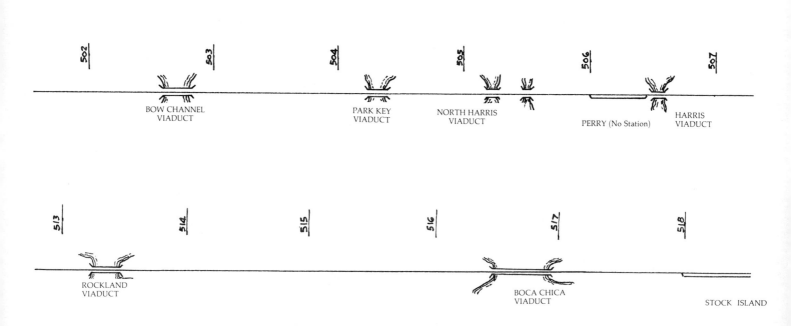

502 503 504 505 506 507

BOW CHANNEL
VIADUCT

PARK KEY
VIADUCT

NORTH HARRIS
VIADUCT

PERRY (No Station)

HARRIS
VIADUCT

513 514 515 516 517 518

ROCKLAND
VIADUCT

BOCA CHICA
VIADUCT

STOCK ISLAND

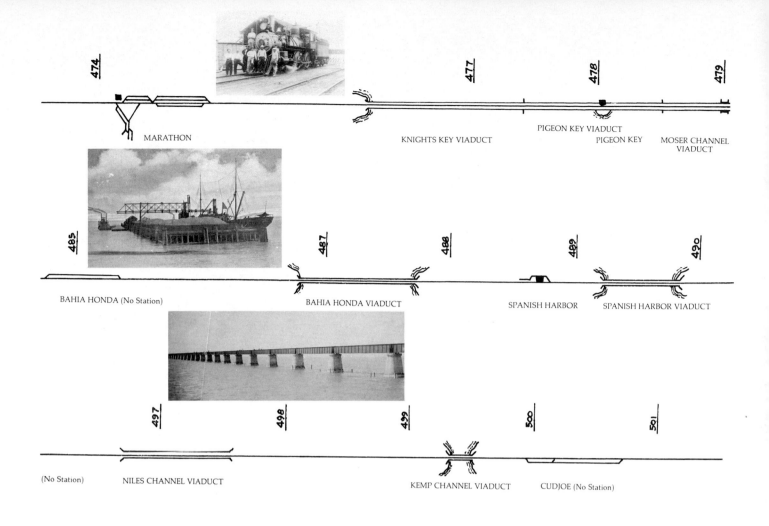

474

477

478

479

MARATHON

KNIGHTS KEY VIADUCT

PIGEON KEY VIADUCT

PIGEON KEY

MOSER CHANNEL VIADUCT

485

487

488

489

490

BAHIA HONDA (No Station)

BAHIA HONDA VIADUCT

SPANISH HARBOR

SPANISH HARBOR VIADUCT

497

498

499

500

501

(No Station)

NILES CHANNEL VIADUCT

KEMP CHANNEL VIADUCT

CUDJOE (No Station)

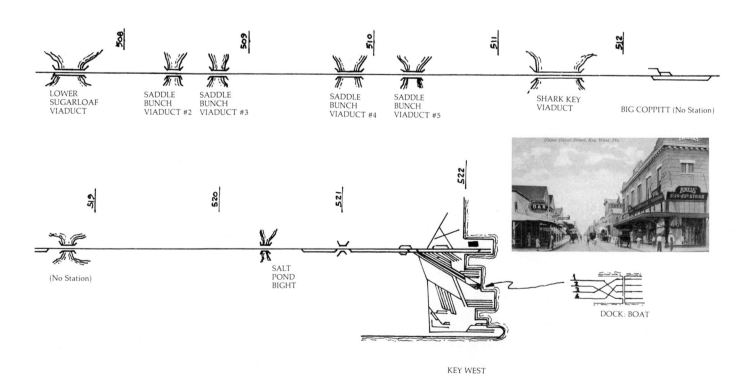

508

509

510

511

512

LOWER SUGARLOAF VIADUCT

SADDLE BUNCH VIADUCT #2

SADDLE BUNCH VIADUCT #3

SADDLE BUNCH VIADUCT #4

SADDLE BUNCH VIADUCT #5

SHARK KEY VIADUCT

BIG COPPITT (No Station)

519

520

521

522

(No Station)

SALT POND BIGHT

DOCK: BOAT

KEY WEST

339

# INFORMATION ON PRIMARY SOURCES

The author's collection of FEC Railway and Florida transportation memorabilia, built up over 45 years, proved to be the main resource for reference material, both written and photographic. Many of the items used as sources are noted in Section III of the Bibliography.

Private collections were a major source. Railroad buffs have built up a vast repository of information and material on the FEC as well as other railroads and street railways. Collections consulted included those belonging to Charles and Richard Beall of Miami; Joseph Bacon of St. Augustine; Roger Schmorr of Hollywood; Ruth and Arthur Marsh, formerly of St. Augustine; and Jonathan Nelson of Miami.

Institutional collections, while duplicating some of the material in private hands, proved to be valuable resources. These facilities included the Miami-Dade Public Library Florida Collection, Miami; the Historical Association of Southern Florida, Miami; "Whitehall," the Flagler Museum and Library in Palm Beach; the Library of the St. Augustine Historical Society; the University of Florida Library, Gainesville; and the State of Florida's Department of Archives, History and Records Management, in Tallahassee.

Though the FEC Railway no longer maintains historical files, they were able to provide some information on various topics.

Finally, though not generally as accessible as the larger historical institutions noted above, due to restricted hours and, generally, almost all volunteer staffs, the various historical societies and associations located along the East Coast of Florida from the Jacksonville Beaches to Key West, were and are fine sources of local information.

For many years, the aristocrat of winter trains, the *Florida Special*, carried musicians and hostesses and for one season in the 30s even boasted a swimming pool. In this photo, we see a musical presentation aboard the recreation car, with an accordianist and hostess leading a singsong. Note the floodlamps used to illuminate the musician and hostess: the lights would be air-brushed out of the final photograph when it was used for promotion.

There are three sections of 88 on this stunning January day in 1936 and the Filipino bands along with the train's hostesses pose for publicity photographs prior to departure.

# BIBLIOGRAPHY

## I. Articles

The author read several hundred articles on all phases of the history of the railroad. The majority of them appeared in *Update*, and *Tequesta*, (Historical Association of Southern Florida); *The Florida Historical Quarterly*, (Florida Historical Society); *Trains* Magazine; *Railroad* Magazine; National Railway Historical Society *Bulletin;* and many of the railroad industry trade magazines, including *Modern Railroads, Progressive Railroading, Railway Age, Railway Locomotives and Cars*, and others. *Time* Magazine provided information on the strike in a 1964 article, and the Brotherhood of Locomotive Engineers monthly magazine had two fine articles on the Key West Extension in 1909 and 1911.

## II. Books and Booklets

Bathe, Greville, *A Brief Account of the St. Johns Railway of Florida* St. Augustine. St. Augustine Historical Society, 1961.

Griffin, Leon Odell. *Ed Ball: Confusion to the Enemy* Tampa Trend House, 1975.

Huffines, Gordon. *Henry Flagler: Empire Builder* City of Publication unknown. In *Ties that Bind*, Published by Federation for Railway Progress. Undated.

Hollowell, Maude Haynes (Editor) *Go to Sea/Key West* Coral Gables. Coral Gables Riviera Publishing. 1939.

Edward G. Budd Manufacturing Co. *Volume Two/The Florida Story/Budd Analysis of Changes in Transportation* Philadelphia. Privately published, 1940.

Rainbolt, Victor. *The Town that Climate Built* Miami. Parker Art Printing Association, 1921.

Pettengill, George W., Jr. *The Story of the Florida Railroads* Boston. R&LHS, 1952.

Redding, David A. *Flagler and His Church* Jacksonville. Paramount Press, 1970.

Packard, Winthrop. *Florida Trails* Boston. Small, Maynard & Co., 1910.

Lovering, Frank. *Hurricane Between* St. Augustine. Privately printed, 1946.

Parks, Pat. *The Railroad that Died at Sea* Battleboro, VT. Stephen Greene Press, 1968.

Stover, John F. *The Life and Decline of the American Railroads* New York. Oxford University Press, 1970.

Harvey, Karen. *St. Augustine: A Pictorial History* Virginia Beach, VA. Donning Co., 1980.

Hellier, Walter. *Indian River: The Belated Paradise* Miami Hurricane House, 1965.

White, Louise and Smiley, Nora K. *History of Key West* St. Petersburg. Great Outdoors Publishing Co., 1965.

Pratt, Theodore. *That was Palm Beach* St. Petersburg. Great Outdoors Publishing Co., 1968.

Browne, Jefferson Beall. *Key West—The Old and the New* City of Publication and Publisher unknown. Ca. 1910.

Volusia County Historical Commission. *Centennial History of Volusia County, Florida. Daytona* College Publishing Co., 1955

Nelson, Edward Akin. *Southern Reflections of the Gilded Age: Henry M. Flagler's System, 1885-1913.* PhD Thesis, University of Florida, Gainesville, 1975.

Strickland, Alice. *The Valiant Pioneers* Miami. Center Printing Co. 1965.

Martin, Sidney. *Florida's Flagler* Athens, GA. University of Georgia Press, 1949.

Sewell, John *Memoirs and History of Miami, Florida* Miami. Privately printed, 1933.

DeCroix, F.W. *An Historical and Progressive Review of Miami....* St. Augustine. Record Co., 1912.

Muir, Helen. *Miami, USA* New York. H. Holt & Co., 1953.

Cohen, Isadore. *Historical Sketches and Sidelights of Miami, Florida* Miami. Privately printed, 1925.

Nash, Charles Edgar. *The Magic of Miami Beach* Philadelphia. The McKay Co., 1938.

Prince, Richard E. *Atlantic Coast Line* Green River, Wyoming. Privately printed, 1966.

Unknown. *The Overseas Railroad* City, Publisher and Date Unknown.

Unknown. *The Overseas Highway* City, Publisher and Date Unknown.

III. **Florida East Coast Railway Material**
Equipment Inventory, 1902, 1915, 1935
Summary of Equipment, 1965, 66, 68, 71, 72-75, 79, 82, 83.
*Bulletin* 1966 through 1974
*Florida: Beauties of the East Coast* JSTA&IR Railway, 1894
Annual Reports: 1912, 1917-68, 1973-74, 1979, 1983.
*Official Industrial and Development Directory*, 1926-27.
*Henry M. Flagler: In Memoriam*, 1913.
*The Story of a Pioneer*, 1935-36, 1946, 1952, 1956.
The Florida East Coast *Homeseeker,* Various Issues.
Passenger Timetables: JSTA & IR, 1893, 1894. FEC, various, 1895-1968.

Employee Timetables: 1919-1983
*East Coast of Florida; Florida East Coast; Florida East Coast Railway and Hotels*, 1895-1958.
Bulletin Books, various years; *Instructions of the Passenger Traffic Department,* various; *Rules of the Passenger Traffic Department,* various; *Rules of the Operating Department* JSTA&HR, 1890; FEC, 1905, 1923, 1962; "Announcement of the Opening of the Key West Extension," 1912; *Official Program and Souvenir, Key West Extension*, 1912, Passenger Traffic Department files, various; Receivership Records, Volumes 1 through 8, and Index; Reorganization Proceedings, Volumes 1 through 10; Booklets, brochures and pamphlets relating to passenger service, freight service, openings of new stations and other pertinent occurrences; Corporate History, June 30, 1916.

IV. **Newspapers**

Indianapolis *Star*
Daytona Beach *Gazette News*
Miami *Herald*
Miami *News*
Jacksonville *Journal*
St. Augustine *Record*
Ft. Lauderdale *News and Sun Sentinel*

*New York Times*
Key West *Inter-Ocean*
Key West *Citizen*
Jacksonville *Florida Times-Union*
Hollywood *Sun-Tattler*
Palm Beach *Post*
The Key West *Morning Journal*

V. **Periodicals**
*Update*, Historical Association of Southern Florida
*Tequesta*, Historical Association of Southern Florida
*The Railway History Monograph*
*The Florida Philatelist*
*Electric Railway Journal* (contained information of the FEC's gas electric car)
National Railway Historical Society *Bulletin*
Railway & Locomotive Historical Society *Bulletin*
National Association of Timetable Collectors, *The Timetable Collector*
Atlantic Coast Line Railroad *Tropical Trips*
Railroadiana Collectors Association, Inc. *The Railroadiana Express*
*Key, Lock and Lantern*, of the National Association of Railroadiana Collectors
*The Florida Historical Society Quarterly*
*Railway Locomotives and Cars*
*The Southern Spike*, Miami Chapter, NRHS
*All Florida Magazine*
*Railway Progress*
*Florida Facts and Fables*

*Railway Age*
*Progressive Railroading*
*Railroad Magazine*
*The Gimlet*
*Trains Magazine*
*Leslie's Weekly*

# ACKNOWLEDGEMENTS

My gratitude to those who assisted with information, photos and ideas for the first edition of *Speedway* remains both intact and unabated, and the reader may note the names of those individuals on page nine of the first *Speedway* As the years have gone by, however, others have come to the fore with additional input, material, information and suggestions, and it is important to not only acknowledge those people warmly, but to again note that there were several so-called historians and/or "buffs" who simply would not respond when called upon, and for them, more is the pity.

It remains as difficult in this edition as it was in the original *Speedway* to list every single individual who has assisted in some way in the preparation of this book, but it is extremely important that I note and acknowledge the following, for their unbounded interest, their never-ending enthusiasm, and their unfailing support.

Robert W. Anestis, Chairman, President and CEO of Industries, who has been completely behind this project and is a long-time railroad historian in his own right;

Roger Barretto, former FEC Vice President, to whom "thank you for everything" is barely enough;

Wayne Blaylock; southern division General Manager, for his never-ending warm welcomes;

Bennett Bramson, my brother, who means so much to me. There is no better;

Leonard and Sue Certain, old and dear friends and FEC buffs;

Ken Charron, Esq., former FEC attorney, without whom Centennial might not have happened;

Marshall Deputy, former FEC Vice President, just a terrific guy;

Dr. Dan Gallagher, who has unearthed treasure troves of memorabilia dealing with the Key West Extension;

Gerry Hall, who never tired of seeing me at Bowden Yard;

Robert Hanson, formerly with the FEC Sales Department, another long-time friend and FEC buff;

Jim Keeley, for many years FEC Police Chief, who supported Centennial totally;

John D. McPherson, President of the railroad, to whom I owe many thanks for many things and trust this will go some small way toward expressing that appreciation;

Robert McSwain, FEC Vice Chairman, for his interest, warmth and never-ending willingness to share;

Jim Misskelley, FEC engineer, who continually provides new tidbits of history on the railroad;

Jonathan Nelson, who never stopped "noodging" me to get in gear and get the job done. It was he who originally suggested the title for this book;

Benjamin Nemser and Saralyn Nemser, my wife's children by a previous marriage, each of whom has not only been loving and supportive, but who have given me my two magnificent grandsons, Joshua Nemser and Harrison Seeman;

Bill Robinson, Amtrak engineer and tireless researcher;

Tom Rountree, Northern Division General Manager, who greets me warmly on each visit;

Roger W. Schmorr, a good friend and true "character" who has been an FEC train rider and buff since childhood;

Steve Spreckelmeier, whose love and interest for FEC steam saved and brought to Miami our 0-8-0 #253;

W. L. Thornton, for whom my respect and admiration are boundless;

Gene and Lenny Wolfe, daughter-in-law and son of the great FEC photographer Harry M. Wolfe, for all that they have done;

Carl F. Zellers, Jr., former FEC President, who was never too busy to share time and insights;

Marcia Zerevitz, Director of the Jewish Museum of Florida, for making the dream of an exhibit honoring Harry M. Wolfe a reality;

The members of the Miami Memorabilia Collector's Club and the now-forming FEC Railway Technical and Historical Society, for their enthusiastic support;

Very special thanks go out to each and every employee, past, present and future, of the Florida East Coast Railway, but I must especially acknowledge with deep gratitude, the following: Pat and Mike Bagley; Tom Ballas; Hank Dickinson; Rudy Dolentina; Bud Harris; Frances Mueller; Marty Robideaux; David Shelley; Bill Stokely and Gloria Taylor. How great you have all been.

Finally, and as before, the most special of all, my bride of more than 25 years, Myrna, whose unending patience, never-ending cajoling, and obvious love for a husband whose house has become the company's archives are finally bearing fruit with the publication of the Revised and Enlarged Centennial Edition.

It's March 1st, 1929 and the flagman is checking his watch as the FEC's "Miamian" prepares to depart America's Playground.